AMERICAN SOUR BEERS

Innovative Techniques
for Mixed Fermentations

MICHAEL
TONSMEIRE

brewers publications

Brewers Publications
A Division of the Brewers Association
PO Box 1679, Boulder, Colorado 80306-1679
www.BrewersAssociation.org
www.BrewersPublications.com

Printed in the United States of America.

10 9 8 7 6 5 4 3 2 1

ISBN-13: 978-1-938469-11-4
ISBN-10: 1-938469-11-9

Library of Congress Cataloging-in-Publication Data

Tonsmeire, Michael , 1983-
American sour beers : innovative techniques for mixed fermentations / by Michael Tonsmeire ; foreword by Vinnie Cilurzo.
    pages cm
Includes bibliographical references and index.
Summary: "American Sour Beers details American innovations and adaptations of traditional sour beer brewing techniques, exploring many processes and ingredients. Advice and practical applications for brewers of all levels are provided"-- Provided by the Publisher.

ISBN 978-1-938469-11-4 (pbk.) -- ISBN 1-938469-11-9 (pbk.) 1. Beer--United States. 2. Brewing--United States. I. Title.

TP577.T63 2014
663'.42--dc23
                                    2014006181

Publisher: Kristi Switzer
Technical Editors: Jennifer Talley, Yvan de Baets
Copyediting: Iain Cox
Indexing: Doug Easton
Production and Design Management: Stephanie Johnson Martin
Cover and Interior Design: Justin Petersen and Kerry Fannon
Cover Photo: Luke Trautwein
    Special thanks to West Flanders Brewing Co. in Boulder, Colorado
Interior images: Michael Tonsmeire unless otherwise noted

To my wife Audrey, my parents Joan and Bob, and a series
of understanding roommates who tolerated my filling the
freezer with hops, the closet with malt, the basement with
barrels, and the air with the smell of fermentation.

TABLE OF CONTENTS

ACKNOWLEDGMENTS

Those of us hooked on brewing sour beer know that it is more than just something enjoyable to drink, it is a passion that mandates a level of patience few hobbies or vocations require. It necessitates years of waiting as an idea slowly emerges into the physical. I am not a religious person, but if there were a god I imagine it to be something like a brewer: setting conditions that yield pleasing results. There is no way to tend to the needs of any individual microbe among the hundreds to untold billions that toil and die in the production of a mixed-fermentation beer, but in return for providing them with a suitable ecosystem the brewer is rewarded with a symphony of flavors that no single species of microbe could produce on its own.

Writing this book has motivated me to research aspects of sour beer production that I would not have otherwise. It forced me to organize my thoughts and opinions in a way that blogging rarely does. I was overwhelmed by the openness of American brewers, many of whom offered detailed information and candid anecdotes unprompted. Several mentioned the generous assistance that other brewers had provided to them when they were starting to brew sour beers. I got a real sense of community, despite the fact that it was often my first time talking to them. I appreciate how lucky I was to gain insight in one hour that had taken these pioneers five, ten, or fifteen years to refine. I hope, as some small compensation for their time, this book provides these brewers and their exquisite beers with well-deserved attention.

I am thankful to the brewers who inspired me with their beers and answered patiently almost every question I asked: Will Meyers, Scott Vaccaro, Ryan Michaels, Gerard Olson, Terry Hawbaker, Ron Gansberg, Tomme Arthur, Ron Jeffries, Jeff O'Neil, Pat McIlhenney, Scott Smith, Eric Salazar, Lauren Salazar, Peter Bouckaert, Tyler King, Patrick Rue, Todd Haug, Jason Perkins, Shaun Hill, Brian Strumke, Gabe Fletcher, Bob Sylvester, Alex Ganum, Chad Yakobson, Jason Davis, Jeff Stuffings, Caleb Staton, Tim Adams, Kristen England, Remi Bonnart, Sebastian Padilla, Levi Funk, Seth Hammond, and Dave and Becky Pyle.

Vinnie Cilurzo deserves special recognition. He personally answered the first question I e-mailed to the generic Russian River e-mail about sour beers on June 30, 2008 (I was planning on adding pluots to my Flemish pale ale at the time). I could never have dreamed that nearly six years later he would be writing the Foreword to my book about American sour beers. Drinking my first bottle of Russian River Supplication in 2005 was one of the experiences that got me hooked on sour beer in the first place. The level of innovation and openness Cilurzo displays continues to impress me.

I appreciate the effort expended by my two technical editors, Yvan de Baets and Jennifer Talley, and publisher Kristi Switzer. Together they did a wonderful job catching my mistakes, debating the finer points of sour beer production, and ensuring this book would not only be technically accurate but also helpful to brewers (craft and home alike). I also want to thank my friends and co-conspirators who filled barrels, inspired me with their homebrews, and shared bottles of sour beers obtained through travel, trade, and tribulation: Nathan Zeender, Alex Howe, Scott Wise, Noah Paci, Tim Pohlhaus, Jeff Long, Zach Brown, Dan Fogg, Eric Denman, Nate Shestak, Dyan Ali, Devin Miller, Dan Fromson, Tammy Tuck, Matt Humbard, and Peter Kay. Without them this would have been a much blander and lonelier adventure.

Thanks to the whizz-bang information superhighway, I was able to sift through a glut of content about each brewery before I talked to the brewers themselves. This preparation allowed me to target my questions, and not waste anyone's time (I hope). This was largely thanks to the podcasters and beer writers who posted interviews, presentations, and other material, especially: James Spencer, Randy Mosher, Jeff Sparrow, Tim Webb, Stan Hieronymus, Steve Gale, Kai Troester, Jeff Bearer, Greg Weiss, Aschwin de Wolf, Adam Nason, Brandon Jones, Justin Crossley, Jon Plise, and Jamil Zainasheff.

The brewing books I value the most are tattered, with dog-eared pages and wort stains from brew-day referencing. I can only hope that this book becomes one of those on your shelf. Even as I was writing, I found myself returning to reread sections when planning batches or answering questions (which gives me hope).

The next step in my sour beer adventure will be applying what I have learned to commercial production. More than a year after I started researching this book, Jacob McKean hired me to consult for his startup brewery, Modern Times Beer. One of the first assignments he gave me was to help develop the sour beer program. I spent the summer of 2013 growing a huge variety of microbes to inoculate the barrels at Modern Times; hopefully at least some of them will have created delicious beer by the time this book is released. American sour beer has gotten to the stage where it is no longer sufficient to brew something that is "just" sour; beer nerds are becoming beer connoisseurs, demanding levels of refinement, balance, and complexity that are challenging to consistently obtain from mixed fermentations. I hope that the brewers at Modern Times and I will be able to rise to that standard, while dealing with the added challenge of me living in Washington, DC while the beers are in San Diego, California.

If you start reading this book before your first taste of sour beer, then I hope you are encouraged to sample a few. If you open this book never having brewed a sour beer, then I hope you are inspired to plan a batch. If you are already a seasoned brewer of sour beer, then I hope that these pages are able to answer questions and spark recipe ideas and process tweaks.

My basement is filled with bottles with various alphanumeric codes scrawled in permanent marker on the caps that allow me to identify what I am opening (I stopped making labels years ago). It is a satisfying feeling to go into the small temperature-controlled basement room to retrieve a bottle filled with beer brewed years earlier. It gives me a chance to reflect on where I was when I brewed that beer and what has happened in my life (brewing and otherwise) since then.

I wish you as much luck on your journey as I have had so far on mine!

FOREWORD

American sour beers are something I started dabbling with in 1999 while working for Korbel Champagne Cellars in the early days of Russian River Brewing Company. I began with just two used Chardonnay wine barrels from a local Sonoma County winery. Since then my collection of wine barrels has grown to over 600. If we had more room I am sure we would own even more. Sometimes I buy or trade beer for barrels when I don't even need them (it does take a lot of great beer to make great wine—ask any winemaker!). Purchasing and collecting wine barrels has become a bit of an obsession, much like your Star Wars figurines or spouse's shoe collection that takes up half the closet. Once you start collecting, you just can't stop!

When I started brewing sour beers there were very few resources like this book. My first barrel-aged beer, called Temptation, was made in those first two Chardonnay barrels that I acquired in 1999. At that time, I only used *Brettanomyces* but no bacteria. (I'm not even sure Korbel knew I was using *Brettanomyces* on the winery property, so we will just keep that to ourselves.) My first rendition of Temptation was one of the earlier examples of a wild beer made in America, but definitely not the first. Although this book focuses on American brewers making sour beer, we are not even close in experience and, to some extent, wisdom as compared to our fellow brewers in Belgium and Germany, who have been making sour beer for a very long time. Let's raise a glass to our friends overseas who have inspired so many brewers around the world.

I feel very lucky to have been at the forefront of the American sour beer movement. At the same time I was learning how to make sour beers, my good friend Tomme Arthur, head brewer (at the time) for Pizza Port in Solana Beach, California, was also starting his journey into the world of sour beers. I remember the many phone calls and discussions we had analyzing different techniques and practices we were either currently using or considering. Thinking back to those early days in brewing also reminds me of all the different hops and hop combinations I discovered early on. It was all a bit overwhelming at the time, but eventually I learned which hops I preferred for bittering and which ones I preferred for aroma. Learning about sour beer production was easily just as intimidating, if not more so.

In 2005 our first batch of Beatification was already in barrels. This batch would end up being the only batch of Beatification into which we pitched yeast and bacteria. All subsequent batches would end up being a blend of what we called Sonambic, our own version of a spontaneously fermented beer. That same year, on a flight home from Belgium, Tomme Arthur and I were discussing everything we had learned the previous week. He brought up the idea of first making a sour mash in the mash tun and then the following day use the mash tun as a horny tank (after the spent grain is removed) to start collecting some wild yeast and bacteria. This is an alternative for those brewers who do not possess a coolship. The wort from that first batch of Sonambic sat in the mash tun overnight and by the next morning, to my surprise, it was fermenting. Once I got it into barrels the batch kept fermenting—bungs were popping out, and beer was spilling all over the place in our barrel room! It was a beautiful sight. We eventually stopped using our mash tun for this purpose and now Sonambic is made in our own version of a horny tank. It is much deeper than a traditional coolship and the shape is not something you would see in Belgium. But, we had to make it work in the space we had available. The spirit of spontaneously fermented beer is now alive and well right here in Sonoma County, California.

This book is a snapshot in time of the current landscape of New World sour beers. Like any good sour beer, the techniques and wisdom of brewers will definitely change over time. I sat on a barrel beer panel at the 2004 Craft Brewers Conference in San Diego, California. At the time, I was advocating for production procedures that are very different from what we now do at Russian River. There was nothing wrong with what I once did, but my thought processes and procedures have evolved over time. In the 15 years I have been experimenting with sour beers I have learned a great deal, primarily from trial and error. But much of my education has come from sharing experiences with other brewers, as well as learning from those who have been brewing these beers for generations. Early on in the learning process we overcarbonated a batch of Temptation bottles. We had to uncork all of the bottles in order to release some CO_2, then recork each one. We did this process by hand four times to over 3,000 bottles before finally adding a new wire hood. Fortunately, it worked and we were able to sell all the beer. That money was likely needed to make payroll back in the early days!

Then there was the time when our first bottled batch of Sanctification (100% *Brettanomyces* beer) formed a pellicle in the neck of the bottle. At the time I had no idea what a pellicle was or what caused it. Then there was our first batch of Compunction, a sour beer aged in barrels with pluots. The first and only time we bottled it, in 2006, I mistook what turned out to be a collection of pectin and other fruit by-products for yeast sediment. In the end there was two inches of sediment in each bottle. The damage was done and we ended up opening all the bottles and dumping them into a tank. Our bottling equipment in those days could not handle carbonated beer, so we ended up filtering it and putting it in kegs. Naturally, Compunction is now available on draft only. I definitely got schooled in the fine art of bottling sour beers and the potential for bizarre results!

While on this funky/sour beer journey, we have created our own process that I like to refer to as the "Russian River Way." My hope is that the technical components and artistry documented throughout this book, along with the real world examples, will inspire you to create your own funky beer-making process. If you are willing to make mistakes and learn from them, you will become a better brewer.

For those of you who are just starting to get "funky," have patience. Use this book to help guide you through this fun and often unpredictable journey. You will quickly learn that sour beers are less about traditional styles and more about "liquid art." Sour beers are the ultimate 10 minutes of drinking pleasure (to paraphrase a quote from Peter Bouckaert). Do not concern yourself right away with all of the nitty-gritty details. These will come to you over time. Sometimes having all the information up front makes you try too hard to control something that really needs to develop a style and technique all its own. That was certainly the case for me. On occasion I would reach out to Peter Bouckaert at New Belgium Brewing Company for advice. In typical Belgian brewer fashion, he never gave me a complete answer, only bits and pieces. I would have to figure the rest out on my own. This limited but useful guidance was essential in helping me develop my own systems for making sour beers. For this, I am grateful.

This book will also be very useful for those who are already producing sour beers. I'm certain this will be a great reference book to add to your library. I found good nuggets of information, both artistic and technical. I am definitely inspired to brew some new sour beers at our brewery.

Above all, never lose respect for the bugs and critters it takes to make these beers. Cross contamination is a real threat and not that uncommon. I strongly recommend you pay close attention to Chapter 2 of this book, and specifically the safety and sanitation part of this chapter. There are many pitfalls you can avoid with a little planning ahead of time. The great beer writer Michael Jackson once compared *Saccharomyces* to a dog and *Brettanomyces* to a cat. *Saccharomyces* is trainable and mostly predictable. Conversely, *Brettanomyces* may, like a cat, run away when you call for her, or scratch you when you pick her up. But sometimes the cat decides to love you and shows great affection. It's all about respect. If you have a healthy respect for *Brettanomyces* (as well as bacteria) and the havoc it could wreak in your brewery, you should remain unscratched.

Grab a bottle of your favorite sour beer and get started on your wild journey into the world of brewing funky beer with this helpful book as your guide!

Cheers,

Vinnie Cilurzo
Russian River Brewing Company

INTRODUCTION

*You know all those brewers who like to be called Master Brewer? For me
a lambic brewer is never a Master Brewer, because a master is someone
who dominates the product. We never dominate the product.*
— *Jean Van Roy (fourth-generation brewer/owner of Brasserie Cantillon)[1]*

In Belgium, brewing and blending *lambic* is regarded as a nearly mystical skill that requires secret knowledge usually passed from father to son. The name of the Belgian brewers' guild is the Knighthood of the Brewers' Mash staff,[2] which gives an indication of how insular they are. They can be mischievously misleading when answering questions from the uninitiated, closely guarding their inheritance. Brewing lambic relies on spontaneous fermentation with wild microbes, predating the study of microbiology and making it more art than science. Lambic brewers who stray from the traditional methods tend to do so to the detriment of the beer, diminishing a fascinatingly tart beverage into a sugary alcopop.

American craft brewers have built their industry by combining and adapting brewing techniques and recipes from all over the world. They often begin their careers brewing reliable ales and lagers, and as a result come to expect a high degree of control over the brewing process. Sour beer resists taming, but this has not stopped American brewers from developing distinctive methods suited to their particular tastes and constraints. Competing in a marketplace dominated by a handful of mega-breweries has also fostered an open and collaborative culture among their small and independent brethren.

My own journey into sour beer began with Jason Steingisser, a childhood friend, who introduced me to "good" beer shortly after my 21st birthday. He and I were home in Massachusetts for the summer before returning for our senior years in St. Paul and Pittsburgh, respectively. At the time I did not have a cerebral interest in beer because I understood the term to refer exclusively to bland, overcarbonated, pale lagers. After tasting the range between beers like Ommegang Hennepin and Dogfish Head Indian Brown Ale, I made it my mission to sample every style. Luckily, back in Pittsburgh, I discovered D's SixPax & Dogz, a bar that stocked a huge variety of single bottles that could be purchased to go (Pennsylvania beer distributors on the other hand are required to sell beer by the case). I went to work, consulting website reviews to find a well-regarded example of each style.

When my quest arrived at fruit lambic I picked the least expensive, Lindemans Kriek. It was slightly tart, but the primary flavors were fruity and sweet. While certainly drinkable, it was not nearly as sour as I expected from descriptions of lambic. A few weeks later I splurged on a 375 mL bottle of Cantillon Kriek 100% Lambic. The acidity was bracing; over the two hours it took me to consume the bottle, all I could do was wonder why anyone would choose to drink something so sour. There was something there though. Maybe it was the challenge, or those long neglected neurons that had not fired since my sister and I competed to see who could keep blue raspberry Warheads® in their mouth the longest. From that point on, every few months I sampled a new sour beer. As my tongue gradually acclimated to the acidity of *gueuze*, Flemish red, and Berliner *weisse*, I began to perceive other complex and surprising flavors that had been previously hidden.

During my senior year at Carnegie Mellon University I brewed my first two batches of homebrew with my friend, Nicole Yeager, as part of a student-taught class, "Beer Brewing and Appreciation." While I was starting to enjoy sour beers, as a college student it was a rare treat at 10 dollars or more for a bottle.

After reading Jeff Sparrow's seminal *Wild Brews: Beer Beyond the Influence of Brewer's Yeast* (Brewers Publications, 2005), I knew that brewing a sour beer was something I had to attempt. At first I was hesitant, because the owner of my local homebrewing shop warned me that doing so would risk turning all of my batches sour. I even read online that I would need to store the fermentors of sour beer in a separate room away from all of my other fermentors, lest the microbes from an *oud bruin* might take to the air to invade an IPA. My excuse finally came a year later during a summer preceding a move to Washington, DC for a new job. During that time I brewed four batches of sour and funky beer (Belgian-style lambic, Flemish red, Belgian strong dark with cherries, and old ale with *Brettanomyces*) to leave aging at my parents' house. Over the next year, every time I returned to Massachusetts I would pull a sample from each of the carboys. When the beers were ready, I bottled them and drove the cases back to DC. The results were pleasant, except for the Belgian-style lambic, and I was hooked. Since then I have continuously experimented, fermenting batches of beer with microbes other than brewer's yeast and writing about my experiences on my blog, *The Mad Fermentationist.*

Why would I write this book when there are already a number of other great books that delve into sour beers? These include, among others, Sparrow's *Wild Brews*, Jean Guinard's *Lambic*, Classic Beer Style Series 3 (Brewers Publications, 1998), Randy Mosher's *Radical Brewing* (Brewers Publications, 2004), and Stan Hieronymus' *Brew Like a Monk* (Brewers Publications, 2005) and *Brewing with Wheat* (Brewers Publications, 2010). After years of researching recipes and blog posts I realized that although some of what I was seeking was spread among these books, there remained a large range of techniques, ingredients, and recipes for American sour beer production that were not covered. This is a developing field, and American brewers, both home and commercial, are pushing the envelope in experimentation with these styles. I wanted to write a book that would provide actionable advice for producing innovative American sour beers with the details in one place.

I set out to write about my own methods and experiences, but the openness of the two-dozen American brewers I interviewed allowed me to write a book with a wider scope than originally intended. Nearly every one of the brewers I contacted were willing, and often excited, to share the granular details of their process. Several of them mentioned that the only reason they had been able to successfully produce sour beers so quickly was the openness of other brewers. Talking to these brewers, many of whom have now been brewing sour beers for a decade or longer, allowed me to document the distinct production methods that each has developed.

This book does not cover the basics of wort production, brewer's yeast fermentation, or sanitation. If you cannot already brew a solid clean beer, this book will not be that useful. My goal is to give brewers who can already brew ales and lagers the information they need to adapt their process to produce sour, funky, and wild beers. If you are not at that point yet, read John Palmer's *How to Brew* (Brewers Publications, 2006) or Wolfgang Kunze's *Technology Brewing and Malting* (VLB Berlin, 2010) and refine your wort production and fermentation skills on beers that have faster turnaround times.

Brewing sour beer depends on experience, feel, and instinct. This book lays out options, differing opinions, and general concepts that you will need to come to your own decisions about. After reading it you should be able to brew a solid sour beer on your first try. However, the skills required to consistently brew superb sour beers cannot be learned solely by reading or observing. Becoming an expert takes years of practice honing your method and training your palate.

About This Book

We begin with an overview of the history of sour beer in Chapter 1. Sour beer is not a modern concept; acidity has been a component of beer's flavor for most of the beverage's history. By the 1980s that tradition had been nearly extinguished by revolutions in pure yeast culturing and sanitation a century earlier, but since then sour beers have experienced a resurgence that continues to accelerate. This chapter includes some background on the current state of mixed-fermentation in Belgium, Germany, Great Britain, and America as well as some suggested beers to sample from each nation. I do my best to describe the hundreds of beers mentioned in the book, but drinking them yourself will make this book much more useful.

Chapters 2, 3, and 4 provide the basic information that the later chapters will draw upon. Chapter 2 aims to get you into the sour beer mindset, answers some basic worries that prevent many brewers from attempting sour beers, and presents a straightforward method for brewing your first sour beer. It also covers important safety and sanitation information and considerations. The remainder of the book is laid out to follow the path a sour beer takes from brew day through drinking. Wort production is the focus of Chapter 3. It covers malt and hop selection, water treatment, and mashing techniques. Once your wort is produced you will need to select what strains of lactic acid bacteria and yeast you want to pitch into it. Chapter 4 contains descriptions of the contributing species of microbes. This chapter also covers techniques for growing and maintaining your own cultures, and obtaining microbes from places other than yeast laboratories.

There is much more variability in the methods used to produce sour beer than most other styles. Many different styles of clean beer are produced with the same basic process, simply by varying ingredients, mash temperature, and fermentation temperature. When it comes to sour beer there are dozens of different methods. Chapter 5 starts with profiles of the general approaches used to produce the four surviving styles of European sour beer. Following that are profiles of American sour beer innovators, including the souring method employed by each. If you have a favorite sour beer producer, read the description of their method, microbes, and ingredients and consider which elements you would like to adopt.

While homebrewers should borrow elements from their favorite commercial producers, not all of the processes and equipment are transferable to small volumes. Because of this, I profile three complete methods tailored to brewing on a small scale in Chapter 6. Some of these techniques may also be valuable for craft breweries that are looking to tinker with sour beers without committing to large volumes.

Chapter 7 deals with an Old World tradition that has gained new followers in America: spontaneous fermentation. This is allowing truly wild microbes from the air to ferment your beer, as is done with traditional lambics. One of the riskiest and most rewarding ways to brew a sour beer, spontaneous fermentation is already producing some remarkable beers in states as far apart as Maine, Michigan, and California.

After a chapter about American brewers borrowing from the past, Chapter 8 covers the American innovation of fermenting beer with nothing but *Brettanomyces*. This so-called wild yeast provides most of the characteristic flavors and aromas of sour beers, other than sourness. If you treat it as you would ale or lager yeast, *Brettanomyces* can produce a wide range of fantastic flavors in a relatively short period of time.

Chapter 9 is all about fermentors and wood. While the flavor contribution and use of barrels is a subject that deserves its own book, I cover the basics. The use of oak barrels is ingrained in the history of sour beer. They provide complementary flavors, a home for the microbes, sugars for them to ferment, and a slow but steady supply of oxygen for their use. While many American brewers have joined this tradition, others opt to ferment their beers in impermeable fermentors with oak cubes, which can produce excellent results as well.

Having covered all of the angles for producing and fermenting sour beer, Chapter 10 delves into the ways in which these beers can be flavored with fruits and vegetables. Ranging from the most traditional, sour cherry, to the borderline crazy, chile pepper, this chapter covers many of the options available in terms of variety, form, and timing.

Chapters 11 and 12 cover how to finish the brewing process, regardless of how the beer was soured or flavored. Blending and aging is covered in Chapter 11. This may not sound like the most exciting subject, but it is possibly the most important. More than anything else, brewing with blending in mind, and possessing an experienced palate to match and adjust beers, is the secret to producing consistently terrific sour beers. Packaging, dealt with in Chapter 12, is a similarly overlooked aspect, but for anyone who has opened a bottle of sour beer that was either dead-flat or gushed, you know how a mistake here can ruin an otherwise perfect beer.

The shortest chapter, and hopefully one you will not need to reference frequently, is the troubleshooting guide in Chapter 13. I have covered the most common flavors and appearances that alarm brewers when making sour beer. In many cases there are solutions, which often involve just waiting, but it is also valuable to know when it is time to cut your losses and dump a batch. If you are worried about a sour beer you are brewing or have a question that this book does not address, please feel free to contact me through www.TheMadFermentationist.com.

Finally, we reach recipes in Chapter 14. I did not include any recipes I have not brewed myself. Recreating a commercial sour beer is a nearly impossible task, even if you have a brewery's exact recipe. As a result, I only included recipes that were inspired by innovative commercial beers, all of which I have actually brewed. If you enjoy the character of a particular brewery's beer it is much more valuable to look at their process and where they source their microbes, rather than mimicking their grain or hop bill. Still, it may be helpful to look at some of the beers I have brewed for inspiration and to get a complete picture of how all of the pieces fit together. Each recipe includes some suggested variations, but in most cases it is best to let your palate guide your choices.

References

1. Jean Van Roy, interview with Tim Webb, *Beer Amongst the Belgians* promotional video, produced by Taylor Brush for Spotted Tail Productions, available as Vimeo video, April 30, 2012, http://vimeo.com/41276710.
2. "The Knighthood of the Brewers' Mash staff," Belgian Brewers, last accessed December 16, 2013, http://www.belgianbrewers.be/en/beer-culture/the-knighthood-of-the-brewers-mash.

SOUR BEERS:
A PRIMER

1

Before digging into the specific details and variations that the rest of this book contains I want to ensure that you have a basic understanding of sour beers. A short introduction to the history of sour beers, some terminology, and cultural exploration will provide a foundation for the remaining chapters.

A Brief History of Sour Beers

Beer was invented (or should I say discovered?) at least 9,000 years ago.[1] However, the grain-based intoxicants enjoyed for most of the subsequent nine millennia would hardly be recognizable to most beer drinkers today. It was only 500 years ago that hops became the default seasoning, and it was just 150 years ago that wort was first pitched with isolated strains of brewer's yeast. Without the antimicrobial properties of the hops, and before the use of sterile culturing techniques, all beer would have begun to sour within days or weeks of brewing. In modern America, to receive label approval from the Alcohol and Tobacco Tax and Trade Bureau (TTB) a beer is legally required to contain hops, and until the 1990s beers fermented with anything other than brewer's yeast had all but slipped from collective memory.

Historically, the complex flavors of well-aged mixed-fermentation beers were appreciated. In England brewers allowed high-alcohol beers to "stale" in oak barrels, where they developed tartness and unique flavors from the resident microbes before being blended with young beer. German and Belgian brewers developed beers known and loved for their acidity, like Berliner *weisse* and *lambic*. However, as the industrial revolution took hold during the latter half of the 19th century, brewers looked for ways to hasten production and consumers increasingly demanded clean and consistent "modern" beers. Thanks to Louis Pasteur's revolutionary *Studies on Fermentation: The Diseases of Beer, Their Causes, and the Means of Preventing Them*,[2] brewers were able to do away with continually repitching mixed house cultures in favor of selecting a single strain of yeast. Brewing scientists later discovered that, while wild yeast and bacteria were responsible for spoilage, some were responsible for those coveted "stale" and tart flavors of aged beers.[3]

Even after most brewers adopted pure yeast strains, tart mixed-culture fermented beers survived, and in some places thrived. The immigrants who flooded America after the Civil War brought with them their taste for the local beers of their homelands. So at the same time that breweries like Pabst Brewing Company (San Antonio, TX) and Anheuser-Busch Brewing Company (St. Louis, MO) were coming to dominate the market with pale lagers from Munich and Prague, other brewers in places like Baltimore specialized in tart Berliner weisse.[4] There were even American brewers who specialized in English-style tart, oak-aged stock ales.[5] In spite of that, because of their relatively small size, none of the American breweries producing sour beer survived the US government's 14-year prohibition of alcohol. In the years immediately following the repeal of Prohibition there were traces of sour beer, like the "Lambic Lager Beer" brewed by Peter Doelger Brewing Company in New Jersey,[6] but I have not found any evidence that names like this were anything other than marketing. Luckily for Americans there were a few holdouts in other countries, places like Berlin and the Senne Valley, where a handful of historic sour beers were sheltered long after they died out elsewhere.

Since the 1970s American consumers have become increasingly interested in the flavor and tradition behind what they eat and drink. Beer was only one of many edible and potable commodities that had become increasingly homogeneous in modern times. As demand slowly swelled for cheeses more complex than Kraft® American Cheese, and loaves chewier than Hostess Wonder Bread®, so it did for more interesting styles of beer.[7] While consumers were originally attracted to German lagers and English ales, eventually small importers like Shelton Brothers, Vanberg & DeWulf, and Merchant du Vin began importing bottles of many of the surviving European sour beers. Years of limited choices provided good beer with something it rarely had before—cachet. Even in Belgium, many of the most traditional and eccentric producers are only able to survive because their beers are sold at much higher margins in countries like America and Japan than is possible in their home market.[8]

In the mid-1990s, as American craft brewers began to master and then adapt many of the traditional beer styles from around the world, there were only a few brewers who started to dabble in sour beer. As recently as the late nineties, no more than a handful of craft brewers were experimenting with microbes other than brewer's yeast. One of the first commercial sour beers to be brewed in America post-Prohibition was by Kinney Baughman of Cottonwood Grille & Brewery, in 1995. The brewery released two sour beers, Belgian Amber Framboise and Black Framboise, created by blending clean beers with a batch accidentally contaminated with the lactic acid bacteria *Pediococcus*.[9] A few years later in 1999, New Belgium Brewing became the first American brewery to release a world-class sour beer with the first bottling of La Folie. Making a beer that stands shoulder-to-shoulder with the best Flemish reds is a major accomplishment, a result achieved in no small part thanks to the time New Belgium's brewmaster, Peter Bouckaert, had spent in the same position at Brouwerij Rodenbach in Belgium.

It was not until 2002 when the Great American Beer Festival® (GABF), already in its 21st year, introduced its first sour beer category. That year, out of only 15 entries, it was no surprise that La Folie won first place, especially considering it had won the more competitive Belgian- & French-Style Specialty Ales category the previous year. Since then the bar has been raised, as breweries such as Russian River Brewing Company, Jolly Pumpkin Artisan Ales, and the Lost Abbey, not forgetting New Belgium as well, have released sour beers that strike off in directions all their own: aged in fresh wine and spirit barrels; flavored with dry hops, local fruits, and spices; and brewed with more assertive malt bills. By 2013 the GABF had taken those beers that had moved beyond pure brewer's yeast fermentation and split them into five separate categories, with a total of 238 entries.[10]

Today it can sometimes appear as though every American craft brewer has released a sour beer, but the required investment in time and space means that few of these brewers devote a large portion of their production to them. The attractive margins and high demand that sour beers command will continue to entice many brewers to increase production.

The yeast and bacteria responsible for sour beer fermentation are capable of producing complex combinations of flavor compounds that cannot be obtained in any other way; because of this sour beers currently enjoy something of a cult status. The flavor profiles of these beers range from simple and quenching to complex and meditative.

Sour Beer Terminology

Here are definitions for seven basic terms used throughout the book to describe flavors and aromas found in sour beers:

Acetic acid. Acetic acid is the same acid found in vinegar. It is sharper than lactic acid and the taste is perceived farther back on the palate. This acidity is complementary in small quantities, where it adds a more assertive, sharper sourness, but it can be unpleasant at elevated levels. It is most closely associated with Flemish reds, but it also plays a small role in many other sour beers. Acetic acid is produced by either the bacteria *Acetobacter* or the yeast *Brettanomyces*, in both cases only in the presence of oxygen. The TTB limits acetic acid levels, indicating it should be no more than 0.15% of a beer.[11]

Clean. Beers that are not sour or funky, that is to say those fermented with a pure culture of brewer's yeast (i.e., *Saccharomyces cerevisiae* or *S. pastorianus*), are described as "clean." This category covers a great majority of the beer commercially brewed today.

Esters. Esters are molecules formed by the combination of an acid and an alcohol. Both brewer's yeast and *Brettanomyces* have the ability to create esters, but only *Brettanomyces* can break them down. Belgian ale yeast strains are prolific ester producers, while one of the goals of lager brewing is to minimize ester formation. The esters we are concerned with in beer are aromatically fruity. Their aroma may not only be reminiscent of a particular fruit but also chemically identical to an ester found in that fruit. For example, the isoamyl acetate produced in German wheat beers is also found in bananas.[12]

Funk. Funk describes a wide range of flavors and aromas not present in beers fermented with *Saccharomyces* alone. Common sensory descriptors include barnyard, horse blanket, and damp basement. Among the various types of molecules that contribute to "funkiness," phenols are of particular interest because of the wide range of sensitivity of beer tasters.[13] As a result, a sour beer that is pleasantly "farmyardy" to one drinker may be reminiscent of a Band-Aid® to another.

Lactic acid. Lactic acid is the same acid found in yogurt, buttermilk, and other soured dairy products (hence its name). Not as sharp as acetic acid, lactic acid has a soft, tangy flavor, although this can become lip-puckeringly sharp at higher concentrations. Lactic acid is one of the primary acids found in sour beers, alongside carbonic acid from dissolved carbon dioxide. It is produced by lactic acid bacteria, specifically species of *Lactobacillus* and *Pediococcus* in the case of beer.

Sour. One of the basic tastes perceived by taste buds is sour. It is described as tart, acidic, tangy, and salivary gland-stimulating. Sour should not be confused with bitter. All beers have a pH below neutral (pH 7) and are thus technically acidic, but only a small percentage have a pH low enough to truly taste sour.

Classic Commercial Examples of Sour and Funky Beers

All over America stores are opening or expanding their offerings to cater to beer enthusiasts. Most carry at least a few sour beers. Exposure to a rich array of sour beers is the only way to determine which flavors you enjoy and which ones you find unpalatable. This "research" is a crucial first step to brewing beers that suit your taste. You cannot select the optimal ingredients or techniques until you have determined what balance or character you are aiming for in your beer.

Take the opportunity to sample in small quantities at better beer bars, high quality beer festivals (e.g., GABF, Great Taste of the Midwest, and those sponsored by Beer Advocate), or with friends. Festivals are often the best places to taste hard-to-obtain and experimentally soured batches. Keep tasting notes for the beers you sample, especially if you are attending a festival that has brewers on hand to answer questions.

Pay attention to the flavors you enjoy and which breweries you gravitate toward. Try sampling a few similar beers from different breweries side-by-side to accentuate their differences.

If you are new to drinking sour beer, what follows is a brief overview of the traditions and beers of Belgium, Germany, Britain, and the US. Many cost less than 10 dollars a bottle, but even the more expensive examples are a worthwhile investment before embarking on the lengthy souring process yourself. As with all of the beers mentioned in this book, the descriptions below are a snapshot as of the writing of this book. Recipes, microbes, and processes change, and beer flavors evolve.

Belgium

Sour beer is most closely associated with the Belgian brewing tradition. This small nation—nestled between France, Germany, the Netherlands, and Luxembourg—is home to the sweet and sour red and brown ales of Flanders, and the sharp lemony lambics of the *Pajottenland*. In addition to the beers that fall into the classic styles, the country is also dotted with a plethora of tiny breweries making acidic and funky beers all their own. Despite its size, Belgium produces a greater variety of beers than any other European country; their brewers simultaneously hold a reverence for tradition and a passion for experimentation. Even several of the most ardently traditional lambic producers brew experimental batches with nontraditional fruits, spices, and barrel aging techniques.

What follows are some classic examples of Belgian beers:

3 Fonteinen Oude Geuze (Beersel, Brabant). This *gueuze* (blended and carbonated lambic), is bright and complex, with lemon, mineral, and classic farmyard funk. It is nicely balanced and not as acidic as some other examples of gueuze. It improves with age, so jump at any opportunity to drink a bottle that is a few years old. If you get your hands on a bottle marked "Vintage," consider yourself lucky because these are blended from owner Armand Debelder's favorite barrels.

Cantillon Kriek 100% Lambic (Brussels, Brussels-Capital Region). Sharply acidic, with enough cherry to let you know it is a fruit beer, but not so much as to mask the rest of the base beer's funky complexities. While sour cherry is the most common fruit added to lambics (and sour beers in general) many of Cantillon's other releases venture away from the norm. Also worth seeking are Saint Lamvinus (red wine grapes), and Fou' Foune (apricots).

De Dolle Oerbier Special Reserva (Essen, Antwerp). A fantastic strong, dark sour beer. One of the most complex beers I have tasted; the best bottles have flavors of port, leather, blue cheese, and rich malt. Try it next to the standard Oerbier to get an indication of the change that microbes and barrel aging can induce in an already marvelous beer. The strain of *Brettanomyces* used in the Special Reserva was originally cultured from a keg of beer that was returned to De Dolle years after it was initially sold.[14]

Orval (Florenville, Luxembourg). * The only widely distributed beer from the Trappist monastery of the same name (Abbaye Notre-Dame d'Orval), this pale beer is so synonymous with *Brettanomyces bruxellensis* that people refer to horse blanket and farmyard aromatics in other beers as "Orval character" (*goût d'Orval*). Orval is hoppy when fresh, growing drier and funkier as the years pass.

Rodenbach Classic (Roeselare, West Flanders). The embodiment of Flemish red. It has a malty sweetness, but not so much that it tastes sugary or artificial like some Flemish reds. Sweetness in a bottled sour beer can only be preserved by pasteurization or filtration. Rodenbach's beers display varying levels of acetic acid character, which gives them a different, more vinegary acid profile than most other sour beers. Rodenbach Grand Cru contains a higher percentage of wood-aged beer than Rodenbach Classic, and as a result is reminiscent of good balsamic vinegar.[15]

Note: If you are interested in the history and evolution of these styles, I recommend you read Jeff Sparrow's *Wild Brews* and Webb, Pollard and McGinn's collaborative effort, *LambicLand: A Journey Round the Most Unusual Beers in the World.*

Germany

Despite the legacy of the rigid *Reinheitsgebot* (beer purity law) and its brewers' renown for clean lagers, Germany has a rich tradition of sour beer production. Berlin's low-alcohol wheat beers and Leipzig's salt and coriander-enriched Gose are the only two surviving styles, with others still waiting to be revived. German sours tend to be more restrained than the

---

* The Belgian province of Luxembourg in Wallonia, *not* the country.

Belgian examples, relying on *Lactobacillus* for sourness and mostly forgoing the complex earthy funk of *Brettanomyces*. If you are new to drinking or brewing sour beers, German styles are a good place to start because their flavors are more approachable and they take less time to mature.

What follows are some classic examples of German sour beers:

Bahnhof Gose (Leipzig, Saxony). The only widely distributed Gose is barely tart, with a refreshing salinity and a pervasive coriander aroma. A resurrection from Leipzig's past, it is not the sort of beer you expect to taste from a German brewery. It was recreated after the style died out in the 1960s, so it is unclear how close it comes to historical examples.

Berliner Kindl Weisse (Berlin). This Berliner weisse is the sole remaining Berliner weisse, with a history stretching back to the style's 19th century heyday. It is low in alcohol and possesses a clean tartness. Until recently it was brewed alongside the now discontinued Schultheiss Berliner Weisse (which had a touch of *Brettanomyces*). The closest example to Kindl Weisse that is still exported to America is Bahnhof Berliner Style Weisse, a *Brettanomyces lambicus*-spiked Special Edition that is closer to the more aggressive Schultheiss.

Professor Fritz Briem 1809 Berliner Style Weisse (Freising, Bavaria). This relatively new entry to the style has more in common with a sour *hefeweizen* than a traditional Berliner weisse. Its flavor exhibits banana, clove, and bready malt, but also a wonderful lactic acid tartness. At 5% alcohol by volume (ABV) it is strong for a modern Berliner weisse, but is still a unique and delicious sour beer.

Note: Stan Hieronymus's *Brewing with Wheat: The 'Wit' and 'Weizen' of World Wheat Beers* relates the history and traditional production of German sour beers better than I could ever hope to do.

Great Britain

England and Scotland have a long tradition of *Brettanomyces*-influenced, strong, wood-aged beers, but any true sour beers they once had have completely died out. British ales with funky characters and minimal sourness are the opposite of the tart beers of Germany. If you are averse to sourness this would be a good place to look for inspiration. There are a handful of British breweries that are brewing sour beers, but they do not have the unbroken lineage of their Belgian and German counterparts.

Below are some examples of classic beers from Britain:

Gale's Prize Old Ale (Horndean, England). While Prize Old Ale is transcendent perhaps a quarter of the time, the rest of the corked bottles do not live up to this experience. It is pretty easy to find vintage bottles at many specialty shops and bars in America, but most fall short of the wonderful leather and damp basement aroma, with flavors more reminiscent of vinegar and musty socks. The one sample I had on cask at a festival still ranks near the top of my favorite glasses of beer.

Greene King Olde Suffolk (Bury St Edmunds, England). Olde Suffolk harkens back to the 18th and 19th centuries, comprising a fresh mild beer blended with a strong ale that has been aged for two years in oak. With hints of sherry and oak, the flavor is reminiscent of Gale's Prize Old Ale, but it is more consistent, and only rarely is it either spectacular or "off." I wish they bottled the 5X (aged portion) straight so I could try it, although on occasion the brewery is known to serve it to visitors.

Le Coq Imperial Extra Double Stout (Lewes, England). With Courage's Russian Imperial Stout no longer brewed with a mixed fermentation as it once was, Le Coq is the closest you can get to a taste of the high alcohol stouts that were shipped to the czars and czarinas of Russia in the 19th century.

Williams Brothers Grozet (Alloa, Scotland). Grozet is a lightly hopped *gruit* flavored with gooseberries. It is a tart callback to the days before hops were the exclusive counterpoint to malt sweetness. Williams Brothers produces several minimally hopped beers (including those flavored with seaweed, pine, and heather), but this is the only one that has perceived sourness.

United States

Serious commercial sour beer production in America only started again in the 1990s. At first, the pioneering craft breweries mimicked the styles and techniques of Belgium, Germany, and Great Britain, but having found their footing many are brewing unique creations, gradually developing their own aesthetic and methods. The best examples often stray from tradition, with unique barrel characters, fruit additions, and base beers. American sour beers tend to be drier and possess a more assertive acidity than Old World examples.

What follows are some noteworthy examples of American sour beers:

The Bruery Tart of Darkness (Placentia, California). Tart of Darkness shows that sour beers now come in all colors. This tart stout is aged in bourbon barrels with a variety of microbes. The result is a marriage of freshly roasted coffee from the malt, vanilla from the charred oak, and fresh cherries from the *Brettanomyces*. That may sound like a mouthful, but at 5.6% ABV it is balanced and approachable.

Jolly Pumpkin Bam Bière (Dexter, Michigan). Bam Bière is low in alcohol, hoppy when fresh, and becomes lightly tart and funky when aged. It is a good beer to search out if you want a gateway to the more aggressive examples. While Jolly Pumpkin's entire production is comprised of barrel-aged sour beers, their beers tend to be among the most approachable.

New Belgium La Folie (Fort Collins, Colorado). The original king of American sour beers, La Folie is at its best when the acidity is potent, with a vinegary sharpness balanced by caramel maltiness. The unpasteurized corked and caged bottles tended to be more complex and aggressive, while the "Lips of Faith" series available in 22 fl. oz. "bombers" are more approachable.

Russian River Supplication (Santa Rosa, California). This brown ale starts with a firm, rounded sourness, followed by distinct dried cherry taste, and finally red wine from the Pinot noir barrels the beer is aged in. All of Russian River's sour beers manage to be both complex and balanced.

The beers described above (and many like them) are the focus of this book. Methods used by American brewers are more applicable to both homebrewers and commercial breweries planning to embark on brewing their own sour beers.

References

1. Patrick McGovern, et al., *Proceedings of the National Academy of Sciences USA* 101(51):17,593.

2. Louis Pasteur, *Etudes sur la Bière*, (Paris: Gauthier-Villars, 1876).

3. Robert Wahl and Max Henius, *American Handy Book of the Brewing, Malting, and Auxiliary Trades.*

4. William J Kelley, 1965. *Brewing in Maryland; From Colonial Times to the Present.*

5. Mitch Steele, *IPA: Brewing Techniques, Recipes, and the Evolution of India Pale Ales.*

6. "Lambic Lager Beer," Tavern Trove, accessed February 24, 2013. http://www.taverntrove.com/item.php?ItemId=60765.

7. John Del Signore. "The Worst Beer In The World, According To Brooklyn Brewery's Garrett Oliver." Accessed December 14, 2013. http://gothamist.com/2011/10/12/garrett_oliver.php.

8. "Bon Beer Voyage's Belgian Beercation Starts in 70 Days!" *Bon Beer Voyage*, accessed December 16, 2013, http://bonbeervoyage.com/new-site/brewery/brouwerij-de-dolle -brouwers/bon-beer-voyages-belgian-beercation-starts-in-70-days.

9. Stan Hieronymus. "A Great Year for Good Beer," *The Beer Connoisseur* (Fall 2010). http://www.beerconnoisseur.com/1995-a-great-year-for -good-beer.

10. "Past Winners," Great American Beer Festival, December 14, 2013, http://www.greatamericanbeerfestival.com/the-competition/winners /past-winners.

11. *Limited Ingredients: Flavoring Substances and Adjuvants Subject to Limitation or Restriction*, prepared by Laboratory – Scientific Services Division for Alcohol and Tobacco Tax and Trade Bureau, U.S. Department of the Treasury (Washington D.C., 2012), Last modified September 4, 2012, http://www.ttb.gov/ssd/limited_ingredients.shtml.

12. McGee, *On Food and Cooking.*

13. Eleanor Snowdon, et al., *Journal of Agricultural and Food Chemistry* 54(18):6465.

14. Peter Bouckaert and Eric Salazar. "New Belgium Brewing" audio podcast. October 19, 2006.

15. Peter Bouckaert. "Brewery Rodenbach: Brewing Sour Ales," April 1996.

GETTING STARTED

2

Before we venture into the step-by-step details of sour beer production, from mashing to packaging, I want to provide an array of general tips and suggestions. Brewing sour beer requires a different mindset than for clean beers, because the time frame for most production methods is measured in months and years instead of days and weeks. Despite the additional wait, most of the basic techniques used for wort production and fermentation are the same as those for other, more common styles. In fact, many clean recipes can be converted into sour beers simply by pitching additional microbes and giving them the time needed to create acids, esters, and phenols. Many breweries do just that, taking wort or beer brewed for regular production and barrel-aging it for months or years with the addition of *Lactobacillus*, *Brettanomyces*, and *Pediococcus*.

General Suggestions for Brewing Sour Beers

For those first starting out on producing sour beers there are some important aspects to keep in mind. Educating your palate, using quality ingredients, and sharing your beers with other sour-heads to obtain feedback, are all vital parts of the process. What follows here are some additional pointers that are useful to remember.

Practice patience. Sour beers will test your restraint—be patient. Avoid pulling samples of a batch frequently, as this serves to introduce oxygen and the end result is that you will steal good beer from your future self. Tasting beer mid-fermentation can also cause unnecessary worry, because off-tasting intermediate by-products or odd textures will come and go as the microbes work. When pulling samples, take a specific gravity (SG) reading to see how much carbohydrates the microbes have remaining. Taking pH readings may be helpful, but many brewers rely primarily on their tongue to gauge acidity (see Measuring Acidity below).

Brew regularly. Start new batches of sour beer on a regular basis to build a production pipeline. It is easy to look forward a few months to the next beer that will be ready, but it will drive you crazy thinking that the beer you are brewing today will not be ready to drink for a year or more. Souring multiple beers simultaneously also opens up the world of blending, an integral part of the process at virtually every commercial brewery (see Chapter 11).

Do not rush packaging. Do not attempt to speed things along by trying to force a sour beer to meet your schedule. Wait for it to be ready (i.e., based on its smell, taste, appearance, and stable gravity) before packaging. Not every sour beer will behave in the same way—even when you brew the same recipe with the same microbes it is unlikely to progress in an identical way every time.

Document the process. Take plenty of notes on the process and flavor at each step to help avoid mistakes or recreate successes in the future. Technique evolves slowly with sour beers because the feedback loop takes years instead of the weeks or months it does with clean beers.

Divide and conquer. Experimentation is made easier by splitting batches to produce multiple beers. Draw a portion of the wort from a clean beer and pitch the microbes required to convert it into a sour beer. For example, Lost Abbey's delicious Red Poppy is nothing but their mild ale (Dawn Patrol Dark) and pale lager (Amigo Lager) blended together, then barrel-aged with additional microbes and sour cherries.[1] Try splitting a sour beer batch and add fruit, spice, dry hops, another beer, wine, or other flavorings to a portion while leaving the remainder as is. Most lambic breweries produce a single base beer which they then blend and flavor in a variety of ways. In this way a brewer can produce several beers without much additional effort. It also allows you to learn by comparing the same beer with and without added flavors.

Measuring Acidity

Most brewers are aware of the impact pH has on enzyme activity in the mash, as well as its impact on hop utilization, Maillard reactions, and protein coagulation in the boil. In addition, checking the pH is one way to monitor the acidity of a sour beer. This allows you to objectively track the progress of the acid-producing bacteria and judge when their work is complete, thus helping to make your results more repeatable.

The pH scale runs from 0 (zero), highly acidic, to 14.0, highly alkaline, with 7.0 being neutral. The pH readings of sour beers generally range from 3.0 to 3.9. At the upper end of this range the beers taste lightly tart, while at the lower end they have a bracing acidity. The pH scale is logarithmic, like the Richter scale, meaning that each decrease of 1.0 indicates a 10 times greater acidity. As a result, while a pH of 3.1 and 3.7 may sound quite close, a beer at pH 3.1 actually contains four times more acidity than one at pH 3.7. If a batch falls below a pH of 3.0 it would probably be best saved for blending, where it can be used to boost the acidity of another batch. One of the most acidic commercial beers is Hanssens Artisanaal Oudbeitje Lambic, at a pH of 2.8.[2]

How acidic a beer is perceived to be is not solely a matter of its pH. Each acid contributes a unique character to the flavor of a beer. A beer that has a pH of 3.5 due to the presence of lactic acid will have a much softer palate than a beer that has the same pH resulting from acetic acid. Residual malt sweetness can balance the acidity, as can the perceived sweetness from herbs and spices. A well-trained palate is your best tool for determining what the final character of a beer will be; pH measurements are a good way to improve your ability to judge acidity.

Scott Vaccaro of Captain Lawrence Brewing Company recommends purchasing a pH meter to monitor the acidity of your beer if you want repeatability.[3] A pH meter is quick and accurate, but they do take effort to calibrate and store. A drawback is that, even with proper storage in a buffered solution, the probe needs to be replaced about once a year. For a variety of reasons (e.g., accuracy, readability, and resolution) pH test strips are a less than ideal way to measure the acidity of a sour beer.

Many vintners rely on titration, rather than a direct measure of pH, to determine the amount of acid present in their grapes and wine. Compared with pH alone, measuring the titratable acidity in terms of chemical equivalents can give a more accurate understanding of exactly what is happening in your souring beer, but requires more effort. Acid–base titration test kits are available from homebrew shops and online suppliers. If your titration kit calculates the titratable acidity as equivalent tartaric acid levels, you may want to multiply the result by 1.2 to convert it to lactic acid equivalents (the primary source of acidity in most sour beers).[4]

Analytically measuring the pH of a beer is of particular importance if you are performing a technique that acidifies the wort before primary fermentation, such as a sour mash or sour wort that uses lactic acid bacteria prior to the main fermentation. With these bacteria quickly producing acid, it can be harder to judge the amount of acid by taste because the sweetness of the wort obscures it. If the pH falls much below 4.0 (the lowest clean beers typically reach) some brewer's yeast strains will have trouble completing a healthy fermentation. Below a pH of 3.5 and there is significant risk of off-flavors and an incomplete brewer's yeast fermentation.

Instead of measuring pH, some brewers prefer to use the titration method when monitoring pre-fermentation souring. Wort contains compounds that buffer against pH changes, which results in a rapid pH drop once the buffering capacity has been expended. You should begin to worry about the primary fermentation if the titratable acidity for lactic acid is above 0.5%—more than that and many brewer's yeasts will have trouble completing a clean fermentation.

Sanitation and Safety

Brewing sour beer brings with it a host of challenges that must be addressed even before you start brewing. These challenges fall into two overlapping categories: sanitation and safety. The wild yeast and bacteria used in the souring process require brewers to take extraordinary steps to keep them from accidentally finding their way into clean beers. The equipment and processes used in the production of sour beers require special attention be paid to safety protocol.

Sanitation

The first anxiety-causing aspect of brewing your first sour beer is not time, variability, or even the risk of bad beer—it is the fear that the "wild" microbes they introduce will ruin other batches of clean beer. This is a legitimate concern. Over the years I have lost a couple of batches to unintentional souring, but the risk is minimal if you follow a few general rules for sanitation and separation of your fermentation equipment.

The same species of yeast and bacteria that are intentionally added to sour beers are found naturally in the environment around you, and the sanitation methods you might typically use are designed to kill them (e.g., Star San®, iodine-based sanitizer, heat, peracetic acid). Read the instructions for your sanitizer of choice and follow the guidelines for concentration, minimum time, and temperature. Using a higher than recommended concentration of sanitizer may not kill additional microbes, and it risks contributing off-flavors to your beer if the residue is not rinsed. Longer contact times, on the other hand, will kill a higher percentage of microbes than the minimum time.[6]

Cleaning your equipment before sanitizing is as important as sanitizing itself. Sanitizers are designed to work on surfaces that are free from the organic and inorganic deposits that provide protective cover for microbes. Cleaning with hot water and either caustic, acid cleaner, Five Star PBW™ (Powdered Brewery Wash), trisodium phosphate (TSP), or Oxyclean Free before sanitizing will remove buildup left behind by the previous batch. Most homebrewers will want to avoid the hazards of working with caustic, but in extreme cases it is available as beer line cleaner. As with the sanitizers, follow the manufacturer's instructions for temperature, concentration, and safety precautions when using cleaning agents.

I have heard several people ask along these lines: "If you can brew a beer with an expressive Belgian yeast strain followed by a clean American strain and not have the second beer taste 'Belgian,' then why worry about contamination?" What these people are missing is that it takes far fewer cells of these non-*Saccharomyces* microbes to create enough fermentation by-products to alter the flavor of the finished beer. These yeast and bacteria are able to slowly reproduce as they metabolize dextrins (long chains of sugar molecules), starches (even longer chains of sugar molecules), and other compounds that no brewer's yeast can ferment. If, on the other hand you accidentally introduce a few thousand cells of a different *Saccharomyces* strain in your wort it will be out-competed by the hundreds of billions of cells from your pitch and not have a noticeable effect on the beer. Peter Bouckaert of New Belgium Brewing Company performed a test that showed how few cells of a non-*Saccharomyces* microbial species are needed to affect the flavor of a beer: he added 100 *Brettanomyces* cells per milliliter to bottles of all of his standard beers in an attempt to see if *Brettanomyces* would delay oxidation by scavenging oxygen. Even at that miniscule pitching rate, the test bottles developed a noticeably funky flavor before the control batches exhibited deterioration from oxidation.[7]

Diligence and a few extra precautions are all you need to keep these additional microbes out of your clean beers. For your mash tun, brew kettle, wort chiller, or anything else that touches the wort before the microbes are pitched, there is no need to have separate equipment. If you are a homebrewer, you should keep a second set of cool-side plastic equipment (e.g., tubing, auto-siphon, bottling wand, bottling bucket, and sample thief) for use only in beers with microbes other than brewer's yeast. You may wish to hand down older clean beer equipment to the sour beer process every year or so. This extends the usable life of equipment past the time it might normally be replaced. Identifying your sour beer equipment with brightly colored tape or a permanent marker ensures you do not mistake it for the equipment used for clean beers.

Stainless steel fermentors are particularly safe because they do not scratch easily, which leaves no place for the microbes to hide from the sanitizer. Keep in mind that glass can still scratch easily if you are not careful. Plastic is risky because even microscopic scratches give shelter to these microbes (some strains of *Brettanomyces* are as small as one quarter of the size of brewer's yeast, with lactic acid bacteria smaller still). Perform frequent visual inspections and discard any damaged plastic. Never clean plastic with anything abrasive.

Most commercial breweries producing both sour and clean beers follow a policy of strict equipment separation. To ensure the *Brettanomyces* and bacteria do not find their way into other beers, both Captain Lawrence Brewing Company (Elmsford, NY) and the Bruery (Placentia, CA) keep two entirely separate sets of gaskets, hoses, pumps, filler parts, and valves for clean and sour beers.[8] Some breweries go further than others—at Russian River Brewing Company (Santa Rosa, CA) the brewers wear different sets of boots, gloves, and goggles depending on what type of beer they are transferring. Employees do not re-enter the regular beer cellar for that day once they have worked with sour beer.

Conical fermentors have numerous small crevices, such as around the *zwickel* (sample port), where microbes can hide. Russian River ferments both clean and sour beers in the same tanks, but all fittings are switched out between batches. They use a color-coded system of buckets, hoses, and Tri-Clamp® gaskets: no marking for clean beers; blue for *Brettanomyces* beers; and red for beers with both bacteria and *Brettanomyces*.[9] It does not take much for contamination to take hold. Russian River suspects that some bottles from an early batch of their strong golden ale, Damnation, contracted *Brettanomyces* from a sight glass that was not swapped out after bottling their 100% *Brettanomyces* beer, Sanctification.[10] At Captain Lawrence only one tank is used for inoculation and aging of sour beers, but other breweries avoid trouble by waiting to pitch souring microbes directly into the barrels.[11] The Bruery uses the same bright tanks for packaging, regardless of whether a beer is clean or sour.[12]

The team at Surly Brewing Co. (Minneapolis, MN), under head brewer Todd Haug, disassembles their Meheen bottler and boils every piece that comes into contact with beer during production. This is to ensure the *Brettanomyces* from their specialty sour beers does not find its way into their clean bottled beers.[13]

There are a couple of breweries that do not separate their equipment. With the exception of the bottling lines, Ithaca Beer Co. uses the same hoses and equipment for both their clean beers and those with *Brettanomyces*. Ithaca's former head brewer, Jeff O'Neil, prefers to sanitize with heat, because it can kill microbes found in cracks and deposits where chemical sanitizers cannot reach. Be careful when exposing plastic to near-boiling water however, as it can melt. Russian River brewmaster Vinnie Cilurzo agrees that sanitizing with heat is smart, but when propagating microbes he uses dedicated kegs and tanks for each microbe and blend.[14]

In addition to doing their best to keep clean beers clean during production, many breweries also have a laboratory to catch issues before beer leaves the facility. The Bruery plates all of their clean beers onto petri dishes to test for wild yeast and bacteria cultures. They also perform microbial cell counts, forced fermentation tests, and even swab hoses for culturing to ensure they are not contaminated.[15] All of this effort is necessary because none of the Bruery's beers are sterile-filtered or pasteurized. Breweries that do kill all of the microbes in their beers have less of an issue with cross contamination, because the microbes have a much shorter window to create off-flavors.

There is a difference of opinion over whether beers using *Brettanomyces* alone or *Brettanomyces* with brewer's yeast, i.e., without bacteria, should fall into the clean beer or the sour beer category. Most brewers I talked to run beers with *Brettanomyces* through their sour beer gear. The Bruery, however, originally allowed *Brettanomyces* beers, even without bacteria to go through their clean fermentors and bottling line. At that point, they packaged their beers that included bacteria on a dedicated six-head gravity wine filler. As these beers became a larger part of the Bruery's output, they purchased a Meheen bottler that they now use for any beers fermented with microbes other than brewer's yeast.[16]

There is no reason to segregate impermeable fermentors into different areas for fermenting and aging clean and sour beers. Nevertheless, home-brewers may wish to store clean and funky beers on different sides of the same room so as not to disturb the sour beer fermentors when moving the clean beers around. *Brettanomyces* is capable of airborne dispersal, so all samples of sour beer should be carefully contained, and be diligent to avoid spilling them on "clean" gear.

Barrels are a special case because they are permeable; do not allow barrels containing clean and sour beer to touch. Many commercial breweries choose to keep sour barrels, *Brettanomyces* barrels, and non-sour barrels segregated in totally different rooms, and in some cases different buildings.

If all of this seems like too much, the other option is to follow the lead of Jolly Pumpkin Artisan Ales or the Anchorage Brewing Company, both of which started by brewing only sour and funky beers. This eliminates the risk of cross contamination, but it may not be the solution for brewers who still want to produce clean beers as well. After almost 10 years at their original brewery, Jolly Pumpkin moved in to a 70,000 sq. ft. (6,500 m²) facility in 2012, where Ron Jeffries oversees the brewing of both sour and non-sour beers.[17]

When brewing spontaneously fermented beers there is an extra layer of sanitation that should be implemented. Proper control of wort pH is crucial to controlling the growth of microorganisms (e.g., *Enterobacter*) that can produce undesirable flavors or aromas as well as biogenic amines. A pH at or below 4.5 will inhibit the growth of these microorganisms in wort.

Safety

Personal and employee safety should be your primary concern no matter what brewing task is being considered. Some things to keep in mind:

- Foster a culture of respect and safety in the brewery with personal buy-in from all levels of employees. This will ensure safety and efficiency, and help to keep a sour program healthy.
- Barrels must be handled carefully—when they are being stacked or unstacked ensure that no employees are standing nearby. If operating a forklift, always consult the equipment instructions before loading/unloading to ensure that the height and weight limits are not exceeded.
    - If you are located in an area with frequent seismic activity, ensure that barrels are stacked in a stable configuration not exceeding four levels.[18] Place the barrels in an area that, if they fell, the only damage would be to the barrels themselves and not people or equipment.
- Mold control in the barrel room is crucial for maintaining health standards. Lowering the ambient humidity reduces the tendency for mold to grow on the barrels and other surfaces. Frequently inspect all surfaces, and apply an appropriate cleaning product to remove any mold found on walls or floors.
- Understand that clean beer contaminated with *Brettanomyces* can undergo attenuation following packaging, sometimes to such an extent that the container may rupture. You must follow rigorous sanitation procedures and carefully control carbon dioxide (CO_2) pressure.
- If you want to try adding *Brettanomyces* to a clean beer you need to start with a beer that is already near 1.000 SG (0 degrees Plato [°P]), and package in heavy-gauge bottles that can handle higher pressure than standard beer bottles. For beers that do not have a suitably low gravity to package with *Brettanomyces*, the yeast should be added to the fermentor and allowed to ferment until the gravity is stable. Over time you will learn at what gravity it is safe to bottle your beer, assuming a consistent recipe and process.
- Brewers with a high number of barrels often transfer beer out of them with a Bulldog Pup® or Rack-it-Teer®. These stainless steel contraptions allow you to push the beer out of the barrel with pressure from CO_2, which has the added benefit of minimizing oxida-

tion. However, use caution when transferring a fruit beer under pressure to avoid clogging the tubing with fruit, which may cause the barrel to burst (Upland Brewing Co. had a barrel burst when a chunk of kiwi clogged the tubing in their Bulldog Pup). Never exceed 5 psi (34.5 kPa), so that even if the transfer does cause a blockage you will be safe.

- Whether homebrewer, head brewer, or owner, it is not enough that you alone are aware of safety procedures—it is crucial that all colleagues and staff are also informed. Devote yourself to ensuring that proper employee training is in place to address all of these potential safety hazards.

Now onto the fun stuff!

Brewing Your First Sour Beer

If you have never brewed a sour beer before, rather than reading this entire book trying to plan a complex and "perfect" sour beer, I advise you brew a basic one now that can age while you read and plan for your second batch. Scott Vaccaro offered some good advice for beginners: avoid starting with a strong base beer (anything over 6.5% ABV) because elevated alcohol makes souring and bottle conditioning more difficult.[5] Avoiding especially dark or hoppy beers is ideal too, as you will read in Chapter 3.

The easiest way to brew your first sour beer is to start with a favorite recipe that fits these constraints: original gravity 1.040–1.060 (10–15°P), fewer than 20 International Bitterness Units (IBUs), color below 25 Standard Reference Method (SRM), and minimal late boil hopping. Brew it exactly like you would normally through cooling the wort. Pitch the standard amount of whatever brewer's yeast strain you usually use, but also add a souring microbe blend from Wyeast or White Labs. You can also add the bottle dregs from two of your favorite unpasteurized sour beers. Allow the beer to ferment for two to three weeks before transferring it to a secondary fermentor with 1 oz. of oak cubes per 5 gal. (30 g per 20 L). Allow the beer to age at room temperature, 60°F–75°F (16°C–24°C), until you are happy with the flavor and the SG is stable (usually 6–12 months), indicating that it is ready to bottle or keg.

You will take away much more from reading this book if you have a batch of beer to observe, smell, and taste along the way. If brewing your own right now is not an option, then sample commercial sour beers to give yourself firsthand experience of the results produced by the methods and ingredients that will be discussed in the chapters which follow.

References

1. "The Red Poppy." Lost Abbey (The). Accessed April 22, 2013. http://www.portbrewing.com/pdf/lost_abbey_red_poppy.pdf.
2. Jeff Sparrow, *Wild Brews: Beer Beyond the Influence of Brewer's Yeast.*
3. Scott Vaccaro, "The Sunday Session" audio podcast, August 31, 2008.
4. Ronald S. Jackson, *Wine Science: Principles and Applications.*
5. Scott Vaccaro, personal communication with author, June 13, 2011.
6. John Palmer, *How to Brew.*
7. Peter Bouckaert and Eric Salazar, "New Belgium Brewing" audio podcast, October 19, 2006.
8. Vaccaro, pers. comm., June 13, 2011; Patrick Rue, "The Sunday Session" audio podcast, November 2, 2008.
9. Peter Bouckaert, Ron Gansberg, Tomme Arthur, Tyler King and Vinnie Cilurzo, "A Comprehensive Look at Sour Ale Production," panel interview, Craft Brewers Conference, San Diego, May 4, 2012.
10. Vinnie Cilurzo, personal communication with author, August 28, 2012.
11. Vaccaro, pers. comm., June 13, 2011.
12. Tyler King, pers. comm., October 19, 2011.
13. Todd Haug, personal communication with author, March 6, 2012.
14. Cilurzo, pers. comm., August 28, 2012.
15. King, pers. comm., October 19, 2011; "Careful Cellaring, Part 1: The Quality Assurance Process for Creating Clean, Living Beer," *The Bruery* blog, December 17, 2013, http://bruery.blogspot.com/2013/12/quality-assurance-brewing-living-beer.html.
16. King, pers. comm., October 19, 2011.
17. Ron Jeffries, personal communication with author, September 26, 2011.
18. Charles Chadwell, Kyle Brennan and Matthew Porter, "Seismic Hazard Mitigation of Wine Barrel Stacks," in *Don't Mess with Structural Engineers: Expanding Our Role*, Proceedings of 2009 Structures Congress, April 30–May 2, Austin, Texas (Reston, VA: American Society of Civil Engineers, 2009), p.1010. doi:10.1061/41031(341)112.

WORT PRODUCTION

3

Wort production for sour beers is very similar to wort production for clean beers. The wort can be produced using the same techniques and ingredients as other types of beer. If you are souring the wort before primary fermentation or employing a more complex mash schedule, there will be twists to the process, but in most other cases the steps are familiar: crushed grains are mashed with hot water, wort is collected and then boiled with hops, before finally being chilled and pitched prior to fermentation.

Recipe Overview

I have brewed and tasted delectable sour beers based on numerous classic styles, including: English brown ale, porter, imperial stout, old ale, wee heavy, *bière de garde*, *wit*, Belgian pale ale, *saison*, Belgian blond ale, *dubbel*, *tripel*, *quadrupel* (Belgian strong dark), and gruit. Brewing the classic sour styles (Berliner weisse, lambic, gueuze, Flemish red, and *oud bruin*) and adhering to their traditional production techniques requires additional work.

The only beers that I avoid souring are those that are aggressively bitter, roasted, spiced, or smoked because these flavors will be exaggerated by the low final gravity (FG) of a traditional sour beer. Sweetness is frequently part of the balance in clean beers, so a holiday spiced ale, double India pale ale, or imperial stout recipe may need to be softened if you want to turn it into a sour beer. Softening can be accomplished by either blending the beer with one that has a mellower character, or reformulating the recipe to diminish the aggressive trait in the base beer.

Completely off-style brewing is welcome for the wort of a sour beer as well. A few of the more "out-there" beers I have soured are: a honey-peach wheat beer, a black cardamom dark saison, a blend of spiced saison and bière de garde, a butternut squash brown ale, and amber buckwheat ale. Not every idea is going to yield a terrific beer on your first try, but there are wonderful combinations waiting to be made that cannot be found either in the style guidelines or in your neighborhood craft beer store.

Designing a Grain Bill

Recipe design for established styles is covered later in this chapter, but first a few general rules for designing the grist for sour ales that do not conform to one of the classic Belgian or German styles. Sour beers can start at a wide range of gravities. I have brewed batches that begin as low as 1.030 SG (7.5°P) and as high as 1.120 SG (28°P). The only major consideration with an original gravity at the high end is the risk that the microbes will not sour the beer if the alcohol level climbs above their tolerance. If you plan to go above 1.070 SG (17°P), you will need to ensure that the microbes you select are suitably hardy.

When designing a recipe, Ron Jeffries of Jolly Pumpkin Artisan Ales suggests: "Think about what each malt is contributing and how much of that particular flavor contribution you are looking for. Think about the beer and how you want it to look, smell, and taste first and then work backwards to a recipe."[1] You also have to imagine how the beer will change as it ferments, carbonates, and ages, and whether you will be adding fruit or barrel character.

Base Malts

Base malts provide starch, the enzymes to convert that starch into fermentable sugar, and the structural malty flavor that support the more intense flavors contributed by the specialty malts. For most sour beers barley comprises the majority of the grist, but many other malted grains contain a sufficient quantity of amylase enzymes to convert their own starches. Continental Pilsner malt is the most traditional base malt for sour beer production, because it has a clean grainy flavor that allows the specialty malts and microbes to express themselves. American pale two-row malt has a similar character that is even more neutral, and is another good choice. Munich malt is ideal for darker sour beers, adding a strong, bready malt character that ages gracefully.

Other base malts, such as Vienna and English pale, can be used if you enjoy their toasty flavors. Consider including American pale six-row malt if brewing a recipe with a high proportion of unmalted adjunct grains, although modern two-row malt has nearly the same diastatic power. There is no real risk with slightly under-converting the starches anyway, because the long-chain carbohydrates which remain will provide additional fermentables for the non-brewer's yeast microbes. Ron Jeffries advocates mixing several base malts, as he does for Jolly Pumpkin's Madrugada Obscura, to add complexity by providing varying degrees of modification, thus replicating the results of poorly controlled historic malting.[2]

Specialty Malts

Specialty malts are used to provide unique malt flavors and color to beer. Although not required for a great sour beer, specialty malts can be used to impart richer flavors such as toffee, chocolate, or dark fruit. With all of the complexity found in sour ales the subtle character of specialty malts is often lost or muddled together; therefore, strive for simple grain bills when possible. Utilizing seven or eight different malts can produce spectacular sour beers if the recipe is constructed skillfully, but in most cases including a greater variety of malts will not enhance the complexity of the finished beer.

Crystal and caramel malts play important roles in the grain bills of many sour beers. They add aromas and flavors reminiscent of caramelized sugar, raisin, and toast, providing complexity to the malt character of the finished beer. When mashed, these malts do not lower the fermentability of the wort by as much as many brewers believe, but the effect is noticeable.[3] While the inclusion of caramel or crystal malts is not an effective method to add fermentables specifically for non-*Saccharomyces* microbes, some of the specialty malt's perceived sweetness will remain even after the mixed-fermentation, helping to balance both alcohol and acidity.

Dehusked (or debittered) roasted malts, like Weyermann Carafa® Special, are a smart choice for dark sour beers because they lack the sharpness of traditional roasted barley, black patent, and chocolate malt.

Minimizing acrid roasted flavors is important when you are brewing a beer that will finish dry. Standard dark grains can be used, but refrain from adding a large quantity unless the grain is cold steeped or you are using a souring process that ensures a suitably high FG. When I brewed a batch inspired by Courage Russian Imperial Stout, I used metabisulfite to kill the *Brettanomyces* when the gravity reached 1.020 SG (5°P) so the large amount of black patent malt would not result in a harsh beer (more on arresting fermentation can be found in Chapter 12). Scott Vaccaro of Captain Lawrence Brewing Company says he finds less roasty beers usually let the aromatics from *Brettanomyces* and the sourness from lactic acid bacteria come through in a "cleaner way."[4]

Toasted specialty malts like amber, biscuit, brown, special roast, and Victory® are not as commonly used in sour beers as they are in clean beers. Small amounts may be used, but be careful because sourness does not complement pronounced toasty flavors. Certain strains of *Brettanomyces* produce similarly toasty flavors in the form of tetrahydropyridines which can lead to flavor overload (in higher concentrations the same compound provides the mousy aromatics that many *Brettanomyces* detractors despise).[5]

Acidulated malt, which has been coated with lactic acid produced by naturally occurring *Lactobacillus*, was originally developed as a way to allow German brewers (who adhere to the Reinheitsgebot) the ability to lower the pH of their mash without necessitating more effort-intensive processes for souring a portion of the mash or wort. For beers without lactic acid bacteria, acid malt is a good choice for adding a light lactic tartness. It can also lower the pH slightly, which enhances *Brettanomyces* fermentation and provides a substrate for the production of the fruity ester, ethyl lactate. The standard rule of thumb is that adding 1% acid malt to the grist will lower the mash pH by 0.1, but this only holds true in a standard mash with a pH of around 5.0–5.5. As pH is a logarithmic scale, you cannot expect a 20% addition of acid malt to lower the pH from 5.2 to 3.2 (lowering the pH by 2.0 requires increasing the amount of acid present by a factor of 100). Despite this, acid malt can be used in larger percentages to provide a portion of the sourness for a beer, as Ithaca does for Brute (for details of their production method, see Chapter 5).[6]

There are numerous other specialty malts available that can be added to sour beers, but remember to account for the low FG of many sour beers accentuating flavors that would normally be balanced by sweetness. Other malts that have been used in sour beers include honey malt, pale chocolate malt, coffee malt, and various smoked malts. Jester King Brewery's (Austin, TX) Salt Lick is a great example of a sour smoked beer. A portion of the base malt is smoked over pecan wood at the Salt Lick BBQ in Driftwood, Texas.[7]

Grains Other than Barley

Brewing evolved out of the necessity to preserve the annual grain harvest for future consumption. While barley was (and still is) the grain best suited for brewing because of its combination of husk, carbohydrates, protein content, and flavor, there are many other grains available. Other cereal grains contribute their own unique flavors, and several have a long history of use in sour beers. Current law requires that beers marketed as lambics in the European Union include 30%–40% unmalted wheat.[8] In America, unmalted grains are often added to sour beer because they contribute starch and dextrins (when used with an appropriate mashing technique) that are unfermentable by *Saccharomyces* but can be consumed by the other microbes.

Another reason that adjuncts have remained popular in sour beer production may be that they lower the buffering capacity of the wort. This means that less acid is required to lower the pH of the beer.[9]

Using truly raw grains takes extra effort during the mash (covered under Mashing later in this chapter), so if that is impractical or too time-consuming for you, more highly-processed grains can be used in their place. Flaked and torrefied grains are still unmalted, but can be added directly to an infusion mash. Malted wheat, oats, or rye can also be used without special mashing procedures. In fact, all of these malts have more than enough enzymes to convert their own starches into sugars, in some cases to a greater extent than malted barley, and as a result can be used for the entire grist. I find that malted grains tend to have a stronger flavor contribution than the same grain unmalted, but provide less body.

Maltsters produce a range of specialty malts using grains other than barley. A few examples include Briess Midnight Wheat, Simpsons Golden Naked Oats, and Weyermann® Carawheat®. These specialty malts should be used as you would crystal and chocolate malts made from barley. The only difference is that, because these malts are huskless, the roasted malts have a smooth flavor that is reminiscent of dehusked barley malts like Weyermann Carafa® Special.

Using large quantities of huskless grains can cause a slow runoff. If this is a concern, add rice hulls to the mash to increase the amount of filter material. The general rule is to add 5%–10% of the weight of the huskless adjunct in rice hulls, because this is the percentage of a whole grain that is husk.

Wheat. Unmalted wheat adds a typical cereal character to the flavor and fullness to the body. In addition, the high protein levels improve head retention. It is a classic addition to many Belgian beers such as lambic, gueuze, and wit, although by law these beers cannot include more than 40% wheat.

Oats. Historically, unmalted oats were used occasionally in lambic grists. Oats are not regularly added to clean pale beers because of the haze they impart, but the microbes present in sour beers and the extended aging period help produce a clear finished beer.

Rye. This underutilized grain contains beta-glucans and is relatively high in protein. Rye often contributes a viscous, almost syrupy, body. I especially like flaked rye in darker beers, which often come across thin after the souring process is complete. Brewed with a substantial portion of rye malt, the Bruery released Sour in the Rye, which has more of the bready/earthy/toasty flavor that I associate with rye bread.

Corn and rice. Either corn or rice is a good addition if you want to dilute the malt character of a beer and ensure a crisp finish. Including these grains in a standard mash will result in the same ratio of sugars to dextrins as using malted barley alone. This is the case because the same enzymes from the malted barley will be working at the same temperature. So, contrary to popular belief, adding any gelatinized grains — those whose starch granules have been swelled to the point of bursting (including flaked or torrefied corn or rice) — to an infusion mash will neither increase nor decrease the fermentability of the wort. Despite the Ithaca Beer Company's practice of adding more than 5% corn to their Brute sour beer, it finishes with a higher FG than most other sour beers.[10]

Sugars

In addition to malts and raw grains, there are other sources of sugars available to add to the wort. When Lindemans (Vlezenbeek, Flemish

Brabant) introduced a bottled version of their classic Faro in 1978, they added 10 oz. of candi sugar per gallon of lambic (75 g per L), enough to raise the gravity by 0.028 SG (7°P)—it is important to note the candi sugar was added after pasteurization had killed the yeast and bacteria.[11] Pure sugars adds sweetness alone, while unrefined sugars, such as honey, agave syrup, palm sugar (e.g., jaggery), maple syrup, and sugar cane derivatives (e.g., molasses and muscovado), each deliver their own flavor. There are also refined sugars, such as dark candi sugar, caramel, and invert sugar, which are treated and cooked to cause sugar molecules to transform into intensely flavorful caramelization and Maillard reaction products. A few examples of American sour beers that include sugars are Bullfrog Brewery's Beekeeper (a blend of honeys, including buckwheat),[12] McKenzie Brew House's Irma Extra (blonde candi sugar and honey), Hill Farmstead Brewery's Ann (20% Vermont wildflower honey),[13] and Cambridge Brewing Company's Resolution #9 (dark candi syrup).[14]

The later the sugar is added in the brewing process the more of its distinctive flavors and aroma will be present in the finished beer. Most brewers I interviewed add granulated sugars and sugar syrups to the boil. You must be careful to avoid sugar sticking to the bottom of the kettle and burning. If sugars are added to the boil or to the primary fermentor they will quickly be fermented by the *Saccharomyces* and will not contribute significantly to the souring process. Honey requires greater care than other sugars because its floral notes are so volatile that it should not be boiled. The contribution of wildflower honey to flavor and aroma will vary depending on the location of the hives and what flowers were in bloom. Sourcing locally produced raw honey may yield more flavorful results, but you should only add it after the primary fermentation or risk the loss of delicate aromatics. Adding honey (or other sugars) after souring for several months will feed the dominant bacteria and *Brettanomyces*.

Classic-Style Grain Bills
The only four classic sour beer styles which survived the lean years have been gaining popularity with the resurgence of craft beer in the United States. There are a few other sour styles not completely lost to history that have been resurrected, like Gose and Lichtenhainer, but there is not an adequate consensus on their production methods and recipes to include them here. Few of these styles were simply created by a brewer one day; most are the

product of slow development over centuries in response to local taste, laws, and availability of ingredients. The best examples were not originally brewed to a prescriptive style, but had been brewed for so long in the tradition of that brewery or area that the style guidelines grew up around them.

Berliner Weisse

This lactic wheat beer is the only sour German beer style that has been continually brewed to present day. While German wheat beers are required by law to contain at least 50% wheat malt, Berliner weisse oddly does not fall into this category.[15] For example, the mash for Berliner Kindl Weisse contains about 25% wheat malt, with the remainder of the grist usually comprised of Pilsner malt.[16] As a *schankbier* (literally "draft beer," but used to refer to beers that are low alcohol) Berliner weisse was for a time strictly defined as starting between 1.028 and 1.032 SG (7°P–8°P). However, since the implementation of the Provisional German Beer Law in 1993 Berliner weisse can start as high as 1.040 SG (10°P), although historically some versions were stronger still.[17,18] In 2012 Southampton Publick House (Southampton, NY) released Überliner, a 6% ABV recreation of these stronger versions.

Lambic and Gueuze

While each Belgian lambic brewer has their own unique recipe and process for brewing their masterpieces, this grain bill is one of the classics: 60%–70% Pilsner malt, with the remainder being unmalted wheat. Low protein, or "soft," winter wheat is said to be the ideal choice, but is not a requirement.[19] The inclusion of raw wheat necessitates a more complex mash because its starch granules are not gelatinized. Flaked and torrefied wheat are already gelatinized, so they can be added directly to an infusion mash. More information about your options for gelatinization can be found in the Mashing section later in this chapter.

Original gravities range from 1.048 to 1.057 SG (12°P–14°P), for the most part, but there are stronger versions available, such as the mushroomy 8% ABV Oude Geuze Mariage Parfait from Brouwerij Boon in Lembeek.

Flemish Red

The grist for a Flemish red is primarily comprised of Vienna and Munich malts, but often Pilsner is included as well. This style is known for deriving some of its malty, sweet character from darker base malts, so consider adding a small percentage of melanoidin or aromatic malt for grists containing more than 50% Pilsner malt. The red color and dark fruit flavors come from medium and dark crystal malts, and caramel malts (especially Special "B"); combined, these malts sometimes reach as high as 20% of the grist. Some Belgian brewers add corn, while American brewers tend to substitute unmalted wheat or leave out the adjuncts entirely. Flemish reds do not have a roasted flavor, so stay away from dark malts unless they have been debittered or dehusked.

While original gravities range from 1.048–1.057 SG (12°P–14°P), there are also breweries that age higher gravity beers for a long time before blending it with a younger, sweeter beer.[20] If you want a beer that cellars well you can push the gravity higher. For instance, Rodenbach's Vin de Céréale is 10% ABV: at that strength you lose the balance of characters that is the signature of the style, but gain a new balance that offsets the bold maltiness with warming alcohol.

Many classic Belgian sour reds have more sweetness and vinegar character. Alcohol is converted to acetic acid by the microbes when oxygen comes into contact with the souring beer, which produces the vinegar flavor. There are many options for controlling acetic acid production, and these are covered in Chapter 9. The sweetness is a result of blending with a younger beer, or adding sugar and then pasteurizing. There are also a few European brewers that add unfermentable artificial sweeteners (e.g., saccharin) to balance the sharp acidity of the aged beer.

Flemish Oud Bruin

The tenuous bruin–red distinction was first codified by influential British beer writer Michael Jackson in 1977.[21] There are many Belgian beers that straddle the line between the styles, but it makes sense to draw a line somewhere between the two general camps of sour beers brewed in Flanders.

The grists of Flemish oud bruins are similar to Flemish reds, starting with a healthy dose of darker base malts (Munich malt is used most often). Oud bruins usually include a smaller percentage of crystal malt, replacing it with dehusked roasted malts to obtain a light cocoa-malt flavor. Additional specialty malts or dark candi sugar are sometimes added to contribute layers of dark fruit and malt complexity.

Oud bruins are often blended from a sour beer and a fresh malty beer, the latter providing sweetness. In the case of Bavik (Bavikhove, West Flanders), they blend a stronger pale sour with a brown ale to produce their Petrus Oud Bruin (the sour pale is sold as Petrus Aged Pale). In Belgium most oud bruins are sweet in character and low in alcohol, but the best versions (like Goudenband from Liefmans in East Flanders) are stronger and more nuanced, which is the direction that most American breweries take with this style. The original gravity for the lower alcohol versions is generally 1.040–1.049 SG (10°P–12.5°P), while the more esoteric versions can run 1.070–1.079 SG (18°P–19°P).

Water

In most cases it is not necessary to aggressively treat your water above and beyond what is required to adjust the pH of your mash or boil. I have not found that it is beneficial to mimic the water that is found in Flanders, Berlin, or any other "classic" region. But it is standard practice for many brewers in the classic sour beer regions to treat their water or to have complex mash regimens to adjust their mash pH.

If any of the minerals in your water, including sulfate (SO_4^{2-}), calcium (Ca^{2+}), chloride (Cl^-), sodium (Na^+), magnesium (Mg^{2+}), or carbonate (CO_3^{2-}), are over 150 parts per million (ppm) consider diluting with distilled or reverse osmosis water. Avoid brewing with water that is high in iron (over 0.05 ppm)[22] or other compounds that contribute off-flavors. A big mineral finish/flavor generally does not enhance the flavor of sour beers as it does for certain clean styles (e.g., Dortmunder export, Burton pale ale). Carbonate acts as a buffering agent, preventing acids from lowering the pH of the wort or beer. As a result, excess buffering capacity could cause problems in beers intended to have only a light tartness. However, I find that brewing with water high in carbonate reduces the acrid flavor resulting from a large percentage of roasted grains in the mash, a flavor especially detrimental to dark beers fermented with *Brettanomyces*.

Ensure that your water is free of the disinfectants chlorine and chloramine. *Brettanomyces* produces copious quantities of phenols that can form chlorophenols when combined with chlorine. Chlorophenols taste strongly medicinal and are never a positive addition to beer flavor.

In addition to its flavor contribution, the water profile also influences mash pH. Treat your water just as you would for any low-hopped beer with a similar grist. If the mash pH is too high (above 5.6 measured at room temperature), you can lower with either calcium salts, acid malt, or food grade acid. In most cases, however, this is not necessary. I talked to brewers both with very hard and soft water who each take minimalistic approaches to water treatment with their sour beer, despite using more aggressive treatment regimens for their clean beers.

Mashing

For a traditional, long-aged sour beer the easiest option is to go with your standard process during the mash, sparge, and boil. When replicating a classic or historic style (e.g., executing a turbid mash for a lambic, or not boiling a Berliner weisse) you can choose to employ a special hot-side procedure, but it is not required. If you are adding flaked grain or undermodified malt, a step-infusion or decoction mash can be employed.

For most grists, a single infusion mash is sufficient. A protein rest to improve clarity is not as necessary for a sour beer as a clean beer, because the microbes and long aging period of sour beers tends to render them brilliantly clear. Transferring hops and protein break material (trub) into the fermentor is not a major concern, but, if you are planning to age a beer in the primary fermentor for the entire duration of the souring process, try to minimize the amount of trub that comes over with the wort.

Many sour beers benefit from starting with a wort high in dextrins. These chains of sugar molecules are too long for brewer's yeast to ferment, but short enough for various other microbes. A saccharification rest in the upper-150s°F (high 60s°C) increases alpha-amylase enzyme activity, creating a higher proportion of dextrins. If you are planning on a quicker sour beer, mashing at a cooler temperature will allow for a more rapid fermentation, but it will also lead to less sourness in the long term. Mash temperature is the most effective way to influence the composition of sugars and dextrins in the wort.

If you enjoy the smoky flavors produced by aggressive strains marketed as *Brettanomyces bruxellensis* and *B. lambicus*, you can begin your mash with a short ferulic acid rest, maximized at 113°F (45°C), and a pH of 5.8.[23] This rest step is also used when brewing hefeweizen to increase the availability of ferulic acid, which leads to greater microbial production of 4-vinylguaiacol. The 4-vinylguaiacol is responsible for hefeweizen's clove flavor, and is also the precursor for smoky 4-ethylguaiacol produced by

Brettanomyces.[24] Despite the prevalence of 4-vinylguaiacol in German wheat beers, ferulic acid can also be contributed by malted barley. However, the addition of wheat malt has been shown to increase the eventual level of 4-vinylguaiacol compared to a similar wort produced with only barley or an equal amount of unmalted wheat.[25] Be aware that the beta-glucan rest used to diminish the gumminess of unmalted oats or rye has a temperature range (98°F–113°F [37°C–45°C]) that overlaps with the ferulic acid rest. If you do not want aggressive smoky aromatics from *Brettanomyces*, you can reduce polyphenol extraction by avoiding the protein rest, over-sparging, sparging hotter than 170°F (77°C), and sparging with high-pH water.[26]

Starch Gelatinization

While the gelatinization temperature range for wheat (125°F–186°F [52°C–86°C]) contains the saccharification range, this is for refined wheat starch and not the effective range for milled grain. If you have ever tried to thicken a sauce with wheat flour you know it will not fully thicken until the liquid has boiled for a few minutes, while refined cornstarch will completely thicken a sauce well below the boil despite a similar gelatinization range of 144°F–180°F (62°C–80°C). This difference is a result of insoluble protein in the flour, which slows the absorption of water. The finer the grind, and the longer and hotter the mash, the more of the starch from the raw grain will be gelatinized and subsequently converted.

Having starch in the wort of a traditionally fermented sour beer is not a bad thing as it will serve as a carbohydrate source for a long, complex fermentation, but starches which have not been gelatinized are difficult to extract with sparge water at standard temperatures. The turbid mashes traditionally used by Belgian lambic brewers get around this by sparging with near boiling water, which is hot enough to gelatinize the starch granules still present and wash them into the kettle. The easiest way around insufficient gelatinization is to include unmalted grains that are either torrefied or flaked, because these grains are gelatinized during processing and thus capable of being added directly to a single infusion mash. If you want to use a raw unmalted grain in your recipe you have several options for how to gelatinize the starches before saccharification. The simplest method is to boil the milled unmalted grain in copious quantities of water for 20 to 30 minutes before adding this porridge to the main mash. The grain will absorb a large volume of water as it boils, so the minimum ratio is 3 qt. of water for each pound of grain (6.25 L/kg grain). When doughing-in remember to include the heat from this porridge in your calculations for the strike water temperature.

Caleb Staton, head brewer at Upland Brewing Co. (Bloomington, IN), starts by boiling the unmalted wheat for their line of Belgian-style fruit lambics with a small amount of malted barley for an hour to gelatinize the starches, before mixing in the remainder of the malt and additional water to stabilize at a saccharification rest of 158°F (70°C). A 200°F (93°C) sparge is used to collect enough wort for a boil lasting more than two hours. Staton says that, "It's kind of like taking a decoction mash and throwing it in a mosh pit!"[27]

Turbid Mash

The final option for incorporating raw grains into your sour beer is to employ the method used by some lambic brewers—a turbid mash. A turbid mash is the traditional technique for producing lambic wort, as well as for several other Belgian beer styles that include raw wheat. It gelatinizes and converts some of the starches in the raw wheat, but leaves a portion unconverted so that the microbes will be able to work on them later in the fermentation process. In essence, it is a modified decoction step mash where liquid (no grain) is removed from the mash and heated. Only a few Belgian lambic producers still perform this traditional method, while most have moved to step-infusion mashes, which are less labor-intensive.

Turbid mashes have a well-earned reputation as complex and archaic, but the process is not nearly as time-consuming as many of the accounts I have read make it sound. The basic idea is to remove a portion of the starchy wort out of the main mash at various points and heat it to prevent the enzymes from converting the starches and dextrins into easily fermentable sugars. Traditionally, a large basket was pressed into the mash to facilitate drawing off the turbid runnings, but you can simply run off liquid through the bottom of the mash tun. When the enzymes have completed their work, the accumulated turbid runnings are added back to raise the temperature of the mash to mash-out. This allows more complex carbohydrate molecules to survive into the fermentor, providing food for the microbes long after *Saccharomyces* fermentation ends.

Sparging the mash with a large volume of water considerably hotter (185°F [85°C]) than would normally be used for a conventional mash gelatinizes any remaining starches and washes them into the kettle. If the grist does not contain any raw unmalted grain there is no benefit to this step, because all of the starches in malted, flaked, or torrefied grains are gelatinized during processing. Do not worry about tannin extraction, a common concern when over-sparging with water hotter than 170°F (77°C), because the long boil and subsequent aging cause most of the tannins to precipitate before the beer is ready to drink. Indeed, a mellow tannic astringency from both the grain and the oak barrels can be a refreshing part of a finished spontaneously fermented beer. The extended boil will also only create a minimal amount of unfermentable dextrins.[28]

The traditional turbid mash schedule requires three vessels, including two that are heated. This requirement is a challenge for many brewers whose systems are designed for infusion mashes. For information on how Allagash Brewing Company, Jolly Pumpkin Artisan Ales, and Russian River Brewing Company conduct the mashes for their spontaneously fermented beers see Chapter 7.

Turbid Mash Instructions

Here is one interpretation of a turbid mash schedule, based on Brasserie Cantillon Brouwerij (Anderlecht, Brussels). The rest times and temperatures were taken from Jim Liddil's *A Liddil Lambic Lesson*.[29]

The metric units are converted to account for a slightly larger target volume of 20 L.

1. Start with the entire milled grist, 5.25 lb. (2.5 kg) of German Pilsner and 2.75 lb. (1.3 kg) of raw hard winter wheat, in the boil kettle.

    The hot liquor tank starts with 5 gal. (20 L) of water, heated to 144°F (62°C).

2. Mix 2.5 qt. (2.5 L) of the 144°F (62°C) water into the grain to get the mash to 113°F (45°C). This is an extremely low water-to-grain ratio of 0.3 qt./lb. (0.6 L/kg), so there is not much free liquor. Grain holds onto approximately 0.4 qt./lb. (0.8 L/kg) at the end of the mash, so this step just gets the grain damp.

3. Mix the water and grain together in the boil kettle before transferring it into the mash tun (if you have an easy way to agitate your mash, you can start in the mash tun).

The water in the hot liquor tank is heated to a boil and held there for the rest of the infusions.

4. After letting the mash rest for 20 minutes, add 4 qt. (4 L) of boiling water to raise it to 136°F (58°C).

5. After five minutes perform a brief *vorlauf* (recirculation) to remove large chunks of grain and pull 1 qt. (1 L) of wort as you would when lautering. Heat the 1 qt. (1 L) of "turbid" wort to 185°F (85°C) in the boil kettle to halt enzymatic action.

    Immediately add 6 qt. (6 L) of the initial amount of water to heat the mash to 150°F (66°C).

6. After 30 minutes pull an amount of wort equal to 4 qt. (4 L) of the volume of water you started with from the mash and combine with the wort pulled earlier in the boil kettle. Increase the heat to get the turbid liquor back to 185°F (85°C).

    Immediately after pulling the second portion of turbid wort, add another 5 qt. (5 L) of boiling water to get the mash to 162°F (72°C).

7. With the final infusion complete, add more water to your hot liquor tank and let it heat to 185°F (85°C) for the sparge. It is helpful to start with more water initially if you are unable to collect and heat water quickly enough for the sparge, but you will need to add water to cool it before starting the sparge.

8. Add all of the starchy 185°F (85°C) wort from the boil kettle to get the mash to 167°F (75°C). This is hot enough that the enzymes will denature before they are able to break apart the starch added back to the mash. Wait 10 minutes before recirculating.

9. After 10 minutes recirculating the wort, start the sparge, draining from the mash tun into the boil kettle.

10. Sparge to collect 9 gal. (36 L) of 1.028 SG (7°P) runnings. At this point bring the wort to a boil and continue with your recipe.

Berliner Weisse Decoction

It can be challenging to successfully produce Berliner weisse. Suggestions often focus on the pitching rates for the yeast and bacteria, but many issues are traceable to wort production. The key to a successful Berliner weisse is keeping the *Lactobacillus*-inhibiting IBUs (international bitterness units) to a minimum, and ensuring a highly fermentable sugar profile. I have had the best results with a decoction mash with hops added to the decoction.

1. Dough-in at 125°F (52°C). After 10 minutes pull a large thick section of the mash (I use 30%) and add a relatively small dose of hops.

2. Heat the hopped decoction to 150°F (60°C) and hold it briefly at that temperature before boiling for 10 to 20 minutes.

3. Add the decoction back to the main mash to raise the temperature to 145°F (63°C). After 45 minutes, add enough boiling water to raise the mash temperature to 158°F (70°C) to finish converting the starch.

This method produces highly fermentable wort and also adds bready flavors that contribute complexity to an otherwise simple style. I do not boil my Berliner weisse wort, but I bring it to just below a boil in order to sterilize before chilling. The hopped decoction probably provides a few IBUs, but not enough to inhibit even the relatively hop-sensitive strains of *Lactobacillus* available from brewing yeast laboratories.

Hops

In most cases, the combination of assertive bitterness and sourness leads to an unpleasant flavor. Low-level sourness can actually enhance bitterness, but the high acidity of sour beers turns firm hop bitterness harsh. For a beer with *Brettanomyces*, but not lactic acid bacteria, the wort can be as bitter as you like, but remember that dryness accentuates bitterness.

Target bitterness for sour beers, therefore, should generally range between 10 and 15 IBUs. One technical reason to hold the IBUs lower is when relying on hop sensitive Gram-positive bacteria, namely *Lactobacillus*, to produce the acidity. Compounds in hops initially inhibit the cells' ability to transport sugars and amino acids. Eventually the susceptible cells lose the ability to respire and synthesize protein.[30] As a result, in cases where you want *Lactobacillus* activity, unless you know your strain is hop tolerant, aim for 5 IBUs or fewer.

One-third of the compounds responsible for the bitterness of hops (*trans*-isohumulones) have a half-life of about a year, while the remaining compounds (*cis*-isohumulones) have a half-life of around five years. As a result, even if starting at 25 IBUs, the bitterness will fall close to the flavor threshold by the time the beer is ready to drink (about 19 IBUs after one year and 15 IBUs after two).[31]

Hop varieties with low levels of alpha acids are most commonly used, especially European varieties and their American derivatives. With these low bitterness levels, even bold American hops like Amarillo and Simcoe can be used without issue. In most cases, a single addition of hops 60 to 90 minutes before the end of the boil is all that is required. The aromatics contributed by late boil additions will dissipate long before a traditionally fermented sour beer is ready to drink.

Even when you cannot directly sense the hop bitterness or aromatics in the finished beer they are not without impact. Some strains of *Brettanomyces* possess an enzyme (beta-glucosidase) capable of liberating aromatic molecules from hop compounds called glycosides. More research is required to determine exactly which *Brettanomyces* strains, hop varieties, and compounds are involved, but a few studies with tantalizing results have already been published.

Aged Hops

Breweries that produce spontaneously fermented beer often add hops that have been aged for several years prior to brew day. Warm temperatures and exposure to air causes the alpha acids in hops to oxidize, reducing the bitterness they contribute. While isomerized alpha acids are also partly responsible for the antimicrobial properties of hops, enough other compounds survive oxidation for the hops to retain antimicrobial activity. Thus, aged hops allow for a higher hopping rate, providing protection against certain microbes without making the beer excessively bitter.[32]

Another group of compounds found in hops, beta acids, have a much lower solubility in wort. Oxidation of the beta acids turns them into more soluble hulupones, which do contribute bitterness. The ratio of alpha acids to beta acids will determine how much bitterness the aged hops will contribute.[33] There is a debate over the character of the bitterness derived from hulupones, with some sources claiming that it is a harsher bitterness than that of iso-alpha acids.[34] Most of the traditional European hop varieties used in lambic production (e.g., Hallertau, Spalt, and Tettnang) contain roughly equal amounts of alpha acids and beta acids. This ratio holds true for many of the American cultivars bred to substitute for them (e.g., Crystal, Liberty, and Mt. Hood). High–alpha acid bittering hops generally do not have proportionally more beta acids.[35]

In addition to the effect that the compounds in aged hops have on microbial ecology during fermentation, they also increase the concentration of certain esters and other compounds in the finished beer. Toru Kishimoto, chief researcher at Asahi Breweries Ltd. (Sumida, Tokyo), studied the effect of an early-boil addition of a hop variety high in alpha acids that he had aged for 30 days at 104°F (40°C). The month of warm storage was enough to reduce the alpha acid content of the hops from 11.5% to 4.1%, but it only reduced the bitterness in the finished beer from 31 to 30 IBUs because of the corresponding increase in non-isohumulone bittering compounds. The finished beer also contained above threshold concentrations of the aroma compounds 3-methyl-2-butene-1-thiol (almond, roasted) and 4-(4-hydroxyphenyl)-2-butanone (citrus, raspberry), while using the same hop variety in cold storage did not.[36] Whether a similar effect is at work in mixed fermentations with wort containing much older hops with lower levels of alpha acids is an area that requires further study.

While aged hops are a traditional ingredient in Belgian lambics, they are not necessary for the vast majority of sour beers, including pitched Belgian-style lambics. When pitching a culture of brewer's yeast along with a variety of other microbes, the wort does not need the antimicrobial protection that traditional spontaneous fermentations require. By contrast, the spontaneous fermentation process calls for a high hopping rate to inhibit certain microbes from becoming dominant before the wort fully cools. The chief concern Belgian lambic brewers have is that wild strains of heat-tolerant *Lactobacillus* will lower the pH of the wort too quickly, thus inhibiting the *Saccharomyces* before it has a chance to complete its fermentation. If you added enough un-aged hops to inhibit the heat-tolerant *Lactobacillus*, the resulting beer would be overly bitter.

For Belgian lambic brewers, 4 oz. aged hops per 5 gal. batch (120 g per 20 L) is the current standard rate (this is equivalent to 25 oz./bbl. [0.6 kg/hL]).[37] American brewers have mostly settled on rates below that, typically using 2.6–3.3 oz. per 5 gal. (80–100 g per 20 L), equivalent to 16.1–20.5 oz./bbl. (0.4–0.5 kg/hL).

Willamette hops aged by the author.

Hoppy Sour Beers

Unless you are employing an accelerated souring method that produces a sour beer within a couple of months (as Colorado Springs' TRiNiTY Brewing Co. does for Red Swingline), you should skip the mid- to late-boil flavor and aroma hop additions. By the time the beer ages enough for sour and funky flavors to develop the volatile compounds contributed by these kettle additions will have dissipated. A sour and funky beer heavily hopped in the kettle can lend an aroma reminiscent of an IPA past its prime by the time it is bottled.

For a sour or funky beer with hop aromatics, the best strategy is to wait until the beer has already fermented and soured fully before adding dry hops. This will provide both a mature acid profile and fresh hop aromatics. There are a few breweries in both America and Belgium that have begun playing with this technique. In Belgium, examples from Brasserie Cantillon include: Cuvée Saint-Gilloise (previously Cuvée des Champions), a two-year-old lambic dry hopped with Styrian Goldings or Hallertau; and Iris, their only frequently brewed non-lambic, a pale sour beer dry hopped with Hallertau. In the USA, Bullfrog Brewing (Williamsport, PA) produced El Rojo Diablo, a sour red ale with three pounds of Amarillo added to the Cabernet Sauvignon barrel; and New Belgium has Le Terroir, their pale sour base beer dry hopped with Amarillo and Citra.

With the current popularity of both IPAs and sour beers it is surprising that there have not been more fusions of these two styles. Bold, citrusy American hops (e.g., Amarillo, Citra, Centennial, and Cascade) add aromatics of grapefruit and orange, which meld naturally with the tartness of the beer. The advantage of the earthy and spicy European hops is that their character tends to age more gracefully than that of American hops. Hops from Australia and New Zealand (e.g., Galaxy, Nelson Sauvin, and Riwaka) are fruitier, often tropical in character, which can be a wonderful addition to the right sour base beer (e.g., Hill Farmstead's Juicy). If you are unsure which hop variety to choose when dry hopping, pull a portion of the batch to run trials with different hop varieties before making your final decision.

When the beer is almost ready to package, add the hops to the fermentor and allow one to two weeks of infusion. Put the hops in a mesh bag to make separating them from the beer easier for you, especially when dry hopping directly in a barrel. To make things simpler, move the beer to a vessel with a wider opening than the bunghole of a barrel (e.g., a vessel with a cleaning port) to allow for easy removal of the hops after they have swelled with beer. Most commercial breweries dry hop either in large oak barrels (called *foeders*), or stainless steel tanks. For homebrewers, a Cornelius keg flushed with carbon dioxide is the best option, because this minimizes oxidation.

Adding dry hops to the serving vessel, be it a cask, keg, or serving tank, is an interesting way to infuse hop aromatics into a sour beer. I have even experimented with adding whole hop cones directly to bottles. One of my favorite batches was a wine barrel-aged sour red with one cone each Simcoe and Amarillo and two cones of homegrown Cascade in each bottle. The bright citrus mingling with the berried tartness of the base beer was transcendent. The only disadvantage of bottle hopping is that it often causes even moderately carbonated beer to gush when opened by providing nucleation cites for CO_2 bubbles to form. Hopping at packaging allows you to create a special portion of the beer that is ready to drink sooner, because the big hop aroma will soften the rough edges that can appear during conditioning.

References

1. Ron Jeffries, "Can You Brew It: Jolly Pumpkin Dark Dawn" audio podcast, October 26, 2009.

2. Ibid.

3. Jeff O'Neil, "The Sunday Session," interview, *Brewing Network*, audio podcast , September 12, 2010, http://thebrewingnetwork.com/shows/669.

4. Scott Vaccaro, personal communication with author, June 13, 2011.

5. Greg Doss, "*Brettanomyces*: Flavors and performance of single and multiple strain fermentations with respect to time," presentation, 2008.

6. Jeff O'Neil, "The Sunday Session," audio podcast, September 12, 2010.

7. Jester King Brewery, "Introducing Salt Lick Pecan Wood Smoked Saison," accessed February 1, 2014, http://jesterkingbrewery.com/introducing-salt-lick-pecan-wood-smoked-saison.

8. Jeff Sparrow, *Wild Brews: Beer Beyond the Influence of Brewer's Yeast.*

9. Tim Webb, Chris Pollard, and Siobhan McGinn, *LambicLand: A Journey Round the Most Unusual Beers in the World.*

10. "How pH Affects Brewing," Kai Troester, *Braukaiser.com*, September 25, 2009, http://braukaiser.com/wiki/index.php?title=How_pH_affects_brewing.

11. Jef Van den Steen, *Geuze & Kriek: The Secret of Lambic.*

12. Terry Hawbaker, personal communication with author, September 16, 2009.

13. "Anna Saison," Hill Farmstead Brewery, accessed March 4, 2013, http://www.hillfarmstead.com/ancestral-series/anna-saison.html.

14. "Resolution #9," Cambridge Brewing Company, accessed April 22, 2013, http://cambridgebrewing.com/beer/description/resolution-9/.

15. "Weissbier," German Beer Institute, accessed December 15, 2013, http://www.germanbeerinstitute.com/weissbier.html.

16. Stan Hieronymus, *Brewing with Wheat: The 'Wit' and 'Weizen' of World Wheat Beers.*

17. Burghard Meyer, "Berliner Weisse," seminar, Craft Brewers Conference, San Diego, May 3, 2012.

18. Hieronymus, *Brewing with Wheat.*

19. Sparrow, *Wild Brews.*

20. Peter Bouckaert, "Brewery Rodenbach: Brewing Sour Ales," April 1996.

21. Michael Jackson, *Michael Jackson's Great Beers of Belgium*.
22. Gregory Noonan, *New Brewing Lager Beer*.
23. Stefan Coghe, et al., *Journal of Agricultural and Food Chemistry* 52(3):602.
24. Doss, "*Brettanomyces*: Flavors and performance," 2008.
25. Coghe, et al., *J Agric Food Chem* 52(3):602.
26. Chad Yakobson, February 2, 2012 (4:43 p.m.) "Primary vs Secondary happenings...," comment on Waylit, "Understanding Brett flavors," *Home Brew Talk*, January 28, 2012, http://www.homebrewtalk.com /f127/understanding-brett-flavors-298943/#post3734990.
27. "Caleb Staton of Upland Brewery Company Q&A!" interview with Brandon Jones, *Embrace the Funk*, October 19, 2012, Caleb Staton, "Sour Ales from the Distant Land of Indiana," presentation, SAVOR Washington, DC, 2012; Staton, "Exploring the American Sour Niche," July/August, 2010.
28. Ankita Mishra, "The Effect of Wort Boil Time and Trub on Barley Malt Fermentability," master's thesis, 2012.
29. Jim Liddil, "Mashing and Wort Composition," *A Liddil Lambic Lesson: The Cult of the Biohazard Lambic Brewers,* website, last modified June 1996, http://www.brewery.org/brewery/library/LmbicJL0696 .html#Mash.
30. M. Teuber and Arno F. Schmalreck, *Archiv für Mikrobiologie* 94(2):159.
31. Denis De Keukeleire (2000), "Fundamentals of beer and hop chemistry," *Química Nova* 23(1):108, doi:10.1590/S0100 -40422000000100019.
32. Sparrow, *Wild Brews*.
33. Horst Dornbusch, "How to Hop," *Brew Your Own Magazine,* October 2001.
34. *Oxford Companion to Beer*, editor Garrett Oliver (New York: Oxford University Press, Inc., 2012), s.v. "hulupones."
35. Stan Hieronymus, *For the Love of Hops*.
36. Toru Kishimoto, "Hop-Derived Odorants," doctoral dissertation, 2008.
37. Sparrow, *Wild Brews*.

KNOW YOUR MICROBES

4

Microbes are the real stars of sour beer production. In the same way that you select particular malts and hops to provide sought after flavors, strains of yeast and bacteria are chosen for their distinctive contributions. The souring method you select will have a large bearing on the species of organisms you pitch, while the flavors and aromas you want the finished beer to possess determines the strain selection.

Saccharomyces

The single genus of yeast responsible for fermenting all clean beers is *Saccharomyces*. It is also responsible for the greatest portion of the gravity reduction and alcohol production in nearly all sour beers, with the few fermented primarily with *Brettanomyces* and *Lactobacillus* as the only exceptions. Any strain of brewer's yeast can accomplish the primary fermentation of a sour beer. Some by-products from the primary fermentation will remain in the finished beer, but many will have been destroyed, dissipated, or altered by the successive waves of microbes that follow.

Many brewers ferment their sour beers with whatever brewer's yeast they have harvested from another batch. The good news is that there is no wrong strain of brewer's yeast that will ruin your beer, although certain primary strains work better with certain types of sour beer. The best practice to ensure a healthy primary fermentation is to pitch at the same rate you would for a clean beer with a similar gravity. Before pitching the brewer's yeast, perform a standard amount of wort aeration/oxygenation to ensure healthy cell division. Adding a yeast nutrient is another worthwhile step to promote healthy and rapid primary fermentation. Hold the fermentation temperature around the same range that you would if using that same strain in a clean beer.

Belgian ale yeasts, including saison, are by far the most popular primary strains for American sour beers. This is partly out of tradition, but their complementary spicy and fruity flavors add complexity to the finished beer. A highly attenuative strain should not be used without taking that characteristic into consideration. The microbes that follow the primary fermentation require residual fermentables to produce acids. Most brewers target a specific gravity (SG) after primary fermentation of at least 1.014 SG (3.5°P), with many targeting 1.020 SG (5°P) or higher. Highly attenuating brewer's yeast strains are often good choices for beers using *Brettanomyces* in the absence of bacteria, because *Brettanomyces* is capable of adding its unique funky flavor even without a substantial drop in gravity. As a result, if all you are looking for is "Brett" character, and not sourness, then the higher the attenuation during primary fermentation, the sooner your beer can be packaged—just remember the cautions about safety in Chapter 2.

There are three options to ensure that adequate fermentables remain to create a sour beer using primary yeast strains with high attenuation. The most common technique, used by both commercial brewers and homebrewers, is to produce highly unfermentable wort by adjusting the mash profile and grain bill. The second option, advocated by several commercial brewers, is to arrest the primary fermentation before the brewer's yeast completes attenuation. This can be accomplished by monitoring the gravity, and then cold crashing, centrifuging, or filtering the beer to remove the yeast cells. Subsequent activity by *Brettanomyces* will diminish any intermediate by-products (e.g., diacetyl, acetaldehyde) that the abbreviated primary fermentation leaves behind. The final option, primarily taken by homebrewers, is to take standard wort and add unfermentable carbohydrates such as maltodextrin or refined starch.

English ale strains work especially well in sour beer production, because most exhibit low attenuation and provide fruity complexities without a distinct character of their own. Jeff O'Neil, previously of Ithaca Beer Company, notes that the vicinal diketones (VDK), including diacetyl, that many English ale strains leave behind when cold crashed mid-fermentation improve the Brett character of the finished beer.[1] This is one of the key steps in the production of Ithaca's Brute, which is fermented with a yeast similar to the Whitbread strain.

American ale strains are not a popular choice for sour beers, but many brewers have experience working with them. These strains are known for their clean neutral character and moderate attenuation. A neutral strain is a good choice when planning to add bold flavors (fruits or spices) that you want to shine through in the finished sour beer. Ale strains marketed as Scottish, Irish, *alt*, and *Kölsch* generally produce clean fermentation profiles and will yield similar results in sour beers.

Hefeweizen yeast strains can be used for the primary fermentation of sour beers, although they are an uncommon choice. Jolly Pumpkin Artisan Ales' Weizen Bam is an excellent example of a soured hefeweizen. Much of the isoamyl acetate, an ester which provides the defining banana character of these strains, will be hydrolyzed (i.e., split into its component acid and alcohol) by the esterase enzyme produced by *Brettanomyces*.[2] Despite this, enough isoamyl acetate usually survives into the finished beer to be identifiable.

Yvan de Baets, of Brasserie De la Senne (Molenbeek-Saint-Jean, Brussels), suggests enhancing *Lactobacillus* performance by pitching it simultaneously with a less flocculent primary yeast strain, because highly flocculent yeast can pull other microbes out of solution. Examples of less flocculent strains are Kölsch, hefeweizen, or Belgian wit yeasts. Removing the yeast after primary fermentation would have a similar effect.[3]

Lager yeast strains tend to produce more sulfur compounds than ale strains, which can give the finished sour beer a delicious stone fruit character. The Lost Abbey used lager yeast to ferment the collaborative Isabelle Proximus, and New Belgium uses it for both of their sour base beers (Oscar and Felix). In most cases, brewers who pitch lager yeast for primary fermentation of their sour beers hold the wort warmer than typical lager fermentations, because the low-ester fermentation character would not carry through into the finished product. There are also sour beers created by blending ale and lager base beers, including Lost Abbey's Cable Car and Jolly Pumpkin's Bière De Mars.

Wine Yeast Strains

Yeast strains (mostly *Saccharomyces cerevisiae*, although *S. bayanus* as well) originally selected for fermenting grape musts can add unique fruit flavors when used to ferment wort. Strains marketed for red wines tend to bestow berry flavors that complement darker sour beers, while white wine strains lean toward lighter apple and pear flavors that benefit pale sour beers. When combining wine and brewer's yeast strains you should select wine yeast that does not produce a "killer" toxin that eradicates susceptible yeast (including most strains of brewer's yeasts). This toxin comes in several variations, but luckily *Brettanomyces* is insusceptible.[4]

Allagash Brewing Company brewed a sour beer, Victor Francenstein (9.5% ABV), that was initially fermented with the wine yeast strain Wyeast 4347 Eau de Vie™ (WY4347). This strain is technically intended for the fermentation of fruits in the production of brandy and other distilled spirits. Victor Francenstein started as Victor, brewed from mostly Pilsner malt, with red Cabernet Franc grapes added to the mash, and hopped with Fuggle and Hallertau. An aggressive yeast strain, WY4347 chews through the simple sugars quickly, but takes several months to complete fermentation.[5] To transform this base beer into Victor Francenstein the brewers aged it in oak barrels with Cabernet Franc grapes and a variety of microbes.

Many breweries add wine yeast to their sour beers to accelerate bottle conditioning. More information on pitching wine yeast during the packaging process can be found in Chapter 12. Russian River experimented with the William Selyem wine yeast strain for primary fermentation, which was also their original bottle conditioning strain. However, the brewers did not care for the poor attenuation it produced.[6] So do not worry if the first wine yeast strain you try does not produce the character you were hoping for—as with brewer's strains, there are dozens to select from.

Brettanomyces

Brettanomyces is the principal wild yeast used in sour beer production. That is right, *Brettanomyces* is a genus of yeast just like *Saccharomyces*, not a bacteria as far too many brewers falsely believe. It is also sometimes referred to by the genus *Dekkera*, which is the sexual reproductive stage of the same organism. Undomesticated *Brettanomyces* was originally introduced to beer by the wooden tanks and barrels that served as fermentors at most breweries prior to the 20th century.

The primary role *Brettanomyces* plays in the fermentation of sour beer is to ferment dextrins (chains of sugar molecules too long for *Saccharomyces* to break down), during which time it produces a wide range of characteristic esters (fruity) and phenols (spicy, funky, and smoky). Available strains are capable of producing aromatics with an immense range, including: lovely ones like pineapple, hay, apple, and pear; those that may be appreciated in low levels, like horse blanket and barnyard; and batch-ruiners, like acrid smoke, Band-Aid, and the dreaded fecal. *Brettanomyces* does not contribute much to the acidity of sour beers—acid production is primarily the purview of bacteria. The only exception is when there is a large amount of oxygen available, which causes *Brettanomyces* to produce acetic acid.

The specific flavors produced depend chiefly on the strain; the common *Brettanomyces* species have a diversity rivaling or even exceeding that of *Saccharomyces*. Of the four scientifically recognized species of *Brettanomyces* there are only two commonly used in brewing: *B. anomalus* (sometimes called *B. claussenii*) and *B. bruxellensis* (sometimes called *B. lambicus*). Even between two members of the same species there are often immense differences in ester and phenol production (in the same way that there are large flavor differences between two *S. cerevisiae* strains, such as spicy Belgian abbey ale and the clean Chico strain). *Brettanomyces* has an even larger intraspecies variation than brewer's yeast as a result of having twice the number of genes.

In beer, *Brettanomyces* tends to produce "higher concentrations of 4-ethylphenol (clove-like, or spicy aroma), while wine contains more 4-ethylguaiacol (medicinal aroma)."[7] Crooked Stave's founder, Chad Yakobson, found in his research that 4-ethylguaiacol is reduced by higher pitching rates,[8] which may partly explain why *Brettanomyces* creates more of this compound in wines, where there are fewer cells present at the start compared with beer. While *B. bruxellensis* is a common agent in wine spoilage, *B. anomalus* has not been isolated from wine to date (although it has been found in cider).[9] The most effective way to control 4-ethylguaiacol is by limiting the amount of precursors in the wort, as discussed in Chapter 3.

There are a few brewers who have started to experiment with the other species of *Brettanomyces* that are known. Al Buck, of East Coast

Yeast, reports that, on its own as a secondary fermenter, his strain of *B. custersianus* produces a complex fruity aroma with "pineapple, green-apple, mango esters, probably some acetaldehyde too."[10] The other identified species are *B. naardenensis* and *B. nanus*, although *B. nanus* was subsequently reclassified as *Eeniella nana*, so genetically it is considered to be distinct from *Brettanomyces*.[11] Buck originally included each of these species in his Bugfarm blends, but has since released all three as single cultures. These are only individual isolates of these species, so they could have the same level of intraspecies variation that the other *Brettanomyces* species exhibit. It will be interesting to see how popular these "new" species become now they are more readily available. It is possible that other species of *Brettanomyces* are out there, waiting to be identified!

In addition to the differences caused by the genetic variation between *Brettanomyces* species and strains, the flavors they produce are also influenced by the acids and alcohols available to be combined into esters. Lactic acid is an especially important substrate for esterification, as its presence allows for the production of fruity-smelling ethyl lactate. Many off-flavored fatty acids become appealing fruity esters when combined with a molecule of ethanol.[12] As a result, do not worry if your sour beer exhibits strange flavors during fermentation, as the *Brettanomyces* will continue to alter the molecules responsible. However, with higher concentrations of lactic acid, production of esters like ethyl caproate and ethyl caprylate (both of which have tropical pineapple-like aromas) is reduced, and conversely production of ethyl acetate (which smells like nail polish remover) is increased.[13] Consequently, to get higher concentrations of the more unique and desirable esters you may need to brew a beer that is not tremendously sour.

When pitching either in tandem with your brewer's yeast or after primary fermentation, the effective pitching rate for *Brettanomyces* should range from 100 cells/mL to 2,000,000 cells/mL. Pitching more cells tends to create a noticeable flavor impact in less time, but not necessarily the same flavors. Several brewers I talked to stressed the importance of healthy *Brettanomyces* cells when pitching into an already fermented beer, because the environment will lack both simple sugars and oxygen.

Brettanomyces and beta-glucosidase

The enzymes produced by a given strain of *Brettanomyces* will determine which carbohydrates the strain is able to consume. Almost all *Brettanomyces* strains produce alpha-glucosidase, which is capable of breaking apart dextrins up to nine glucose molecules long.[14] Some studies indicate that this enzyme is capable of working on even longer chains, just not efficiently.[15] In addition, some *Brettanomyces* strains produce beta-glucosidase, which breaks beta(1→4) bonds between a molecule of glucose and another simple sugar. For brewers, the most relevant example of a disaccharide that falls into this category is cellobiose (two glucose molecules linked with a beta bond), which is found in oak barrels. Maltose is also composed of two glucose molecules, but the type of linkage (alpha bond) is different. Lactose, refined from milk, is another example of a disaccharide formed by two sugars (galactose and glucose) linked with a beta(1→4) bond. If your wort contains a strain of *Brettanomyces* that produces beta-glucosidase, lactose becomes a carbohydrate to feed a sour beer, rather than a sweetener.

Beta-glucosidase-positive strains are also able to break apart glycosides, odorless molecules where a sugar (in this case glucose) is bonded to a non-carbohydrate aglycone. Glycosides in beer are contributed by spices, fruits, and hops. Once the glucose molecule is removed and fermented, the aromatic aglycone remains. Research focusing on the classic addition of Schaerbeek cherries to Belgian kriek has shown that beta-glucosidase-positive strains are able to release more "important contributors to sour cherry aroma such as benzaldehyde, linalool and eugenol" during refermentation when compared with beta-glucosidase-negative strains.[16] Research on coriander, the most common spice in Belgian beers, produced similar results.[17] There are studies which suggest beta-glucosidase activity on hop-derived glycosides yields some appealing aromatics, but more study on the specific hop varietals is needed before specific advice can be given.

The strains that produce beta-glucosidase include those classified as *B. claussenii*, which are not commonly found in lambic production.[18] However, a research group found that seven out of ten of the strains of *B. intermedius* (*B. bruxellensis*) they analyzed had high beta-glucosidase activity.[19] Another study showed that a particular strain of *B. custersii* (a *B. bruxellensis* variant isolated from a lambic fermentation)[20] is particularly effective at releasing aglycones (this strain, *B. custersii* CMBS LD72, was obtained from the Centre for Malting and Brewing Science in Leuven, Belgium).[21] There are few specifics available on exactly which commonly used commercial strains produce beta-glucosidase, which is a good reason to pitch multiple *Brettanomyces* strains into a single beer if you are counting on beta-glucosidase activity.

Brettanomyces reproduces at a slower rate than *Saccharomyces* and prefers a lower pH environment. As a result, it can take months for *Brettanomyces* to assert its character. *Brettanomyces* is able to absorb nutrients that are released when *Saccharomyces* cells undergo autolysis (die), so to encourage more Brett character allow your beer to age in the primary fermentor without removing the yeast. Upon its death, *Saccharomyces* also releases caproic, caprylic, and capric acids from its cell walls, which can be converted into esters by *Brettanomyces*.[22] The only sour beers traditionally left in the primary fermentor for the entirety of their aging are lambics, where a powerful fruitiness and rustic funk are the signatures of the style.

Brettanomyces can be pitched in the absence of *Saccharomyces* to complete the fermentation on its own. When aerated, *Brettanomyces* will produce a small amount of acetic acid, the signature acid of vinegar. While many brewers do everything they can to avoid acetic acid production, Chad Yakobson says that the small amount of acetic acid produced during a well aerated primary fermentation (45–150 ppm) is soft and complementary. During his research, Yakobson did not see a strong correlation between pitching rate and ester or higher alcohol production.[23] However, he did warn that over-pitching can lead to a more acetic character, but only as a result of the acetic acid produced during the aerated propagation. More information about 100% *Brettanomyces* fermentations can be found in Chapter 8.

Lactobacillus

There are two genera of bacteria, *Lactobacillus* and *Pediococcus*, responsible for lactic acid production in sour beers. Best known for its role in the production of tart dairy products like yogurt, *Lactobacillus* is capable of quickly producing lactic acid without contributing other potent flavors. It is an aerotolerant anaerobe, meaning it does not require oxygen, but also is not harmed by it (although, anecdotally speaking, not all strains grow as quickly when aerated). Despite this, the only styles that rely on *Lactobacillus* as the primary souring microbe are in the German tradition

(Berliner weisse and Gose). In most other worts the IBUs are high enough to inhibit the majority of *Lactobacillus* species. In fact, the chief preservative effect of hops is their ability to restrain the *Lactobacillus* living on malt and thus commonly found all over most breweries. However, this readily available source of *Lactobacillus* is useful for techniques such as sour mashing that contribute acidity before hops are added to the wort.

Lactobacillus thrives and works quickly at temperatures between 100°F (38°C) and 120°F (49°C). Below about 55°F (13°C) most strains go dormant. Peter Bouckaert at New Belgium found *Lactobacillus* grows most effectively on complex media, so he suggests using malt-based fermentable substrates for the starter.[24] While as few as 8 IBUs are enough to inhibit most commercial strains of *Lactobacillus*, more are needed to inhibit the wide range of species that exist in the wild. Hops become more effective at inhibiting *Lactobacillus* as the pH of the beer drops, so even if you notice a strong initial fermentation by the bacteria, lackluster souring could be the result of having too high of a hopping rate.[25]

Lactobacillus is a diverse genus, and individual species or strains may exhibit atypical properties. For example, there are species, such as *L. brevis*, that can tolerate more hops than others.[26] Some strains of both *L. brevis* and *L. delbrueckii* are also capable of producing the dextrin-reducing enzyme alpha-glucosidase, the same as *Brettanomyces*.[27] While the strains of *Lactobacillus* marketed by brewing yeast labs tend to be rather alcohol intolerant, some strains are able to sour beers exceeding 10% ABV, with some *saké* strains tolerating in excess of 20% ABV.[28]

The biggest concern when souring a beer with *Lactobacillus* is that it can lower the pH too rapidly, leading to an unhealthy primary fermentation. There are brewers who pitch *Lactobacillus* several days in advance of the primary yeast strain, but this can cause problems if you do not closely monitor the pH. One of the main reasons Belgian lambic brewers add a large quantity of aged hops to the boil is to prevent *Lactobacillus* from souring the slowly cooled wort before yeast has a chance to become established.

There are two general categories of *Lactobacillus* strains, homofermentative and heterofermentative. Homofermentative strains generate only lactic acid with no other by-products; according to Al Buck, these strains tend to have higher nutritional requirements.[29] Heterofermentative strains produce other compounds in addition to lactic acid, usually including CO_2 and ethanol. Heterofermentative strains can even be used with good results for primary fermentation in low alcohol beers, as the Bruery does for their Berliner weisse, Hottenroth. Their *Lactobacillus* strain is able to consume dextrins within a relatively short timeframe, yielding a final gravity of 1.002 (0.5°P) after a month.[30]

If you want to find out which category your *Lactobacillus* falls into, ferment starter wort with it. If you see either the gravity of the liquid fall or gas production indicated by a kraeusen that looks like thick soapsuds, you will know that you have a heterofermentative strain. Sourness alone with no change in gravity or CO_2 production indicates a homofermentative strain, and no change at all suggests dead bacteria.

Lactobacillus cannot thrive in a beer with a pH as low as *Pediococcus* can, but most of the strains used in brewing can lower the pH to around 3.3–3.4, which makes for a truly sour beer. Some brewers describe the lactic acid character produced by *Lactobacillus* as being softer and tangier than that produced by *Pediococcus*. However, there must be another factor causing this perceived difference because the lactic acid produced by these two bacteria is identical.

While the *Lactobacillus* strains used in the production of fermented dairy goods are able to consume lactose, not all of the strains sold to brewers will. If you want to use *Lactobacillus,* try several strains to determine which one works best for your application: this will depend on the hop and alcohol tolerances, hetero- or homofermentative nature, and ability to metabolize certain sugars.

Pediococcus

Pediococcus is the other common lactic acid bacteria used in sour beers. Other culinary roles include contributing to the acidification of sauerkraut and traditional dried sausages. The long aging time required by many traditional beer souring methods is partly a result of the months it takes for *Pediococcus* to initiate a dramatic lowering in the pH of the beer. This plodding pace is an advantage, as it allows time for the primary yeast strain to complete its fermentation before the substantial drop in pH occurs. While *Pediococcus* may take longer than *Lactobacillus* to sour a beer it is both more hop and acid tolerant, able to produce sharply acidic beers with a pH lower than 3.0.

The fundamental drawback of acidifying with *Pediococcus* is that most strains produce concentrations of diacetyl above the taste threshold. Unlike brewer's yeast, *Pediococcus* will not enzymatically reduce diacetyl by converting it to less-flavorful by-products (as yeast would, i.e., converting to acetoin, and then 2,3-butanediol); instead, it leaves the butter-flavored diacetyl behind.[31] The only remedy is to include *Brettanomyces* in beers that are pitched with *Pediococcus*, where the *Brettanomyces* serves the role of eliminating diacetyl. This process takes a varying amount of time, so do not be alarmed if you taste movie theater popcorn in a young sour beer.

Pediococcus is microaerophilic, which means it is a microbe that requires oxygen to survive but at a lower concentration than what is found in the atmosphere. *P. damnosus* (the hop tolerant species most often used in brewing, also known as *P. cerevisiae*) are aerobic Gram-positive cocci.[32] As a result, you can pitch it in the primary fermentation without concern for the bacteria being harmed by the initial aeration, although if you are worried the souring blend can be added after the onset of fermentation.[33]

Some strains of *Pediococcus* other than *P. damnosus* can produce acetic acid in the presence of oxygen, but none of these are found in brewing.[34] Many brewers describe the acid character from *Pediococcus* as being more aggressive and sharp than that from *Lactobacillus*. This could be due to either the lower pH generated by *Pediococcus*, or the sub-threshold presence of acetic acid from the *Brettanomyces* that would not always be found in beers soured with *Lactobacillus*.

Exactly what *Pediococcus* is capable of consuming is highly dependent on the strain. Generally, *P. damnosus*: "does not hydrolyze arginine, arabinose, ribose, xylose, or lactose. Some strains metabolize maltose and sucrose, and most strains ferment fructose, galactose, and glucose to form DL-lactate."[35] On the other hand, *P. dextrinicus* (originally *P. cerevisiae* sp. *dextrinicus*), often found in "beer, beer bottles, silage, and spent grains" is capable of hydrolyzing carbohydrates as large as starch.[36] As *Pediococcus* is most active after the simple sugars in the wort are consumed the strains used for brewing should be able to ferment complex carbohydrates.

Only some strains of *Pediococcus* produce a condition in aging beers, commonly called being "sick" (from "Sarcina sickness")[37] or "ropy," that is the result of their production of exopolysaccharides. The effect is a beer that is viscous, syrupy, and slimy. Exopolysaccharides are mainly produced during the bacterial growth phase, with higher production occurring at 54°F (12°C) compared to 77°F (25°C), and at higher glucose and nitrogen concentrations.[38] Some species of *Lactobacillus* are also capable of exopolysaccharide production, although it is relatively uncommon in the species used in sour beer production. *Brettanomyces* eventually breaks down and ferments the exopolysaccharides, another reason to always include it in beers where *Pediococcus* is present. It usually only takes a few weeks for the viscosity to return to normal, so even if your beer becomes sick you may not notice.

Acetobacter

The activity of *Acetobacter* is held to a minimum in the fermentation of most sour beers because it consumes ethanol to produce harsh-tasting acetic acid. These bacteria require a steady supply of oxygen to perform the oxidative fermentation that converts ethanol into acetic acid. *Acetobacter* is commonly airborne, so even if none is pitched it will easily establish itself in barrels that sit empty for several days before refilling. New Belgium is the only brewery I spoke with that does not try to eliminate *Acetobacter* from their beers. Brewmaster Peter Bouckaert suggests always including *Brettanomyces* with *Acetobacter* to yield more interesting beers.[39]

Adding or allowing production of acetic acid pre-boil is not recommended because of its high volatility and nostril-stinging smell. *Acetobacter* will not do much early in fermentation, because positive pressure due to carbon dioxide production prevents oxygen from coming in contact with the beer. After primary fermentation is complete, the lack of pressure will allow oxygen to start seeping into the fermentor, entering through the wood of the barrel, a faulty seal, or an empty airlock.

Acetobacter prefers warm temperatures, so controlling the aging temperature of barrel-aged sour beers is especially important. At temperatures within *Acetobacter aceti*'s ideal growth range of 77–86°F (25–30°C), and with access to oxygen, an offensive vinegar character can develop in only a matter of days.[40] At cellar temperature, with unrestricted access to oxygen, a beer can still become unpleasantly acetic in a matter of weeks.

A low level of acetic acid is an important flavor component of traditional Flemish reds, and, to a lesser extent, Belgian lambic. If your goal is to create a vinegar flavor, add a small amount of unpasteurized vinegar (which contains live *Acetobacter*) when you pitch the other microbes. With this *Acetobacter* present in your beer, the oxygen that permeates through the fermentor or that enters when the bung is removed will be enough to generate noticeable acetic-acid sharpness. However, a safer route to achieve the same goal is to blend the batch with homemade (or commercial) malt vinegar to taste at bottling (see Chapter 13).

Other than the flavor itself, the other concern over the presence of acetic acid is that *Brettanomyces* can form ethyl acetate (an ester) from acetic acid and ethanol. Ethyl acetate smells like pear at low levels, but quickly becomes reminiscent of nail-polish-remover solvent in excess.

Oxidative Yeast and Enteric Bacteria

There are other minor microbial players involved in certain sour beers, particularly early on in those that are fermented spontaneously; Jeff Sparrow's *Wild Brews* is a good resource, giving descriptions of what oxidative yeast and bacteria in the Enterobacteriaceae family contribute. Their presence is not required to produce complex aromatics in a finished sour beer.

Sherry Flor

Flor encompasses a number of yeast species, including *Saccharomyces cerevisiae,* and can be used in beer.[43] Sherry flor are the yeast strains active during the long aerobic fermentation stage that gives sherry its distinctly nutty aroma. Flor can ferment anaerobically initially, but then needs oxygen to produce aldehydes (especially acetaldehyde). Sherry is aged in barrels that are left partially filled (approximately five-sixths full) to allow a larger surface area, and the bungs are left only partially closed to allow air to enter. The flor yeast thrives around 15% ABV, but can contribute complexity when added to a lower alcohol mixed fermentation. Randy Mosher's *Radical Brewing* advocates fortifying a beer to reach the ideal alcohol content for sherry flor, but a stronger base beer would also be an option. Flor yeast is included in the Wyeast Roeselare Blend to add complexity.

Another option is to consider pitching a flor strain for primary fermentation. As a pure liquid culture it is only available to homebrewers from White Labs as WLP700 Sherry Flor Yeast. Dried flor does exist, but Red Star has discontinued their version, and Vierka's is not widely available.

Malolactic Bacteria *(Oenococcus oeni)*

Lactic and acetic acid are not the only acids present in sour beers that include fruit. Some fruits (e.g., apples and grapes) contribute malic acid, which has a sharp flavor often used to sour candies. If the sourness of a malic fruit beer is too sharp, it can be converted into softer tasting lactic acid by pitching a culture capable of malolactic fermentation. While both *Lactobacillus* and *Pediococcus* are capable,[44] they are not the only option.

Especially in beers where fruit is added after the souring is complete, the pH or alcohol tolerance of the lactic acid bacteria may be exceeded. In these cases, *Oenococcus oeni* can work in as little as two weeks, but some commercial yeast labs indicate that their strains may take as long as three months to complete malic to lactic acid conversion. *Oenococcus oeni* is commonly used in wine production, and can be purchased as White Labs WLP675 Malolactic Cultures (which is tolerant to 15% ABV and a pH as low as 3.0),[45] Wyeast Vintner's Choice Malo-Lactic Cultures (tolerant to 15% ABV and a pH of 2.9),[46] or Lalvin Bacchus Malolactic Bacteria Culture (tolerant to 13.5% ABV and a pH of 3.1).[47] The *Oenococcus oeni* bacteria in these cultures produce diacetyl, which may need additional time for the *Brettanomyces* to reduce (as it does when using *Pediococcus*).

Microbe Sources

Now that you know about the species of yeast and bacteria involved in the fermentation of sour beers, it is time to cover selecting and procuring specific strains. While spontaneous fermentation of the sort used to produce Belgian lambic is gaining popularity in the production of American sour beers (see Chapter 7), most breweries still pitch microbes in one way or another. A combination of commercial cultures and microbes harvested from bottles of unpasteurized sour beer is a good place to start. In most cases, the microbes sold by Wyeast and White Labs are less aggressive than those found in bottle dregs. However, these fresh commercial cultures are valuable, because they ensure a full complement of species and improve repeatability. There is also a wide range of other sources of microbes that are worth experimenting with. Pitching multiple strains of each desired microbe species provides the best chance for the beer to develop sufficient sourness and personality over a reasonable aging period. Fermentation characteristics of the wide variety of microbes available can be found on the relevant supplier websites, and also from the record of my experiences online at the *Mad Fermentationist*.[48]

Wyeast Laboratories

The 100 mL Wyeast homebrewing *Brettanomyces* cultures are packaged at 750 million cells per milliliter (75 billion cells total), while the bacteria are packaged at 150 million cells per milliliter (15 billion cells total). In both cases, this is substantially fewer cells than their standard *Saccharomyces* Activator™ packs; Wyeast ale and lager strains are 95 mL and packaged at about 1.2 billion cells per milliliter, with a 30 mL nutrient pack.[49] Far from being low, however, a 100 mL *Brettanomyces* culture added to 5 gal. (18.9 L) of wort is equivalent to nearly four million cells per milliliter, which is about double the most aggressive pitching rate I have encountered for a mixed fermentation at a commercial brewery. This number of cells is perfect for larger batches or preparing a starter for a 100% *Brettanomyces* fermentation (see Chapter 8). Wyeast commercial cultures are larger in volume, but packaged at the same cell densities.

White Labs

The single-strain *Brettanomyces* tubes and bacteria tubes that White Labs sells to homebrewers have far fewer cells than those from Wyeast, only 50–80 million cells per milliliter in a 35 mL homebrew tube (1.8–2.7 billion cells total); compare this to 1.5–4 billion cells per milliliter for their brewer's yeasts.[50] For 5 gal. (18.9 L) this is a pitching rate of 95,000–140,000 cells per milliliter, which is on the low-to-medium end of the range suggested by craft brewers for a traditional *Brettanomyces* secondary fermentation. White Labs Sour Mix 1, which includes *Saccharomyces*, has a higher concentration to account for the multiple microbes, being packaged at 200 million cells per milliliter in a 35 mL homebrew tube (7 billion cells total). While White Labs includes *Pediococcus* in blends (e.g., WLP655 Belgian Sour Mix 1), they do not sell it to homebrewers as a pure culture.

East Coast Yeast

Al Buck started by providing microbe cultures to homebrewers on the Burgundian Babble Belt HomeBBBrew board in return for a promise to send a sample of whatever they brewed with it. His East Coast Yeast *Brettanomyces* cultures (ECY04 and ECY05) have approximately the same cell density as his brewer's yeast cultures, so they are an easy option for 100% *Brettanomyces* fermentation.

Buck has also worked with breweries such as Goose Island Beer Co. (Chicago, IL) and the Bruery on sour beer projects, but he does not frequently provide cultures for large production batches.

As far as the blend ratios go, I use certain strains together as their growth kinetics observed are approximately the same. [With] ECY04 for example [I have] found that all three strains grow and ferment at a similar rate, ECY05 are much slower than the ones in ECY04. For the more complex blends (ECY01/20) there is no rhyme or reason because there are too many strains to precisely balance. (Al Buck, personal communication with author, January 11, 2012)

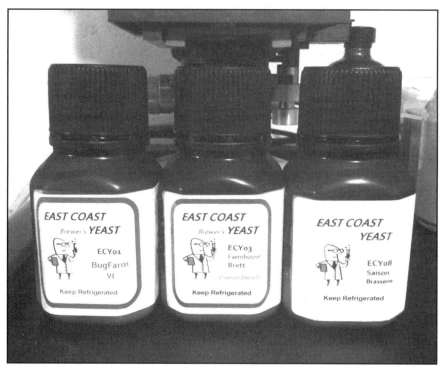

Several vials of East Coast Yeast in the lab. (Courtesy of Al Buck, East Coast Yeast)

Brewing Science Institute

BSI sells their cultures primarily to commercial breweries. The minimum size pitch is packaged for a pitching rate of 7 million cells per milliliter in 1 bbl. (1.2 hL) of wort. In addition to *Brettanomyces* Drie, they sell several other *Brettanomyces, Lactobacillus,* and souring blends that I have not worked with. BSI also works with craft brewers to bank proprietary microbes and produce custom blends of microbes to suit a brewery's needs.

Other Strains

The four laboratories mentioned above carry numerous strains, but there are many more held by small yeast labs, culture banks, and in the private collections of microbe hunters. Nicholas Impellitteri has isolated dozens of strains of yeast, some of which he sells through his company, The Yeast Bay. In Sweden, Maarten Vanwildemeersch started Saccharolicious to sell brewer's yeast. Saccharolicious also sells two strains of *Brettanomyces*: Brett I is from Orval,[51] while Brett II is a unique isolate from Brasserie à Vapeur Cochonne (Pipaix, Leuze-en-Hainaut, Belgium). Vanwildemeersch describes the character of his Brett II as reminiscent of French cider.[52] Another microbe hunter named Jeff Mello, who runs the online supplier Bootleg Biology, has isolated some strains from sour beers, but also from wild honey, kombucha, and his own backyard.

I had the opportunity to use strains of *Brettanomyces* isolated from bottles of Cantillon by two New Yorkers, Jason Rodriguez and Dmitri Serjanov. Rodriguez isolated two strains from Cantillon Blåbær Lambik; CB1 was too urinal cake–forward for my tastes, but CB2 produced a wonderful blend of funky aromatics in a surprisingly short amount of time. Neither strain is highly attenuative, making them good choices for bottle conditioning, where they produce aromatics but no excess carbonation. Serjanov isolated three *Brettanomyces* strains from Cantillon Iris, which give surprisingly fruity flavors, with lots of strawberry and sweet melon.

We have many of these microbes working in our barrels at Modern Times Beer in San Diego, CA.

Harvesting Bottle Dregs

I have soured beers with microbes from many different sources, and many of my best results have come from pitching the dregs from bottles of unpasteurized sour beer. The thin layer of sediment found at the bottom of a sour beer contains many of the microbes responsible for transforming the bland wort into a complex finished beverage. These microbes are often faster, hardier, and produce a greater range of by-products than their "domesticated" brothers available from larger yeast labs. As a bonus, the dregs also come with a free beer to drink! A list of unpasteurized sour and funky bottled beers that you may be able to harvest yeast from can be found on the *Mad Fermentationist* blog.[53]

Fresh bottles of lower alcohol beer are best for harvesting. They contain the highest viability cells and have a more representative selection of the microbes that fermented the beer (instead of only those cells that survived months or years in an alcoholic and low pH environment). If you are buying a bottle with the intent of harvesting the dregs it is certainly worth checking the bottling date. Dregs from bottles with a few months or even a year of age often yield positive results, but avoid anything older than two years unless you are pitching dregs from multiple bottles. This is not to say that older or stronger beers will not have any microbes left alive. Kris Herteleer, the brewer of De Dolle (Esen, West Flanders, Belgium), enjoyed the Brett character in an old returned keg so much that he decided to save the yeast. The isolated strain is now added to the barrel-aged Reserva versions of his beers.[54] Professor Methner at the University of Berlin was even able to culture *Brettanomyces* from a 30-year-old bottle of Berliner weisse (it was the only remaining viable microbe).[55]

To harvest dregs, let the bottle sit upright somewhere cool for a couple of weeks to allow most of the cells to collect on the bottom. Sanitation here is not as crucial as it is when trying to culture a brewer's yeast strain, but it is best practice to wipe the lip of the bottle with sanitizer, or flame it, before pouring to minimize the chances of introducing unwanted

Brewer Ryan Michaels adding bottle dregs from one of the author's own beers to one of the souring barrels at McKenzie Brew House.

microbes. Decant the beer into a glass (or glasses) with a single slow pour, leaving a half-inch (1.25 cm) of beer behind. Stop pouring sooner if you see sediment streaming towards the neck of the bottle. If you have a batch ready, swirl the remaining beer in the bottle to suspend the microbes and pour them directly into your wort or beer. Pitching bottle dregs directly into the fermentor is commonly done by homebrewers, as well as brewpubs such as Cambridge Brewing Company (Cambridge, MA), McKenzie Brew House (Malvern, PA), and Iron Hill Brewery & Restaurant.

Add the dregs along with the primary yeast strain once the wort is chilled to give the microbes time to grow with the oxygen and simple sugars available. The dregs can also be added later for less impact. If you do not have a beer ready, prepare 8 fl. oz. (0.25 L) of 1.040 SG (10°P) starter wort to pitch the dregs. Seal the starter with an airlock both to keep oxygen out and because even below 40°F (4°C) the microbes can still produce CO_2. Keep the starter cool in the refrigerator until you are ready to pitch it. This will prevent the bacteria from outcompeting the yeast. Bringing pressure-canned wort is a great way to harvest dregs from a tasting or trip to a beer bar.

When making a starter with the dregs do not worry too much about how it tastes and smells, because the microbes take months to reach their potential. The one exception is if you detect a terrible off-flavor like ethyl acetate. A starter is not necessary except when planning a primary fermentation with bottle dregs alone. Many American sour beers are bottle conditioned with the addition of wine yeast. Adding a healthy culture of a killer wine yeast strain could disrupt primary fermentation (see Wine Yeast Strains above), so do not make a starter with the dregs from any beer bottled with a wine strain. If added directly to the primary the few wine yeast cells in harvested dregs will not start working quickly enough to cause a problem for the sensitive brewer's yeast, but given time to multiply in a starter they could dominate the primary fermentation.

Despite the benefits of pitching bottle dregs, they cannot be relied upon to deliver exactly the same sour and funk character as the bottle they were harvested from. The pitching rate, timing, wort composition, and aging conditions have as much impact on the final character of a sour beer as the strains pitched. If you want to mimic the character of a specific brewery's beers, then avail yourself of the information about their method (several are discussed in Chapter 5). To exactly emulate many breweries' methods using harvested dregs you will have to go through the effort of isolating and culturing the individual strains from their bottles, but that is beyond the scope of this book. Chad Yakobson's *Brettanomyces* master's dissertation[56] and Chris White and Jamil Zainasheff's *Yeast: The Practical Guide to Beer Fermentation*[57] are the best resources if this is a subject that interests you.

Yakobson's work isolating different morphologies within *Brettanomyces* cultures is fascinating, and has yielded several strains which he is now pitching at his brewery, Crooked Stave Artisan Beer (Denver, CO). If you are interested in isolating your own strain of *Brettanomyces*, Yakobson suggests starting with a bottle of gueuze or lambic, or even trying Australian wines, because most American sour beers will yield strains that are closely related to those available from yeast laboratories.[58] If you want to try harvesting *Brettanomyces* from wine, products from wineries that minimize sulfite additions are ideal.

Other Sources of Microbes

The same species of yeast and bacteria responsible for producing the alcohol, acids, and esters in sour beer are also used (either alone or in combination) to produce many other types of food and drink. The unique abilities of these distinctive strains and species can often be harnessed for the production of sour beer.

The yeast used to raise bread dough is the same species as ale yeast, *Saccharomyces cerevisiae*. Baker's yeasts have been selected for their ability to ferment quickly rather than for alcohol tolerance or flocculation as brewer's yeasts have, but they can still be used to produce unique rustic ales. For a simple low gravity sour beer, dried active bread yeast is an interesting option. The process used to dehydrate bread yeast is not as sanitary as the one designed for brewer's yeast. As a result, *Lactobacillus* is usually present in high enough numbers to sour a beer not protected by an elevated hopping rate. If you are not pitching other souring microbes, keep the IBUs close to zero to ensure that the *Lactobacillus* will flourish; conversely, if your goal is to brew a beer that is not sour using bread yeast, aim for at least 15 IBUs. Sourdough bread starters contain a mix of yeast (usually including both *Saccharomyces* and other wild yeast species) and lactic acid bacteria (primarily *Lactobacillus*).

Kombucha is a tart tea that is fermented by a symbiotic colony of bacteria and yeast (known as "SCOBY"), sometimes referred to as a mushroom. This gelatinous puck contains a menagerie of acetic and lactic acid bacteria in addition to wild yeast. The brewers of Dogfish Head in Delaware and the founders of Beer Advocate collaborated to brew Fungus Tea'Mungus, a beer fermented by both kombucha SCOBY (from Katalyst Kombucha) and Dogfish Head's house ale strain. They also included black (Assam) and green (Sencha) teas as well as lemon zest.[59] This tandem fermentation yielded a relatively mild sourness, most likely a result of anaerobic fermentation in a stainless steel tank. If you want to attempt this method, try fermenting low gravity wort with a kombucha SCOBY alone—avoid a traditional kombucha open fermentation as it yields a vinegary result.

If fermenting an entire batch of beer with a kombucha SCOBY seems like too much of a gamble flavor-wise, then already fermented commercial or homemade kombucha can be blended into a batch of beer to contribute acidity and complexity. Three beers that take this course are Goose Island Fleur, Jester King Buddha's Brew, and importer Vanberg & DeWulf's Lambrucha (which includes lambic brewed by De Troch's brewery in Wambeek, Flemish Brabant). In the case of the first batch of Buddha's Brew, Jester King blended a base beer reminiscent of their Bonnie the Rare (Berliner weisse fermented with *Lactobacillus* and *Saccharomyces*) with 10% of a locally produced plain kombucha from the Buddha's Brew Kombucha company. The base beer was already pretty dry at 1.004 FG (1°P), but Jester King allowed the blend to sit for a week in a packaging tank so that any residual sweetness contributed by the 1.010 SG (2.5°P) kombucha could ferment out.[60] While the kombucha added a hint of acetic tartness, its main contribution was a more dynamically funky aromatic profile, which was clearly reminiscent of kombucha. If you attempt a similar method, keep the beer away from oxygen after blending to prevent an increase in acetic acid. You may choose to pasteurize the kombucha before blending to remove this risk entirely.

Many tart dairy products, such as yogurt, buttermilk, and sour cream, are fermented by *Lactobacillus*. It is best to use fat-free versions to source your bacteria, otherwise the butterfat in normal dairy products will reduce head retention and eventually go rancid. Dairy *Lactobacillus* strains tend to be hop-intolerant, so they are a good choice if you are concerned about cross contamination with your clean beers. They also have the ability to consume lactose, something the strains more commonly used in brewing cannot do.

There are other microbes to be found if you know where to look. To discover microbes for New Belgium's young souring program, Peter

Bouckaert went microbe hunting at bars on Tuesday mornings; the beer sitting in the lines overnight is often teaming with hop tolerant microbes capable of growing in beer.[61]

Like traditional Belgian lambic brewers do, collecting wild microbes that live in the local air is an option that is rapidly gaining favor with the best American sour beer producers. There is much more complexity and risk involved in this technique than the other microbe sources. Chapter 7 details how to harvest wild microbes from fruits and naturally fermented wines and ciders.

Repitching slurry from a previous batch or reusing barrels is the best way to develop a house character. After months or years the microbes will not have the same viability as a fresh culture, so unless you are pitching on slurry that recently finished primary fermentation you should pitch a healthy culture of brewer's yeast, before or along with the old microbes. Bacterial reproduction will outpace yeast in the short term, so even if you are repitching mixed-microbe slurry from primary fermentation you may still want to augment it with additional brewer's yeast. This dispropor-tional growth rate can cause tremendous batch-to-batch deviations, so exercise caution if seeking a consistent character.

Repeated repitching may eventually lead to an equilibrium based on frequency, temperature, aeration, and wort composition, amongst other factors. How long this takes, and whether this ratio of microbes will produce desirable finished beers reliably, is hard to predict. Before he started brewing professionally, Brian Strumke, founder of the itinerant Stillwater Artisanal Ales, repitched the same mixed-culture from one batch of homebrew to the next, "kinda like a Friendship Bread starter," for years without issue. For commercial beers he opted for a variety of *Brettanomyces* strains, mostly from East Coast Yeast. Strumke would love to include *Lactobacillus* and *Pediococcus* as well, but most of the breweries where he rents space do not allow him to ferment with bacteria (one of the drawbacks of gypsy brewing).[62]

Maintaining Cultures

Brewing sour beer can become pretty expensive when including optional extras like barrels, a second set of gear, and fruit, not to mention the time and space. There are, however, a few areas where saving a couple of dollars will not mean sacrificing the quality of your beer. Maintaining your own microbial cultures and having starters of *Brettanomyces*, *Lactobacillus*, and *Pediococcus* on hand saves money, adds convenience and allows for more spontaneity.

Maintaining cultures is only worthwhile if you brew sour beers at least once every couple of months and know which strains have the flavor and fermentation characteristics you like. If you are just starting out, it is worth brewing beers with as many different strains as you can to discover which ones work for your palate and brewing style before you commit. For convenience and consistency, cultures are often purchased from yeast labs. While they maintain their own mixed house culture of lactic acid bacteria at Russian River, Cilurzo says, "For the *Brett* we often purchase fresh cultures from the yeast supplier and culture it up with wort from whatever we are brewing."[63]

There are two options for keeping several strains on hand at pitchable quantities: either propagate the individual strains separately or as a single mixed "house" culture. Individual strains are easier to maintain because each microbe has certain ideal conditions that are often at odds with those of other species. Separate cultures also give you more flexibility if, for example, you want to ferment a beer with *Brettanomyces* but not *Lactobacillus* (or vice versa). A mixed house culture allows you to maintain a more complex blend of microbes because a huge number of strains can be combined into a single vessel (although it is difficult to keep the ratios of the various microbes from changing over time). There is no reason that you could not keep single microbe cultures of a few favorite strains in addition to a mixed microbe culture. You can maintain a variety of mixed cultures besides, such as keeping a starter with several strains of *Brettanomyces*, or one with both *Lactobacillus* and *Pediococcus*.

For storing yeast, craft breweries often use carboys or even tanks to allow them to maintain a large enough quantity of microbes to inoculate multiple barrels. Production breweries tend to pitch their cultures frequently enough that they can simply refill with fresh media (e.g., wort) each time they draw off a portion of the starter to pitch. Growlers, 750 mL bottles, or 1 gal. (4 L) glass jugs work well for homebrewers. No matter what vessel you pick or the type of microbes you are growing, affix a stopper and airlock to prevent oxygen and other microbes from getting into the culture. If you go a long time between feedings it is good to double the size of the cultures each time you feed them. Drain enough of the culture before feeding so that there is no risk of needing a blowoff tube.

Sanitizing the mouth of the starter vessel each time you open it is best practice. You are afforded more leeway than culturing brewer's yeast because the acid production, high attenuation, and naturally funky character that these microbes produce will minimize the risk of other strains that find their way in becoming established and having an impact on the beer. However, with long-term storage of these cultures wild microbes could survive and even thrive, which can be for better or worse.

Many breweries feed their cultures with whatever moderate gravity, low IBU wort they have available. Brewers at Captain Lawrence Brewing Company originally kept cultures of *Brettanomyces* in 15 gal. (57 L) carboys. They fed these cultures with wort from Liquid Gold (which has moderate hopping, gravity, and color) a few days before they were used to ensure the *Brettanomyces* was actively fermenting when it was pitched. They added more wort to return the culture to its original volume after each pull. They have since switched to buying fresh cultures for each batch to be completely confident that the intended strain is in good health.[64]

Several breweries use slightly more elaborate media than wort for their bacteria cultures. For example, Cilurzo at Russian River uses "one part (unfiltered) apple juice to four parts low gravity wort for bacteria."[65] In addition to adding simple sugars, the apple juice dilutes the IBU level of the wort, which makes it less stressful for *Lactobacillus*.

Brettanomyces. *Brettanomyces* is the easiest microbe to maintain because it is content to slowly ferment complex dextrins. After using my *B. bruxellensis* starter, I replace the removed volume with an equal amount of 1.030 SG (7.5°P) wort produced from either light dried malt extract or final runnings. I include a teaspoon of Wyeast yeast nutrient per gallon of replacement wort (1.3 mL per L). If I have not done this in two months, I dump half the culture before replenishing with fresh wort. Once the starter wort is chilled, add it to the culture and then shake to dissolve some oxygen to encourage cell proliferation. A cool cellar temperature slows the metabolism of *Brettanomyces* and extends the time needed between feedings. If you need a large *Brettanomyces* culture in a hurry, grow it on a stir-plate at a temperature around 82°F (28°C).[66] *Brettanomyces* exhibits two-stage (diauxic) growth: the cells first convert carbohydrates to ethanol, and then that ethanol is converted to acetic acid. Maximum cell density should be reached in about a week, but you may notice lags along the way. Because of the acetic acid you may wish to decant the starter wort before pitching.

Lactobacillus. The ideal temperature range for *L. delbrueckii* growth is 104°F–111°F (40°C–44°C),[67] but it will continue to grow at considerably cooler temperatures. Refrigerated storage slows the lifecycle, preventing it from dying between infrequent feedings. A couple of brewers recommended adding chalk to buffer against the lactic acid produced by the culture, but you may not find it necessary. You can decant apple juice based starters to reduce the amount of malic acid that reaches the beer, but a small amount has never caused a problem for me. Pasteurized apple juice is sterile when first opened, so it can be added directly to the starter, which makes the frequent feedings required much easier. *Lactobacillus* does not need oxygen to reproduce as yeast does, but it is also not harmed by it. Some even benefit, for example *L. brevis* yields 50% more cells when aerated.[68]

If you do find a strain of hop-tolerant *Lactobacillus* that you want to keep that way, always propagate it in a media that contains hops. According to Peter Bouckaert, for practical applications in the short term, it can take as little as one generation for *Lactobacillus* to lose its hop tolerance when propagated in a hop-free media.[69] A study published in the *Journal of the Institute of Brewing* indicates that it can take up to a year of culturing in unhopped media to remove the culture's hop tolerance completely, but even before this point it may require culturing in a low-hopped wort to sufficiently prepare the cells to ferment hopped beer.[70] Studies have also shown that by slowly building the hopping rate of the culturing media you can increase the hop tolerance of *Lactobacillus* by eight to twenty times.[71]

Pediococcus. Wort or apple juice with yeast nutrient are both suitable starters for *Pediococcus*. While certain species (e.g., *P. pentosaceus*) are capable of producing acetic acid in the presence of oxygen,[72] the strain most commonly used in beer, *P. damnosus*, cannot. *P. damnosus* is a facultative aerobe,[73] meaning it can survive in either the presence or absence of oxygen, though it prefers a low-oxygen environment. The only real concern when culturing is that the bacteria will produce enough lactic acid to inhibit its own growth, so a few grams of chalk per liter would not be a bad idea (5.5 is the optimal pH for growth).[74] The ideal temperature for growth is 86°F–90°F (30°C–32°C); lower temperatures will cause it to reproduce at a slower rate. Do not worry if the culture smells buttery, which is due to the bacterial culture having no *Brettanomyces* to reduce the diacetyl being produced.

Mixed culture. Cultures containing both yeast and bacteria are best kept refrigerated because the cold slows the metabolism and reproduction of the bacteria, preventing them from overwhelming the yeast. Al Buck of East Coast Yeast confirms, "An easy thing to do is periodically decant off 'old' starter media from the sediment and add fresh media with plenty of nutrients added—say every other month or so. Refrigerate afterward until ready to use. What will happen over a couple of years is anyone's guess."[75]

Starting with the slurry from a favorite batch of beer is the best idea because you know that it contains a successful blend of microbes. Another option is to keep an "everything" culture into which you pitch commercial cultures and the dregs from your favorite sour beers as you open them, allowing the microbes that thrive to become dominant. Either way, always pitch fresh brewer's yeast to ensure a healthy primary fermentation.

Buck uses a more cautious and reliable tactic when producing blends to sell. Each yeast strain is grown individually before they are combined in approximately equal amounts (for simplicity). This culture of mixed yeast strains is then propagated into a larger quantity. Buck says that, "Waiting to add the lactic acid bacteria allows them [the bacteria] to be propagated with their own unique set of conditions, and allows the amount of [bacterial] cells to be more carefully controlled."[76]

To distribute their cultures to homebrewers, both Buck and Cilurzo have soaked oak cubes and chips in their mixed cultures and then dried them. This method allows for easier sharing of mixed cultures, because the dried microbes will not reproduce so the ratios of the various microbes will not change. The dried cultures still need to be refreshed every few months to prevent a significant decrease in viability; this is done by re-culturing in wort before drying once more. Drying the microbes onto oak is more time consuming for long-term storage, because it periodically requires growing a fresh culture from the chips and then having to dry them on a rack again.

Keeping microbes streaked on agar plates or slants (in tubes) is another option, though it requires special equipment (although not a huge investment) and additional time to build a culture back to a pitchable quantity. If you get a particular strain that you love that is not available from a yeast laboratory, it is worth keeping plates to allow you to periodically start over with the known culture. If this is something that you are interested in, refer to White and Zainasheff's *Yeast: The Practical Guide to Beer Fermentation*, or you can pay a yeast laboratory to bank strains for you.

No matter what sort of microbes you are growing, always feed the culture a few days before you plan to pitch it to ensure the cells are alive and active. This is especially important any time you are relying on the microbes to start fermenting rapidly, such as doing a 100% *Brettanomyces* fermentation or a quick souring method with *Lactobacillus*. If you notice issues with your cultures, e.g., sluggish performance or major off-flavors, then start over with a fresh culture. The cost of buying new microbes is dwarfed by the money and time wasted brewing and aging a beer that does not turn out well.

References

1. Jeff O'Neil, personal communication with author, December 21, 2011.
2. Jeff Sparrow, *Wild Brews: Beer Beyond the Influence of Brewer's Yeast.*
3. Vinnie Cilurzo, Yvan de Baets, Jean Van Roy, "Barrel-Aged Sour Beers from Two Belgian's Perspectives," panel interview, 2011.
4. "Brewing beer with wine yeast and proper oaking techniques with wine consultant Shea Comfort," interview on "The Sunday Session," audio podcast, *Brewing Network*, November 23, 2008, http://www.thebrewing network.com/shows/The-Sunday-Session/The-Sunday-Session -11-23-08-Shea-Comfort.
5. Jason Perkins, personal communication with author, October 7, 2011.
6. Vinnie Cilurzo, personal communication with author, June 7, 2013.
7. Pascal Chatonnet, et al. *Journal of the Science of Food and Agriculture*, 60(2):165.
8. Chad Yakobson, "Pure Culture Fermentation Characteristics of *Brettanomyces* Yeast Species and Their Use in the Brewing Industry," master's thesis, 2010.
9. Chris D. Curtin, et al. *FEMS Yeast Research*, 7(3):471.
10. Al Buck, personal communication with author, March 5, 2012.

11. Maudy Th. Smith, Wilma Batenburg-Van der Vegte, W.A. Scheffers, *International Journal of Systematic and Evolutionary Microbiology* 31(2):196; Yuzo Yamada, Minako Matsuda, Kozaburo Mikata, *Journal of Industrial Microbiology* 14(6):456.

12. Sparrow, *Wild Brews.*

13. Yakobson, "Pure Culture Fermentation Characteristics of *Brettanomyces.*"

14. Yakobson, personal communication with author, December 3, 2011.

15. H.M.C. Shantha Kumara, S. De Cort, and H. Verachtert, *Applied and Environmental Microbiology* 59(8):2352.

16. Luk Daenen, et al., *FEMS Yeast Research* 8(7):1103.

17. Ronnie Willaert, et al., "Bioflavouring of Food and Beverages," *Applications of Cell Immobilisation Biotechnology*, vol. 8B, 355.

18. Yakobson, "Pure Culture Fermentation Characteristics of *Brettanomyces.*"

19. H. McMahon, et al. *Journal of Industrial Microbiology and Biotechnology* 23(3):198; Anna K. Mansfield, Bruce W. Zoecklein and Robert S. Whiton, *American Journal of Enology and Viticulture* 53(4):303.

20. Maudy Th. Smith, M. Yamazaki, G.A. Poot, *Yeast* 6(4):299.

21. Luk Daenen, et al. *Journal of Applied Microbiology* 104(2):478.

22. Chad Yakobson, "Brewing with *Brettanomyces*: the horse the goat and the barnyard," presentation at the National Homebrewers Conference, Seattle, 2011, YouTube video (13:59), http://www.youtube.com/watch?v=D8D4t-UJ5Nw.

13. Yakobson, "Pure Culture Fermentation Characteristics of *Brettanomyces.*"

24. Peter Bouckaert and Eric Salazar, "New Belgium Brewing," audio podcast, October 19, 2006.

25. W.J. Simpson, *Journal of the Institute of Brewing* 99(5):405.

26. Kanta Sakamoto, "Beer Spoilage Bacteria and Hop Resistance in *Lactobacillus brevis*," doctoral thesis, 2002.

27. S. De Cort, H.M. Kumara and H. Verachtert, *Applied and Environmental Microbiology* 60(9):3074.

28. National Research Institute of Brewing, "Kusazo lactic acid bacteria strain list," [in Japanese], archived website, accessed April 23, 2013, http://web.archive.org/web/20060601125049/http://www.nrib.go.jp/ken/Lacto.html.

29. Al Buck (as "Al B"), August 09, 2011 (12:01 p.m.), comment on Jim L. Berliner Weisse Success, *Burgundian Babble Belt* homeBBBrew message board "Re: Berliner Weisse Success," accessed February 01, 2014, http://www.babblebelt.com/newboard/thread.html?tid=1108752780&th=1309210030&pg=2&tpg=1.

30. Tyler King, personal communication with author, October 19, 2011.

31. Sparrow, *Wild Brews*.

32. David A. Bruckner, Paul Colonna and Bradley L. Bearson, *Clinical Infectious Diseases* 29(4):713.

33. Al Buck, personal communication with author, January 11, 2012.

34. Paul De Vos, et al., eds., *Bergey's Manual* 2nd edition, vol.3, 513–532.

35. Y. H. Hui and George G. Khachatourians, eds., *Food Biotechnology: Microorganisms*.

36. Werner Back, *International Journal of Systematic Bacteriology* 28(4):523.

37. George Fix, "Diacetyl: Formation, Reduction, and Control," *Brewing Techniques*, vol. 1, no. 2.

38. Maite Dueñas, Arantza Munduate, Aidé Perea, Ana Irastorza, *International Journal of Food Microbiology* 87(1–2):113.

39. Peter Bouckaert, personal communication with author, March 2, 2012.

40. United States Environmental Protection Agency, "*Acetobacter aceti* Final Risk Assessment."

41. Vinnie Cilurzo, "Brewing Sour Beers at Home Using Traditional & Alternative Methods," presentation at the NHC San Diego, 2011; "Vinnie Cilurzo 2011 NHC Keynote," presentation, audio podcast, Basic Brewing Radio, July 7, 2011, http://www.basicbrewing.com/index.php?page=basic-brewing-radio-2011; "Brewing Sour Beers at Home Using Traditional & Alternative Methods," PowerPoint® presentation, accessed December 17, 2013, www.babblebelt.com/newboard/brew_resource/RRsour_beer_presentation.ppt.

42. P. Romano, et al., *International Journal of Food Microbiology* 86(1–2):169.

43. Ian Spencer Hornsey, *The Chemistry and Biology of Winemaking*.

44. "Malolactic Fermentation," in *Handbook of Alcoholic Beverages*, ed. Alan J. Buglass, 1:96–113.

45. "Non-Saccharomyces and Malolactic Cultures," White Labs, accessed March 12, 2013, http://www.whitelabs.com/wine/malolactic.html.

46. Greg Doss, personal communication with author, March 15, 2013.
47. "Bacchus Malolactic Bacteria Culture: *Oenococcus oeni*," Lallemand Inc., accessed March 12, 2013, http://www.lalvinyeast.com/bacteria.asp.
48. "Commercial Brett, Lacto, and Pedio Descriptions," Michael Tonsmeire, *Mad Fermentationist*, accessed January 14, 2014, www.themad fermentationist.com/p/commercial-cultures.html.
49. Doss, pers. comm., March 15, 2013.
50. Neva Parker, personal communication with author, November 14, 2011.
51. "Products," Saccharolicious, accessed April 24, 2013, http://www .saccharolicious.com/products.
52. Maarten Vanwildemeersch, personal communication with author, April 10, 2013.
53. "List of Unpasteurized Sour and Funky Bottled Beers," Michael Tonsmeire, *Mad Fermentationist*, accessed January 14, 2014, www.themad fermentationist.com/p/dreg-list.html.
54. Bouckaert and Salazar, "New Belgium Brewing," October 19, 2006.
55. Frank-Jürgen Methner and K. Wackerbauer, "The microorganisms of 'Berliner Weissbier' and their influence on the beer flavour," EBC Microbiology Group Meeting, Wuppertal, Germany 13–15 June 1988.
56. Yakobson, "Pure Culture Fermentation Characteristics of *Brettanomyces.*"
57. Chris White, Jamil Zainasheff, *Yeast: The Practical Guide to Beer Fermentation.*
58. Chad Yakobson, "The Sunday Session" audio podcast, Brewing Network, April 15, 2012, http://thebrewingnetwork.com/shows/866.
59. BeerAdvocate. "'Kombucha Brew' - BeerAdvocate & Dogfish Head," Vimeo video (5:12), posted March 11, 2011, 3:58 p.m., http:// vimeo.com/20934308.
60. Jeff Stuffings, personal communication with author, October 30, 2012.
61. Bouckaert and Salazar, "New Belgium Brewing," October 19, 2006.
62. Brian Strumke, personal communication with author, May 1, 2012.
63. Vinnie Cilurzo, personal communication with author, June 11, 2011.
64. Scott Vaccaro, personal communication with author, June 13, 2011.
65. Cilurzo, pers. comm., June 11, 2011.
66. Yakobson, "Pure Culture Fermentation Characteristics of *Brettanomyces.*"

67. Jacques-Edouard Germond, et al. *Molecular Biology and Evolution* 20(1):93.

68. J. R. Stamer and B.O. Stoyla, *Applied Microbiology* 15(5):1025.

69. Hilde Martens, "Microbiology and Biochemistry of The Acid Ales of Roeselare," doctoral thesis, 1996.

70. J.L. Shimwell, *Journal of the Institute of Brewing* 42(5):452, cited in Kanta Sakamoto, "Beer Spoilage Bacteria and Hop Resistance in *Lactobacillus brevis.*"

71. M. Richards and R.M. Macrae (1964), "The significance of the use of hops in regard to the biological stability of beer II. The development of resistance to hop resins by strains of lactobacilli," *Journal of the Institute of Brewing* 70(6):484. doi:10.1002/j.2050-0416.1964.tb06353.x.

72. T.D. Thomas, L.L. McKay, H.A. Morris, *Applied and Environmental Microbiology* 40(2):908.

73. De Vos, et al., eds., *Bergey's Manual* 2nd edition, 513–532.

74. Ibid.

75. Al Buck, personal communication with author, March 13, 2011.

76. Ibid.

COMMERCIAL
METHODS OF SOURING

5

Now we arrive at the heart of sour beer production, the methods employed by commercial breweries. Each brewer I interviewed embraces a unique combination of wort production, microbes, timing, and aging to produce their sour beers. First though, a brief refresher on the production methods used to produce the classic sour beer styles of Belgium and Germany. These time-tested European methods have been covered thoroughly by Jeff Sparrow in *Wild Brews* and by Stan Hieronymus in *Brewing with Wheat*, but it is difficult to understand and appreciate where American innovation is today without some familiarity with traditional practices.

Classic European Methods

There are variations between the methods employed at the breweries producing each of these beer styles, but not to the same extent that the techniques of American brewers have diverged. Many European styles and methods were originally developed in response to limitations imposed by equipment or taxation, but they have lasted because of the wonderful flavors they create. Despite this, unconstrained by history, you may not choose to stay entirely faithful to traditional methods, even when attempting to produce beers that conform to the classic styles.

Berliner Weisse

Berliner weisse is the only classic sour beer style that always relies wholly on *Lactobacillus*, in the absence of *Pediococcus*, for lactic acid production. As a result of the high sensitivity of *Lactobacillus* to hops, the IBUs of the wort should be kept to a minimum. Aged hops retain their *Lactobacillus* inhibiting properties, so there is no benefit to using them either when brewing Berliner weisse.

In the past many of the breweries in Berlin did not boil their wort, which allowed the wild *Lactobacillus* living on the malt to survive into the fermentor. In modern times, however, most breweries maintain cultures of *Lactobacillus*, although in at least the case of Professor Fritz Briem's 1809 Berliner Style Weisse the strain was originally isolated from malt.[1] Most modern German breweries either pitch *Lactobacillus* into the wort along with the ale yeast, or the wort is divided and fermented with *Lactobacillus* and brewer's yeast separately.[2] While there are both breweries and yeast labs that use hefeweizen yeast strains, the more traditional choice is neutral ale yeast. A handful of Berliner weisse exhibit a touch of earthy or floral *Brettanomyces* aromatics, which I enjoy, but is not a requirement. Indeed, the sole remaining brewer of the style in Berlin, Berliner Kindl Weisse, does not include *Brettanomyces*, although Professor Burghard Meyer of VLB (Versuchs- und Lehranstalt für Brauerei) asserts that *Brettanomyces* is essential to the traditional character.[3]

Start a traditional Berliner weisse brew with a decoction mash, adding a small dose of hops to the first pull. After the wort is collected heat it to 210°F (99°C) to sanitize, but do not boil. Skipping the boil preserves malt aromatics reminiscent of fresh bread dough. (Anecdotally, despite the Pilsner malt base, dimethyl sulfide [DMS] is not an issue with this method.) Chill the wort to 68°F (20°C) then simultaneously pitch *Lactobacillus* and an attenuative ale yeast—in this case, highly attenuative strains like Fermentis Safale US-05 or Wyeast 3711 French Saison are good choices. Starter cultures are important when fermenting with *Lactobacillus* and ale yeast to ensure both are active when pitched. You can also opt to pitch a small amount of *Brettanomyces* at the same time. While there are brewers who advocate pitching *Lactobacillus* a few days before the ale yeast, avoid this unless you are prepared to monitor the pH. *Lactobacillus* is capable of producing lactic acid rapidly, which can stress the ale yeast and cause it to leave behind off-flavors.

Quoted in *Brewing with Wheat*, Kristen England at Pour Decisions Brewing Company (Roseville, MN) suggests pitching *Lactobacillus* and *Saccharomyces* together at a ratio of 5:1.[4] England says his ratio is based on cell counts, not volume. When pitching by volume you must account for the fact that *Lactobacillus* cells are only about 10% of the size of ale yeast cells, which means a bacteria-to-yeast ratio of 1:2 would be required to achieve a microbial cell ratio of 5:1, assuming equally dense slurries. England is especially fond of the more aggressive *Lactobacillus* species like *L. brevis* and *L. casei*, and suggests bottling only a few days after brewing, saying that, "I find that the beers sour quicker with less time spent 'conditioning' in secondary or the like. They take on a better character, pear/lemon."[5] Bottling a sour beer this young requires producing highly fermentable wort, and enough confidence with your process to know when fermentation is complete. I opt for the safer option, allowing my Berliner weisse a couple of months of cellar-temperature aging before bottling.

Wyeast employee Jess Caudill ran tests to look at what fermentation methodology produced the most reliably tart Berliner weisse in the mold of the now discontinued Schultheiss Berliner Weisse. He discovered that Wyeast 1007 German Ale (WY1007) was the yeast strain that resulted in the lowest final pH when pitched with Wyeast 5335 Lactobacillus (WY5335). However, he found that even more acidity could be generated by inoculating the wort with WY5335 and allowing it to ferment at 68°F (20°C) for a week before pitching WY1007. Caudill suggested pitching 10 million *Lactobacillus* cells per milliliter (about a 1 qt. [1 L] starter in a 5 gal. [18.9 L] batch) to ensure a rapid pH drop. With the increased acid from using this pre-inoculation method, and with a stable gravity, Caudill found that pitching *Brettanomyces* at one million cells per milliliter at bottling gave his desired level of flavor by-products after six months.[6]

Belgian Lambic, Gueuze, and Kriek

By definition, Belgian lambic, gueuze, and kriek are fermented spontaneously by wild microbes. However, the largest producers blend in a portion of clean beer to increase production, as the Belgian labeling law states that these style names are reserved for "sour beers wherein spontaneous fermentation played a part in the production process."[7] All but one of the producers who brew or blend at least one completely spontaneously fermented lambic banded together to form HORAL (De Hoge Raad voor Ambachtelijke Lambiekbieren—The High Council of Artisanal Lambic Beers). Brasserie Cantillon, one of Belgium's most respected craft producers, is the only holdout, in protest of member breweries that produce both traditional and faux-lambics. HORAL was able to successfully lobby for an "Oude" Traditional Specialty Guarantee. As a result Oude (*Vielle* in French) may now only be used to label Belgian lambic, gueuze, and kriek (it does not protect *framboise*) blended exclusively from spontaneously fermented beer.

The most traditional wort production process calls for boiling the turbid mashed wort for several hours with aged hops. All of the traditionalists cool their wort slowly overnight in a coolship where local microbes are allowed to land in the wort. The next day the cooled wort is usually pumped into a "horny" tank to homogenize it, and later that day it is pumped into used barrels for the long fermentation. Other than the microbes in the air, those living in the horny tank, and those living in the wood from the previous batch, no other yeast or bacteria is pitched. Less artisanal lambic production methods, such as those used by Belle-Vue (a brewery in Brussels owned by Anheuser–Busch InBev), call for inoculation by bubbling unfiltered air through the force-chilled wort contained in stainless steel fermentors.[8]

In America, the most common technique is to pitch a cultured blend of half a dozen microbes. While this can produce similar flavors to spontaneous fermentation, replicating the exact character is impossible with such a small selection from the dozens of strains of wild microbes involved in producing a true Belgian lambic. Chapter 7 discusses the new wave of spontaneous fermentation methods being used in America.

Belgian lambics are left in the same barrels for their entire fermentation, routinely sitting on the flocculated yeast for one to three years. The molecules released when *Saccharomyces* cells undergo autolysis nourish the *Brettanomyces* and help create a unique rustic funk not found in other styles. The hulls of the dead yeast cells will absorb some substances toxic to *Brettanomyces*, such as octanoic and decanoic fatty acids.[9]

While both old and young lambics are sold unblended and lacking carbonation, the majority are blended to create highly carbonated gueuze. Most of the best examples of gueuze use lambics of different ages (often one, two, and three years), with the youngest Belgian lambic providing yeast and residual dextrins that eventually carbonate the beer during an additional year of conditioning in the bottle. Information on estimating the carbonation contributed by blending old and young beer is found in Chapter 12. Adding priming sugar is an option to carbonate unblended lambic; Cantillon's wonderfully oaky Lou Pepe Gueuze is produced by taking their best two-year-old lambic and allowing its wild yeast to consume the dose of priming sugar.

Fermentation and blending are so important to the process that a number of excellent gueuze producers, such as Hanssens Artisanaal (Dworp, Beersel) and De Cam Geuzestekerij (Gooik, Flemish Brabant), do not brew their own wort. Instead, these producers ferment lambic wort purchased from Brouwerij Girardin, Brouwerij Boon, and Brouwerij Lindemans (all located in Flemish Brabant), later blending it to create the final gueuze. Gueuze blenders use tanker trucks to collect the cooled wort at the brewery, pumping it into their own barrels for fermentation and aging. Cantillon is the only other brewery that allows a blender to buy wort from them, and in their case it is only Gueuzerie Tilquin (Rebecq, Walloon Brabant).

Belgian lambics also serve as the base for many fruit beers, most traditionally kriek (sour cherry), and framboise (raspberry). While the less traditional producers are making overly sweet, often artificially flavored spontaneously fermented beers like apple, cassis (currants), peach, and banana, other breweries, such as Cantillon and 3 Fonteinen, are adding wine grapes, bilberries, and rhubarb to produce delicious modern classics. The traditional producers do not add fruit until the beer is at least a year old. The beer and fruit are allowed to ferment for another few months before they are separated and the fruit lambic is packaged. Much more on adding fruit to sour beer is found in Chapter 10.

Flemish Red

Belgian Flemish reds that contain raw corn require a cereal mash to fully convert, while many artisanal producers rely on an all-malt grist and an infusion mash. This is followed by a standard length boil of the wort. Despite the persistent rumor that their red color results from many hours of boiling, the truth is that it is created by the combination of darker base malts, like Munich and Vienna, as well as a high percentage of crystal malt. While historically these beers were cooled in coolships, the remaining breweries today rely on heat exchangers.[10]

Flemish reds are pitched with mixed cultures that contain full complements of yeast and bacteria. Flemish red brewers generally allow the brewer's yeast to complete its fermentation in stainless steel before transferring the beer into foeders (large oak tanks). The vinegar character that results is caused by air coming in contact with the beer as it ages (see Chapter 9).

Bottled Flemish reds are often blends of an older (around 18 months), highly acidic oak-aged beer with a younger, sweeter stainless steel fermented beer, which are blended at packaging.[11] This tempers the harsh acetic acid by diluting it and adding sweetness, but requires pasteurization or filtration to prevent the microbes from consuming the dextrins in the younger beer. Most American versions of the style are fermented to a lower sweetness and contain sub-threshold acetic acid.

Adding fruit for complexity or sweetness is another option. Brouwerij Rodenbach Alexander was a cherry flavored variant of Rodenbach Grand Cru, and retains a cult status despite having been last produced in the late 1990s. Redbach, which replaced it, lacks the same complexity because it is based on younger beer and pasteurized to retain the sweetness of the 25% cherry juice blended in at packaging.

Flemish Oud Bruin

Oud bruin recipes tend to be all malt, so an infusion mash is all that is required. After a standard boil, the wort is chilled and pitched with a mixed-culture similar to the ones used for Flemish reds. Other than the differences in their malt characters, the main distinction between the two styles is that the acid character of oud bruins is softer than Flemish reds. The majority of oud bruins are now aged in stainless steel, which eliminates the vinegar character by minimizing oxygen exposure.[12] Oud bruins also tend to have a subdued *Brettanomyces* character, although it is not clear whether this is the result of the microbes used, or the conditions under which they are aged.

Brouwerij Liefmans Goudenband is the classic example of the provision-strength variation, i.e., those strong enough to benefit from extended storage. Fermented and aged in stainless steel tanks with a mixed culture (originally from Rodenbach), the finished beer is produced by blending differently aged batches of the same recipe. The result is malty, slightly tart, and rich in dark fruit character. In 1992 the beer was boosted to 8% ABV, which was done to improve its aging potential.[13] Other breweries' methods, like the one Brouwerij Bavik uses for Petrus Oud Bruin, call for blending a wood-aged sour beer with a young, malty beer to provide sweetness.[14] Oud bruins serve as the base for fruit beers as well, but most of these are sweetened (sometimes partly artificially), like Liefmans Kriekbier and Frambozenbier.

American Breweries' Methods

The production of sour beers by American craft brewers has come a long way since the beginning of the craft beer resurgence. Starting with techniques cribbed from Europe, American breweries have developed their own methods that range from simple to incredibly complex. Some methods can produce a finished beer in as little as a few weeks, but most require months or even years. A handful of American brewers are making beers of a similar quality to the best European examples, with a greater level of experimentation.

There are dozens of American breweries innovating and producing sour beers. Out of those, I selected 10 that employ distinct production methods that result in a range of quality beers (Figure 1). The ensuing discussion is limited to each brewery's processes that are integral to their results. For example, the way that a brewery cleans its barrels can have a profound impact on other aspects of their process, while bottle conditioning is relatively standalone (and thus most of the information on it is relegated to Chapter 12, Packaging). There are also chapters to follow that detail specific types of fermentations, such as spontaneous and 100% *Brettanomyces*, so a brewery's section may contain a note directing you to other chapters where more information on their beers is located.

While researching this chapter, in addition to listening to interviews and reading articles, I talked to at least one brewer from each brewery. Everyone I spoke to was generous with their time, details of their production, and opinions. I feel that the production method each brewery employs is more valuable than the specifics of the grains and hops used to produce the wort. If you like the sour beers brewed by one of these breweries then design your own recipe, but brew and ferment it with that brewer's techniques. Do not feel that these are the only possible souring methods, or that you must follow one of them to the letter (although this is not a bad idea for your first few batches). Once you understand why each method works, you can mix and match their elements to develop a personal style that suits your equipment, tastes, and time constraints.

At the end of each brewery's section there is a swim lane process flow diagram that provides an overview of the production timeline. Each row (or "lane") indicates when the included set of steps is to be performed, with arrows directing the overall flow. For the breweries that employ multiple methods, this diagram only describes the production of the beer that is the most representative. A few of the simple variations between beers (e.g., adding fruit or dry hops) are included as gray boxes.

At each of these breweries the refinement of their process is still very much ongoing. While the information presented is up to date as of the time of publication, there will certainly be changes as these breweries increase their production and refine their results over the years to come. While the methodology and art of these breweries will evolve and change over time, it will fortunately not change the fact that these processes as presented here will still yield terrific beers!

Figure 1—A map of the American sour beer producers featured in this chapter.

1. New Belgium Brewing Company
2. Jolly Pumpkin Artisan Ales
3. Russian River Brewing Company
4. The Lost Abbey
5. Cambridge Brewing Company
6. Captain Lawrence Brewing Company
7. The Bruery
8. Cascade Brewing
9. Ithaca Beer Company
10. Allagash Brewing Company

New Belgium Brewing Company

In 1999, Colorado's New Belgium Brewing Company became the first American brewery to release a world-class sour beer. This was no coincidence—their brewmaster, Peter Bouckaert, had been employed in the same position at Brouwerij Rodenbach until 1996, where he brewed Belgium's most celebrated Flemish reds. It is easy to see the similarities the original New Belgium sour beer, La Folie, shares with Rodenbach's Grand Cru. Bouckaert and the rest of the staff did not stop there though; since 1999 they have continued to create style-agnostic sour beers that push both the science of brewing and the art of blending.[15]

When New Belgium started producing sour beers they were aged in standard wine barrels, but as production increased these were replaced with larger vertical oak tuns called foeders. They still have some smaller barrels used to age experimental batches, but retired ones have gone to breweries like Russian River, as well as local homebrewers. Moving to foeders is a different strategy to the one pursued by most other brewers, who instead have added hundreds or thousands of 53–120 gal. (200–454 L) barrels to boost their sour beer capacity. Demand continues to increase, and in 2013 New Belgium added 32 French oak foeders, bringing their total potential aging capacity to 7,670 bbl. (9,000 hL), making them one of the largest American producers of sour beer. The cellar team has found that the larger a foeder is the longer it takes for the beer to be ready to package.

All of the sour beers that New Belgium releases are based on an "Odd Couple" of base recipes, Felix (light) and Oscar (dark). From these two beers come numerous variations brought about through blending with clean beers, aging on fruit, and dry hopping. Oscar (grain bill: pale, Munich, CaraPils®, caramel 80, and chocolate) is sold as La Folie, while Felix (grain bill: pale, wheat, caramel 80, CaraPils, and oats) is dry hopped to create Le Terroir. Wort production at New Belgium aims for highly fermentable wort using a "low and slow" mash. This is followed by a short boil that sees the wort run over a super-heated cone as part of their Merlin boiling system, which quickly volatilizes the DMS and isomerizes the alpha acids. A traditional boil would accomplish the same objectives, but takes longer and requires more energy.

The sour base beers are both initially fermented with a house lager strain in stainless steel tanks at a slightly elevated temperature. Once fermentation is complete the yeast is removed by rough filtration. Early in the development of La Folie, New Belgium refilled their barrels with unfiltered beer, allowing the yeast to accumulate at the bottom. The growing bed of yeast led to autolysis, and what Bouckaert described as "burnt, wet-dog-like off-flavors." The fermented and filtered beer is transferred to a holding tank to await space in a foeder.

Having fermented beer ready in tanks ensures that it is always available to refill the barrels when a foeder is ready to top-off, blend, or package. This system works especially well for New Belgium, because their brewhouse is on a tight schedule producing wort for standard releases (primarily their flagship Fat Tire). Eric Salazar, the brewer in charge of the barrel cellar, explains:

> *We have been experimenting with the idea of dosing a bit of* Lactobacillus *into stainless holding vessels [after filtering] with the intention of having a head start filling recently emptied foeders. The foeders are likely to dry out quickly in this climate when left empty for too long so with this beer we can fill them right away without taxing production. At least that's the idea, thus far the beer doesn't really wait in those vessels very long as production of sour beers has been quite steady in the past year.*

When New Belgium began experimentally souring beer, Bouckaert sourced microbes from culture banks. They tested each organism in its own jar to see what character it produced, tasting and taking analytic measurements weekly. This produced a pile of data, but the actual flavors only got interesting when they combined strains—Bouckaert discovered that single microbe tests gave little indication of how they would perform in combination.

The resident house cultures responsible for souring New Belgium beers today were developed organically. The process started with inoculating each barrel with microbes sourced from either commercial cultures or fresh Belgian lambic, or even hop-tolerant microbes cultured from dirty tap lines. One of their favorite cultures came from a keg of Fat Tire, which was returned sour but lacking diacetyl. As the inoculated barrels fermented, they kept the ones that produced beers with better sensory profiles while discarding the ones that did not.

When the New Belgium brewers get a new foeder, after cleaning, they fill it with fresh beer from a stainless steel fermentation along with 10% sour beer from one of their favorite established (at least two-year-old) barrels to act as a starter. This makes expanding the cellar a challenge, as each new foeder requires hundreds of gallons of beer that would otherwise have been packaged.

Despite their well-trusted microflora, not every foeder makes desirable beer on the first fill. In the case of foeder #9, the first batch aged in it had to be dumped because the beer was not satisfactory. Following this, New Belgium aged a high bitterness (60 IBU) beer in foeder #9 for a year to inhibit the growth of hop-sensitive microbes. All told, it took seven years from the purchase of this foeder to the release of a beer aged in it. This is one of the drawbacks of aging beer in large barrels:

A few of the foeders at New Belgium Brewing Company. (Courtesy of New Belgium Brewing Company)

it concentrates risk. However, foeder #9, or Cherry Go Lightly as it is named, has become one of Lauren Salazar's favorites. She described the flavors it produces as "delicate cherry, almond, and cherry pit." In her job as both wood cellar manager and blender/specialty brand manager of the Lips of Faith series (which includes New Belgium's sour beers), and previously as sensory specialist, Lauren Salazar has years of personal relationship with each foeder.

The room where the foeders were originally stored experienced large ambient temperature swings, into the 90s°F (low 30s°C) during summer days, although with their large thermal mass the temperature of the beer itself does not fluctuate nearly as drastically. This is in stark contrast to the constant 59°F (15°C) that the beer at Rodenbach enjoys as it ages. In mid-2012 the foeders were each emptied and moved to a room with a more consistent temperature around 65°F (18°C).

Originally, foeders were only topped off when their flavor indicated they were getting too much oxygen; there was no set schedule. However, the new stainless steel holding tanks have allowed the brewers to top-off each foeder monthly. Eric Salazar and Lauren Salazar work in tandem, with one up on a ladder peering into the bung to estimate the space remaining, and the other operating the pump that pushes from a holding tank into the bottom of the foeder.

When the brewers remove soured beer from a foeder, they can leave up to 10%–20% of the volume to ensure that the young beer transferred from the holding tank to the foeder gets a good blend of microbes. In some cases they leave much more beer behind, and have been surprised by how quickly the beer is ready to package again. The brewers found that as the barrels become more established they are able to leave less beer in them, and, since 2013, some do not require any leftover beer at all thanks to the cultures living in the wood.

New Belgium has one of the more interesting and advanced blending programs among American sour beer producers, which is covered in depth in Chapter 11. Despite her training in the science of taste, Lauren Salazar takes a traditional approach to blending: "When I started blending La Folie I would note the wide range of chemical compounds, [but since then] I have changed to using more actionable identifiers."

A large portion of the blend for La Folie is approximately three-year-old Oscar, which adds a firm acidity. Lauren Salazar looks for a signature character within each vintage of La Folie. For example, one year they had a foeder with a strong blackberry flavor, while another year one had a unique pineapple-*Brettanomyces* character (they usually do not have much *Brettanomyces* character from the foeders). After choosing a base beer, she will work in beers from other barrels to tweak the character or stretch the amount. Lauren Salazar always has an idea of what La Folie should be, and because she has blended it so many times it now only takes 30 minutes to determine the ratio.

Le Terroir is Felix that has been dry hopped with Amarillo and Citra (the original test batch used only Amarillo), which gives it the citrusy nose of an IPA but with a balanced acidity in place of bitterness. It was inspired by Lauren Salazar's realization that a particular foeder had fruity aromatics (peach, citrus, and mango) reminiscent of Amarillo. She created a five gallon test batch in a carboy, followed by a few special releases at festivals, before it was eventually released to full distribution. The dry hops (1 lb. Amarillo and 0.25 lb. Citra/bbl. [0.4 kg Amarillo and 0.1 kg Citra/hL]) for Le Terroir are added using New Belgium's "dosing system" after transfer into stainless steel. After four days the beer is centrifuged and bottled.

Eric's Ale starts as Felix as well, but instead of dry hops it is aged on fresh peaches; the resulting fruit beer is blended with strong golden ale to lower the acidity (the original batch was close to undrinkable before blending). The beer's creator, Eric Salazar, says,

> *Fruit is generally added as the beer makes its way to the stainless cellar via the pasteurizer but has also been added using the same method as dry hopping. I have found that it helps to add a bit of yeast to the blended product and go through another fermentation at temp[erature] to consume some residual sugars. This will obviously dry out the final product and make for a more balanced flavor profile.*

One of their more recent sour beers grew out of a homebrew by Lauren Salazar and a friend, a spiced Belgian imperial stout that was blended with 20% Oscar. Lauren Salazar loved the result, but the character of the stout was subdued before it reached market. Brewed in collaboration with the blues/rock band, Clutch, New Belgium Clutch is a tart stout that is not hugely complex (cherries, cocoa, and bready malt), but retains a modest residual sweetness, which is key to producing a balanced beer that is both acidic and roasty.

For the first 10 years of production, La Folie was blended and bottled straight from the foeders, re-yeasted with Champagne yeast, primed with sugar, and hand bottled in the most stunning corked and caged 750 mL bottles a beer has ever seen. Since switching their sour beers to the Lips of Faith series (packaged in capped bombers) the beer is flash pasteurized for safety, partially force-carbonated, and then re-yeasted and primed.

Today, New Belgium's sour beers are bottled on the same line as their clean beers. Other than the change in the appearance of the bottle, Lauren Salazar says that she prefers the new method because it allows her to focus on blending the best beer without worrying about carbonation or flavor stability (as a result, what you drink is closer to what she intended). Flash pasteurization also allows the inclusion of clean beers and residual fruit sweetness in bottled blends. With a lower risk of excessive carbonation developing, less expensive packaging also allows these beers to be more accessible; Lauren Salazar lamented consumers' tendency to hang onto the old corked-and-caged bottles too long waiting for the perfect occasion to drink.

New Belgium also brews a few *Brettanomyces*-finished beers that are not soured, like Biere de Mars (which is finished with *B. bruxellensis*). The brewery keeps a library of numerous *Brettanomyces* strains so they can choose the right strain for a given batch.

New Belgium's method is tailored for a brewery that is dedicated to sour beers and has the funds and space to invest in foeders (Figure 2). However, even a smaller brewery or homebrewer could borrow the basic idea of having a couple of base sour beers to blend and flavor in a variety of ways. New Belgium's choice to have only two base sour beers also provides insurance, because when the beer in any individual barrel is not ready this does not prevent any of their range of beers from being released. Having larger foeders allows for a simpler blending process because there are fewer beers to be sampled and combined. As a homebrewer you could treat this as a modified *solera*, keeping carboys of beer ready to rack into the barrel each time the beer in the barrel is ready to package.

New Belgium Souring Method

Pros: Complexity, sharp acidity, quicker blending

Cons: Equipment costs may be prohibitive, blending skills required

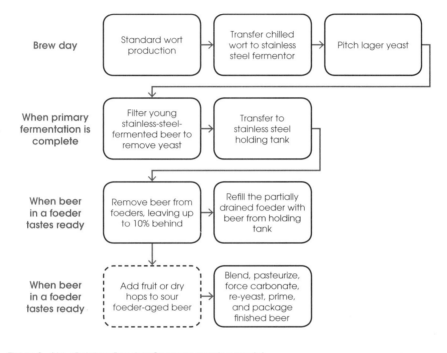

Brew day	Standard wort production → Transfer chilled wort to stainless steel fermentor → Pitch lager yeast
When primary fermentation is complete	Filter young stainless-steel-fermented beer to remove yeast → Transfer to stainless steel holding tank
When beer in a foeder tastes ready	Remove beer from foeders, leaving up to 10% behind → Refill the partially drained foeder with beer from holding tank
When beer in a foeder tastes ready	Add fruit or dry hops to sour foeder-aged beer → Blend, pasteurize, force carbonate, re-yeast, prime, and package finished beer

Figure 2—New Belgium Brewing Company souring model.

Jolly Pumpkin Artisan Ales

Since the mid-to-late 1990s, hundreds of America's over 2,700 breweries have experimented with creating sour and barrel-aged beers. When it opened in 2004, Jolly Pumpkin Artisan Ales was the first producer to focus on producing barrel-aged mixed-fermentation beers exclusively (in 2011 Anchorage Brewing became the second). This brewery in Dexter, MI produces a wide variety of beers ranging from lightly tart to acerbic. Malt bills vary from simple to complex, and founder and brewmaster Ron Jeffries is a master of subtle spicing, but generally avoids adding fruit to his beers. However, since the opening of pubs in Ann Arbor and Traverse City, Jeffries has kegged a few fruit beers, such as their sour red La Roja aged on cherries.[16]

The pubs have also caused Jolly Pumpkin to diversify into brewing clean, stainless steel-aged beers marketed under other brand names (including North Peak, Golden Manatee, and Tortuga). This forms an even larger part of production now that their new facility, comprising a larger brewhouse and two bottling lines, is operational. The new facility is just one and a half miles (2.4 km) from the original facility, and has room for expansion up to 150,000 sq. ft. (14,000 m²).

Jolly Pumpkin produces sour beers in a shorter time frame than most other breweries that ferment with the full complement of lactic acid bacteria and wild yeast. This allowed Jeffries to win his first Great American Beer Festival® (GABF) gold medal with the original batch of Oro de Calabaza less than a year after opening, a remarkable achievement. Production starts with a thin single-infusion mash, with the saccharification rest around 147°F–149°F (64°C–65°C) to promote beta-amylase activity. Beta-amylase creates more maltose than alpha-amylase, allowing higher attenuation by the primary yeast strain. This approach leaves fewer dextrins for the other microbes to eat, which in turn facilitates bottling younger beer. This wort production diverges from the most common approach, which produces wort rich in complex carbohydrates that are unfermentable by brewer's yeast.

Jolly Pumpkin's house ale yeast strain started out as White Labs Belgian Ale (WLP550), but has adapted to the brewery through repeated top cropping and repitching. The brewers aim to pitch once the wort is chilled to 64°F–66°F (18°C–19°C), at which point the temperature is allowed to rise freely as high as the heat generated by the yeast takes it. Primary fermentation is carried out in open fermentors, which are about as wide as they are tall. The wild yeast and bacteria are obtained by running the HVAC system so that it pulls in cool nighttime air from outside the brewery, circulating it over the fermenting beer. Jeffries credits the undomesticated microbes for producing beers with more character and complexity than he ever could with the commercially available strains he pitched at previous breweries.

Once primary fermentation is complete, brewers transfer the beer to barrels. In addition to several hundred regular-sized wine and spirit barrels—many second hand from other breweries like Founders Brewing Company (Grand Rapids, MI) and Firestone Walker Brewing Company (Paso Robles, CA)—Jolly Pumpkin also ages beer in larger oak tuns that range between 264 and 3,100 gallons (1,000–11,734 L). The oak in the barrels comes from a large number of places, including America, France, Austria, and Germany.

Through multiple fillings the oak has come to harbor billions of wild microbes, increasing the speed and consistency of the souring process. Most of Jolly Pumpkin's year-round and seasonal beers spend from a few weeks to a couple of months in barrels. The relatively short time spent in contact with wood adds a touch of oak flavor, but has the primary purpose of ensuring that each beer is inoculated with the full range of house microbes. This has a lot in common with traditional lambic fermentation, where the wood of the barrel also takes the place of pitching cultured microbes.

After a barrel is emptied it is cleaned with 160°F–165°F (71°C–74°C) water generated by an industrial on-demand hot water heater. Jeffries would prefer to use 180°F (82°C) water to better control the microbes, but the local municipal water source contains so much calcium that it precipitates out at such high temperatures, clogging the hot water heater. As the hot water is produced the brewers collect it in a tank with a heating element to continue raising the temperature, but since cleaning is started immediately the water does not get hotter than 165°F (74°C). This hot water cleaning step serves as population control, preventing the microbes from reproducing unchecked.

While many other brewers control the temperature and humidity of their barrel rooms, Jolly Pumpkin does not. Jeffries says, "I think fluctuations in heat and humidity are a part of barrel aging." While temperature changes can have positive effects, such as causing the beer to move in and out of the pores of the wood, extremes can cause the microbes to produce undesirable flavors. The original brewery had three areas where barrels age: the backroom (60°F–75°F [16°C–24°C]); near the packaging line (65°F–80°F [18°C–27°C]); and by the brewhouse, which is similar to packaging, but with greater daily swings resulting from the heat generated during the boil. Jeffries has not noticed significant differences between the barrels stored in the various parts of the brewery. Differences may exist, but he does not take comprehensive notes on where a barrel was stored or the specific flavor attributes it produces during each fill. No attempt is made to keep the barrels in the same area from batch to batch. Even if there was subtle character variance, each release is blended from barrels aged all over the brewery.

If a beer in a smaller barrel does not work in the current blend, Jeffries leaves it in the hope that he will eventually be able to find an appropriate place to include it. In a case where no fit is found, he eventually surrenders and dumps the contents of the barrel. When I talked to Jeffries, he was preparing to empty barrels of six-year-old Lambicus Dexterius (a completely spontaneously fermented beer covered in detail in Chapter 7) that had never come around. These unsuccessful barrels are cleaned with hot water and reused. Most barrels are emptied young, so if a problem developed later in aging the same microbes may not have a chance to cause problems on subsequent fills. Jeffries has only had to throw away a small number of barrels because of the off-flavors they imparted.

It is easier to notice the seasonal variation of the beer aged in the large tuns because they are so big that these batches are often bottled unblended. Experience has taught Jeffries that certain beers work best in a particular tun at certain times of the year. For example, their white ale (Calabaza Blanca) fares best aged in one of the large tuns during the summer, where it derives an intense lactic sourness.

Jolly Pumpkin dry hops Bam Bière, the 4.5% ABV featherweight of the lineup, while it is in oak. Adding a huge hop sock to a large oak tun that has a manway makes this process much easier than trying to force mesh bags full of hops through the small bungholes of normal-sized barrels. This step accelerates production by allowing Bam Bière to continue extracting wood character as it gains hop aromatics. The Bam line of lower alcohol beers includes several other variants, including Weizen Bam (50% wheat malt, 50% Pilsner), E.S. Bam (an extra special bitter recipe which has been a surprising hot-seller), and Bam Noire (a beer that is dark, but not roasty). Jeffries calls these true farmhouse ales, unlike so many strong beers carrying the label on the market today, as he related to me,

> *High-alcohol versions of farmhouse ales are a trend I don't agree with. These are rustic beers, from the pastoral days (that may have never existed). They had poor extraction. Six to nine percent alcohol does not make sense for a beer to drink with crusty bread before you go plow the field.*

The bold coffee and chocolate additions that work so well in big sweet stouts do not succeed when combined with a dry and sour base. Success depends on subtlety and subterfuge, which Jolly Pumpkin achieves with cacao, cinnamon, and sweet orange peel in their Maracaibo Especial.

Seasonal sour beers are a rarity, but Jolly Pumpkin releases one for almost every time of year. Their fall seasonal, Fuego del Otono, contains 10% chestnuts in the mash, and Jeffries considers increasing the amount one day in the future. He has tried several products from Michigan's Chestnut Growers Incorporated: the sliced dried chestnuts contributed more of a raw chestnut flavor, while the chips were toastier (Jeffries' preference). The chips are marketed to brewers and include the pellicle (a thin skin that forms between the nut and its shell, not to be confused with a pellicle that forms on fermenting beer), which intensifies their flavor and color contributions. For spices "subtle is the best way to go," says Jeffries, with Fuego del Otono also receiving small amounts of ginger, star anise, and cinnamon. Jolly Pumpkin also used chestnuts in the collaborative Special Holiday Ale (with Stone Brewing Company and Nøgne Ø), along with white sage, juniper berries, and lots of rye malt.

While some of Jolly Pumpkin's beers are bottled unblended from the big tuns, others are the results of more complex blends; for example, releases of La Roja from the original brewery were blends from five or six oak barrels. The larger facility and new equipment allow Jeffries to create blends from up to 30 barrels (in each case about 20% of the beer has aged more than one year). While Jeffries strives for simplicity in his process, it did not work out that way for a few beers, like Bière De Mars. The origins of this spring seasonal started with two identical mashes fermented with different yeast strains (one ale, one lager). After primary fermentation the two batches were combined into a single 528 gal. (2,000 L) tun, where the beer aged for one month. At that point the beer was distributed into nine 60 gal. (227 L) barrels for at least three additional months of aging. Each barrel was tasted and two or three separate blends were crafted.

All of Jolly Pumpkin's beers are unfiltered, unpasteurized, and conditioned in the bottle or keg. Kegged beer is often much fresher (three to four weeks out of oak) than the bottled beer, which tends to mature longer before distribution. Many of Jolly Pumpkin's beers have minimal sourness and funk when they are bottled, as a result of the more fermentable wort and short barrel aging. While the beers are delicious fresh, their wild character develops with additional age.

The Grand Reserve versions of Jolly Pumpkin's standard base beers spend a couple of years in barrels, where they become among the sourest and most barrel-forward beers I have sampled. The Perseguidor series are blends of Grand Reserve barrels of several different beers, with some components often nearing three years in oak at the time of bottling. Despite all of this age, I found Perseguidor #5 (a blend of Bam Bière, La Roja, and Luciernaga) to be beautifully balanced. Sadly, at this point, both the Grand Reserve and Perseguidor releases are only available directly from the brewery.

You can develop your own local microbe culture in the same way, but it is much easier to use Jolly Pumpkin's microbes by culturing the dregs from their bottles (which as a result of their freshness are some of my favorites to pitch). While their souring technique (Figure 3) allows for a quick turnaround, it can also result in overcarbonated beer if a batch is bottled before the microbes have consumed nearly all of the fermentables. You could end up with exploding bottles depending on how much carbohydrate remains at packaging.

Jolly Pumpkin Souring Method

Pros: Quick, complex flavor compared to other quick methods, beers change more as they age

Cons: Risk of overcarbonation, not enough time for substantial oak character, beers change more as they age

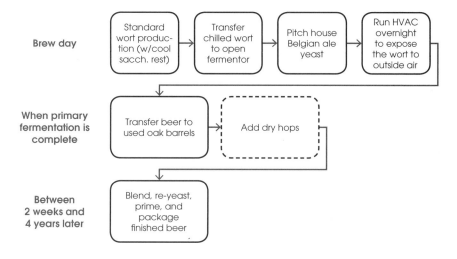

Figure 3—Jolly Pumpkin Artisan Ales souring model.

Wine barrels at Russian River Brewing Co. (Courtesy of Russian River Brewing Co.)

Russian River Brewing Company

Vinnie Cilurzo, who serves both as Russian River's brewmaster and co-owner with wife Natalie, may be the most respected American brewer when it comes to both sour and hoppy beers. He consistently creates some of the country's most complex, balanced, and nuanced sour beers. Cilurzo started brewing for Russian River in 1997, but it was not until he bought the rights to the name from the owners, Korbel Champagne Cellars, in 2003 and subsequently opened a brewpub in Santa Rosa, CA in 2004 that he became a household name among beer nerds. The 20 bbl. (23 hL) brewhouse at the pub only had enough excess capacity for occasional bottlings. In 2008 he opened a production facility nearby, which houses a 50 bbl. (59 hL) brewhouse, purchased from Dogfish Head, and 600 wine barrels of souring beer.[17]

Located in Sonoma County with close proximity to dozens of vineyards, Russian River has easy access to freshly emptied wine barrels. Their three best-known sour beers are each aged in wine barrels that previously held a varietal complementary to the character of the beer: Chardonnay for the blonde Temptation; Pinot noir for the brown, dried sour cherry-permeated Supplication; and Cabernet Sauvignon for the dark, strong, dried Zante currant-infused Consecration.

Coming from a winemaking background, Cilurzo's aversion to acetic acid is the reason behind many of the decisions he makes, saying:

> *I personally do not like acetic acid, a little bit is good but I really do not like the vinegar character it can contribute to certain styles of beer. Some brewers really like this character which just goes to show how subjective these types of beers are. There really is no right or wrong way to make them—that is what makes these beers so fun and personal.*

Temptation, Supplication, and Consecration are all mashed with a single infusion around 158°F–159°F (70°C–71°C). Russian River uses aged hops for all of their sour beers, with measured IBUs of 10 to 15 before aging. This moderate bittering charge, for a sour beer, is high enough to mostly inhibit *Lactobacillus*, but low enough that after a year of aging it falls below the flavor threshold. Restraining *Lactobacillus* allows *Pediococcus* to take the lead in lactic acid production, which Cilurzo says lends a "deeper" acidity compared to the lighter, crisper sourness produced by *Lactobacillus*.

The Russian River souring method takes a more managed approach than the other breweries I spoke with. Temptation, Supplication, and Consecration undergo clean primary fermentations in stainless steel tanks with a Belgian ale strain (after experimentation they have settled on White Labs Abbey Ale WLP530 for most batches). After the terminal gravity is reached, usually 1.012–1.016 SG (3°P–4°P), the primary yeast is removed with a centrifuge (in the past fining and filtration have also been employed).

The bright beer is then transferred into barrels. Most of these were originally constructed of French oak, because its highly porous nature allows the microbes to penetrate deeper into the wood. However, Russian River has since changed to include American oak barrels, because their lower permeability reduces the production of acetic acid. Aging a beer for a year in a barrel fresh from the winery lends heavy wine and oak characters that can overpower a delicate beer. To reduce the oak character of the finished beer each barrel is reused for the aging process three times, so that every batch of beer is aged in a combination of fresh barrels and those which have already aged one or two previous batches (approximately one-third each of first-use, midlife, and final-use barrels). After a barrel has run its course most of the oak and wine character will have been depleted. At this point some of the barrels are used to hold spontaneously fermented Beatification, the full production details of which are found in Chapter 7.

At the same time that the beer goes into the barrel it receives one million *Brettanomyces* cells per milliliter. This pitching rate is the same regardless of which beer they are making (other than the 100% *Brettanomyces* Sanctification, which is covered in Chapter 8). When he started the barrel program, Cilurzo performed experiments with all of the commercially available strains of *Brettanomyces,* both individually and in combination, to determine which he preferred. *Brettanomyces* starter cultures are kept going in-house for pitching, but Russian River periodically replaces these cultures with fresh pitches from a lab to ensure the flavor and fermentation characteristics do not stray. For Consecration and Supplication, the dried fruit is added to the barrel at the same time as the *Brettanomyces.*

The *Brettanomyces* works for several weeks or months before a large pitch of their house culture of lactic acid bacteria ("Funky Bunch") is added to each barrel. This culture is mostly *Pediococcus*, but also has "a hodgepodge of bacteria and wild yeast," including truly wild microbes captured through spontaneous fermentations. When I asked Cilurzo how much of the culture they add, he responded, "We do not use pitch rates for the bacteria, as our supply of house culture is always at different levels of acidity and we tend to make pitch rate decisions for bacteria more on taste." Unlike their *Brettanomyces* strains, the "Funky Bunch" culture is kept going in a 3 bbl. (3.5 hL) tank indefinitely, because it has large number of strains that have "fused together" and mutated. To add it to the beer they fashioned a length of hose inserted into a cobra tap to minimize pellicle disruption.

With all of the microbes introduced, the beer is barrel-aged between six and twelve months. Two to three months after pitching the bacteria, the *Pediococcus* produces copious amounts of buttery diacetyl, which is slowly reduced by the *Brettanomyces*. After a few years of production Russian River found their beers started to go through a ropy phase that takes three to four months to pass.

The barrels are not allowed to rise above 62°F (17°C). At the pub, they installed an air conditioning unit to keep their barrel room at 58°F–62°F (14°C–17°C). At the production facility barrel storage, both temperature and humidity are controlled. Even though this low temperature decelerates fermentation, Cilurzo favors it because it discourages the growth of *Acetobacter*. After some experimenting, Russian River did not find much difference between the character of the beers when they topped off the barrels or left them alone. As a result, they have gone back and forth on topping-off, although they always do it at least once when the bacteria is pitched. At most, they will top-off monthly with an active *Brettanomyces* fermentation (usually Sanctification). If you choose to top-off, Cilurzo suggests racking beer in, rather than pouring it, to minimize disruption to the pellicle.

Between the initial first and second batches of Supplication the barrels were rinsed out, but not sulfited, before being left to sit empty for a month. This exposure to oxygen in the air allowed *Acetobacter* to grow, which caused the second batch to become more acetic than Cilurzo wanted (although the beer still received positive reviews). Even after that incident, Russian River did not aggressively clean their barrels between fills, instead relying on quick refills to prevent *Acetobacter* from gaining a foothold. This practice has changed dramatically over the last few years. The brewers now clean each barrel with a high pressure wine barrel washer that sprays 150°F–160°F (66°C–69°C) water all over the interior at up to 1,200 psi. Aggressive cleaning reduces acetic acid production, and kills the weaker strains of the beneficial microbes.

Russian River's Temptation starts with a relatively simple recipe of base malt (Pilsner and pale) and unmalted wheat to produce a 1.062 OG (15.2°P) wort, which is hopped with Sterling and Styrian Golding. It is the aging process that transforms it into a complex tart and funky beer. After primary fermentation the batch receives *Brettanomyces* at the same time that it is transferred into Chardonnay barrels. Like most Russian River barrel beers, Temptation is topped-off after two to three months with bacteria and more *Brettanomyces* beer. The pH is also adjusted by blending in highly acidic beer at bottling.

The 1.060 OG (14.7°P) wort for Supplication gets its color from a range of malts, including crystal 40, Vienna, and Carafa Special. After the Belgian ale yeast completes the primary fermentation the beer is transferred to Pinot noir barrels along with three strains of *Brettanomyces* and dried cherries (25 lb. per 60 gal. [11.3 kg per 230 L]). Two months later it receives bacteria and additional *Brettanomyces*. Supplication ages for a total of 9 to 12 months in the barrel before blending and bottling.

In 2007, for the Toronado's 20th anniversary, Russian River released a special one-off beer as a thank you for this San Francisco beer bar's early support. The beer was conceived, brewed, and blended with the assistance of Dave Keene, the Toronado's owner, who challenged Cilurzo to brew something dark, funky, higher in alcohol, and barrel aged. The result was a blend of five beers each aged between 12 and 18 months. The main component was a 12% ABV quadrupel aged in barrels that were previously part of Firestone Walker's union fermentation system; however, after four months the beer was so oaky that it had to be moved to more neutral Merlot wine barrels and cut with the stainless-steel-aged portion of the batch. The remaining components comprised: two Belgian strong darks (8%–9% ABV) in neutral barrels with resident microbes; spontaneously fermented Sonambic (the base beer for Beatification) for acidity, because it is hard to get lactic acid bacteria to work in a high alcohol beer; and Sanctification to soften the dark flavors and lighten the color. Only 150 cases of Toronado 20th Anniversary Ale were produced.

Consecration was inspired by Toronado 20th, but is slightly lighter and aged in Cabernet Sauvignon barrels with the addition of dried Zante currants (which are not true currants, but in fact small grapes). Most of its color comes from dehusked roasted malt, and it is one of the few Russian River beers to include Special "B" in the grist. Primary fermentation takes it from 1.078 OG (19°P) to 1.012–1.016 SG (3°P–4°P), at which point the beer is put in barrels with *Brettanomyces* and the currants. Again, like other Russian River barrel beers, bacteria and more *Brettanomyces* are added to Consecration several months later. Consecration is barrel-aged for a further six to nine months before packaging. The beer shows a surprising amount of range, sometimes being more barrel-, currant-, or malt-forward.

Five years after Toronado's 20th anniversary, Cilurzo and Keene collaborated again to blend Toronado 25th Anniversary Ale. This took a similar direction to the original, being blended from six barrel-aged components (36% strong pale ale, 28% ale aged with currants, 16% blonde ale, 12% strong dark ale, 4% Sonambic, and 4% Baltic porter).[18]

Out of all the beers I have tasted from Russian River, my favorite was the first batch of Beatification. This was a completely different beer to the spontaneously fermented one they have released for all subsequent batches. Batch 001/PH1 was created by aging Redemption (a Belgian single) in two barrels that had been previously employed by New Belgium to age La Folie. The PH1 barrel was one of the favorites of New Belgium's Lauren Salazar, and I can see why, as it produced a remarkable beer with floral notes, an intense sourness with a hint of vinegar, and minimal funk.

Surprisingly, the mixed fermentations do not bring Russian River's beers below 1.006 FG (1.5°P). To produce the final blend, Cilurzo tastes each barrel to determine whether or not to include it. There is no magic in what Cilurzo does—most of the time too much acetic acid is his prime concern, and he simply tosses out any barrel which tastes off. Once the remaining barrels are blended he adjusts the acidity by either lowering it with stainless-steel-fermented *Brettanomyces* beer, or increasing it with strongly acidic beer fermented with the "Funky Bunch" culture. Russian River keeps a stock of "orphan" beers left over from other batches (with extra microbes to pitch in them) to use for blending, which undergo tasting to try to find releases where they will fit.

The finished blend is primed with sugar and re-yeasted with dry wine yeast. More info on Russian River's packaging process is found in Chapter 12. They do not experience a huge amount of character change after bottling these long-aged sour beers, other than the addition of carbonation. Russian River's website includes a bottle log that provides information for each of their releases (brewing/bottling date, primary yeast strain, and batch notes), a valuable feature that I wish more breweries would add.

Bottles of Russian River become pricier the farther away you travel from the brewpub, and are difficult to find even in the few markets they do distribute to, but if you have a chance to sample their sour beers they rarely disappoint. Their production method is one of the most difficult to replicate because of the staggered pitching (Figure 4), but their commitment to consistency is an example for the rest of us.

Russian River Souring Method

Pros: Controlled/reliable, complex results

Cons: Requires time and effort to maintain and pitch multiple cultures

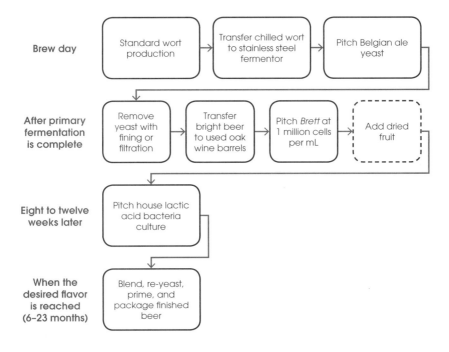

Figure 4—Russian River souring model.

The Lost Abbey and Pizza Port

Southern California's The Lost Abbey is the definition of a brewery obsessed with experimentation. Even though the brewery houses close to 1,000 oak barrels, their highly sought-after releases are often produced in ultra-low quantities. This is a testament both to the huge range of beers they produce and their love of blending. Their director of brewery operations, Tomme Arthur, honed his skills as head brewer at the Pizza Port brewpub in Solana Beach for a decade, before opening the Port Brewing production facility that now produces the Lost Abbey brand. I happened to visit Pizza Port Solana Beach in the fall of 2005, where I tasted a few of the last batches that Arthur brewed before his transition. The production brewery is in the same building that previously housed Stone Brewing. Luckily, Arthur has managed to carry that same "flavor-driven" (as he describes it) attitude into his new role, and is still producing beers focused on character rather than style guidelines.[19]

While brewing at Pizza Port, Arthur kept three strains of *Brettanomyces* (*B. bruxellensis*, *B. lambicus*, and *B. anomalus*) propagated in Cornelius kegs that were always available for pitching. In order to maintain the strains, he pitched them on a regular basis, adding fresh wort when more was needed. The original *B. bruxellensis* culture, which the Lost Abbey has maintained and repitched since Arthur moved there, has been allowed to mutate into a house strain; this *Brettanomyces* strain is available, mixed with saison yeast, as White Labs WLP670 American Farmhouse Blend.

The brewers at the Lost Abbey pitch 400,000 *Brettanomyces* cells per milliliter to allow the strains to establish themselves in first-use wine and spirit barrels. *Lactobacillus* and *Pediococcus* add the sourness to their beers, with about a third of a gallon (1.25 L) of their mixed house culture ("thick but not yogurt thick") added to each barrel the first time that a sour beer is aged in it. The house culture has developed organically. Arthur says, "We harvest the slurry from the bottom of our favorite barrels. It becomes a mixture of cultures over time. From time to time, we will add more *Brettanomyces* cultures to the barrels if we think that they are missing that aspect [i.e., Brett character]." Used barrels are rinsed with hot water and then a sulfur wick is burned inside each before they are either refilled or put into storage. For subsequent barrel fills the Lost Abbey brewers rely on only one-third of the pitching rate that they do for first-use barrels.

Barrel aging times range from as little as six months to as long as two years. As Arthur explains, "100% *Brettanomyces* fermentations are fast (typically less than a month if pitched properly) while secondary or tertiary *Brettanomyces* ferments (barrel type) take six to nine months to manifest true *Brettanomyces* flavors." The aging barrels at the brewery do not receive any additional temperature control above and beyond making it comfortable for the brewers and patrons. They also lease additional warehouse space for barrel storage that naturally varies from 50°F–68°F (10°C–20°C) depending on the season.

Many of their sour beers are barrel-aged versions of their low-hopped (around 1 lb. of Magnum per 30 bbl. batch is standard [0.45 kg per 35 hL]) clean year-round or seasonal beers. For example, the Lost Abbey's Red Poppy starts life as an English mild (Dawn Patrol Dark), with a two-week clean fermentation in stainless steel. This dark ale is blended with their Amigo Lager and transferred into used French oak wine barrels for a year of aging with their house microbes on 30 lb. (13.6 kg) of sour cherries. The Lost Abbey's answer to Rodenbach Alexander, Red Poppy is the sharply acidic descendant of Le Woody Brune, which Arthur first brewed at Pizza Port Solana Beach in 2002. The Lost Abbey occasionally releases a special draft-only version of Red Poppy, which receives double the amount of fruit.

Tomme Arthur's signature creation, Cuvée de Tomme, starts as Judgment Day, a Belgian strong dark with raisin puree added at the end of the boil (malt bill: American two-row, wheat, medium and dark English crystal, Special "B," chocolate malt, and dextrose, resulting in 1.092 OG [22°P]). Back in the Pizza Port days, when it was first brewed in 1999, the base beer was called Mother of All Beers. The fermented beer is aged in barrels on sour cherries with their three house strains of *Brettanomyces*. Early batches were aged exclusively in bourbon barrels, but more recent releases have introduced wine barrels as well. Wine barrels were included as a way of diluting the distinct character of the fresh bourbon barrels that the Lost Abbey had to buy as they increased production. Even after more than 10 years, Arthur still uses some of his original barrels to brew sours because of their mellow oak contribution.

In addition to whole fruit, several of The Lost Abbey's sour beers (e.g., Cuvée de Tomme, Red Poppy, Framboise de Amorosa) have also received 100% fruit juice concentrate at packaging. Arthur feels that this final dose of fruit allows the beer to trap more ephemeral fruit flavors that are usually driven off by fermentation. If you want to attempt this method, you will need to account for the sugar in the fruit concentrate itself when determining the amount of priming sugar (see Appendix A).

The Lost Abbey's most highly regarded beers are often available in minuscule quantities by production brewery standards, but that only serves to add to their cult status. Most famously, Yellow Bus, a peach-flavored sour, was never officially released for sale to the public. Yellow Bus highlights the value of sourcing the best quality fruit. A single 55 gal. (208 L) red wine barrel was created by souring a yellow base beer on about 60 lb. (27 kg) of heirloom white peaches picked from the tasting room manager's century-old tree. Sadly the tree died shortly thereafter, but cuttings from the tree had previously been grafted onto rootstock. Arthur has vowed that he will not brew another batch of Yellow Bus until these reincarnated trees yield fruit.

When the Lost Abbey brewers have barrels whose flavor does not fit into a blend for a production beer they hang onto these orphans until they find them a home in another blend. One of the ways they have devised to utilize spare barrels is to release beers that always have a similar concept but are blended each year from different base beers and barrels. Permitting the blend to stray from year to year gives the blender the opportunity to blend the best possible beer from the components available, rather than trying to reproduce a successful batch from components that do not taste exactly the same. Two examples of this are Cable Car and Sinners Blend.

Cable Car, blended for the Toronado beer bar's anniversary each year since 2007, is always a pale to amber sour. The first batch included barrel-aged versions of Red Barn (spiced saison), Avant Garde (lager yeast fermented bière de garde), and Amigo Lager. Each year the brewers taste the available barrels and create a beer that is in the same category, but is not trying to be exactly the same. In 2011 the Lost Abbey also released a special version of the beer aged on cherries, Cable Car Kriek.

Sinners Blend, released annually to the Lost Abbey's now defunct Patron Sinners Club, was always a darkish barrel-aged beer blend, although it was not always sour. Sinners Blend 2010 consisted of a mix of brandy-barrel-aged Angel's Share barleywine, sour beer on Cabernet Franc grapes, and their Gift of the Magi holiday ale, aged in a red wine barrel with *Brettanomyces.*

One of Arthur's unique skills is his ability to create interesting flavors by combining his sour beers with other beverages, including mead. He treats these as he would any other beer, getting the context right and not over-selling the flavors. This is something that is fun to play with, but it is easy to obscure the flavors of the base beer if you are not careful. Let your palate determine which combinations and flavors work for you.

The Veritas series is the showcase for these blending experiments (Table 1). They are often culled from orphaned barrels and only rarely are they distributed outside of the brewery's tasting room. Production is always limited, a scant 70 cases being the largest run, with others as modest as six cases (002 and 005 were not officially released). David Meyers of Redstone Meadery helped blend his Black Raspberry Mead into Veritas 002. They found that the addition of Old Viscosity, a clean bourbon-barrel-aged black barleywine, brought out the fruitiness of the mead. Going into these blending sessions without a target volume means that the best blend is chosen without concern for a low yield.

Table 1—The First 11 Veritas Releases by the Lost Abbey

Batch #	Description
001	Equal blend of three beers (now lost to the pages of history) barrel-aged on cherries.
002	Barrel-aged Avant Garde, Old Viscosity, and Redstone Black Raspberry Mead.
003	Angel's Share, Amazing Grace, Cuvée de Tomme, plus a "funky aged beer."
004	Yellow sour beer with peaches.
005	A sour base beer aged on wild native Southern California grapes (*Vitis girdianas*).
006	Phunky Duck aged on mandarin tangerines and raspberries, and blended with Cuvée de Tomme, raspberry mead, and Angel's Share aged on Cabernet Franc grapes. The successor to Sangre del Cristo and precursor of Framboise de Amorosa.
007	A pale sour beer with Cabernet Franc grapes.
008	Mellow Yellow (soured Amigo Lager), aged in jars with black tea and lemon zest.
009	Strong, dark ale aged in bourbon barrels, followed by aging in Syrah barrels with sour cherries.
010	A sour beer barrel-aged with yellow peaches.
011	Barleywine aged in Cognac barrels with fresh nectarines and *B. claussenii*.

Veritas 008 stands out as a particularly unique beer; it was produced by taking sour beer and giving it the ice tea treatment, with lemon and tea bags added to jars of beer that were placed by the brewery's windows. While this may sound gimmicky, it produced a balanced beer that was highly drinkable, with a uniquely complex ice tea and beer flavor. Until 2010, Lindemans produced a beer with a similar concept called Tea Beer by infusing their lambic with tea leaves and adding lemon juice, a creation that was especially popular in Japan.

While Arthur is known for brewing outside of the style guidelines, the collaborative Isabelle Proximus, inspired by Belgian-style lambics, showed he is capable of brewing a straightforward sour beer that is world class. The sole batch was brewed in November 2006. While the grist was relatively traditional (70% American pale malt and 30% unmalted wheat), the 10-day primary fermentation with lager yeast at 80°F (27°C) was anything but. The beer was aged at the Lost Abbey in a total of 18 inoculated barrels contributed by the brewers from Russian River, Avery, Allagash, and Dogfish Head, as well as the host. This is a brilliant idea, because the microbes from each brewery produced their signature characters, giving the beer much greater complexity than if it had been inoculated with cultures from only one brewery. It is similar to the method gueuze blenders use, who buy already inoculated wort from multiple lambic breweries. Isabelle Proximus spent 16 months aging in the mix of American and French oak barrels (four from each brewery except Dogfish Head, who donated two). When it was finished souring in the spring of 2008, only one barrel was not included in the final blend, which yielded 400 cases.[20] If you have a house culture, consider inoculating a few of your batches or barrels with a completely different set of microbes to give your beers more range and open up new blending possibilities.

Duck Duck Gooze proves that the Lost Abbey is also capable of making a wonderful pale sour beer with just their own in-house microbes. It is always a blend of approximately one, two, and three-year-old pale sour beers aged in French oak red wine barrels. The first batch included young Mellow Yellow, middle-aged Phunky Duck (7.0% ABV, brewed as the backbone for this blend), and old, soured Avant Garde. Starting with the 2013 release, their spontaneously fermented "Project X" was incorporated into Duck Duck Gooze. Beer from Project X was first commercially released as Cable Car 2012, blended with soured Avant Garde.

In 2004, Arthur was also a pioneer in 100% *Brettanomyces* fermentations when he and Peter Bouckaert brewed Mo' Betta Bretta at Pizza Port Solana Beach. Originally, the Lost Abbey website indicated this would return as the renamed Golden Rule, but it took a second collaboration with Bouckaert in 2012 to finally produce a second batch under the original name. For more production details on Mo' Betta Bretta see Chapter 8. The yeast from that second batch was passed onto New Belgium, where the two brewers combined on a second collaboration, this time called Brettanomyces Beer.

Despite all of their critical success, the Lost Abbey has fought a mundane production issue, carbonation levels. Several of their batches were undercarbonated to the point of being still, while others were overcarbonated enough to gush. The difficulty stemmed from the ale yeast strain they were adding at bottling, which worked well in their moderate-gravity clean beers, but had problems in the harsh environments of sour and high-alcohol beer. In addition, the Zahm and Nagel CO_2 Volume

Meter that they originally used did not accurately measure the low level of carbonation remaining in beers right out of the barrel.

To overcome these problems, the Lost Abbey now checks to see that the final gravity is low enough before pitching Champagne yeast, and sometimes a fresh *Brettanomyces* culture is also used to ensure proper carbonation. A sophisticated CO_2/O_2 Gehaltemeter (all-in-one CO_2/O_2 meter) ensures they are at 1.5 volumes of CO_2 before packaging, and John Mallett's (of Bell's Brewery) spreadsheet with a corrective factor determines how much dextrose they add to reach the target carbonation. The bottled beers are then held in the warm room at 75°F (24°C) for two to four weeks to condition. While the Lost Abbey's clean beers are now somewhat widely distributed, the low production volume of their sour beers means they are still only rarely available outside of southern California. Hopefully this will change, because in 2013 Arthur began searching for a second facility for clean beer production that would allow them to devote the original brewery entirely to sour beers.

 The Lost Abbey Souring Method

Pros: Complex flavor results, relatively hands-off aging process
Cons: Blending takes experience, skill, and a large number of components

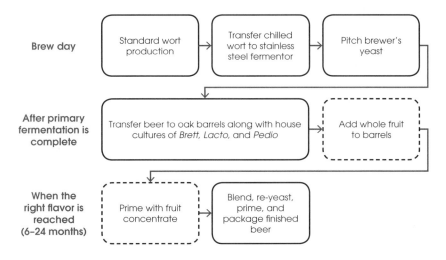

Figure 5—The Lost Abbey souring model.

Cambridge Brewing Company

In 1990, Cambridge Brewing Company was the first American brewery to brew Belgian-style beers, and they have not stopped breaking new ground since. At any given time the brewpub, located right around the corner from the Massachusetts Institute of Technology (MIT) campus, has multiple beers on tap that blend traditions, styles, and ingredients. Serving their unique creations only feet from the brewhouse allows the brewers to produce beers that would be problematic on a larger scale or with wider distribution. Some of their most interesting releases have been those aged in Madeira barrels, flavored with hand-harvested heather, and blended with the solera method.

Cambridge Brewing Company's longtime brewmaster, Will Meyers, and his staff employ a variety of techniques to sour the beers brewed on their 10 bbl. (12 hL) brewpub system. Unlike many of the other breweries featured in this chapter, Cambridge does not have a single souring method or house culture that it employs on all of their beers. Meyers focuses on brewing the types of sour beer that he enjoys drinking.

The barrels are stored in the brewery's cellar, a 110-year-old crawl-space that is not climate-controlled, which has a stone foundation and only five feet (1.5 m) between the floor and ceiling. Originally the space had a dirt floor, but plywood was eventually laid on top. The evaporation caused by this ambient temperature storage forces the brewers to top-off their barrels regularly.

From the point of view of the production process, the most unique and interesting beer made by Cambridge is Cerise Cassée. First brewed in 2004, this sour brown ale is aged with cherries in three sets of wine barrels, and blended by the solera method (each set consists of five barrels). It is easiest to explain this system if I start at the end: when the beer in the oldest set of barrels is ready to package, a portion of each is drawn out, blended, carbonated in the tank, and served from the bright beer tank. Beer from the middle set of barrels is then transferred to refill the oldest barrels. This leaves empty space in the middle barrels that is replaced with beer from the youngest set. The youngest set is refilled with fresh wort.[21]

With all of the solera barrels once again full of beer, they are allowed to age until the contents of the older barrels are ready for the process to be repeated. As Meyers puts it, "Proportional blending has become the norm, as certain barrels have expressed a propensity for producing higher

Will Meyers in the barrel cellar at Cambridge Brewing Company. (© Rachel Carrier)

acid concentrations than others, or result in a more attenuated beer, and a balanced and consistent beer is the goal every year." Cerise Cassée is worth the effort, with loads of dark fruit flavors, in addition to the bright sour cherry, a touch of acetic bite, and some yeastiness. More information about starting and maintaining a solera is found in Chapter 12.

Originally, a few days before blending and packaging Cerise Cassée, wort production for the new batch would begin with a sour mash (Figure 6, p. 116). This is no longer the case, but it is still a valuable technique to be aware of. When done incorrectly sour mashes are highly variable and stink (literally), but when done correctly they are reliable and clean smelling enough to perform in a busy brewpub. The way Cambridge performs sour mashes was inspired by Jean-François Gravel's method for producing his Berliner weisse at the Dieu Du Ciel! brewpub in Montreal, Canada. Air is the archenemy of a sour mash, because oxygen allows foul smelling aerobic bacteria to compete against the clean smelling facultative anaerobic *Lactobacillus*. Cambridge flushes the mash tun's head space with non-reactive gas. By minimizing oxygen contact the gas prevents aerobic bacteria and mold from reproducing as the mash sits.

For most brewers, CO_2—which is heavier than air—is the most readily available option for displacing oxygen. Purging is only effective if you have an airtight mash tun. Remember to flush with non-reactive gas again each time you open the lid to test the pH or temperature. If you do not have an airtight mash tun, the best option is to run the gas at the lowest possible pressure into the head space to create positive pressure, which prevents air from entering. If you do not have a kegging system, adding seltzer water to cool the mash will also serve to release enough carbon dioxide to purge the head space initially. Dry ice (solid CO_2) is a third option, but because of its frigid temperature (at atmospheric pressure sublimation occurs at −109.3°F [−78.5°C]) you will need to find a way to suspend it above the mash.

The actual mechanics of the sour mashes performed at Cambridge Brewing Company are relatively straightforward. The brewers hold the entire mash at the saccharification rest temperature, 154°F (68°C) in the case of Cerise Cassée, until it is converted, then they heat it to 170°F (77°C) for mash-out. With the enzymes denatured, the mash is cooled to 120°F–125°F (49°C–52°C) by cycling the wort through the heat exchanger and back into the mash tun. With the mash now cooled to the optimal temperature range for *Lactobacillus*, a bag of crushed pale malt is stirred in to introduce the wild bacteria that cling to the grains. Next, the temperature naturally cools over approximately 72 hours to 100°F (38°C), and the pH drops to 3.4–3.5. As the mash sours, Meyers takes periodic samples, writing times and tasting notes with a dry-erase marker on the side of the mash tun.

With the desired flavor and pH achieved, the mash is reheated to ensure good extraction and a quick runoff. The brewers then boil the wort to kill the microbes that were active during the sour mash. The wort is chilled, aerated, and mixed with an organic 100% cherry juice concentrate. The chilled wort is used to refill the youngest set of barrels immediately after their beer is moved to the middle set. The beer ferments in the barrels without the addition of fresh yeast or bacteria.

Meyers has inoculated his barrels with a wide variety of microbes. A few examples include slurries provided by New Belgium, Chad Yakobson's variant of the *Brettanomyces* Drie strain, and custom blends produced by Brewing Science Institute (BSI). The BSI blend is similar to Wyeast's Roeselare, but contains additional *Brettanomyces* strains in place of brewer's yeast. Whenever someone brings in a good bottle of lambic to share, the dregs often get run to the basement and tossed into a barrel.

The same sour mashing method that began the production of Cerise Cassée could be executed without the subsequent barrel souring to produce a quick sour beer, but doing it this way could result in some slightly funky off-flavors. For Cambridge beers that do not go through a secondary souring, like their Berliner-weisse-inspired Berliner Kendall, Meyers chooses to sour the wort rather than the mash. For more information on his technique, see the Sour Worting section later in this chapter.

Cambridge Brewing Company produces numerous traditionally soured beers as well, although many of these are one-off experiments with a total production of just a few barrels. While Cambridge uses only wine barrels to age Cerise Cassée, many of their other beers employ barrels that previously held spirits or fortified wines. If a beer does not have enough oak character, oak spirals are occasionally added. Cambridge's weighty Benevolence straddles the line between the English and Belgian traditions. It starts as a dark, malty sour beer that is fed with raisins, dates, and honey as it sours. This portion of Benevolence is aged in spirit barrels that had previously held a strong beer at another brewery. At kegging, this dark sour ale is blended with young strong ale to cut the sourness and return both body and sweetness.

The lightly spiced Resolution #9 was aged in two Madeira barrels. It was brewed with pale, caramel, roasted malt, and Belgian dark candi syrup, hopped with Hallertau, and spiced with a touch of coriander, orange peel, and ginger (1.075 OG, 1.008 FG, 8.8% ABV). Meyers pitched mixed-microbe slurry provided by his friends at New Belgium into the first-use barrels. The beer initially developed unpleasant phenolic and sulfur characters as well as massive acidity. The off-aromatics eventually volatilized, but the huge acidity remained. For years it was used as an acid beer, to sharpen fruit beers and other batches that required more balance to their residual sweetness. After five years of aging, however, on what may have been its final chance, Meyers enjoyed a sample so much that he decided to serve the beer straight.

The Colonel is Meyers' loose interpretation of a historical vatted porter. The first batch was aged in fresh bourbon barrels with *Brettanomyces* and *Lactobacillus* for six months, but ensuing batches have aged for as long as 18 months in the now well-used barrels. The beer was named in honor of Colonel Albert Bacon Blanton, who founded the Buffalo Trace distillery where Cambridge Brewing Company sourced the barrels. They have also taken The Colonel and added pumpkin, cinnamon sticks, and candied ginger to transform it into O.P.P. (Olde Pumpkin Porter), which combines the roasty sour porter flavors with subtle, earthy sugar pumpkin and spice. There was only a single batch produced, but it was doled out over a couple of years at their annual Great Pumpkin Festival, with the final keg consumed in 2011.

Cambridge Brewing Company also produces several beers based on a spontaneously-fermented strong lambic, which is detailed in Chapter 7. It is impossible to list, let alone detail, all of the sour beers that Cambridge has produced, but each one has relied on Meyers' passion for experimentation and emphasis on letting the beer age until he is happy with the flavor.

Cambridge Brewing Souring Process (Cerise Cassée)

Pros: Steady stream of blended beer with less intensive blending required

Cons: Risky, time-consuming production

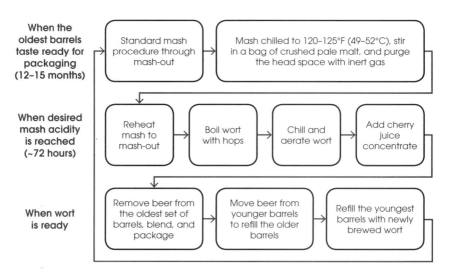

Figure 6—Cambridge Brewing Company souring model.

Captain Lawrence Brewing Company

Scott Vaccaro, the founder and head brewer of Captain Lawrence Brewing Company, has admitted the difficulties he had finding success with souring beers during his time as a homebrewer. Despite these struggles, Vaccaro won a GABF gold medal in 2007 for his first commercial effort, Cuvee de Castleton. Vaccaro founded Captain Lawrence in 2006, and for the first six years of operation he brewed on a 20 bbl. (23.5 hL) system cobbled together from used equipment purchased from various breweries. After outgrowing the original location in Pleasantville, NY, Captain Lawrence moved to a larger facility with a 40 bbl. (47 hL) brewhouse five miles away in the city of Elmsford. The new brewery also includes a 7 bbl. (8 hL) brewhouse that allows for more one-off batches, including experimental sour beers.[22]

Many of the sour beers produced by Captain Lawrence start as one of their clean beers. For example, Cuvee de Castleton begins life as their Belgian blond, Liquid Gold (Pilsner and Vienna, 1.063 OG [15.5°P], 15 IBUs), which is then aged in French oak wine barrels with *Brettanomyces* and 1 lb./gal. (0.12 kg/L) of Muscat grapes. Vaccaro selected Muscat for its juicy apricot flavor and perfume aromatics. The grapes are shipped from California to the winery next door to Captain Lawrence's original brewery, the same place they source the wine barrels (good neighbors to have).

The original batch of Cuvee de Castleton was fermented to dryness, 1.008 SG (2°P), with White Labs WLP530 Abbey Ale before it was transferred to barrels. The *Brettanomyces* was pitched into the barrels and allowed to work for eight months prior to the introduction of the grapes. By the time the beer was ready to bottle the gravity was at 1.000 (0°P).

For more recent batches the primary fermentation is cut early by crashing the temperature at

Barrels stacked four high at Captain Lawrence Brewing Company. (Courtesy of Captain Lawrence Brewing Company)

80°F–90°F (27°C–32°C) down to 50°F–60°F (10°C–15°C). Vaccaro has found that cutting the primary fermentation short in this way reduces *Brettanomyces* lag time, minimizes autolysis, and reduces the time needed for aromatic molecule formation. This results in a different character, more tropical fruit when compared with adding *Brettanomyces* to a dry beer. To further reduce autolysis, Captain Lawrence filters certain sour beers, like Little Linda's Liquid, to remove *Saccharomyces* before the *Brettanomyces* is pitched. For certain batches Vaccaro employs both of these techniques for portions aged in different barrels, which produces a wider range of blending options. Vaccaro suggests that if you are unable to halt the fermentation, a good alternative is to produce dextrinous wort, waiting until it drops clear before racking to secondary and pitching *Brettanomyces*.

The brewers pitch several strains of *Brettanomyces* in various combinations for their sour beers, including *B. bruxellensis*, *B. claussenii*, and *B. bruxellensis* var. Drie. Vaccaro puts an emphasis on pitching healthy cells. They do not pitch *Lactobacillus* or *Pediococcus* into most of their beers, instead relying on bacteria introduced by the wood or fruit to cause the pH to drop to somewhere around 3.5. Captain Lawrence does keep a house "mother" culture that has a huge variety of microbes from a wide range of sources. It is used when they want high acidity.

The closest sibling to Cuvee de Castleton is Rosso e Marrone, which is produced by aging St. Vincent's Dubbel in red wine barrels with 1 lb. of wine grapes, Zinfandel and Merlot, per gallon (0.12 kg/L) for 18 months (although Vaccaro is considering reducing the aging time). The combination of dark fruit from the malt and red wine from the grapes is spectacular. These wine grape sour beers develop only a moderate acidity because neither is pitched with lactic acid bacteria. Captain Lawrence also brews sour beers with cherries (Little Linda's Liquid) and peaches (Flaming Fury), and these are considerably more acidic than Cuvee de Castleton and Rosso e Marrone. Other than the grapes, most of the fruit is locally sourced from New York State vineyards and orchards. Vaccaro feels that the extra effort they put into obtaining high quality fresh fruit pays off with greater nuances in the final product.

The majority of Captain Lawrence's sour beers are aged in standard sized wine barrels, although others are rested in used spirit barrels or a single 800 gal. (3,000 L) oak tank. At the original brewery the barrels were scattered throughout the building, which had ambient temperatures ranging from 55°F in the winter all the way to 100°F in the summer (13°C–38°C).

Vaccaro says that he has found this fluctuation extracts character from the barrels (temperature changes cycle beer in and out of the wood). He also puts a lot of emphasis on minimizing acetic acid by ensuring the barrels are topped off and the airlocks remain filled. At the Elmsford brewery Vaccaro plans to eventually install temperature-controlled barrel storage, but this upgrade is not an initial priority.

All of the Captain Lawrence sour beers age for at least a year in oak (Figure 7). When it comes time to blend Cuvee de Castleton it is a relatively simple process: they toss out the barrels they do not like, and blend the rest. For other beers, like Barrel Select, it is personal preference; Vaccaro tastes all the available barrels of sour brown ale and determines a blend that suits his palate. The first bottling of Barrel Select was aged in oak wine barrels. This is one of their only beers pitched with lactic acid, which explains its more aggressive sourness. The second batch left out the lactic acid bacteria and was split to age on cherries (moderate cherry, slight acetic sourness) and raspberries (raspberry-seed, soft sourness). Their sour beers are bottle conditioned and usually improve with an additional year or two of age.

Captain Lawrence Souring Method

Pros: Complex flavors

Cons: Moderately high effort, variable acid production

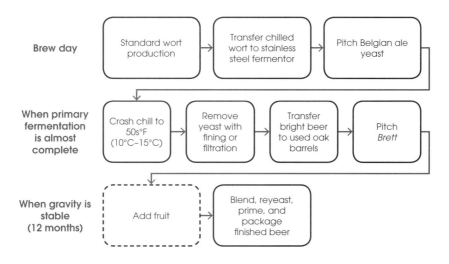

Figure 7—Captain Lawrence Brewing Company souring model.

A bottle of The Bruery's Oude Tart. (Courtesy of The Bruery)

The Bruery

Since founding southern California's the Bruery in 2008, Patrick Rue and his Sr. Director of Brewing Operations, Tyler King, have earned a reputation for brewing a wide range of beers that stand out for their uniqueness. Their sour beers include both ones brewed to classic styles and boundary-pushing experiments. In its first three years the brewery acquired and filled nearly 1,000 oak barrels, and that number has only grown since the addition of a 12,000 sq. ft. (950 m²) temperature-controlled warehouse. By 2013, the combination of clean and sour beers aged in oak represented half of their total production.[23]

The most approachable sour beer that the Bruery produces is Hottenroth, their take on a Berliner weisse. Most batches start with a single infusion mash at 158°F (70°C), but when they have enough time the brewers will include an overnight sour mash at 120°F (49°C). The only hop addition is a small amount of Strisselspalt in the mash. After conversion the wort is boiled for just 20 minutes, the shortest boil of any of their beers. The wort is fermented with a house culture of *Lactobacillus* that includes a small amount of *B. bruxellensis*. Each time the blend is harvested and repitched for the next batch, the fast-growing *Lactobacillus* can be seen to be outcompeting the *Brettanomyces*. Hottenroth includes no *Saccharomyces*, making it the only commercial beer I am aware of that has the bulk of the fermentation completed by bacteria rather than yeast. Hottenroth ferments and ages for a month in a tank before it is packaged. When the beer was first brewed the amount of sulfur produced by the fermentation required a few additional weeks of aging to dissipate, but the blend has adapted and now completes a cleaner fermentation. Despite the hot saccharification rest the beer finishes at 1.002 FG (0.5°P). The combination of the short boil and the *Brettanomyces* provides a fresh cereal character, adding complexity to what is usually a straightforward beer style. This is a good method to try if you experience the common difficulty of souring a Berliner weisse. If you want to attempt this you need a highly-attenuative, heterofermentative *Lactobacillus* strain, like White Labs' WLP677 (possibly blended with another *Lactobacillus* that produces a higher level of acidity).

According to Professor Burghard Meyer of VLB, the only major issue with pitching *Lactobacillus* for primary fermentation is that the bacteria will produce a proteolytic enzyme that degrades all of the protein in your beer, leading to poor (or even non-existent) head retention. This is especially problematic at higher fermentation temperatures between 113°F and 122°F (45°C–50°C). To prevent this, Professor Meyer suggests lowering the pH of the wort slightly to 4.5–4.8 before fermentation. In addition, he suggests adding chit (undermodified) malt.

The Bruery maintains four strains of *Brettanomyces* in-house: *B. anomalus*, *B. bruxellensis*, *B. lambicus*, and Fantôme (a strain isolated by East Coast Yeast that is similar to *B. anomalus*). They also maintain strains of *Lactobacillus* and *Pediococcus*. When they are not brewing Hottenroth or a 100% *Brettanomyces* beer, the Bruery pitches a clean American ale strain for primary fermentation of their sour beers. They do not use their usual house ale yeast, which is a descendent of the Duvel strain.

The Bruery's best regarded sour beer is Oude Tart, which is based on Flemish reds and won a gold medal at the 2011 GABF. It is one of the closer American examples to the traditional Belgian style, with a balance of sweetness and acidity. Tyler King was inspired by reading *Wild Brews* and aged the original homebrewed test batch for three years before the Bruery opened. It starts with a mash of American pale two-row, unmalted wheat, Vienna, CaraMunich® 45, and Special "B." The wort was originally pitched with Wyeast's Roeselare Blend, but the Bruery now individually propagates and pitches a neutral yeast strain in the stainless steel primary. This is followed by several strains of *Brettanomyces*, *Pediococcus*, sherry flor, and *Lactobacillus*, after transferring to well-used Cabernet Sauvignon barrels (Figure 8, p. 124). To produce beer with higher acidity the brewers ferment a portion of the wort spontaneously, racking into previously used barrels without pitching additional microbes.

The brewers try to avoid rinsing barrels unless they previously held fruit beer, in which case each barrel receives a few minutes of cold water spray just to remove the chunks of fruit. As time goes by the brewers have relied more on the microbes living in the wood and less on pitching. Previously, microbes were pitched by volume, but in 2012 the Bruery hired its first quality control employee to run trials to determine the optimal pitching rates for the various microorganisms. Once customized pitching rates are implemented for each beer, King hopes to achieve better consistency and quality.

Early batches of the Bruery's barrel-aged sour beers occasionally had too much acetic acid because the aging beer was not temperature controlled or topped off. The Bruery's new barrel aging warehouse has two temperature zones, 72°F (22°C) for their sour beers, and 65°F (18°C) for their clean bourbon-barrel-aged beers. They have also started a regular schedule of topping off each barrel, allowing for higher quality and more consistency in their sour beers. In 2014, the Bruery began shifting both the aging and packaging of their sour beers to a completely separate facility to minimize the risk to their clean beers.

Part of the secret behind Oude Tart is blending barrels of beer that were brewed in different ways to construct the finished beer. Each release contains batches of several ages (e.g., 10 months and 15 months). The older components are brewed to be maltier, and the younger batches are brighter and more acidic. A small amount of Sour Blonde (a pale spontaneously fermented beer) is included to lighten the flavor. A version of Oude Tart called Gypsy Tart skips the wine barrel aging; a version of Oude Tart aged with sour cherries is also available once a year.

The beer that best exemplifies the Bruery's style is Mélange #1, a blend of Oude Tart and Black Tuesday, the latter a bombastic 19% ABV bourbon-barrel-aged imperial stout. Mélange #1 was originally blended out of necessity when King needed a special firkin for their tasting room, but only had these two beers, both of which were too young to serve on their own. The "moderate" alcohol content (less than 10% ABV) points to the 7.5% ABV Oude Tart comprising the majority of the blend, but the precise ratio remains undisclosed. The test blend was hugely popular, and has since been blended on a larger scale for bottling.

The Wanderer, winner of a silver medal at the 2011 GABF in the Wood- and Barrel-Aged Sour Beer category, was blended from three different beers, one of which contained two different kinds of fruit. It was created in collaboration with Craig Wathen from City Beer Store in San Francisco for the store's fifth anniversary. Half of the blend was Sour Blonde, aged on blackberries and Bing cherries (bought at a farmer's market by Wathen), with the remainder being Oude Tart and the Bruery's strong, malty anniversary beer (Coton/Cuir). The Wanderer had a subtle fruit character, which King generally favors, although he does believe that there is a place for over-the-top fruit, such as the 30% raspberry and tart cherry puree blended into BeRazzled, described by King as a "sour fruit beer smoothie." For most of their fruited beers, the brewers aim to let the beer age for three months on fruit, enough time to ferment out the sugars, but not so much that the fresh flavor fades. However, BeRazzled is bottled as soon as the fruit settles, usually about three days.

The Bruery also releases unblended sour beers. This includes a 5% ABV sour stout named Tart of Darkness, which was aged in second-use bourbon barrels with their house blend of souring bacteria and yeast. For this beer the brewers perform a concentrated boil, diluting the wort with water to allow them to fill more barrels from a single brew. I found this beer to have a clean, snappy acidity, and a rich dark cherry character, especially as it approached room temperature.

In 2010, Rue and King collaborated with their counterparts at Tampa's Cigar City Brewing to produce Marrón Acidifié. They created a strong oud bruin inspired by the style's standard-bearer, Liefmans Goudenband. Their targeted flavor profile was based on Cigar City's reputation for producing outstanding brown ales and the Bruery's expertise in malty sour beers. Together, the brewers decided on a recipe that included higher percentages of roasted and crystal malts than the Bruery usually uses. They produced four batches of 30 bbl. (35 hL) each, which were fermented with *Lactobacillus* and *Brettanomyces bruxellensis* (no brewer's yeast or other microbes were pitched). The beer was aged in a combination of wine and bourbon barrels, which had previously aged Cuir and Black Tuesday. After souring was complete the brewers found they had too much beer to produce a single blend for their bottling line, so it had to be bottled in multiple runs, which they made as consistent as possible. The result was a toasty, dark malt character, sharp sourness, and an earthy funk.

In addition to Marrón Acidifié, the collaboration yielded a fruited variation named ISO:FT (for the abbreviations Internet beer traders use to mean "in search of" and "for trade"). Their original plan had been to include black sapote (a Floridian fruit with cocoa notes), but a cold snap that winter prevented them from obtaining high quality examples of the fruit in the quantity required. Instead, they added guava from Florida and dates from California, then aged it in former bourbon barrels. When the souring was complete the beer was coarsely strained, resulting in a small amount of fruit making it into the bottles. The guava brightened the beer, making it lighter and more complex than Marrón Acidifié. The breweries also collaborated on a second recipe, this time brewed at Cigar City's brewery and called Dos Costas Oeste. It was aged on a variety of woods; more on the subject can be found in Chapter 9.

The Bruery has managed to place the spirit of experimentation and innovation above the desire to increase production. While I am excited to see even wider distribution of their barrel-aged beers in the years to come, I hope they do not lose the drive to keep discovering new combinations of flavors.

The Bruery Souring Method (Oude Tart)

Pros: Complex flavors, variety of blending options

Cons: Moderate difficulty, blending skills required

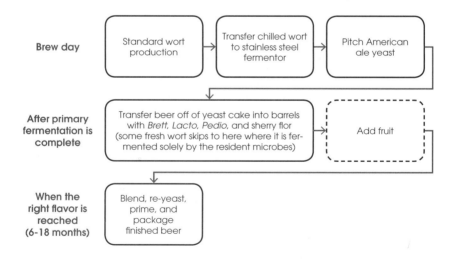

Figure 8—The Bruery souring model.

Inspecting apricots for Cascade Brewing's Apricot Ale. (Courtesy of Cascade Brewing Company)

Cascade Brewing

Portland, Oregon is known for having one of the strongest craft brewing cultures in the country. While there are a few breweries in town that brew sour beer, Cascade Brewing truly specializes in sours. Their beers are available bottle-conditioned, and on tap at Cascade Brewing Barrel House (where they store most of their barrel-aging sour beers).[24]

Most of Cascade's sour beers have a clean sourness and an assertive flavor component provided by fruit, bourbon barrel aging, or spicing. Their distinctive balance has led to several GABF medals, including in 2009 when they took both the gold and silver medals in the Wood- and Barrel-Aged Sour Beer category. The Cascade beers obtain their unique character from souring with *Lactobacillus brevis*, without pitching *Brettanomyces* or *Pediococcus*. Head brewmaster Ron Gansberg feels that this microbe gives his beers a well-defined acidic crispness (he never adds refined lactic acid) while preserving the malt backbone. It also eliminates the *Brettanomyces* "horsiness" character. Another advantage of this method is that the *Lactobacillus* will not create as much acid as *Pediococcus*, so the beers rarely become overly acidic. The combination of flavors Gansberg achieves is particularly striking in high alcohol, lightly-spiced beers like Vlad the Imp-Aler and Bourbonic Plague. Their fruit beers contain more fruit flavor and residual sweetness than most American sour beers, but do not come off as sugary.

Wort production on Cascade's 10 bbl. (11.7 hL) steam-heated brewhouse is relatively standard. The brewers execute a step-mash to create wort that has the desired level of fermentability. During the boil, small additions of aged hops keep the IBUs to a minimum (in most cases between 8 and 13 IBUs) to ensure that *Lactobacillus* will not be inhibited. After the clean primary fermentation with Belgian ale yeast is complete, the now 1.020–1.024 SG (5°P–6°P) beer is chilled and allowed to settle. The clear (bright) beer is then transferred to barrels along with the house *Lactobacillus* culture. This method would not work with any of the timid commercially available strains of *Lactobacillus*. Gansberg would not reveal the original source of his alcohol-tolerant and aggressive strain, but it can be harvested from bottles of their beer.

The beers age in a variety of barrels, including those that previously held either wine or bourbon. Barrels at the brewery are stored at ambient brewhouse temperatures (although being in the Pacific Northwest this is rarely too hot). At the Cascade Brewing Barrel House facility, which houses 400 barrels, the temperature is controlled around 60°F–64°F (16–18°C). While the beers age the bungs of each barrel are kept propped slightly open with hollow plastic cotton swabs that have had one end cut off. According to Gansberg, this allows the pressure inside and outside the barrel to equalize. The remaining cotton head allows carbon dioxide produced by the *Lactobacillus* to escape. When the weather cools, a small amount of air can flow into the barrel without allowing wild yeast or bacteria access to the beer. If you choose to follow this method, be cautious—if microbes other than *Lactobacillus* are present in the beer there is a high likelihood of acetic acid production.

The base beers are allowed to sour in the barrels before they are racked into large tanks, where they are then combined with fresh fruit. Before bottling, the beer spends about four months on either apricots for Cascade's Apricot Ale, or cherries for their Kriek Ale. Dried fruit is often used for barrel aging, for instance, Bourbonic Plague's strong porter base spends 14 months on dates in wine and bourbon barrels before it is blended with a vanilla–cinnamon porter. Gansberg does not suggest adding fruit to hide

Tapping a beer "live from the barrel" at the Cascade Brewing Barrel House. (Courtesy of Cascade Brewing Company)

flaws: "When we put fruit to beer it is only the absolute best beer because the fruit is an additional investment in labor, time, and expense."

Many of Cascade's releases are blends of more than one base beer. There are blends that were inspired discoveries, while others were the result of experimentation. When blending, Gansberg tastes for different characters (more or less acidic, lemony, and aged character, for example) and "uses them to build a sum greater than the individual parts." A percentage of each base beer put into barrels is earmarked for a certain blend or set of blends (Table 2).

After blending, the barrel-aged sour beers to be bottled are first dosed with American ale yeast to ensure carbonation. While some experimental beers and blends are only served on tap, the Cascade Brewing Barrel House also serves beers "live from the barrel" unblended, simply drawn from a spigot near the bottom of the barrel that the beer was aged in.[25]

In addition to barrel-aged sour beers, Cascade produces several tart stainless-steel-fermented beers. These include four seasonal Gose variations that are not bottled (Table 3). The Summer Gose contains the traditional seasonal additions, and exhibits an assertive lactic sourness from the mixed fermentation with *Lactobacillus* at 70°F–75°F (21°C–24°C).

Table 2—A Selection of Cascade's Sour Beers

Beer Name	Base Beer	Aging - Addition
Kriek Ale	Northwest-Style Sour Red	Oak barrel-aged, then on cherries
Sang Rouge	Northwest-Style Sour Red	Barrel-aged
Sang Noir	Northwest-Style Sour Red	Aged in bourbon and Pinot noir barrels, then on Bing cherries
Sang Royal	Northwest-Style Sour Red	Aged in port and Pinot noir barrels, then Cabernet Sauvignon grapes
Apricot Ale	Tripel	Wine barrel-aged, then on apricots
The Vine	Tripel, Blonde Quad, and Golden Ale	Barrel-aged, then fermented with white wine juice
Cuvée du Jongleur	Northwest-Style Sour Red, Tripel, and Blonde Quad	Barrel-aged

Table 3—Cascade Brewing Seasonal Gose

Beer Name	Additions
Spring Gose	Chamomile, lemon peel, as well as golden and purple culinary lavender
Summer Gose	Coriander and salt
Fall Gose	Orange peel, nutmeg, and cinnamon
Winter Gose	Cranberries, hibiscus, cinnamon, sweet orange peel, and a slightly higher alcohol level

The Cascade Brewing souring method does not create the wide range of esters and phenols found when using a more diverse range of microbes, so it is best for sour beers that have a strong character of their own. If you want to try this method (Figure 9), start with the dregs from one of their bottles and keep the IBUs of the wort to a bare minimum.

Cascade Brewing Souring Method

Pros: Sourness without funk, more complex flavor than pre-boil souring methods

Cons: Sourness without funk, longer aging required than pre-boil souring methods

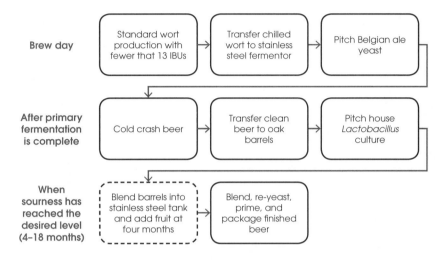

Figure 9—Cascade Brewing Company souring model.

Ithaca Beer Company

Located in upstate New York, Ithaca Beer Company did not release their first sour beer until 10 years after it was founded in 1997. Most of Ithaca's production capacity is devoted to a solid lineup of clean beers, including one of the East Coast's best IPAs, Flower Power.

The golden-hued Brute was the first sour beer Ithaca released in bottles. The grist includes corn (5%) and wheat (12%). Former brewmaster Jeff "Chief" O'Neil developed a unique method to sour this beer that does not rely on lactic acid bacteria. Instead, a large portion (13%–14%) of acidulated (*sauer*) malt is added to the mash to contribute lactic acid. Weyermann acidulated malt was added to the first batch, but in following years they sourced from Best Malz®. The acid malt lowers the pH of the mash, which reduces the efficiency of the enzymes provided by the Pilsner base malt. This is compounded by the hot saccharification rest, which is

129

Funky Brewster, the tank that Ithaca Brute was aged in each year. Now used for other sour beers. (Courtesy of Andrew Schwartz, Ithaca Beer Company)

conducted at an almost unheard of temperature of around 160°F (71°C). The combination of these factors ensures low attenuation by the primary yeast strain, leaving a large amount of dextrins for the *Brettanomyces* to follow. O'Neil refers to it as a "cheater's version of a classic turbid mash."

In addition to including local unmalted grains, Brute is hopped with New York State-grown Willamette, Hallertau, and Cascade hops. The hops are aged in open Mylar bags for a couple of years in the boiler room to reduce their alpha acids and mute their flavor. Aged hops are not strictly required for this method, as they are for spontaneous fermentation, but like any sour beer a low level of bitterness is best for flavor considerations. The boil raises the gravity of the wort to around 1.057 OG (14°P).

Primary fermentation takes place in stainless steel with Ithaca's house yeast, a Whitbread-related English ale strain. The fermentation temperature is allowed to free rise to around 90°F (32°C) to encourage a fruitier profile. Once the desired gravity is reached, 1.028–1.032 SG (7°P–8°P), the beer is crash cooled. This rapid chilling mid-fermentation causes VDKs (e.g., diacetyl) to remain in the wort, which O'Neil values as an additional substrate for *Brettanomyces* flavor development. After fermentation is halted, the 25 bbl. (29.3 hL) batch of bright beer is transferred onto a vigorous 1 bbl. (1.2 hL) starter of *Brettanomyces* Drie, a pitch of about 2 million cells per milliliter. This high pitching rate reduces the amount of time it takes the beer to reach final gravity. A new pack of six lightly-toasted French oak spirals were added to the tank for the first few batches. What was the dedicated Brute tank (a uni-tank with a manway on the top—nicknamed Funky Brewster) sat in the brewery's driveway for a few years after the glycol jacket imploded before O'Neil figured out how to put it to good use. The surface of the fermentation sits 1 ft. (0.31 m) below the top of the tank.

The annual batch of Brute is brewed near the end of each summer, and allowed to age until late spring the following year. O'Neil feels that the seasonal temperature progression is a big part of the success of the beer. It starts at 90°F (32°C) in the summer and then goes down to 54°F–59°F (13°C–15°C) in the winter, before a final burst of activity as the ambient temperature starts to rise in the spring. During the spring the brewers witness one final gravity and pH drop. Despite the long aging with *Brettanomyces,* the finishing gravity is higher than most moderate-gravity sour beers, approximately 1.016 FG (4°P). The final pH is on the high end for sour beers, 3.6–3.7.

Once the *Brettanomyces* completes its work, CO_2 is used to push the batch out of the tank. This means there is no oxygen exposure between the time when the old batch is bottled and the next batch is moved into the tank. The brewers did not clean the tank after the first two batches, so the oak spirals continued to collect. The third batch turned slightly acetic, so before the fourth batch the 18 old oak spirals were removed and the clean-in-place (CIP) system was run on the tank. O'Neil was able to judge the age of each spiral from the progressive consumption of the wood by the *Brettanomyces*.

None of Ithaca's sour and funky beers are filtered, although they do filter several of their year-round and seasonal beers. Brute is bottle conditioned with a blend of three Champagne yeast strains and kraeusened with fresh wort, usually from their Apricot Wheat. The total production of Brute each year is only 250 cases, most of which is sold at the brewery. The result of Ithaca's innovation (Figure 10) is a beer with a sharp acidity, a big, funky nose, and fuller body than many other *Brettanomyces* fermented sour beers. It is not a sweet beer; given the flavor most people are surprised to find out how high the final gravity is. However, Brute does not age quite as gracefully as many other sour beers, developing a slight cider vinegar character after a couple of years.

Ithaca also brews LeBleu, a blueberry sour beer that begins production as wort diverted from their Apricot Wheat. The grist includes 35% wheat malt and 5% acid malt, and gives a starting gravity of 1.044 OG (11°P). It is hopped with 15 IBUs of Northern Brewer. No *Saccharomyces* is pitched, only *Brettanomyces* Drie, but the beer has tested positive for the presence of bacteria as well. Primary fermentation is completed in a variety of local wine barrels, all well used, including both French and American oak. The barrels are stacked four to five high on racks and stored at ambient brewery temperature. If you are not temperature controlling your barrel room be aware of how much hotter the barrels at the top of stacks may become. Because the wort for LeBleu was so frequently brewed the barrels were regularly topped off as they aged.

Each bottling of LeBleu is a blend of multiple vintages of the same beer. For example, the 2010 release was a blend of beer put into barrels in 2007, 2008, and 2009. The barrels selected for a release each receive 50 lb. (22.5 kg) of hand-crushed raw blueberries for the last few months of the *Brettanomyces* fermentation. The blueberries come through as woodsy-spice, lacking the fresh berry flavor you might expect. The blueberries also contribute a striking pinkish-red hue that lets you know they did not skimp on the fruit. Each barrel is reused for several turns before it is retired when there is no wood character left to give.

Ithaca also brews a strong (8% ABV) Belgian pale ale with *Brettanomyces* called White Gold. It is brewed with Pilsner, wheat, and a small amount of acidulated malt. The New York mega-collaboration Super Friends, a 100% *Brettanomyces* fermented IPA, was brewed at Ithaca (see Chapter 8).

After leading Ithaca Brewing into the world of sour beers, O'Neil left his position as brewmaster to take up the same role at a small brewpub just outside New York City called Peekskill Brewing. Both breweries are thriving. Ithaca recently completed building a new facility with a dedicated space for barrels. O'Neil's move to Peekskill Brewing provides a new building with a rooftop beer-garden overlooking the Hudson River and more room for creativity, not to mention a coolship.

Ithaca Souring Method (Brute)

Pros: Quicker than most, acid level is easier to control

Cons: More residual sweetness, does not age well long term

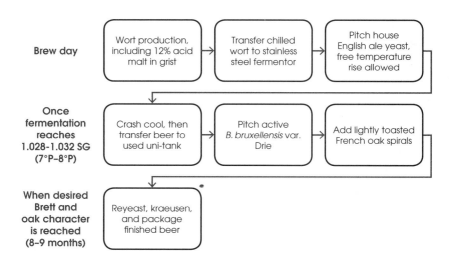

Figure 10—Ithaca Beer Company souring model.

133

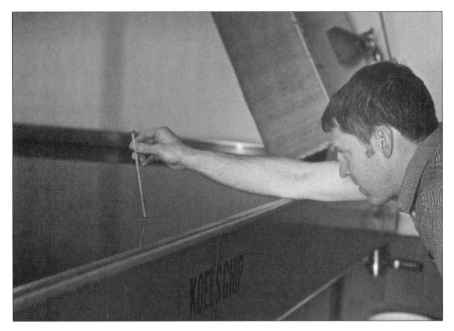

Jason Perkins measuring the temperature of the wort in Allagash Brewing Company's coolship. (Courtesy of Allagash Brewing Company)

Allagash Brewing Company

When they opened in Portland, ME in 1995, Allagash was one of the first American breweries to specialize in producing Belgian styles. Allagash White is reliably one of the best American examples of Belgian wit, and accounts for the majority of their sales. After focusing on clean Belgian beers for a decade, Rob Tod, the founder, and Jason Perkins, the brewmaster, began experimenting with mixed-fermentation beers. Most of these highly sought after beers have been one-off brewery-only releases of just a few hundred bottles. They do ferment two beers with *Brettanomyces* that see wider production and distribution, namely Interlude and Confluence.[26]

In 2005 Allagash brewed the first batch of Interlude, a beer that was intended to be a clean saison. When the *Saccharomyces* stalled half-way through fermentation (a common occurrence with fussy saison strains) the beer was left in the tank for three months. When a brewer happened to notice that the tank had started producing CO_2 again they assumed that the primary yeast had restarted fermentation, but a taste revealed a flavor reminiscent of *Brettanomyces*. Only later did the brewers discover that the tank had a loose fitting lid, which had allowed air to be pulled in as the beer cooled.

Not wanting to leave the unique and delicious flavor as a one-off, Allagash contracted two yeast laboratories to isolate and analyze the uninvited microbe; one thought it was *Brettanomyces*, while the other concluded it was a wild *Saccharomyces*. Jason Perkins now suspects that it is *Dekkera*, the spore forming form of *Brettanomyces* (for simplicity referred to as *Brettanomyces* for the remainder of this section). The strain is only mildly funky, adding flavors mostly reminiscent of bread, ripe fruit, and SweeTarts®, along with minor barnyard funk. Perkins also found it to be a sluggish strain that needs to be pitched with a good deal of fermentables remaining in the beer. While a yeast laboratory banks and propagates this strain for the brewery, it is not commercially available (although it is available to harvest from their bottles).

On ensuing batches of Interlude this house wild yeast is pitched after primary fermentation stalls, 10 days after the initial pitch of saison yeast. When the beer has aged 10 months in stainless steel, 15% of the volume is transferred to a holding tank. The remaining 85% is blended with the reserved 15% from the previous batch, which by this point has been aged for an additional 10 months in French oak barrels that previously held Merlot and Syrah at the PlumpJack Winery in Napa Valley, CA. The barrel-aged portion provides oak flavors, additional funky complexity, and further dryness to the finished blend. The 15% reserved from the current batch is used to refill those French oak barrels, and is left to age until it is time to blend the next bottling (Figure 11).

Confluence, the other widely distributed beer that features Allagash's house *Brettanomyces*, starts with a mash of imported Pilsner, domestic pale, and caramel malt. The wort is hopped with Tettnang and East Kent Goldings in the kettle. The fermentation differs from Interlude in that Confluence is pitched with both their house Belgian ale strain and house wild yeast simultaneously. The pitching rate is split roughly evenly between the strains, but the two yeasts are treated differently; the wild yeast is readied with four days of propagation in low-hopped wort with several oxygen additions, while the ale yeast comes right out of cold storage. This method gives their wild yeast strain enough of an advantage to compete, but the ale strain still ferments more rapidly. The wild yeast works slower, taking five months to finish its fermentation. When the gravity is stable,

Confluence is dry hopped with Glacier for two weeks to give it fresh hop aromatics to complement the fruity and funky *Brettanomyces.*

In addition to the two beers with wild yeast, Allagash has also released several excellent mixed-fermentation sour beers. Gargamel (9.2% ABV, American two-row barley, both raw and malted wheat, and caramel malt) was aged in five oak barrels with raspberries and their house *Brettanomyces.* However, because of a large variation between the barrels only three were combined for the final blend. Vagabond, another strong sour at 10% ABV, was aged for four years in a single American oak barrel, but despite this long aging the beer had a superb oak flavor without tasting like lumber. One of my favorites of Allagash's one-off beers was Tripel Roselaire (spelling intentional), a draft-only version of their Tripel Reserve, aged for two years in a wine barrel with Wyeast's Roeselare Blend. These beers are mostly experiments of the type homebrewers do, playing with different strains and base beers in an attempt to figure out what works and what does not.

For Allagash's research projects using small batches, some barrels see *Brettanomyces* and lactic acid bacteria added along with the beer, while other previously used barrels are filled with fresh beer and the microbes in the wood allowed to work. The brewers keep the barrel room at or below 62°F (17°C), and regularly top-off their barrels to reduce oxidation and acetic acid production. The sour beers are all bottled unpasteurized using equipment (12-head rotary filler, gaskets, and pumps) that never touches the clean beers.

Rob Tod and Jason Perkin's spirit of experimentation and risk-taking is on full display with their spontaneously fermented Coolship series of beers. The success of their wild yeast increased their confidence that spontaneous fermentation in Maine could produce delicious results. After getting encouragement from the Van Roy family of Cantillon, they decided to build a traditional coolship and see how the classic Belgian lambic methods for wort production, inoculation, aging, and blending would translate to America. The complete details of these beers are found in Chapter 7.

Most of Allagash's year-round clean beers do not stray far from the Belgian tradition, but their sour and funky beers, while rooted in the Old World, have a distinctive American spark. Having their own proprietary wild yeast strain while there are still only a handful of strains available commercially helps set Allagash beers apart from the rest.

Allagash Method (Interlude)

Pros: Adds aged character without the long-term evolution of a true solera

Cons: Involves both a regular fermentor and barrels, relatively large production required

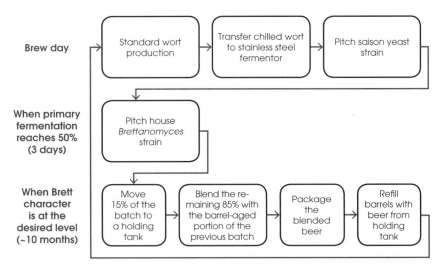

Figure 11—Allagash Brewing Company souring model.

Sour Worting

Employed by several breweries, most notably Cambridge Brewing Company, sour worting is similar to sour mashing in that both methods produce all of their acid prior to primary fermentation. Sour worting is quick, completed in days rather than the months or years required for traditional sour beer production. This method does not require a prolonged mixed fermentation, so the pH drop is easier to control. However, beers produced by sour worting followed by a clean ale or lager yeast fermentation do not attain a complex fermentation character, so the method is best utilized for souring beers that exhibit other assertive characters.

Although similar to sour mashing, sour worting has several advantages when the two techniques are compared. Sour worting eliminates most of the problems associated with the sour mash method, such as inconsistent sourness, off-flavors, and stuck sparges. This is accomplished by separating the wort from the spent grain, pasteurizing it, and then inoculating it in a fermentor with *Lactobacillus*. Once the desired acidity is reached, the wort is pasteurized a second time before the fermentation is completed by brewer's yeast. Sour worting allows for relatively standard wort production, freeing the mash tun for production of other beers.

To sour his Berliner weisse at Cambridge Brewing Company, Will Meyers cools the 10 bbl. (12 hL) batch of boiled Berliner Kendall wort with a heat exchanger and then pitches a strong 30 gal. (114 L) culture of *Lactobacillus*. When the wort has soured to the desired level, he heats it to 180°F (82°C) to kill the bacteria. The acidic pH (as low as 3.2) can cause issues for the *Saccharomyces*, so Meyers adds extra yeast nutrient and uses a higher pitching rate to ensure a healthy fermentation. The pH of the beer actually rises to 3.5 while the ale yeast ferments.[27] The result is a clean, tart, lightly bready wheat beer, finishing at 1.005 FG (1.25°P).

A pure commercial culture of *Lactobacillus* is reliable, but the less expensive and more efficient method is to ferment the wort with wild *Lactobacillus* found living on malt. While it is possible to inoculate the wort directly with a small amount of crushed grain, it is far less risky to select for *Lactobacillus* by making a starter first.

To make the starter, you will begin with a small volume of low gravity, 1.030 SG (7.5°P), unhopped wort. As a general rule, the starter should be about 2.5% of the wort's volume. When the starter wort has cooled below 120°F (49°C) combine it with 25% of its own volume of crushed base malt. Incubate the starter in the optimal range for *Lactobacillus*, 104°F–111°F (40°C–44°C), to encourage its growth at the expense of the other microbes living on the malt. Homebrewers can try using a heating pad to maintain the warm temperature, but a ceramic reptile heater, or Brew Belt attached to a temperature controller, would work equally well. If you are able to hold the starter anaerobically by flushing with CO_2, this will further select for the oxygen-ambivalent *Lactobacillus*. After three days the starter should taste sour. The low pH (3.3–3.5) will inhibit or kill most of the aerobic microbes responsible for the garbage-dump-in-summer smell that improperly conducted sour mashes are reviled for. Do not worry if not much CO_2 is produced or if the gravity of the starter does not drop (either of these simply indicates you have a homofermentative strain of *Lactobacillus*—see Chapter 4). At this point get the starter ready to pitch by straining and discarding the grain.

With your starter all set, prepare the wort through the sparge as normal. You will not have the additional attenuative power of a mixed fermentation, so perform a relatively cool saccharification rest, although this will ultimately depend on your choice of yeast strain and desired balance of sweet and sour. You can either complete the boil before or after souring; postponing the boil ensures that there is no risk of inhibiting the *Lactobacillus* with hops. If you do boil first, keep the bitterness below 4 IBUs. Even if you are not going to boil the wort, you should heat it to 180°F (82°C) to kill any microbes from the grain or mash tun. Force chill the wort to around 100°F (38°C), then transfer it with the starter to a fermentor that has been flushed with CO_2. For added insurance against oxygen getting in, you can purge the fermentor by bubbling CO_2 through the wort. Try to keep the wort warmer than 80°F (27°C) while it sours. Warmer temperatures than this will cause the souring process to proceed more rapidly, but this can be difficult to achieve because most brewers do not have the equipment needed to safely maintain a large volume of wort above 100°F (38°C). Be careful not to allow the wort to get above 120°F (49°C) or you will risk impairing the *Lactobacillus*.

Monitoring acid levels is important. If the wort gets extremely sour, below a pH of 3.4, the acidity can cause fermentation problems for most strains of brewer's yeast. Alternatively, for pre-fermentation souring, you might prefer to measure the acid level of the wort directly by measuring tritatable acidity rather than measuring pH. Titration can be more useful when monitoring acidity, because although the amount of acid increases roughly linearly with time, when the buffering capacity of the wort is exhausted, the pH can plummet rapidly. It is safest to stay below 0.5% lactic acid to avoid problems with the brewer's yeast fermentation. If you overshoot your desired acidity, blend in clean wort between pasteurization and primary fermentation to dilute the lactic acid and raise the pH.

The lower bound for acidity, taken with the pH rise during primary fermentation, means that sour worting on its own is only a good method for adding light to moderate acidity. If your goal is to produce a grippingly sour beer, you will need to select another souring method.

Once the desired level of lactic acid is obtained, transfer the wort back into the kettle and complete the boil, adding hops as desired. If you boiled the wort before souring, you only need to hold the soured wort at 160°F (71°C) for 20 minutes, or briefly at 180°F (82°C), to pasteurize. Take care anytime you are heating soured wort—if you pitched a heterofermentative strain that produced alcohol this can be dangerous, as alcohol vapors may ignite. From this point, the wort is treated the same as it would be for any clean beer. In most cases, the sterile soured wort is chilled and then pitched with a healthy culture of brewer's yeast.

Souring wort is an option for brewers who do not have enough storage space to allow long-term aging, and for those brewing stronger beers that have enough alcohol to inhibit lactic acid bacteria after primary fermentation. While the method does not produce the same complex ester and phenol profiles of a traditional mixed fermentation, it is possible to produce a sour beer that takes only a few days longer than is needed to ferment a clean batch of beer. The finished beer is also free of wild microbes, so you do not have to worry about contaminating your kegging or bottling equipment.

My results with this method were solid, but unspectacular. In fact, the brown ale I soured with *Lactobacillus* grown from a small amount of Maris Otter took several months to age out the fresh worty aromatics. So, in the end, I did not realize any substantial time saving over the more traditional souring process.

If you want to create a quickly fermented beer imbued with both sourness and funk, then there is one final option. Soured wort serves as an excellent base for 100% *Brettanomyces* fermentations. This combination is a relatively quick way to produce a complex sour ale. *Brettanomyces* can thrive at a pH as low as 3.1, so this is a way around the pH floor mentioned earlier. Crooked Stave and Pizza Port have both completed sour worting before starting 100% *Brettanomyces* primary fermentations. For more information about this see Chapter 8.

Sour worting can serve as a standalone method for brewers looking to minimize aging time or worried about introducing bacteria into their post-boil equipment. Do not expect a remarkably complex beer from this quick method, but it is a more honest way to produce clean, safe, and quick sour beers than resorting to dosing a clean beer with food grade lactic acid. It can also serve as a safety measure for spontaneous fermentations; pre-souring the wort prevents harmful bacteria from growing before the wild *Saccharomyces* begins fermenting. Where sour worting shines, however, is as a way to add lactic acid to a beer as part of a more complex process, where it can be substituted in place of sour mashing as a way to lower the pH before continuing on to mixed-microbe fermentations.

Sour Worting Method

Pros: Quick, high level of control over acid level

Cons: More residual sweetness, does not age well long term

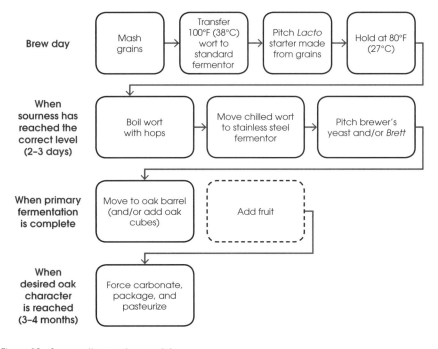

Figure 12—Sour worting souring model.

References

1. "1809 Berliner Weisse Style," *B. United International Inc.*, last accessed April 24, 2013, http://www.bunitedint.com/information/brands/description/103/.
2. Stan Hieronymus, *Brewing with Wheat: The 'Wit' and 'Weizen' of World Wheat Beers.*
3. Burghard Meyer, "Berliner Weisse," seminar presentation, Craft Brewers Conference, San Diego, May 3, 2012.
4. Kristen England, quoted in Hieronymus, *Brewing with Wheat*, 173.

5. Kristen England, personal communication with author, March 7, 2011.

6. Jess Caudill, "Perspective on Brewing Berliner Weisse Style Beer," presentation, National Homebrewer's Conference, San Diego, 2012, posted by NorthernBrewerTV, YouTube video (20:36), August 3, 2012, http://www.youtube.com/watch?v=_hClp9huB1M.

7. Tim Webb, Chris Pollard, Siobhan McGinn, *LambicLand: A Journey Round the Most Unusual Beers in the World.*

8. Jef Van den Steen, *Geuze and Kriek: The Secret of Lambic.*

9. S. Lafon-Lafourcade, C. Geneix and P. Ribéreau-Gayon, *Applied and Environmental Microbiology* 47(6):1246.

10. Jeff Sparrow, *Wild Brews: Beer Beyond the Influence of Brewer's Yeast.*

11. Peter Bouckaert, "Brewery Rodenbach: Brewing Sour Ales."

12. Sparrow, *Wild Brews.*

13. Michael Jackson, *Michael Jackson's Great Beers of Belgium.*

14. Ibid.

15. Much of the information in the New Belgium section was taken from: Peter Bouckaert, personal communication with author, March 2, 2012; Lauren Salazar, personal communication with author, October 19, 2011; Eric Salazar personal communication with author, January 16, 2012; "Lauren Salazar of New Belgium Q & A," interview with Brandon Jones, July 26, 2012; Peter Bouckaert and Eric Salazar, "New Belgium Brewing," interview, October 19, 2006; Peter Bouckaert, Ron Gansberg, Tomme Arthur, Tyler King and Vinnie Cilurzo, "A Comprehensive Look at Sour Ale Production," panel interview, 2012; "SDBW: Tasting with Eric Salazar of New Belgium," Jeffrey Crane, *Bikes Beer & Adventures* blog, November 17, 2010, http://jeffreycrane.blogspot.com/2010/11/sdbw-tasting-with-eric-salazar-of-new.html; Peter Bouckaert, "Key Note," presentation, National Homebrewers Conference, Denver, 2007, Basic Brewing Radio, MP3 audio, http://media.libsyn.com/media/basicbrewing/bbr06-28-07nhckeynote.mp3.

16. Much of the information in the Jolly Pumpkin section was taken from: Ron Jeffries, personal communication with author, September 26, 2011; Ron Jeffries, "Can You Brew It: Jolly Pumpkin Dark Dawn" audio podcast, October 26, 2009; Ron Jeffries, "Can You Brew It: Jolly Pumpkin Bam Biere" audio podcast, October 12, 2009; "Beers," Jolly Pumpkin Artisan Ales, accessed December 15, 2013, http://www

.jollypumpkin.com/artisanales/beers.htm; "'Autumn Fire' Catches On," Michelle Hall, *Chestnut Grower,* Winter 2009.

17. Much of the information in the Russian River section was taken from: Vinnie Cilurzo, personal communication with author, June 28, 2008; ibid. June 11, 2011; ibid. June 7, 2013; ibid. February 22, 2012; Peter Bouckaert, Ron Gansberg, Tomme Arthur, Tyler King and Vinnie Cilurzo, interview with Brandon Jones, January 9, 2012; Peter Bouckaert, Ron Gansberg, Tomme Arthur, Tyler King and Vinnie Cilurzo, "A Comprehensive Look at Sour Ale Production," panel interview, 2012; Vinnie Cilurzo, "The Sunday Session," audio podcast, August 14, 2005; ibid., "The Sunday Session: First Russian River Appearance," June 26, 2005; "Brewing Sour Beers at Home Using Traditional & Alternative Methods," Vinnie Cilurzo, Key note presentation NHC, San Diego, 2011; Tomme Arthur and Vinnie Cilurzo, "Cult Beers of California," Craft Beer Radio, MP3 audio, 2009; "Brewing Sour Beers at Home Using Traditional & Alternative Methods," Vinnie Cilurzo, PowerPoint® presentation, accessed December 17, 2013, www.babblebelt.com/newboard /brew_resource/RRsour_beer_presentation.ppt.

18. Jason Henry, "Russian River Toronado 25th Anniversary Beer: Deconstructed."

19. Much of the information in the Lost Abbey section was taken from: Tomme Arthur, personal communication with author, June 2, 2013; ibid., December 12, 2011; "Brew Stories - Lost Abbey - Yellow Bus with Tomme Arthur," interview by Dan Sullivan, posted by Brewdies, YouTube video (5:01), September 2, 2010, http://www.youtube .com/watch?v=lHKFEc_lr3c; Tomme Arthur and Vinnie Cilurzo, "Cult Beers of California," Craft Beer Radio, MP3 audio, 2009; "Feb 17: A flight from Lost Abbey: with special guest Tomme Arthur on location at The Lost Abbey," interview with Stephen Johnson, John Holzer, Brad Kohlenberg, Dr. Bill Sysak, posted by New-BrewThursday, YouTube video (36:16), February 18, 2012, http:// www.youtube.com/watch?v=T0b-ZONZg9c.

20. "Brett Pack Beer Dinner," *Basic Brewing Radio* podcast. November 27, 2008.

21. Much of the information in the Cambridge Brewing Company section was taken from: "La Método Solera," Will Meyers, *Cambridge Brewing Co.* blog, December 1, 2010, http://cambridgebrewing .com/blog/details/la-metodo-solera; Will Meyers, personal communication with author, November 14, 2011.

22. Much of the information in the Captain Lawrence section was taken from: Scott Vaccaro, personal communication with author, June 13, 2011; Scott Vaccaro, "The Sunday Session" interview, audio podcast August 31, 2008; Patrick Rue and Scott Vaccaro, "A Study in Barrel Aging with Captain Lawrence and The Bruery," presentation at SAVOR Salon, Washington, DC, 2011, *Craft Beer Radio* MP3 audio, http://www.craftbeerradio.com/SAVOR2011-Salon-barrelstudy.mp3.

23. Much of the information in the Bruery section was taken from: Tyler King, personal communication with author, October 19, 2011; Rue and Vaccaro, "A Study in Barrel Aging," SAVOR Salon, 2011; Patrick Rue, "The Sunday Session," audio podcast, November 2, 2008; New Brew Thursday, "Sept 29 : Oude Tart : The Bruery on location with Tyler King," interview by Stephen Johnson and John Holzer, Vimeo video (22:57), September 27, 2011, http:// vimeo.com/29687671.

24. Much of the information in the Cascade section was taken from: Ron Gansberg, personal communication with author, June 13, 2011; "The Brewing Network on the Road," interview with Ron Gansberg, audio podcast, *Brewing Network*, August 5, 2011, http://thebrew ingnetwork.com/BN-Army-Blog/The-BN-On-The-Road-2011 -Cascade-Brewing-Barrel-House.

25. Ritch Marvin, "Cascade Barrel House: 'Live from the Barrel' Tapping," *Behind the Pint*, posted by Dantenatas, YouTube video (2:30), November 24, 2010, http://www.youtube.com/watch?v=fsM-PYxI2zs.

26. Much of the information in the Allagash section was taken from: Jason Perkins, personal communication with author, October 7, 2011; "All About Allagash," Jeff Alworth, *Beervana* blog, December 01, 2008, http://beervana.blogspot.com/2008/12/all-about-allagash.html; "#32 – Spontaneous Fermentation," Peter Kennedy, Simply Beer podcast, May 13, 2010, http://www.simplybeer.com/2010/05/13 /simply-beer-podcast-32-spontaneous-fermentation;

Rod Tod and Adam Smith. "Even Cowgirls Get the Brews," SAVOR Salon presentation, Washington, DC, 2012, *Craft Beer Radio* MP3 audio, http://www.craftbeerradio.com/savor/savor2012.html; "D. Edgar on Beer: Make it Funky!" David Edgar, *Craft Beer Quarterly,* vol.10, no.1 (Spring 2011), http://www.yeastbank.com/cbq/Second2011.pdf.

27. Will Meyers, personal communication with author, November 14, 2011.

HOMEBREW METHODS OF SOURING

6

Many commercial sour beer production methods covered in Chapter 5 are adaptable to brewing at home, but homebrewers have never been content to just mimic commercial breweries. The first intentionally sour beer produced in post-Prohibition America was almost certainly brewed in a homebrewer's kitchen or garage, and thousands continue to push boundaries of this category today. But there are also aspects of the process that are much easier on the larger scale of a craft brewery, such as barrel aging, performing cell counts, maintaining cultures, and souring enough beer for elaborate blending schemes.

I have tasted numerous homebrewed beers that stand toe-to-toe with the best commercial sour beers. The most successful homebrewers play to the strengths and advantages of their lower capacity, and have developed methods that produce their desired flavor profile, despite their limitations. It is also easier and less expensive to tailor a specific process for each recipe, rather than relying on the same techniques and microbes for every batch as many commercial brewers do.

Mad Fermentationist (My Method)

I have settled on a general methodology that works for my system and palate, but I still dabble with new techniques once every few batches. However, when I am focusing on the recipe and the ingredients I go with the method described here, which is somewhere between Jolly Pumpkin, Russian River, and traditional Belgian lambic producers. It is simple and yet produces beers with terrific complexity (Figure 13).

I usually conduct a single infusion mash because most of the malts available today do not require anything more involved. The only major exceptions are when I am brewing with a large amount of wheat, such as a turbid mash for a spontaneously fermented beer, or a decoction for a Berliner weisse (both of which are covered in Chapter 3). Minimal hopping is the rule, usually between 10 and 15 IBUs; I tend to add whatever excess hops I have from a bulk order.

I have had the best results when pitching *Lactobacillus*, *Pediococcus*, and *Brettanomyces* at the same time as the brewer's yeast and after force cooling the wort. Any brewer's yeast will work for primary fermentation, so I do not have a standard strain; I tend to pitch whatever strain I have on hand from a recent clean beer. If I am pitching a highly attenuative strain, I go out of my way to produce a less fermentable wort. I do not normally make a starter for the microbes unless I am working with a pure culture for something like a 100% *Brettanomyces* beer, or I am relying on *Lactobacillus* alone for sourness.

I often use a three-headed pitch consisting of a pure culture of brewer's yeast, a commercial mixed culture, and the dregs from two or three bottles of unpasteurized sour beer (either commercial or my own). The brewer's yeast ensures a quick start to fermentation, and the commercial souring culture provides a good base of healthy microbes from each species. Bottle dregs contain heartier microbes that are more resistant to high alcohol, hopping, and low pH. Despite pitching souring microbes early, they will have little effect during primary fermentation, but access to oxygen and simple sugars allows them to prepare for their task ahead.

The few times I have waited until after a clean primary fermentation to pitch the microbes in carboys it did not produce enough sourness for my taste. However, I have found a clean primary fermentation has worked well when souring in barrels.

I usually rack sour beers to secondary on the same sort of schedule I use for standard ales, which is when primary fermentation is mostly complete and a good deal of the yeast and trub has settled out (usually between two and three weeks). Do not worry about leaving the *Brettanomyces* and bacteria behind in the primary fermentor when you rack, there will be plenty of cells carried over in suspension. In most cases my secondary fermentor is a 5 gal. (18.9 L) BetterBottle®, to which I add oak cubes and attach a standard stopper and airlock. I age the beers in my basement, where the temperature ranges from around 55°F (13°C) in winter to 68°F (20°C) in the summer (constrained by an air-conditioning unit).

Unlike barrels, the permeability of glass and plastic fermentors is not affected by the fill level. Head space in a barrel allows the wood to dry, eventually opening up gaps between the staves that increases the rate at which oxygen can enter. So while I try to ensure barrels are filled completely, I do not worry if carboys are half a gallon (2 L) short of being full.

Rather than blend to adjust the acidity, as many breweries do, I tweak my process to accomplish a similar goal. If after six months the beer has not started souring, I will often add the dregs from a few more bottles of unpasteurized sour beer to try to move things along. If the gravity is below 1.005 SG (1.25°P) and there is not enough sourness for my taste, I add malt extract or wort to feed the microbes. Malt-based fermentables are a good choice because they contain dextrins that the microbes can slowly work to break down and consume.

Mad Fermentationist Souring Method

Pros: Simple, high level of sourness
Cons: Less control over balance and consistency

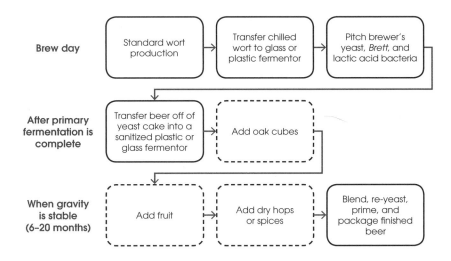

Figure 13—Mad Fermentationist souring model.

Fruit is low in dextrins, but it is a good choice for boosting acidity. I usually wait until the beer is almost ready to bottle, at which point I rack half the batch onto fruit, usually in a 3 gal. (11.4 L) carboy, then bottle the remainder, mixing it with table sugar and a few grams of rehydrated wine yeast in the bottling bucket. The portion on the fruit is allowed to ferment until the gravity is stable, usually two to four months, before bottling. If I have several batches ready to bottle at the same time, I will blend them to taste, always leaving a portion of each batch plain for comparison.

Other Homebrewers

Commercial breweries are not the only ones who have their own unique methods of souring beers. America has plenty of talented homebrewers, and I am by no means the only one who loves brewing sour beers. Indeed, a big part of the reason that I have been able to brew sour beers successfully is the support and encouragement of other homebrewers, both locally and over the Internet. I decided to profile two souring methods that have been used to win the American Homebrewers Association® (AHA) National Homebrew Competition's Homebrewer of the Year award.

Dave and Becky Pyle

In 2005, Dave and Becky Pyle's Straight (Unblended) Belgian-style Lambic earned them the AHA National Homebrew Competition's Homebrewer of the Year honors. It was the first time they had entered the competition, but their spontaneously fermented beers have won many awards both before and since in other competitions, including another gold in Sour Ales during the final round of the 2006 AHA competition.

Dave and Becky Pyle had four barrels of spontaneously fermented beer aging in their garage when I visited them.[1] Each barrel is a decommissioned bourbon barrel that Dave Pyle and a friend disassembled, decharred, re-toasted, and reassembled. This recoopering worked well, but has its risks—they lost an entire batch a few years ago when one of the barrels sprung a leak. After barrels have gone through three cycles of filling, fermenting, and emptying, each cycle lasting three years, Dave and Becky start adding a small amount of French oak cubes to them.

The Pyles' grist is equal parts Pilsner malt and wheat. Whether malted or unmalted, the wheat is mashed in exactly the same way: it is milled and added directly to an average temperature single infusion mash. Unlike many

Becky and Dave Pyle blending beer in their garage.

other brewers, the Pyles do not execute a complex, step, cereal, or turbid mash. Dave Pyle is the primary wort producer in the relationship, and he uses a 20 gal. (76 L) MoreBeer! BrewSculpture to boil the final runnings in the hot liquor tank, producing enough wort in two days to fill a barrel.

Dave Pyle worked for Hopunion for many years, and takes credit for convincing the owner, Ralph Olson, to sell old bales of German hops, which had been discarded by Budweiser, as lambic hops. In their garage, the Pyles have a personal stash of aging hops in plastic bags and mason jars; some are more than a decade old. Dave Pyle calculates the hop additions by feel more than anything else. To fill half of a 53 gal. (201 L) barrel, his usual target is about 1 lb. (450 g) at 60 minutes from the end of the boil and half that amount with 30 minutes remaining. However, when I brewed with him, he was adding Magnum hops, which, even if well-aged, still contain enough alpha acids to impart excessive bitterness at the aforementioned rate. As a result, Dave reduced the amount to 7 oz. (198 g) at the start of the boil and 2 oz. (57 g) at the midpoint.

Asked where the authentic loamy character of his spontaneously fermented beer comes from, Dave Pyle's canned response is that he will get ready to brew a batch by wearing the same outfit "for about six weeks" to get his clothes funky enough to add to the mash. The truth is that the loamy character comes from a completely spontaneous fermentation (Figure 14). Over 10 years ago the Pyles bought commercial-sized pitches of the various microbes responsible, and since then they have simply relied on the microbial residents of the barrel and about 25 fl. oz. (0.75 L) of beer from an older batch—no other yeast is pitched. The boiled wort is run through a plate chiller to cool it to around 68°F (20°C) and sent directly into the barrel without additional aeration. So just like a real Belgian lambic brewery, each of their barrels has developed its own unique house character.

Even though their garage is not temperature controlled, Dave and Becky Pyle do not top-off barrels to account for evaporation or the removal of beer, although they do avoid starting fermentation during the hot Mid-Atlantic summer. They allow aging to continue in partially filled barrels until the last of the beer is blended off; this exposure to oxygen in the head space probably explains why their older beers develop a harsh acetic character (vinegars are often aged in partially-filled barrels to encourage the formation of acetic acid). The level of acetic acid would be prohibitive if you wanted to enjoy their oldest Belgian-style lambic straight (the sample I had in 2010 from their 2006 barrel was close to undrinkable), but it becomes a positive addition to a blend.

Watching Dave and Becky Pyle blend their spontaneously fermented beer into gueuze is impressive. With more than 15 years of experience blending together they are able to quickly agree on the desired ratio. Becky explains that they can each blend gueuze on their own, but working together they are both happier with the end result. Their blending method grew from tasting the beers separately at first, to where they now fill their bottling bucket with an approximate blend, tasting and adding more until they reach the flavor they are looking for. They are careful to leave extra space in the bottling bucket initially to ensure there is room to adjust the blend.

The product of Dave and Becky's efforts is remarkable. On first whiff it is a complex amalgamation of bright lemon and damp decaying soil. However, the more you drink of it the more those fruit flavors come out. The flavor has a similar sharpness to Hanssens Artisanaal Oude Gueuze, which is to say quite sour in comparison to less acidic gueuze from 3 Fonteinen and Lindemans.

The combination of aromatics in the Pyles' spontaneously fermented beer is enhanced by the subtle additions of fruit. This is accomplished in the case of their kriek with cherry juice added for priming, but other fruits are added fresh or pureed to carboys of blended spontaneously fermented beer.

Dave and Becky Pyle's Method

Pros: Amazingly complex, funky aromatics from a simple method
Cons: Requires blending skill, oak barrels, and both the acidity and other flavors can become aggressive

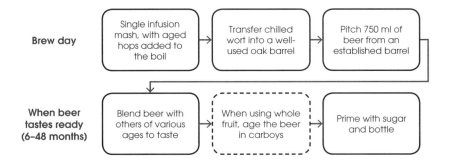

Figure 14— Dave and Becky Pyle's souring method.

Remi Bonnart

In 2010, Remi Bonnart won the AHA National Homebrew Competition's Homebrewer of the Year title with his Flemish red that is aged on Calvados-soaked French oak. Sadly, I have not had the chance to drink any of his beers, but winning Homebrewer of the Year is not a fluke. Much of Bonnart's approach is standard, like adding bottle dregs and oak cubes, but he incorporates a few techniques (especially force carbonation) that are not a part of most homebrewers' processes (Figure 15).[2]

> *The main character that I really love in sour beer is the complex interaction between all of the components including: acidity (predominately/exclusively lactic), sweetness (sometimes there isn't much/any), fruitiness (from fruit, malt, yeast components, hops), Brettanomyces funk (barnyard, sweaty horse, earthiness, sometimes even tropical fruit), malt (breadiness, dried fruits) and anything else the brewer decides to throw in there (dry hops, spices, etc.). (Remi Bonnart, personal communication with the author, February 22, 2012)*

For his Flemish red, Bonnart starts with a hot, hour-long saccharification rest. The wort is fermented to completion with a clean ale strain (Wyeast 1764 Pacman) at 60°F–65°F (16°C–18°C) and transferred to a glass carboy. Bonnart says, "I like to ferment in glass mainly because I think you can get more predictable results and you don't have to deal with the maintenance and variability of oak barrels, not to mention using a 5 gal. [18.9 L] barrel is not very practical." The carboy is pitched with Wyeast Roeselare Blend and 8 fl. oz. (237 mL) of slurry from his previous batch. Reusing microbes from a previous batch is a good way to simulate the effect of aging in a well-used barrel. Rather than a standard airlock, Bonnart opts for a Ferm-Rite vented silicone stopper. This removes the effort required to top-off a water-filled airlock, but also lets

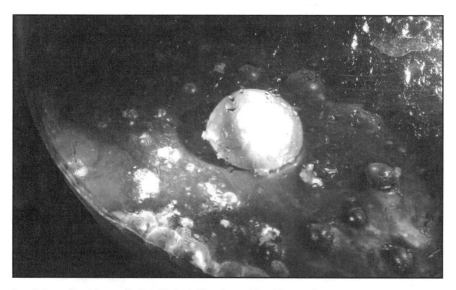

A pellicle on Remi Bonnart's Flemish Red. (Courtesy of Remi Bonnart)

a minute amount of oxygen into the aging beer, although not enough to produce a prominent acetic character. While the beer ages at 65°F–70°F (18°C–21°C), he adds dregs of his favorite sour beers (commercial and homebrew), because "there may be 'bugs' in the dregs that might add another dimension and aren't necessarily present in the mixed-culture."

To replicate the wood flavors contributed by a barrel, Bonnart adds 2 oz. (57 g) medium-toast French oak cubes along with the Calvados that he soaks them in. The beer is aged on the oak until the character is at the desired level, then he racks the beer to a keg and force carbonates. Bonnart first enjoys the beer on tap "as a reward for the

Remi Bonnart's Method

Pros: Consistent results

Cons: May not develop as much over time without bottle conditioning

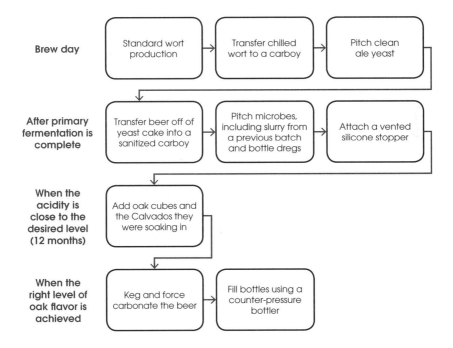

| Brew day | Standard wort production | → | Transfer chilled wort to a carboy | → | Pitch clean ale yeast |

| After primary fermentation is complete | Transfer beer off of yeast cake into a sanitized carboy | → | Pitch microbes, including slurry from a previous batch and bottle dregs | → | Attach a vented silicone stopper |

| When the acidity is close to the desired level (12 months) | Add oak cubes and the Calvados they were soaking in |

| When the right level of oak flavor is achieved | Keg and force carbonate the beer | → | Fill bottles using a counter-pressure bottler |

Figure 15—Remi Bonnart's souring model (Flemish red).

long waiting period," before counter-pressure bottling the remainder for additional aging. On the subject of bottle conditioning, Bonnart explains: "I like to be able to adjust carbonation to exactly the level I want, have less sediment in the bottle and not have to deal with the sometimes unpredictable results of bottle conditioning sour beer." His method allows for greater control and ease of carbonating compared to bottle conditioning, but requires considerable time and equipment. The National Homebrew Competition's winning batch was bottle-aged for an additional eight months.

References

1. Dave Pyle and Becky Pyle, personal communication with author, April 18, 2010.
2. Remi Bonnart, personal communication with author, February 22, 2012.

SPONTANEOUS FERMENTATION

7

Out of all of the ways to sour a beer, the most romantic is to let fresh wort ensnare wild yeast and bacteria from the chilly nighttime air. The vision of spontaneous fermentation that most people have is of leaving wort exposed as it slowly cools, allowing whatever yeast and bacteria happen to be floating in the air to ferment its sugars. Unfortunately, creating something drinkable from a fermentation by wild microbes is not quite so effortless.

While spontaneous fermentation has been practiced for millennia, it has been brought to its highest form by Belgian lambic producers, whose best offerings have a balance of acidity and complexity that is unrivaled by any other beverage. Their methods had not been attempted outside the Senne Valley (the home of Belgian lambic), until the turn of this millennium. Since then, a small but increasing number of American brewers have not only started to experiment with the practice, but have succeeded with their own spontaneous fermentations. Despite the risks outlined in Chapter 2, commercial breweries like Allagash Brewing Company, Anchorage Brewing Company, Cambridge Brewing Company, Flat Tail Brewing, Indigo Imp Brewery, Jolly Pumpkin Artisan Ales, Russian River Brewing Company, and several others have all conducted fermentations influenced by their own local microflora.

The Basics

Wild yeasts were responsible for fermenting the first beers and are the forebears of every brewer's yeast strain available from a laboratory today. However, the isolated strains of brewer's yeast that we pitch into our ales and lagers have characteristics that took untold generations for brewers to select for, important properties like alcohol tolerance, flocculation, and desirable flavor profile. Finding a wild yeast strain with all of these same attributes is as likely as dropping a net onto a prehistoric field and having the first animal you catch be as easy to raise and delicious to eat as a modern cow. This is because the characteristics we like in brewer's yeast are not necessarily beneficial to the survival and reproduction of wild *Saccharomyces* species (just as a modern cow set free would not survive for long in the wild). In fact, genetic research has shown that lager yeast (*Saccharomyces pastorianus*) is actually the result of hybridization between two yeast strains (*S. eubayanus* and *S. cerevisiae*), which took place in a vat of beer sometime during the 16th century.[1]

Even if spontaneous fermentation appeals to you, wait until you have brewed several successful sour beers using more predictable microorganisms. Fermentation with truly wild microbes is riskier than pitching known cultures from either a laboratory or bottle, because you do not know exactly what strains are native to your local ecosystem. Even under the best-case scenario, Belgian lambic brewers blend batches and barrels to produce the finished beer, and still they are forced to throw away unsuitable barrels.[2] If you want to tackle spontaneous fermentation in a serious way, you will need to invest time in fermenting numerous batches to provide enough blending options.

Belgian lambic is the only surviving style of beer to be fermented spontaneously, although depending on how you look at the process you might conclude that lambic brewers are actually fermenting with a carefully selected and propagated house culture. At most Belgian lambic breweries the wort cools overnight in the shallow metal coolship. There is usually exposed wood above the coolship, onto which steam is allowed to condense and drip back into the cooling wort. The specific dimensions of the coolship are less important than the effect they have, allowing the wort to cool quickly, but not too quickly.

At Cantillon, the coolship is not large enough to hold all of the wort from a single brew, so the remainder is pumped into a receiving tank. Once the wort in the coolship reaches the desired temperature, it is mixed with the wort in the receiving tank.[3] Later that day the young beer is transferred into barrels. For decades lambic brewers and blenders have been reusing those barrels that produce delicious beer, while getting rid of the ones that do not (burning them for fuel in the case of Cantillon).[4] First-use barrels (mostly from wineries or Pilsner breweries) are often inoculated with microbe-laden beer from an established barrel to give them the best chance to produce high-quality lambic. Belgium lambic brewers also allow kraeusen to overflow from barrels and then dry, creating a yeast-laden dust which finds its way into new batches.[5] All of this effort is to reduce the role luck plays by providing each batch with proven microbes. This technique is similar to seed saving; the best batches are kept, so allowing a positive house microflora to develop over many generations, while the less delicious beers are discarded. Unfortunately, when you brew your first batch of spontaneous beer you will not have this luxury.

There is nothing unique about the wild microbes floating around Belgium; the same species of the key sour beer fermenters—*Saccharomyces, Lactobacillus, Pediococcus*, and *Brettanomyces*—are found all over the world. It is the selective pressure that Belgian lambic brewers have placed on these microbes living in their barrels and walls (as well as their masterful post-fermentation blending) that allows the production of such consistently remarkable sour beers.

In a study published in 2012, Bokulich et al. demonstrated that many of the same families of microbes are at work in American coolship-inoculated ales (in Maine) as in Belgian lambic fermentation.[6] Bokulich et al. go on to say that,

> *Viewed at higher taxonomic levels . . . the microbial succession of ACA [American coolship ale] fermentation appears to closely parallel that previously observed in lambic: a brief, early bloom of enterobacteria before LAB [lactic acid bacteria] and* Saccharomyces *conduct the main fermentation, and finally domination by* Brettanomyces *during the long maturation period. However, lower-level taxa reveal subtle differences between these fermentations. (Bokulich, Bamforth and Mills (2012),* PLoS ONE *vol.7, no.4, e35507: 7)*

Dissimilarities include the species of enterobacteria active during the early fermentation, and a greater presence of *Lactobacillus*, in addition to *Pediococcus*, as the fermentation progresses. The difference in lactic acid bacteria is likely a result of the lower hopping rate used by the American brewery compared to their Belgian counterparts.

Even though these key microbes are widely established, it does not mean that you can simply leave standard pale ale wort exposed to the air and expect it to become a drinkable beer. There are a number of wort production techniques you can employ that will increase the chances of your fermentation having a similar microbial progression. Producing a less fermentable wort ensures that carbohydrates survive the initial burst of fermentation to sustain the slower growing microbes through the long fermentation as the beer ages. For spontaneously fermented beers this is traditionally accomplished with a turbid mash, which carries unconverted starch into the boil. A turbid mash is not required, but at a minimum, select a saccharification rest no lower than 158°F (around 70°C).

Spontaneous fermentation is the only souring technique that greatly benefits from aged hops. Properly aged hops do not impart an off-putting bitterness, even at the high rate required to prevent thermo-philic (heat loving) *Lactobacillus* from reducing the pH of the wort too far before *Saccharomyces* has sufficient time to complete its fermenta-tion. A long boil is the traditional method for concentrating the large volume of runnings collected from a turbid mash, and extracting the maximum preservative effect from the aged hops (while simultaneously volatizing their undesirable aromatics). More details on turbid mashes and aged hops can be found in Chapter 3.

There is debate over the best location to expose your cooling wort for inoculation. Tradition holds that areas near orchards or vineyards are ideal, because the same sugar-loving yeasts that ferment the fallen fruit are well suited for fermenting beer. Urbain Coutteau of De Struise Brouwers (Oostvleteren, West Flanders) claims that cities are a better option, because their high level of activity ensures there are more sugar loving microbes in the air.[7] This is supported by the fact that Brasserie Cantillon is in an urban part of Brussels where few cherry trees remain—not the bucolic landscape that is evoked by their labels. Breweries will also have their own unique microflora from the presence of the pitched strains, something which may or may not be desirable. If you brew sour beers, odds are that your fermentation room already has its own unique resident microflora. If you want to enhance the local microflora, spray a few ounces of unpasteurized sour beer onto the walls and floor (a few lambic brewers have gone so far as to take the unpainted ceiling beams from above their coolship with them when they move it to a new building).

Outside temperature is the key indicator for determining the best time to capture wild microbes. Jeff Sparrow reports in *Wild Brews* that lactic acid bacteria are too prevalent for successful spontaneous fermentation during the hot summer, although there are also brewers who suggest that *Acetobacter* is the bigger issue. Hot temperatures also slow natural cooling, which allows thermophilic bacteria more time to thrive before the wort cools below 100°F (38°C) where yeast thrive. Whatever the reason, most Belgian lambic producers take the summer off from brewing, which is a sensible practice to follow. At the other end of the thermometer, if the temperature is below freezing there may not be enough wild microbes to ensure a quick start to fermentation, although this risk may be overstated.

You should cool the hot wort in a wide vessel to speed the dissipation of heat and provide more surface area for microbes to land on. Homebrewers can use their boil kettle as an acceptable option. If cooling indoors, open a window and run a fan to speed cooling and bring more microbes into contact with the wort. Alternatively, consider repurposing an aquarium pump to bubble unfiltered air through the wort once it has chilled.

For professional brewers without a shallow vessel, colder temperatures are an advantage. Shaun Hill of Hill Farmstead says, "Our coolship is not so much a ship as an old mash tun. Mash tun goes into the yard, in front of the brewery, during a cold spell of weather. Knock out into the tun in the late afternoon. Try to aerate well." Located in northern Vermont, Hill starts spontaneous fermentations when the temperature outdoors is as low as 0°F (–18°C), and on the coldest days, "By 7 a.m.," says Hill, "the temperature [of the wort] drops from 200°F+ (93°C+) to somewhere below 50°F (10°C)." The dry air causes significant evaporation in that time before the chilled wort is racked via gravity to oak barrels. Hill uses the cultures from these spontaneously fermented beers to inoculate most of his other sour beers, producing a character he describes simply as, "Beautiful. Lactic."[8]

Barrels of wort being exposed to the Alaskan air by Anchorage Brewing. (Courtesy of Anchorage Brewing Company)

If you do not have high hopes for the microbes living around your brewery or home, take a page from Gabe Fletcher of Anchorage Brewing in Alaska. He cut small squares around the bung of several barrels, before filling them with fresh wort and driving the barrels several hours outside of Anchorage into the wilderness near the village of Slana.[9] Once there, Fletcher parked his truck in the woods near wild blueberry bushes and removed the small square of wood from each barrel, covered each hole with a piece of mesh, and left the wort exposed to the air for two days. With no additional yeast pitched, the wild microbes took a week to show initial signs of fermentation, but eventually they fermented out fully.

After the wort is completely chilled (usually in fewer than 24 hours) it should be moved to a closed fermentor. Exposing the beer to air for too long will allow aerobic microbes to start producing acetic acid and other undesirable flavors. Well-used barrels are the traditional choice, but any fermentor that you are comfortable leaving a beer in for a year or longer will work.

Spontaneous Fermentation Safety

An oft-repeated reassurance to most beginning brewers is that no matter how bad a beer tastes it will not sicken you, but when it comes to spontaneous fermentation this is not always the case. For the first few weeks of fermentation there is a chance that pathogenic enteric bacteria like *Escherichia coli (E. coli)* and other members of the Enterobacteriaceae family can subsist in the wort. Controlling the wort pH is crucial to controlling Enterobacteriaceae bacteria, which can produce undesirable metabolites such as biogenic amines. As soon as the pH starts to drop due to yeast fermentation and alcohol production the danger is over. Lowering the pH below 4.5 pre-inoculation will prevent enteric bacteria from reproducing, and is a good safety measure no matter what spontaneous fermentation method you are attempting.[10] This can be accomplished before chilling by using a sour mash, sour worting, acid malt, or food grade lactic acid.

At this stage, once the wort is in the fermentor, your work is complete for a year or more. Spontaneously fermented beer is traditionally left in primary so that the *Brettanomyces* and other wild yeasts can benefit from the nutrients ejected by *Saccharomyces* cells undergoing autolysis. This contributes a more rustic, funky character than racking after primary fermentation is complete. For a cleaner character, rack off of the trub after the initial vigorous fermentation subsides. After fermentation slows, top-off the barrels to minimize the amount of head space. Cantillon's beers became softer and less acetic when they started topping off their barrels and sealing them immediately after the initial burst of fermentation, rather than their previous method of waiting to seal partially-filled barrels on the same day at the end of the brewing season.[11]

Achieving successful results from spontaneous fermentation takes commitment, and a large investment in fermentors and time. To create a wider variety of characters to blend, try to inoculate batches in different locations or at different times of the year. Even the best Belgian lambic breweries have barrels that are so acidic the only value their contents have is in shining the copper kettles. Only the very best barrels, a tiny percentage, do not benefit from blending.

If you opt for a coolship, it is not just a single purpose vessel. At Peekskill Brewery, Jeff O'Neil uses his coolship on the third floor for more than just introducing wild microbes into beers destined for the cellar. It also serves as a hot liquor tank, a settling tank (a replacement for whirlpooling), and even a primary fermentor for top cropping yeasts like hefeweizen, saison, and English beers.[12]

American Wild Ales

Breweries in every corner of America (including Alaska, California, Colorado, Maine, Massachusetts, Michigan, Texas, Washington, and Wisconsin) have proven the microbes that are native to this country can produce interesting sour beers. So far, most of these craft breweries have mimicked the recipes and production methods of Belgian lambic brewers, but with time they are adapting their recipes and processes to match their own equipment and tastes.

Jolly Pumpkin Lambicus Dexterius

Jolly Pumpkin's Lambicus Dexterius is brewed only during the fall and spring, when the weather is cool but not freezing. Brewmaster Ron Jeffries brewed the first batch in October 2005, but he did not release his first bottled blend until the end of 2009. The brew starts with a turbid mash, following the schedule described in *Wild Brews*, which is similar to the one in Chapter 3. The grist is composed of 70% Pilsner malt and 30% raw wheat, and the mash takes four hours to complete instead of one hour for the single infusion mashes of their other beers. While the brewers have made a few subtle changes to the process based on advice from Yvan De Baets (the hugely influential beer scholar and brewer at Brasserie de la Senne in Brussels), Jeffries says that he has been reluctant to change the process much because of the long aging. His worry is that if he makes a change that negatively affects the beer he will be left thinking, "We shouldn't have done *that* two years ago."[13]

Brewing a beer using a turbid mash on a brewhouse not designed for it can be trying. Lambicus Dexterius mashes start with doughing-in with water from the kettle to hit their first rest. The brewers heat the remaining water to a boil in the kettle and then move it to a holding tank. To raise the temperature for the remaining rests, water from that holding tank is fed in through the bottom of the mash tun as the brewers vigorously stir. Holding the hot water in another tank frees the kettle for heating the starchy runnings that are drawn out at various points during the process. If these runnings accidentally reach a boil, the brewers lower the heat to avoid excessive evaporation and scorching the starches.

Once the mash is complete and the wort has been collected it is boiled for three hours. Most batches are hopped with pre-aged hops that Jeffries buys in 13 lb. (5.9 kg) boxes; for ease, the brewers have settled on one box per 10 bbl. (11.7 hL) batch (3.4 oz per 5 gal. [0.1 kg per 20 L]).

When the boil is complete, the wort is sprayed into a shallow open fermentor to initiate cooling. Cooling continues naturally overnight as the brewery's HVAC system draws in microbe-laden air from outside; the cool wort is pumped into well-used barrels the next morning.

The brewers are even more careful than usual when selecting which barrels to empty to ensure that the best barrels are available to receive the spontaneous wort. Jeffries chooses the barrels whose pellicles look "freaky and alien-like" and whose beers taste strongly acidic, both features indicating strong microbial colonization. The barrels are cleaned with 160°F–165°F (71°C–74°C) water, which is not hot enough to sanitize them. No other microbes are pitched besides the ones living in the wood. Fermentation has usually started in the oak barrels by 24 hours, or 48 hours at the most. Jeffries credits the quick onset to the microbes in the wood rather than the cells that land on the cooling wort.

Once fermentation begins, the brewers ignore the beer until it is at least one year old. When Jeffries decides that it is time to bottle a batch of Lambicus Dexterius, they taste all barrels older than a year to determine the blend. It is bottled without additional priming sugar, relying on the sugars in the younger beer for carbonation. For the first batch mostly long-aged barrels were blended and as a result there was not enough refermentation to carbonate the beer. That batch was sharp, strongly acidic, with a wonderfully funky nose despite the minimal carbonation. For future blends Jeffries plans to include a higher percentage of young beer to ensure more residual fermentables. It is always a delicate balance though, as adding too much young beer generates excessive carbonation, risking the integrity of even heavy bottles.

In addition to producing Lambicus Dexterius, Jolly Pumpkin has also blended the same spontaneously fermented beer to add acidity and complexity to other beers. An example of this is Bambic, the first batch of which included 15% spontaneously fermented beer blended into Bam

Bière. Jeffries has never pitched cultured wild yeast or bacteria at Jolly Pumpkin, so his is a particularly authentic commercial attempt at spontaneous fermentation with wild American microbes.

Cambridge Imperial Lambic

Cambridge Brewing Company in Massachusetts uses exposure to the air to initiate spontaneous fermentation for their potent "imperial" (9%–10% ABV) spontaneously fermented base beer. The resulting beer is flavored with fruit to produce Kriek du Cambridge (cherry), and Rosé de Cambrinus, the latter taking both its name and inspiration from Cantillon's cherry- and raspberry-infused Rosé de Gambrinus (although more recent batches of the Cantillon beer have left out the cherries). Honey Badger, which starts as the same imperial lambic base, is similar in concept to Hanssens Artisanaal's Mead the Gueuze (spontaneously fermented beer blended with mead). Honey Badger is so named because it receives raw local honey on the third day of fermentation, allowing the wild yeast it contains to help spur fermentation.[14]

Over the years the method that brewmaster Will Meyers and his staff employ has evolved into its current unique form. Following their 2011 batch of imperial lambic base, it started with a turbid mash, which was a challenge on a brewing system intended for English-style single-infusion mashes. The oak barrels were sprayed out and filled with boiling water to kill the microbes living in the wood (in theory), then the water was emptied out and each barrel filled to one-fifth capacity with near-boiling wort directly from the kettle. The bunghole of each barrel was covered with cheesecloth to prevent insects from flying inside; the goal was to allow air to be sucked into the barrel as the wort and steam inside cooled and contracted.

The remaining 80% of the batch was pumped into the mash tun, which served as a makeshift coolship. The manway was left open, as were the doors and windows of the brewpub, and the fans were run to introduce wild microbes. A day later the cool wort in the mash tun/coolship was pumped into the barrels until they were filled entirely. For four days there was no sign of fermentation, but on Meyers' final check of the cellar before leaving on Friday night he saw kraeusen erupting from all five barrels (Meyers left his none-too-pleased wife alone at the bar on date night while he cleaned).

Cambridge leaves their barrels to age for a year or two before they are ready to fruit, re-ferment, blend, and keg. The Kriek du Cambridge and

Rosé de Cambrinus portions are transferred into clean barrels containing the fruit three months before blending. Meyers always has younger beer available for blending if the acidity of any of the beers needs to be softened.

Russian River Beatification

Russian River's brewmaster (and co-owner) Vinnie Cilurzo on spontaneous fermentation in America:

> *I remember several years ago Jean Van Roy at Cantillon telling me, 'You can spontaneously ferment in the United States, but, keep in mind that it probably won't be the same way we do it here. You might have to come up with your own program.' In the case of Allagash, they've pretty much been able to copy how it is done in Belgium and they are getting amazing/similar results as our friends in Belgium. For us [Russian River], we've had to come up with a couple of hybrid methods to make it happen. (Vinnie Cilurzo, personal communication, February 21, 2012)*

Before it is blended and packaged to create the final product, Russian River's Beatification starts off life as Sonambic, their unblended base beer. Sonambic starts with a complex step mash with 60% pale barley, 40% unmalted wheat. Originally, when the starch conversion was complete the mash was left to sour overnight, which lowered the pH of the wort and prepared the mash tun for its role as makeshift coolship. (The sour mash step has since been omitted with the installation of a dedicated coolship, described below.) The following morning the mash was sparged (without heating back to mash-out) and given a three to four hour boil with 10-year-old Hallertau from Hopunion (the opened bale of Hallertau sits in the rafters of the brewery).[15]

While the wort was boiling, the mash tun would be emptied and then rinsed with cold water. This ensured all of the spent grain was removed, but the lactic acid bacteria that multiplied during the sour mash were still present. Once the boil was complete the wort was pumped back into the mash tun. When Russian River made their first batch, the wort was moved over too hot, which resulted in a violent fermentation by the next morning with the wort still at 85°F (29°C). The ensuing rapid pH drop prevented the *Brettanomyces* from fermenting effectively. For each subsequent batch the brewers tried slightly cooler knockout temperatures: for example, the second batch went in at 70°F (21°C) and took five days to start fermenting. They eventually settled on 60°F (16°C), which delayed peak fermentation for a couple of weeks.

After spending the night in the mash tun the wort was pumped into barrels that are set aside for Beatification, these barrels having already aged several batches of sour beer so that they are saturated with microbes and nearly devoid of oak character. The standard souring microbes impart that big citrus character that Beatification often displays. This citrus character is enhanced by warmer fermentation temperatures, which explains why the first spontaneously fermented batch (002) had a grapefruit character reminiscent of a Cascade-hopped IPA.

In late 2011, Russian River installed a 19 ft. by 4 ft. (5.8 × 1.2 m) coolship in which all subsequent batches of Beatification have begun their spontaneous fermentation.[16] As the sour mash was undertaken primarily to inoculate the mash tun with microbes, it is no longer part of the process. Cilurzo is experimenting with various temperatures for the wort going into the long narrow stainless steel trough. To increase exposure to the air the wort is agitated every few hours. Despite the substantial changes in process, Beatification batch 006, the first to be started in the coolship, had a remarkably similar character to the early batches. Russian River is also considering employing the coolship to introduce wild microbes into other beers that will subsequently be pitched with *Brettanomyces* and brewer's yeast.

Once the spontaneous fermentation is complete, barrels from multiple batches of Sonambic are blended together, allowing Russian River to achieve a balanced flavor profile. Beatification batch 002, a blend of batches ranging from 13 to 18 months old, was among the sourest beers I have tasted. Batch 003, a blend of beers between seven and fifteen months old, was much more balanced thanks to the lower knockout temperature. While undeniably sour, it had the depth, funk, and complexity that batch 002 lacked.

Particularly sour barrels of Sonambic are reserved to boost acidity when blending other beers that are not sour enough. Russian River also aged a few barrels of Sonambic on raspberries to produce the first batch of Framboise for a Cure, which was sold as a fundraiser for breast cancer research. The second batch of this beer was based on Temptation (tart, Chardonnay-barrel-aged blonde) instead, and had a gorgeous red color and juicy fresh fruit. More recently, Russian River has used a blend of

Sonambic and Temptation to make Framboise for a Cure. This is one of the only beers the brewery produces where fruit is added in a stainless steel tank after the beer completes barrel aging.

Allagash Coolship Series
In 2007 Allagash constructed a traditional coolship in a small room off the side of the brewery. This shallow stainless steel basin (12 ft. by 8 ft. and 1 ft. deep [3.6 × 2.4 × 0.3 m]) can easily hold a 20 bbl. (23.5 hL) batch of wort. A coolship works by providing ample surface area for cool air to pass over the wort, carrying away heat and delivering wild microbes; it is the way that the highest quality Belgian lambic and gueuze are chilled (and was the way many other beers were chilled before the invention of heat exchangers). Allagash's coolship cools numerous batches of their spontaneously fermented Coolship series of beers.[17]

The first two batches using the coolship were brewed in the fall of 2007, followed by two more in the spring of 2008. Despite not knowing how the beer would turn out, brewmaster Jason Perkins and founder Rob Tod wanted to brew enough batches early on to accumulate a library of barrels for future blending sessions. The first bottles were not released commercially until 2011, but for a couple of years before that test blends sporadically appeared at events in both America and Belgium. Before undertaking this project, the brewers compared their weather pattern in Portland, Maine, to that of Brussels, Belgium, the epicenter of lambic brewing. For most of the year the two regions are similar, but because Maine is much colder in the winter and Belgian lambic brewers do not brew in the heat of the summer, Perkins and Tod decided to avoid these two periods. Perkins considers an outside temperature of 35°F (2°C) to be ideal, because the good microbes are still active, but the wort chills quickly and there is a minimal amount of *Acetobacter* present.

To produce the wort for their spontaneously fermented beers Allagash starts with a turbid mash using a grist comprised of about 40% unmalted wheat and 60% Belgian Pilsner malt. The thick mash starts with a rest at 115°F (46°C) for 15 minutes, followed by hot water infusions to reach the protein and saccharification rests. The brewers decoct (boiling 25% of the mash for 10 minutes), before returning the decoction to the mash tun to raise the mash temperature from the saccharification rest (145°F [63°C]) to mash-out (170°F [77°C]).

Once the mash is complete, the wort is collected and boiled with hops that have been aged for a minimum of three years. Allagash's first few batches were brewed with a high enough hopping rate that the resulting beer possessed an astringent flavor, so as time went on the amount of hops was reduced. As of 2011, at the start of the boil the brewers were adding 1 lb. of 4 to 5-year-old hops (mostly Hallertau) per barrel of wort (0.39 kg/hL), equivalent to 2.6 oz. per 5 gal. (80 g per 20 L).

Coolship room at Allagash Brewing Company. (Courtesy of Allagash Brewing Company)

When the three-and-a-half hour boil is complete, the wort is pumped into the coolship while attempting to leave most of the spent hops behind in the kettle. The wort is sprayed into the coolship through a screen to catch any hops that may have transferred over (clearly they do not worry about hot-side aeration). The wort is allowed to sit undisturbed in the coolship with the room's windows open and an exhaust fan running until it cools to 65°F–70°F (18°C–21°C). The exact amount of time this takes depends on how cold it is outside, but 12 to 18 hours is expected. Once the wort is cool, it is moved to a stainless steel tank briefly to ensure that the microbes that landed on its surface are evenly distributed among the barrels.

Before the barrels are filled, they are cleaned with 190°F (88°C) water, which is surprising considering most breweries doing spontaneous fermentation do not try so hard to sanitize the wood. As of 2011, the brewery had 50 to 60 barrels aging coolship-inoculated beer, including barrels that previously aged other Allagash beers as well as newly introduced wine barrels. Perkins has not noticed variation in sourness or funk character between the two types of barrels, which indicates the barrel-cleaning process is successful in killing most of the microbes resident in the barrels themselves. The wort is pumped from the tank into the barrels and allowed to ferment at 60°F (16°C). According to Perkins, the cool temperature limits *Acetobacter* activity and produces a more desirable finished beer. Barrels include both standard size examples (approximately 60 gal. [227 L]) and ones that are twice that size; Perkins says the larger barrels tend to produce beers with a less phenolic, more refined flavor.

The fastest Allagash has seen active fermentation begin is three days, but other barrels require up to a week to show visible signs of activity. Once it does start, fermentation is often so vigorous that the kraeusen overflows. The active stage lasts for 10 to 11 days, at which point 80% of the apparent fermentables have been consumed. The beer is left in the barrel on the yeast until it is ready to bottle. Near the start of fermentation the barrels experience butyric acid production (reminiscent of rancid butter), although luckily this acid is eventually turned into a tropical-fruity ester (ethyl butyrate) by the *Brettanomyces*. After six to eight months classic *Brettanomyces* character starts to emerge, but before that the phenols they produce are reminiscent of plastic. It is one year into aging before apparent acidity emerges. The character and progress of the Coolship beers is different from other blends of microbes the brewers have worked with; individual barrels have surprised them with significant jumps in flavor over only a couple of weeks. There is also huge variation in final flavor barrel-to-barrel (let alone batch-to-batch). The wild yeast and bacteria eventually dry the beer out fully, finishing between 1.000–1.004 FG (0°P–1°P).

When the beer has reached the desired acidity, flavor, and gravity it serves as the base for four Coolship series beers. Resurgam, the non-fruit version, is produced by blending several vintages, for example, barrels from batches that are 24, 18, and 6 months old. The nose is really bright, lemon, and subtle acidity in line with 3 Fonteinen, although oakier and without quite the depth of funk. Allagash also produces three fruited versions: Red (raspberries—bright, fresh, slightly more acidic), Cerise (Montmorency cherries, which give only a light pink color, but a great fresh cherry flavor, even a hint of cinnamon), and Balaton (Balaton cherries). The brewers add 2–3 lb. of locally-sourced fruit per gallon (0.24–0.36 kg/L). Before you ask, Rob Tod has sworn off the idea of adding the ubiquitous Maine blueberry, stating it is too trendy. Jason Perkins has also sworn off Maine blueberries, but because he does not feel the fruit works well in sour beers.[18]

Fruit is added when the beer is mature; the first batch of Cerise was blended mostly (90%) from two-year-old beer. The beer sits on fruit for three months until the secondary fermentation is complete, or slightly longer until the staff has time to bottle. Fruit beers are passed through a metal canister with a screen to ensure that no chunks of fruit reach the bottles, but are otherwise unfiltered. The remainder of that first batch of Cerise was six-month-old beer, which assisted in bottle conditioning. Blending in young beer is yet another authentic step that brings Allagash nearer to the more traditional Belgian production methods. In addition to the four Coolship beers, Allagash also brews Ghoulschip, a beer that includes both raw pumpkin and toasted pumpkin seeds. This beer has a slightly different fermentation than the beer discussed above; while it is cooled in the coolship it is subsequently pitched with their house ale yeast.[19] This dual inoculation is a good way to diminish the risks and inconsistencies associated with spontaneous fermentation.

Allagash Coolship Cerise. (Courtesy of Allagash Brewing Company)

Spontaneous Homebrew in America's Capital

DCambic (DC Lambic)

After reading about and tasting several spontaneously fermented commercial American beers, I knew it was something I had to try for myself. Many homebrewers I talked to who relied on truly wild microbes reported poor results from the combination of the traditional open cooling and inoculation step with fermentation in a carboy or bucket. Professional brewers have a substantial advantage, with larger surface areas and being able to ferment in barrels with established microbe populations. Even the relatively small commercial operations often have

Inoculation of a spontaneous starter in the author's basement.

many times the number of fermentors than an average homebrewer, and this allows them greater blending possibilities.

I decided to execute a less traditional, but more reliable, method for my first attempt at fermenting a sour beer with only local (Washington, DC) microbes. To reduce the risk of major off-flavors, I captured microbes in multiple starters to propagate and sample before pitching into the cooled wort.

A few weeks before brew day I created a half gallon (1.9 L) of low gravity wort (1.030 SG [7.5°P]) from light dried malt extract, 0.5 oz. (14 g) three-year-old hops, and a pinch of yeast nutrient. The substantial dose of aged hops (Willamette) was intended to prevent *Lactobacillus* from lowering the pH of the starter before the yeast was able to start its fermentation. It is not strictly necessary for the hops to be aged when using this method, because the bitterness that fresh hops impart will be diluted when the starter is pitched into the main wort. However, I wanted to see what sort of character the three-year-old Willamette hops would contribute before adding them to a full batch.

After boiling, I divided the wort into three sanitized metal pots to make three separate starters, and covered each with a layer of cheesecloth secured by a rubber band (to prevent insects from getting into the wort as it cooled). I divided the starters between various locations: my backyard (42°F [6°C]), my living room (62°F [17°C]), and my basement barrel room (57°F [14°C]). The following morning, with the wort in the pots cooled and teaming with life, I poured each starter into its own growler and left them at 62°F (17°C) to begin fermenting. I did not give the wort additional aeration except for what it received during funneling into the growlers. I attached stoppers with airlocks to reduce the chance that aerobic microbes would dominate.

It took a couple of days for the first signs of activity to appear in all three of the starters (small kraeusen and occasional burps of the airlocks). I left them alone for three weeks, enough time for the yeast and lactic acid bacteria to generate sufficient alcohol and acidity to inhibit enteric bacteria. Even at this point I did not feel safe tasting the starters, and I immediately dumped the "living room" starter because it had grown black mold and smelled foul. The "backyard" starter had a spotty white film and smelled spicy, while the "barrel room" starter had no mold and smelled like over-ripe fruit, so I kept both.

I took the two keepers and doubled their volume with fresh unhopped starter wort, and moved each to a sanitized clear 1 gal. (3.8 L) glass jug so I could monitor their progress. Instead of an airlock, I capped each jug with a piece of aluminum foil and shook them occasionally to aerate. Both starters resumed fermenting quickly and smelled clean and pleasant. The backyard starter fermented slightly more rapidly and produced a mild sulfur aroma, while the barrel room starter worked more slowly and produced more fruity and funky aromatics. When fermentation slowed I reattached the airlocks to limit additional oxygen exposure, so preventing mold and other aerobic microbes from appearing. After two more weeks I finally felt it was safe to drink a small sample of each; I was relieved to find that they had both developed a light, lemony tartness.

Now that I had an idea of how the two cultures performed and what they tasted like, I decided to use both starters to pitch a 5 gal. (18.9 L) batch of wort. I used a traditional lambic grain bill of raw wheat and Pilsner malt in a turbid mash, followed by a long boil with aged hops (even though their antimicrobial properties are not needed for this method). After force chilling the wort to 65°F (18°C), I pitched 32 fl. oz. (0.95 L) from each of the two starters. While there was what looked to be yeast flocculated at the bottom of each starter, I chose not to decant them because the hazy liquid indicated there were still microorganisms that had not settled out.

Visible fermentation took 24 hours to appear. During the first week I held the ambient temperature at 65°F (18°C) to give the yeast the best chance to complete a healthy primary fermentation, letting it rise slightly after that time. While it lasted, the kraeusen was composed of large, delicate bubbles (a sign that the strains at work are less flocculant than brewer's yeasts). For the first few months the beer had a strong tropical fruit aroma combined with moderate clove, but this faded as the beer aged and became funkier. My batch did not show signs of acidity until six months into aging.

I bottled half of the batch with a small addition of priming sugar at the one-year mark. The flavor of this batch is tart, but not sharply sour, reminiscent of Belgian lambic, with dried hay and over-ripe fruit; it also has some unique green tobacco aromatics I have not tasted in a gueuze. I racked the remaining two gallons (7.6 L) of beer onto mulberries harvested from my backyard. They provided a stunning purple color, slightly higher acidity, and the earthy/fruity flavor of ripe mulberries, softening the more unusual aromatics of the base beer.

Using this technique is no guarantee of success, because you will not be able to tell how the character of the captured yeast and bacteria will change with additional time, but it will reduce the chance of producing an undrinkable beer. If you get a culture you enjoy, follow the lead of other brewers of spontaneously fermented beer by repitching your microbes into future batches rather than starting from scratch each time. Remember that a one-year-old spontaneous fermentation is still young—hold onto these beers and see how they develop over a few years before making the decision to dump anything that does not taste good.

Other Sources of Wild Microbes

Rather than rely entirely on chance, the brewers at Jester King Brewery placed uncovered wort on the roof of their Austin, Texas brewery at various times. After sitting overnight, the inoculated wort was sealed in jars and sent to the Brewing Science Institute in Colorado. The yeast laboratory

Catching wild yeast on the roof of Jester King Craft Brewery. (Courtesy of Jester King Brewery)

was able to isolate a total of 24 strains of acid-producing wild yeast from the samples collected, which may or may not be *Brettanomyces*. After fermentation trials, the brewers at Jester King decided on three of the strains to use as their house culture. This wild yeast blend is usually pitched into barrel-aged sour beers following primary fermentation with a French saison yeast. It typically takes six to eight months at 64°F (18°C) for these local strains to contribute their soft funky character to the Jester King beers.[20]

Belgian-style lambic is not the only spontaneously fermented alcoholic beverage in the world. For centuries both grape wines and apple ciders have been fermented without the addition of cultured yeast. In these cases, rather than wild yeast in the air, it is the yeast on the skins of the fruit that completes fermentation. Garrett Oliver, of Brooklyn Brewery in New York, is working on a project to harness these wild strains with the assistance of the vintner at the nearby Red Hook Winery. The first batch, Crochet Rouge Rose, was created by taking the brewery's already fermented Brooklyn Local 1 and aging it in barrels with the lees from Red Hook's naturally fermented Chardonnay and Pinot noir; according to Oliver, after a few months the wild microbes added a complementary funk. For the second batch he added fermenting wine to wort to build a starter for a fully wild fermentation.[21]

In 2011, the American importer B. United Inc. began the Zymatore Project to barrel-age some of the beers in their portfolio.[22] Of the ones I have tried, my favorite was Birrificio Barley's Friska, created from an Italian brewed wit aged in a barrel that previously held Ramato wine at Channing Daughters Winery on Long Island, NY.[23] The inclusion of the lees from the wine added a tart, citrusy funk that mingled nicely with the refreshing base beer.

Using a cider fermented solely by the yeast living on apple skins (and on the cider press) could work equally well. Remember that fermenting a beer with these cultures is likely to produce a beverage with more acidity and funk than the original. This is because of the higher percentage of complex sugars in wort compared to fruit juice.

If you do not have access to a naturally fermented wine or cider, inoculate a starter directly with local fruit. Just pick a few wild berries (or buy from a local farmer who does not spray with pesticides) and add the unwashed fruit to a small test tube or other small container with enough wort to cover. One research group found that ripened wine grapes that had been damaged had a 25% chance of harboring *Saccharomyces*, while immature grapes only had a 0.05% chance.[24] Once you see activity you should increase the volume with fresh starter wort, evaluating the flavor before pitching it into a batch in the same way I describe for airborne starters.[25]

Mystic Brewery (Chelsea, MA) is one of the few breweries to have released beers fermented with yeast strains isolated from fruit. Vinland One was fermented with yeast isolated from a plum purchased at a farmers market, and Vinland Two with a strain cultured from blueberries.[26] The peppery saison-like yeast character of Vinland Two earned Mystic a gold medal in the Indigenous Beer category at the 2013 GABF. [27]

Rather than isolate a strain, the Italian brewery LoverBeer (Torino, Italy) adds freshly crushed local Barbera wine grapes to spark a spontaneous fermentation in oak vats of their BeerBera.[28] The result exhibits a vinous aroma, jammy flavor, oak spiciness, and slight tartness. The overall balance of BeerBera has much more in common with a red wine than most beers flavored with wine grapes, thanks to the wild yeast living on the skin of local grapes.

Conclusion

Like most aspects of brewing sour beer, there is no single preeminent method for starting a spontaneous fermentation. What works for one location or brewer may not work for all. It is important to focus on the general principles, i.e., ensuring a quick start to fermentation while avoiding too much early activity from *Lactobacillus*. Once fermentation starts, you should heed the advice found in other sections of this book on minimizing oxygen exposure, monitoring the progress of the microbes, and always being aware of the risks outlined here and in Chapter 2. This style of fermentation demands caution, patience, blending ability, and the willingness to dump beer, but with both skill and luck you can fashion a beer that is more exciting and rewarding than anything fermented with cultured microbes.

References

1. Diego Libkinda, et al., *Proc. Natl. Acad. Sci. USA*, 108(35):14539.
2. Jeff Sparrow, *Wild Brews: Beer Beyond the Influence of Brewer's Yeast.*
3. Vinnie Cilurzo, Yvan de Baets, and Jean Van Roy, "Barrel-Aged Sour Beers from Two Belgian's Perspectives," panel discussion, Craft Brewers Conference, San Francisco, 2011.
4. Nathan Zeender, personal communication with author, April 6, 2011.
5. Cilurzo, et al., "Barrel-Aged Sour Beers from Two Belgian's Perspectives."
6. Nicholas A. Bokulich, Charles W. Bamforth, David A. Mills, *PLoS ONE* 7(4):e35507.
7. Urbain Coutteau, "The Sunday Session" audio podcast, Brewing Network, March 23, 2008, http://thebrewingnetwork.com/shows/The-Sunday-Session/The-Sunday-Session-De-Struise/Ebenezers-03-23-08.
8. Shaun Hill, personal communication with author, January 15, 2012.
9. Gabe Fletcher, personal communication with author, February 18, 2012; Interview on "Episode 91 – From Italy to Alaska," *Beer Sessions Radio* MP3 audio (starts 18:59), November 29, 2011, http://www.heritageradionetwork.com/episodes/2081-Beer-Sessions-Radio-TM-Episode-91-From-Italy-to-Alaska.
10. P. Small, et al., *Journal of Bacteriology* 176(6):1729.
11. Jean Van Roy, "The Sunday Session," audio podcast, May 8, 2011.
12. Jeff O'Neil, personal communication with author, December 21, 2011.

13. Ron Jeffries, personal communication with author, September 26, 2011.

14. Will Meyers, multiple personal communications with author, 2011.

15. Info on Beatification from: Vinnie Cilurzo, interview with Brandon Jones, *Embrace the Funk* blog, January 9, 2012; Keynote presentation at NHC 2007, *Brewing Network*, MP3 audio, July 7, 2007; Tomme Arthur and Vinnie Cilurzo, "Cult Beers of California," *Craft Beer Radio*, MP3 audio, 2009.

16. Cilurzo, *Embrace The Funk*, January 9, 2012.

17. Jason Perkins, interview with James Spencer, *Basic Brewing Radio*, MP3 audio, April 30, 2009; Jason Perkins, personal communication with author, October 7, 2011; "Coolship," *Allagash Brewing Company*, accessed April 25, 2013, http://www.allagash.com/beer/coolship; AllagashBrewing, "Allagash Brewing's First Traditional Spontaneous Brew," YouTube video, December 13, 2007.

18. Perkins, pers. comm., October 7, 2011.

19. Allagash Brewing, "Allagash Ghoulschip Brew Day," Vimeo video (2:32), November 2, 2012, http://vimeo.com/52688021.

20. Jeff Stuffings, personal communication with author, October 30, 2012.

21. "Wild Yeast Collaboration with Brooklyn Brewery," Jason Rodriguez, *Brew Science – Homebrewing Blog*, April 2, 2012, http://sciencebrewer.com/tag/crochet-rouge-rose.

22. "Zymatore Project," *B. United International Inc.*, accessed March 15, 2013, http://www.bunitedint.com/zymatore.

23. "Zymatore Project Showcase," *The Farmer's Cabinet*, accessed March 15, 2013, http://www.thefarmerscabinet.com/zymatore-project-showcase/891.

24. Robert Mortimer and Mario Polsinelli, *Research in Microbiology*, vol. 150, issue 3, 201–202.

25. "Yeast Hunting: Update," Jean-Claude Tetreault, *Trillium Brewing Company*, company blog, October 20, 2010, http://trilliumbrewing.blogspot.com/2010/10/yeast-hunting-update.html.

26. Christopher Staten, "Native ales: A new state of beer," *Draft Magazine*, March/April 2013, http://draftmag.com/features/native-ales-yeast.

27. "GABF Winners," Great American Beer Festival® (GABF), accessed February 2, 2014.

28. "BeerBera: Fruit Beer," [in Italian] *LoverBeer Brewery*, accessed March 15, 2013, http://www.loverbeer.com.

100% *BRETTANOMYCES* FERMENTATIONS

8

The characteristic earthy funk of *Brettanomyces* has been a component of beer for hundreds, if not thousands, of years. *Brettanomyces* is a close cousin to *Saccharomyces*, being in the same taxonomic family. Both types of yeast consume sugar, producing alcohol and carbon dioxide (CO_2) as a result. *Brettanomyces* was identified in 1904 by N. Hjelte Claussen,[1] a few decades after Pasteur had first described *Saccharomyces*. Despite Claussen's discovery and the recognition that it was responsible for the unique flavors of aged beers in three of the principal European brewing traditions (English, Belgian, and German), *Brettanomyces* was not used to ferment a commercial beer in the absence of *Saccharomyces* until a century later.

The way individual *Brettanomyces* cells behave is affected significantly by the way they are treated and what compounds are available for ester and phenol production. As you have read in Chapters 5 and 6, traditionally a small number of *Brettanomyces* cells are pitched into a beer either at the same time as brewer's yeast or following it. As a result of competition from the brewer's yeast, the *Brettanomyces* cannot take full advantage of the easily fermentable mono- and disaccharides present in the wort, or the dissolved oxygen it requires for rapid reproduction. After the brewer's yeast has fermented the chains of certain sugar molecules short enough for its enzymes to tackle, the *Brettanomyces* will continue to slowly ferment the longer chains that remain. The brewer's yeast also supplies *Brettanomyces* with by-products, particularly various esters and phenols, that serve as substrates for further flavor development.[2] Over several months the secondary *Brettanomyces* fermentation results in a dry beer, which contains a large variety of flavorful by-products.

For a 100% *Brettanomyces* fermentation a large pitch of the cultured wild yeast is added to the wort in the absence of *Saccharomyces*. This gives the *Brettanomyces* exclusive access to the oxygen and simple sugars. As a result, the *Brettanomyces* does not ferment as many of the complex (long-chain) carbohydrates as it does when pitched in combination with brewer's yeast. The higher number of cells used for the pitch also allows the *Brettanomyces* to complete its fermentation and achieve a stable final gravity within weeks instead of months. However, this more rapid fermentation in the absence of substrates usually supplied by brewer's yeast results in lower levels of the fascinating esters and phenols that are *Brettanomyces'* signature. It is also important to remember that while *Brettanomyces* will produce acetic acid when oxygen is readily available,[3] bacteria are required to produce the lactic acid of a true sour beer.

One hundred percent *Brettanomyces* fermentations are a good technique for brewers just starting to produce funky beers, because the time required is on the same scale as that of a lager fermentation. Research into 100% *Brettanomyces* beers is still in its infancy, and many of the practices are still anecdotal. While most of the scientific research on *Brettanomyces* is still funded by winemakers who are trying to determine how to prevent wild yeast from spoiling their product, there is increasing research on *Brettanomyces'* role in primary fermentation as 100% *Brettanomyces* beers gain commercial viability. For example, Chad Yakobson researched and wrote his dissertation, "Pure Culture Fermentation Characteristics of *Brettanomyces* Yeast Species and Their Use in the Brewing Industry," while completing his master's degree at the International Centre for Brewing and Distilling in Edinburgh, Scotland, before going on to start the Crooked Stave Artisan Beer Project in Colorado, which specializes in 100% *Brettanomyces* beers.

When paired with an aggressive pre-boil souring technique (e.g., sour mashing, sour worting, or acid malt) a 100% *Brettanomyces* fermentation is a good solution for making a complex sour beer without waiting as long as you would for a traditional mixed fermentation. Pre-boil souring is especially effective, because *Brettanomyces* is able to complete a healthy fermentation in wort with a starting pH that is too low for brewer's yeast. Given the popularity of sour beers today, it is surprising that this is not a more common method for commercial breweries.

Strain Selection

As a general rule, *Brettanomyces* strains in primary fermentation produce a softer variation of the same types of flavors as when pitched in combination with brewer's yeast. For example, the classic horsey flavors of *B. bruxellensis* are muted in primary fermentation, allowing more fruit to come forward. Wyeast's *B. lambicus* moves from a cherry and funk combination to become so cherry pie-forward that you might be able to pass it off as a fruit beer.

The milder strains, those marketed as *B. claussenii* and *B. anomalus*, are good choices if you want a restrained Brett character. When pitched for primary fermentation in a malty or hoppy beer, it is difficult to discriminate between the flavors they produce and those produced by Belgian brewer's yeast strains (especially when the beer is young). This may not be what most brewers want from the effort of brewing a 100% *Brettanomyces* beer, but it is a good way to complement the flavors of hops or spices.

The most popular strain for primary fermentations at commercial breweries is *Brettanomyces* Drie (a.k.a. *Brettanomyces* Trois, Dr. Drie). This is a variant of *B. bruxellensis* that Adam Avery had Brewing Science Institute (BSI) isolate from a bottle of 3 (i.e., Drie) Fonteinen J & J Oude Geuze Blauw (a gueuze that was blended to celebrate the marriage of Joost and Jessie, the owners of De Heeren Van Liedekercke).[4] Avery Brewing Company (Boulder, CO) first employed the strain for the primary fermentation of Fifteen (which included white pepper, figs, and hibiscus). Other examples of *Brettanomyces* Drie fermented beers are the Super Friends IPA (a collaborative effort), and recent batches of Russian River's Sanctification, which have included some *Brettanomyces* Drie along with other strains.[5] The *Brettanomyces* Drie strain is prized for its rapid fermentation and highly aromatic bready, tropical fruit, and mildly funky aromas. Commercial pitches are available to brewers through BSI, and to both commercial and homebrewers from White Labs as WLP644 *Brettanomyces bruxellensis* Trois.

If no single strain seems like the right choice for your batch, the final option is to blend strains together to impart a unique fermentation profile. Including *B. anomalus* can soften the more aggressive flavors produced by *B. bruxellensis* for example. At Crooked Stave, Chad Yakobson fermented his early batches with a blend of five *Brettanomyces* strains in an attempt to ensure rapid attenuation and production of his desired range of flavors. As time went on he removed one strain that was not making a substantial flavor contribution. Yakobson's current combination that he uses for beers like Surette, Wild Wild Brett Rouge, and WWB Orange, is a "close to even" mix of BSI *Brettanomyces* Drie, his own Drie isolate (CMY001), Orval's *B. bruxellensis*, and *B. custersianus* from East Coast Yeast.[6] In other cases, Yakobson has pitched as few as two strains, for example, the highly tropical duo of CMY001 and CMY007 (another proprietary strain). Many other breweries pitch blends of strains as well; with so few strains of *Brettanomyces* available this is often the best option for getting the preferred fermentation profile.

Propagation and Pitching

To compensate for a slower growth rate you can pitch 100% *Brettanomyces* beers at the same rate by volume that you target for lagers, which is about twice the standard pitching rate for ales. Yakobson conducted the research for his thesis using ale pitching rates, but now suggests, "Right in between an ale and lager pitching rate, so 1.25×10^6 cells/mL per °P."[7] At Crooked Stave he has observed much faster fermentations when repitching *Brettanomyces*, so if you are brewing another batch by repitching the yeast you may want to reduce the rate. Al Buck of East Coast Yeast recommends pitching at the same rate by volume for *Brettanomyces* as *Saccharomyces* for primary fermentation, about 34 fl. oz. of slurry per barrel (0.8 L per hL).[8]

Like brewer's yeast strains, the more cells you pitch the cleaner the fermentation will be, with lower fusel alcohol and ester production. Pitching a lower number of cells than the amount suggested can result in a beer that takes longer to attenuate, but produces a more classically "Bretty" aromatic profile. Even at lower pitching rates, however, a *Brettanomyces* primary fermentation still produces a much milder profile than you would expect considering the quantity of the fermentables it consumes compared to a traditional long secondary fermentation. According to Yakobson, this milder character is a result of the reduced level of 4-vinyl derivatives usually produced by primary fermentation with a Belgian ale strain, which certain strains of *Brettanomyces* can convert into pungently funky 4-ethyl derivatives.[9]

If you do not own a hemocytometer to perform cell counts you will have to rely on a pitching rate calculator to correlate starter size with cell count. The physical size of the individual cells is the key factor in equating the peak cell density of a starter. *Brettanomyces* cells can vary from about the same size as brewer's yeast, to one quarter of their size. Yakobson was able to reach peak densities of 6.5×10^8 *Brettanomyces* cells per milliliter in continuously agitated starters.[10] This is more than three times the cell density of brewer's yeast, which peak around 2×10^8 cells/mL given similar propagation techniques.[11] Without knowing exactly how large your *Brettanomyces* cells are it is hard to quantify exactly how much you will need to account for this difference, but depending on your results you should consider making a slightly smaller starter by volume than what a calculator or formula designed for brewer's yeast suggests.

While the information in Chapter 4 on maintaining *Brettanomyces* cultures provides information on basic propagation techniques, growing the huge number of cells required for primary fermentation necessitates additional tips. It can take a few weeks to grow a standard culture into an adequate cell count, especially if you are a homebrewer starting from a White Labs *Brettanomyces* culture, which contains far fewer cells than their brewer's yeast (homebrewers can expect 1.8–2.7 billion cells per tube compared to around 100 billion for brewer's yeast). Patrick Rue of the Bruery suggests homebrewers step up White Labs *Brettanomyces* cultures first to 50 mL and then to 150 mL when prepping for a five gallon batch.[12]

A *Brettanomyces* starter culture can be created and stepped up using similar techniques to ale yeast propagation, but each growth step takes longer. Moderate gravity, 1.036–1.048 SG (9°P–12°P), un-hopped wort with an addition of yeast nutrient works well. In his research, Yakobson found that on average it took between seven to eight days at 82°F (28°C) with continuous aeration for *Brettanomyces* cultures to reach maximum cell density. The time required differed by strain, for example, BSI *Brettanomyces* Dric was the slowest at the start, but yielded the most cells by the end.[13] If you do not have a stir-plate, or another method to continuously aerate the starter, then a simpler method can work (such as periodic shaking or bubbling air through the culture), but will not result in as dense of a culture.

Some brewers worry that the acetic acid *Brettanomyces* produces under aerobic propagation is enough to stall growth; they suggest adding a small amount of chalk to buffer against a pH drop, but this is not always necessary. In fact, most strains of *Brettanomyces* grow fastest at a pH in the low 3.0s, according to Yakobson's research, although not to the extent that he suggests adding acid to the starter.[14]

When you have propagated enough cells for your batch, taste the starter beer before deciding whether or not to decant. If you like a hint of acetic acid in your beer, you can pitch the entire starter. To reduce the amount of acetic acid in the finished beer, allow the starter to sit for several days and decant off as much of the starter beer as you can before pitching the slurry. Settling the *Brettanomyces* into a compact layer will take longer than for most brewer's yeasts, because *Brettanomyces* cells are smaller and have not been selected for high flocculation. Many brewers report that chilling *Brettanomyces* reduces fermentation vigor, so chilling the starter is not suggested to accelerate flocculation. If you do choose to chill the starter, feed the decanted and warmed culture several hours before pitching it into the main wort.

Fermentation

The initial pH of the wort will have a large impact on both the speed of fermentation and the character of the resulting beer. A lower pH tends to increase the rate of fermentation, although the intended tartness of the finished beer should be your primary consideration (i.e., if you do lower the pH to speed up fermentation, your beer may end up being very sour). Yakobson found that, for most strains, the lowest pH (3.08) in his trials resulted in both marginally less time to reach a terminal gravity and increased attenuation, but consequently also lowered production of several key esters.[15] Vinnie Cilurzo of Russian River suggests a minimum pH of 3.4.[16]

While food grade acids are an option for lowering the pH, a quick souring method implemented prior to primary fermentation with *Brettanomyces* produces more interesting results. A White Labs *B. bruxellensis* (WLP650) fermentation of un-hopped wort that I produced, using the sour worting method described in Chapter 5, yielded a beer with much more stone-fruit character than I expected; this strain usually expresses primarily farmyard and horse blanket. A lower pH can also be obtained by adding *Lactobacillus*, either during pre-boil wort acidification (as Pizza Port did with Mo' Betta Bretta) or into the fermentor (as Russian River does with Sanctification). Similar results can be accomplished with either a sour mash method in the style of Cambridge Brewing Company (see Chapter 5) or an acid malt addition as per Ithaca Beer Company's Brute (although in the case of the latter ensure complete starch conversion has taken place before adding the acid malt). I have not had an issue with attenuation when starting with a "standard" wort pH, but having at least a small amount of lactic acid present in the wort enables the creation of ethyl lactate, an ester which has a fruity aroma that is one of the signature components of sour beer.

The amount of oxygen dissolved in the wort at pitching will have a significant impact on the character produced by the *Brettanomyces*. If you aerate as you would for a normal beer the *Brettanomyces* will be healthier and ferment more quickly, producing less of the character it is known for. Several brewers pointed out that many people's instincts are backwards when thinking about the role of oxygen. As Cilurzo has said, "Increasing oxygen . . . will increase the cell count, but it doesn't necessarily bring up the flavor, and if anything it will go [in the] opposite [direction]."[17] Reducing or eliminating wort aeration will stress the *Brettanomyces*, which does cause higher production of its characteristic flavors, but also a longer and less reliable fermentation. Yakobson recommends aerating at 10–12 ppm oxygen for all strains.[18] However, I have also had good results holding aeration to a minimum, especially when dealing with milder strains at high pitching rates.

The last major variable that influences *Brettanomyces* character is fermentation temperature. Hotter temperatures will result in a more rapid attenuation, but too hot will cause the production of unpleasant fermentation by-products reminiscent of burnt rubber bands. I achieved the best results with White Labs *B. claussenii* (WLP645) by slowly increasing the fermentation temperature to 80°F–82°F (27–28°C), which produces abundant peach and tropical fruit esters. However, Wyeast *B. anomalus* (WY5110, now discontinued) performed better at a lower fermentation temperature, around 68°F (20°C). In most cases, you are safer fermenting cooler rather than warmer; at Crooked Stave most of the 100% *Brettanomyces* beers are pitched around 68°F (20°C) and allowed to warm a few degrees as fermentation progresses.[19]

In my experience, primary fermentations with most strains of *Brettanomyces* result in about 80%–90% apparent attenuation (similar to many saison strains). This is lower than the nearly 95%–100% apparent attenuation that is achieved by many beers fermented with both *Brettanomyces* and brewer's yeast. If you want to produce a dry 100% *Brettanomyces* beer you will need a long cool saccharification rest. A slightly higher finishing gravity may actually be helpful though, because *Brettanomyces* does not exhibit glycerol production, whereas *Saccharomyces* does.[20] Glycerol enhances body and mouthfeel, so 100% *Brettanomyces* beers tend to taste even thinner than their already low finishing gravity would suggest.

A healthy *Brettanomyces* primary fermentation will look similar to that of a standard ale (substantial kraeusen and rapid CO_2 production). When the pitching rate as suggested above is followed, a stable gravity is most often reached within two weeks. In Yakobson's experiments, fermentation times with the various strains ranged anywhere from less than a week to over a month,[21] but this was with a pitching rate lower than either he or I now recommend. When fermentation is complete, *Brettanomyces* flocculates better than expected compared with being in a mixed or a secondary fermentation, but most strains are still no faster to drop than low flocculating brewer's yeast.

Even after visible fermentation has ceased you should monitor the gravity for several weeks before packaging to ensure that there is no further attenuation, especially if you are bottling. Once you are confident that the gravity is stable you can package as is, or attempt to clear the beer with cold conditioning, fining, filtration, or centrifuging.

For bottle conditioning, the standard formula for calculating the priming sugar addition works, although it may take slightly longer to reach full carbonation. I have several 100% *Brettanomyces* batches that were bottled a month after brewing (with no additional yeast pitched) that have maintained a stable level of carbonation despite more than six years in the bottle. However, Pizza Port took the step of bottling their first batch of Mo' Betta Bretta with an American ale yeast to ensure proper carbonation. Recent reports on this bottled batch, now more than eight years old, suggest it has become overcarbonated,[22] possibly as a result of the fermentables released as the ale yeast undergoes autolysis. For more information on packaging see Chapter 12.

The flavors of 100% *Brettanomyces* beers hold relatively steady as they age. Over the first six months they tend to move from fresher and fruitier towards the classic leather, barnyard, and horse blanket. Wyeast

B. lambicus (WY5526), for example, exhibits classic kriek flavor early on, but over time the fruit fades, to be replaced by earthier flavors. Although it does increase, the funk never reaches the same level as beers with a slow secondary *Brettanomyces* fermentation. If you like the character of a young 100% *Brettanomyces* beer, store it cold to retard this flavor evolution. Killing the *Brettanomyces* is a more extreme option if you want to preserve the current character, or retain more residual sweetness and body.

Commercial Examples

In 2004 the Lost Abbey's Tomme Arthur became one of the pioneers of 100% *Brettanomyces* fermentations when he and Peter Bouckaert, brewmaster of New Belgium Brewing, collaborated on Mo' Betta Bretta at Pizza Port Solana Beach—the first commercially bottled 100% *Brettanomyces* beer.

Unsure how dry Mo' Betta Bretta would ferment, Arthur and Bouckaert included flaked oats and CaraPils® in the grist to increase the mouthfeel. They wanted a small amount of lactic acid in the wort to promote the formation of ethyl lactate, but did not want to brew a truly sour beer. To accomplish their goal they took a portion of the first runnings and diluted it with water to reach 1.040 SG (10°P), to which they pitched a dense 68 fl. oz. (2 L) slurry of *Lactobacillus amylovorus*. This hop-sensitive lactic acid bacteria was selected to reduce the risk of cross contamination (hop-sensitive strains like this are commonly found in cheese making). While the remainder of the wort was boiled and lightly bittered with Magnum hops, the *Lactobacillus*-inoculated portion was held warm at 99°F–118°F (37°C–48°C). Servomyces® yeast nutrient was added to the boil to encourage a quick fermentation and improve flocculation. The noticeably soured wort was combined with the rest of the wort near the end of the boil to kill the bacteria before it reached the fermentor.[23]

Bouckaert suggests that as little as 100 ppm of lactic acid in the pre-fermentation wort is enough for the *Brettanomyces* to generate above-threshold ethyl lactate, because the ester has a much lower flavor threshold than the acid itself. The cooled wort was pitched with what Arthur believed was *B. anomalus*. However, Bouckaert suspected that the strain is actually a variant of *B. bruxellensis*, something that was confirmed with Wyeast's discovery that the *B. anomalus* strain they had originally cultured from Mo' Betta Bretta had been misidentified.[24]

The two brewers collaborated again on two recipes that were brewed in 2012. For the Lost Abbey, Bouckaert and Arthur resurrected the original recipe, once again naming it Mo' Betta Bretta.[25] The beer brewed at New Belgium on the other hand, dubbed straightforwardly as Brett Beer, was all pale malt, hopped with Target, Centennial, and Sorachi Ace, and fermented with two *Brettanomyces* strains, one contributed by each brewery.[26] In the case of Brett Beer, multiple batches were required to fill the large fermentor, so wort from the first batch was soured and added to the boil of the final batch 12 hours later.[27] While neither beer had an expressive Brett character, I found Brett Beer to be drier and livelier next to the recreated Mo' Betta Bretta, which came off slightly tarter, more phenolic, and sweeter.

Beer enthusiasts rave about the original Mo' Betta Bretta's dominant tropical-pineapple aromatics, most likely the esters ethyl caproate or ethyl caprylate, and replicating this aroma has become an obsession rivaling Captain Ahab's for some homebrewers. A good place to start, according to Chad Yakobson's research, would be fermentation with WLP653, BSI *Brettanomyces* Drie, or WY5526, which are the only strains currently commercially available that he found capable of producing above threshold concentrations of the two esters thought to be in Mo' Betta Bretta.[28] Even Arthur had problems recreating this magical flavor on the second batch of Mo' Betta Bretta, which lacked prominent fruitiness.

In late 2004, following on the heels of Arthur and Bouckaert's success, Vinnie Cilurzo brewed his first batch of Russian River Sanctification. This pale tart beer is an example of the fruity and funky flavors produced by the best 100% *Brettanomyces* fermentations. The grist includes 5% acid malt to lower the initial wort pH. Sanctification is pitched with an evolving blend of *Brettanomyces* and lactic acid bacteria.[29] Initially, the same strain of *B. anomalus* (or whatever it was) that fermented Mo' Betta Bretta was included, but this strain was eventually removed from the mix.[30] The fermentation temperature is held between 68°F to 80°F (20–27°C).[31] According to Cilurzo, after a long lag time the yeast flies to 1.020 SG (5°P), before slowly attenuating the rest of the way over the next few weeks. After their new production facility allowed Russian River to have sour barrel-aged beers available year round, Cilurzo differentiated Sanctification, making the beer much less sour than it had previously been.[32]

Chad Yakobson has been applying the knowledge he gained completing his master's dissertation to the Crooked Stave Artisan Beer Project, the brewery he founded and opened in 2011. His Wild Wild Brett (WWB) series is a showcase for 100% *Brettanomyces* fermented beer, each one flavored by ingredients of a particular color. The first few releases included WWB Rouge (hawthorn berries, rose hips, and hibiscus), WWB Orange (Minneola tangelos, bitter orange peel, and coriander), and WWB Green (4 lb. of hops per barrel [1.55 kg/hL]). Each is fermented with a blend of *Brettanomyces* strains he selected to enhance both the flavor and rate of attenuation. Yakobson's standard process is to knockout around 68°F–69°F (20°C), letting the fermentation climb to 73°F–74°F (23°C). The gravity takes two to three weeks to level out, but there is still some slow fermentation for a few weeks after that.[33]

A quickly fermented pale beer is not the only option for a 100% *Brettanomyces* fermentation. Surly Brewing Co. in Minneapolis took their fifth anniversary beer, Five, in a different direction from the strong malty ales they had brewed in previous and subsequent years. Five was a 7.5% ABV, 100% *Brettanomyces*, wine-barrel-aged brown ale that was brewed with three malts (dark Munich, Carafa III, and Special "B"), and 14 IBUs of Willamette hops.[34] The primary fermentation was conducted with a huge pitch of *B. claussenii* and *B. anomalus* in stainless steel. After seven days fermenting in tanks attenuation appeared complete, and after 14 more days the beer was racked to red wine barrels for extended aging. The brewers repitched the slurry into oxygenated (10–15 ppm) wort for a total of three batches. The combination of the extra oxygen and nearly a year of barrel aging provided enough oxygen for the *Brettanomyces* to produce a mild, but noticeable, amount of acetic acid. The resulting beer had a wine-berry character from the barrels and a pleasant acidity. The fermentation left more body than most mixed-fermentation sour beers, which worked well with the rich bready flavor of the Munich malt. The success of the anniversary release inspired a similar recipe from Surly Brewing—Pentagram—which involved repitching the same mixed *Brettanomyces* culture as for Five.

An easy way to get started with 100% *Brettanomyces* fermentation is to divert a portion of wort from another batch, as the Bruery does with 100% *Brettanomyces* versions of a few of their seasonal beers (including Autumn Maple, Trade Winds Tripel, and Saison de Lente). A 100% *Brettanomyces* pitch can successfully ferment just about any wort, because, unlike sour beers, its character does not clash with higher amounts of hops, roast, or spice. *Brettanomyces* is alcohol tolerant, so you could even ferment a strong beer. It is also important to remember that 100% *Brettanomyces* beers age more like clean beers than those where *Brettanomyces* plays a secondary role in fermentation.

If a 100% *Brettanomyces* fermentation fails to attenuate properly, or you are under time constraints that even this relatively speedy technique will not satisfy, consider taking a page from Oxbow Brewing Company's playbook (Oxbow are in Newcastle, ME). Co-founder and head brewer Tim Adams explained to me that they start several of their "American farmhouse ales" with a large pitch of *Brettanomyces* (usually the Drie variant of *B. bruxellensis*). When the beer reaches 1.016–1.020 SG (3°P–4°P), attenuation slows to a crawl. When this happens they add a full pitch of their house saison strain to finish the fermentation.[35] This method can rapidly produce moderately Brett-forward beers that, thanks to the glycerol production of the saison yeast, do not exhibit a watery mouthfeel.

100% *Brettanomyces* IPAs

One recent trend is for hoppy 100% *Brettanomyces* beers. When done well, the *Brettanomyces* adds a layer of complexity beneath the bold hop aroma, but when executed poorly the hop aromatics oxidize and fade before the beer is packaged. The ability of *Brettanomyces* to scavenge oxygen also leads to a fresher hop aroma for a longer period of time than an identical beer fermented with brewer's yeast.

Super Friends IPA is a 2010 collaboration of five New York area breweries (Brewery Ommegang, Captain Lawrence Brewing Company, Flying Fish Brewing Co., Ithaca Beer Co., and Southampton Publick House), along with Steve Altimari, who is currently the brewmaster at High Water Brewing in Redding, CA. Their goal was to combine the tropical mango and citrus hop flavors with earthy Brett character. They started with a simple grist comprised of pale American two-row and Dingemans crystal 20, and hopped with the boldly fruity Citra variety. They blended strains of *Brettanomyces*, including several *B. bruxellensis* strains (one of which was Drie for its complementary pineapple esters) and *B. claussenii*.

The day before brewing Super Friends, Ithaca's brewmaster Jeff O'Neil added the mixed *Brettanomyces* culture to 2 bbl. (2.4 hL) of wort so that the yeast would be at high kraeusen when it was pitched the following day. O'Neil estimated that they pitched enough cells for a 75 bbl. (88 hL) batch of ale into just 45 bbl. (53 hL) of wort. The 1.061 OG (15°P) wort started fermenting at 68°F (20°C) for the first few days before it was allowed to rise to 71°F–73°F (22–23°C).

After 12 days the fermentation was complete at 1.014 FG (3.4°P), and the beer was dry hopped with more Citra. The resulting IPA had loads of tropical hop aromatics, something any hophead would enjoy, but with enough funk to give it an additional layer of complexity. The key was that the Super Friends brewers pitched enough yeast that it was ready to keg after only three weeks.

Conclusion

Over the last few years 100% *Brettanomyces* fermentations have gone from being a curiosity to a relatively common technique attempted by dozens of American breweries and a handful of others around the world. The speed with which they can go from brewing to drinking makes them an ideal choice for a first step into brewing sour beers. If you want to learn the most from the process, find a strain (or blend) that you enjoy and stick with it, taking time to alter the fermentation regime (pitching rate, temperature, and aeration) to discover the combination that produces the flavors that you enjoy most.

References

1. N.Hjelte Claussen, *Journal of the Institute of Brewing* 10(4):308.
2. Greg Doss, "Brettanomyces: Flavors and performance of single and multiple strain fermentations with respect to time."
3. M. Aguilar Uscanga et al., *Applied Microbiology and Biotechnology* 61(2):157.
4. "Brett Pack Beer Dinner," *Basic Brewing Radio*, MP3 audio, November 27, 2008.
5. "Bottle Logs," hyperlink via "Brews", *Russian River Brewing Company*, last accessed February 5, 2014, http://russianriverbrewing.com/bottle-logs/.
6. ChadY, February 7, 2012 (7:10 p.m.), comment on brewinhard, "Bretts in Chad's Crooked Stave?" *Burgundian Babble Belt* homeBBBrew board, February 7, 2012, http://www.babblebelt .com/newboard/thread.html?tid=1108752780&th=1326031057.

7. Chad Yakobson, personal communication with author, December 3, 2011.

8. Al Buck, personal communication with author, January 11, 2012.

9. ChadYakobson, February 2, 2012 (4:43 p.m.) "Primary vs Secondary happenings...," comment on Waylit, "Understanding Brett flavors," *Home Brew Talk*, January 28, 2012, http://www.homebrewtalk .com/f127/understanding-brett-flavors-298943/#post3734990.

10. Chad Yakobson, "Pure Culture Fermentation Characteristics of *Brettanomyces* Yeast Species and Their Use in the Brewing Industry," master's thesis, 2010.

11. Chris White and Jamil Zainasheff, *Yeast: The Practical Guide to Beer Fermentation*.

12. Patrick Rue, "The Sunday Session," audio podcast, *Brewing Network*, November 2, 2008.

13. Yakobson, "Pure Culture Fermentation Characteristics of *Brettanomyces.*"

14. Ibid.

15. Ibid.

16. Vinnie Cilurzo, Keynote presentation at National Homebrewers Conference 2007, *Brewing Network*, MP3 audio, July 7, 2007, http:// thebrewingnetwork.com/shows/The-Sunday-Session/The-Sunday -Session-07-07-07-Meltdown-and-Sour-Beer.

17. Ibid.

18. Yakobson, pers. comm., December 3, 2011.

19. Ibid.

20. Chad Yakobson, "Crooked Stave Brewing Network," interview, "The Sunday Session," audio podcast, *The Brewing Network*, April 15, 2012, http://thebrewingnetwork.com/shows/866.

21. Yakobson, Pure Culture Fermentation Characteristics of *Brettanomyces.*"

22. "Mo' Betta Bretta," *The Lost Abbey* blog, last accessed April 25, 2013, http://lostabbey.com/mo-betta-bretta/.

23. Peter Bouckaert and Eric Salazar, "New Belgium Brewing," MP3 audio, *Basic Brewing Radio*, October 19, 2006.

25. "Mo' Betta Bretta," *Lost Abbey.*

26. "Brett Beer," New Belgium Brewing, last accessed March 17, 2013, http://www.newbelgium.com/beer/detail.aspx?id=751a53c5-5cdc -4ca0-bb68-fb98c4a56aee.

27. Peter Bouckaert, personal communication with author, March 2, 2012.

28. Yakobson, "Pure Culture Fermentation Characteristics of *Brettanomyces.*"
29. "Vinnie Cilurzo of Russian River Q&A!" Interview by Brandon Jones, *Embrace the Funk* blog, August 2, 2011, http://embracethe funk.com/2011/08/02/vinnie-cilurzo-of-russian-river-qa.
30. Vinnie Cilurzo, "The Sunday Session: Vinnie Returns to the Session," interview, *Brewing Network*, MP3 audio, January 17, 2010, http:// thebrewingnetwork.com/shows/596.
31. "The Sunday Session: Belgian Beers with Vinnie Cilurzo," MP3 audio, August 14, 2005.
32. Cilurzo, "Vinnie Returns to the Session," January 17, 2010.
33. Yakobson, pers. comm., December 3, 2011.
34. Todd Haug, personal communication with author, March 6, 2012; "Surly Turns Five: An Interview with Omar Ansari and Todd Haug," interview with Michael Agnew, *A Perfect Pint*, August 25, 2011.
35. Tim Adams, personal communication with author, February 21, 2013.

FERMENTORS AND WOOD AGING

9

Aging in oak barrels is not required when brewing a sour beer, but it is no mere coincidence that so many of the brewers I spoke with act as if it is. Oak barrels can serve to harbor the souring microbes at the same time as isolating them from clean beers, provide micro-oxygenation, contribute tannins, add complex flavors, and introduce variance within batches to increase blending options. Used oak barrels are relatively inexpensive, especially compared with buying additional stainless steel fermentors, although they do not last as long and require more time and expertise to maintain.

Sour beers share an ancient and intricate relationship with wooden barrels. Long before stainless steel conical fermentors became the commercial brewing standard, barrels provided both a place for beers to ferment and a home for the responsible microbes. You can do anything from primary fermentation to secondary aging in barrels. During primary fermentation, CO_2 production limits the amount of oxygen in the air that diffuses through the porous wood, but when allowed to age in a barrel this oxygen can slowly diffuse into the beer. For most types of beer post-fermentation oxygen exposure should be kept to a minimum to improve shelf stability, but in sour beers oxygen allows *Brettanomyces* to thrive. Too much oxygen though and a sour beer can be transformed into malt vinegar.

Toasted oak, the wood typically used in barrel construction, promotes complex flavors and serves as a source of fermentable sugars for

Brettanomyces. Oak also contributes tannins, which at the right level add body to sour beers left thin by high attenuation.

Despite these advantages, aging in barrels is not as effortless or risk-free as using durable modern fermentors. Barrels can leak, harbor *Acetobacter*, allow evaporation, and take more effort to fill or empty. There are techniques to minimize the difficulties, but barrels will never produce beer as easily or consistently as impermeable metal or glass fermentors.

Oak Barrels

While neither barrels nor wood are a requirement for sour beer, it is very telling that many of the best sour beers are aged in barrels. Toasted or charred oak barrels are the traditional aging vessels for many Western alcoholic beverages, from the red wines of Burgundy to the bourbons of Kentucky. Oak imparts a wide range of flavors that include spice, vanilla, roasted coffee, and caramel. The permeability of oak is low enough to prevent rapid oxidation and evaporation (although both processes do happen slowly).

Oak even serves as a food source for strains of *Brettanomyces* that produce beta-glucosidase, an enzyme capable of breaking down cellobiose (wood sugars),[1] which explains why *Brettanomyces* is sometimes present even in brand new barrels.[2] *Brettanomyces* forms biofilms and pseudohyphae, both multicellular structures that allow the yeast to better adhere to the interior of a barrel.[3] The small size of *Brettanomyces* cells, and even smaller size of bacteria, enable them to travel with the beer into the wood of the barrel as deep as 0.3 in. (8 mm).[4] As a result, once you introduce microbes to oak it is impossible to remove them completely, although a large percentage can be killed with hot water or steam. Far from this being a problem, many breweries rely on the microbial residents of established barrels to promote consistency. A few brewers spoke of their barrels like pets, each one having its own personality and will.

When selecting a barrel, there are five things to consider: the species/origin of wood it is made from, the toast, the previous contents, how old it is, and the volume. Each of these properties of a barrel will have an impact on the final flavor of the beer aged in it.

The barrels used to age most sour beers have already been used for several years by the time they arrive at the brewery. After aging wines, distilled spirits, or non-sour beers for years, there is only a small fraction of the originally intense oak character remaining. The restrained malt character and low finishing gravity of most sour beers leave them unable to support the same level of oak character suitable for more assertive beverages. Belgian lambic brewers often reuse their barrels for decades. After many years, these barrels do still contribute elusive nuances of flavor, but their primary role is to house microbes and allow oxygen to diffuse into the beer. This "micro-oxygenation" allows *Brettanomyces* to replenish its cell walls and continue fermenting despite the low pH and minimal residual extract. The oxygen enters slowly, so it is quickly absorbed by the *Brettanomyces* before the beer oxidizes significantly.

Many American breweries, and a handful in Belgium and Italy, are releasing sour beers aged exclusively in fresher barrels, which impart a more assertive oak character and residual flavor from the previous contents. At the right level these flavors add depth and dimension to beer. If the barrel character is too potent, however, it can eclipse the delicate complexities of the base beer. Many producers choose to age the same beer in barrels that range from fresh from a winery or distillery, to more neutral barrels that no longer impart a significant oak character. These can then be blended to fine-tune the level of barrel character.

The two most common types of oak used to construct barrels are American and French. There are flavor differences resulting from the species of oak and from the treatment of the wood before it is coopered (e.g., split vs. sawn, aged vs. kilned). American oak tends to be more aggressive, imparting bold vanilla and coconut flavors, while French oak is spicier and more balanced. American white oak barrels allow less oxygen diffusion as a result of their higher concentration of sap-conducting xylem.[5] This vascular tissue carries the sugars produced by photosynthesis in the leaves to the rest of the tree, and when the sugar dries it forms an impermeable layer. If you have problems with excessive acetic acid production, American oak is a good choice. Hungarian oak has flavor characteristics that fall between French and American and is a good choice as well.

A newly coopered oak barrel can contribute excessive lumber-like flavors in the time it takes for beers to age, which can be months or years. Brand new 60 gal. (227 L) barrels are also expensive, usually costing at least US$400 for American oak and as much as US$1,000 for French oak. These costs are several times that of used barrels.

There are several breweries that age clean beers in new American oak barrels before using them for sour beers. Odell Brewing Co. (Fort Collins, CO) ages their Woodcut series in medium-toast barrels from Canton Cooperage,[6] before the barrels are then used to age Friek, a sour cherry and raspberry beer.[7] Despite this, I still found Friek to have a heavy oak character, even after the strong clean beers had stripped out a considerable amount of the oak flavor and tannins from the barrels. Hair of the Dog Brewing Company (Portland, OR) uses new medium-toast barrels to age several batches of their barleywine Fred, to create Fred From the Wood, before using them to age the sour red Michael, which is heavy on oak flavor and light on sourness.[8]

Barrels are available in a wide range of toast levels, from lightly toasted to heavily charred. As the oak is heated over a fire the sugars and other compounds in the wood undergo pyrolysis, which changes the flavors imparted from woody and fruity, to caramel and spice, and all the way to roasted nuts and charcoal at the high end. However, because the beer is able to penetrate deep into the wood through the toasted layer, even heavily charred barrels can impart vanilla and coconut if given adequate time. As a rule of thumb, lighter toast levels work better with paler beers, and darker toasts complement roastier beers.

Most breweries procure used barrels from wineries, distilleries, or other breweries (Belgian lambic brewers have long prized the barrels which lager the most traditional Czech Pilseners). The main advantage of these barrels is that the fresh wood flavors have already been extracted; ironically, this is why they are no longer useful to their original owner. Second- or thirdhand barrels are much more economical as well, with prices ranging from US$50 to US$125. These barrels can be pressed into service immediately for a sour beer, but many brewers choose to age one or two batches of clean beer in them first to further soften the character. A number of breweries specializing in sour beer (e.g., Cambridge Brewing Company, Jolly Pumpkin Artisan Ales) buy spirit barrels from other breweries that had used them for the potent character first-use barrels impart to their strong clean beers.

Most wineries reuse their barrels to age a couple of vintages, so their barrels tend to have a mellow oak character by the time they are sold. The most common size is 58 gal. (220 L), but slightly larger sizes are often available as well. On the first use they will impart a moderate character reminiscent of the wine that they previously contained, along with oak character. Assuming each beer ages for a year, by the third fill these barrels generally have only minimal oak character remaining, and by the fifth they are effectively neutral.

Depending on your location, spirit barrels can be tougher to acquire (compared to wine barrels) because there are fewer distilleries than wineries in America. The one exception is bourbon barrels, because by law bourbon must be aged in new charred oak barrels.[9] As a result of this definition, bourbon distilleries' 53 gal. (201 L) barrels are widely available and relatively inexpensive. Distillers of other spirits often buy used bourbon barrels to age their products. Many apple brandy, rum, and Scotch distillers favor the character that charred American oak imparts to their spirits.

Jason Perkins of Allagash Brewing Company prefers barrels larger than the more commonly available standard sizes.[10] Many breweries producing spontaneously fermented beers age their beer in barrels called pipes, which have volumes two to three times greater (108–172 gal. [410–650 L]) than standard wine barrels. This larger size, and inherently lower surface-to-volume ratio, reduces the amount of evaporation and oxygen exposure, making them especially valuable for beers that will be aged for more than two years.

Always select a barrel whose character will complement the beer you are planning to age in it. Do not forget to consider the spices, fruits, or other flavorings you plan to add. First-use spirit barrels are best suited for stronger, darker sour beers as a result of the distilled liquor's potent varietal character. The character of first-use bourbon barrels is especially potent, with notes of vanilla, coconut, and plenty of booze; select a base beer that will benefit from these bold flavors. The lone exception is hard-to-obtain gin barrels, which lend a lighter, herbal character that can complement paler sour beers, especially those that are already spiced. A few examples of gin-barrel-aged sour beers are Upright Brewing's Special Herbs, Jester King's Viking Metal, and B. United International's Zymatore series version of 1809 Berliner Style Weisse.

Do not limit yourself to those barrels that are easiest to acquire: consider that brandy, Scotch, rum, and others will all lend distinctive flavors. There are distilleries and wineries making interesting products all over America, so see what barrels local producers have available rather than going with one of the more common choices. For example, one of my local wineries, Potomac Point, uses bourbon barrels to age their port-style wine, and these are perfect for a strong red sour.

Terry Hawbaker, formerly of Bullfrog Brewery and now head brewer at Pizza Boy Brewing Co. (Enola, PA), prefers well-used barrels, mostly bourbon and red wine (some French oak, but primarily American). Even after

Cramped barrel cellar at Bullfrog Brewery in Williamsport, Pennsylvania.

three turns at a local winery he finds that they still have abundant character, especially the American oak. Like many brewers, for bourbon barrels
Hawbaker often puts a strong clean beer through a barrel first to soften the
oak and spirit characters before aging a sour beer.[11]

Wine barrels that have already aged a couple of clean or sour beers are the
best choice for batches requiring less barrel character. If a beer derives enough
barrel character before the gravity stabilizes, you should transfer the beer to a
neutral barrel, or another type of fermentor. Blending is the best option if a
particular barrel becomes overly oaky.

For added complexity, there are a few sour beers that are aged consecutively
in multiple barrels. This is a technique usually reserved for strong dark beers
that are capable of long-term aging. The Lost Abbey's strong dark ale, code-
named Knights Templar, KT for short, spent more than a year in bourbon
barrels before aging an additional 15 months in French oak Syrah wine barrels. Sour cherries were added three months before the beer finally emerged
as Lost Abbey's Veritas 009.[12] More frequently, the same beer is divided into
several types of barrels for aging at the same time. For example, when my friend
Nathan Zeender and I collaborated with McKenzie Brew House (Malvern,
PA) on Irma Extra, we aged the same batch of tart amber saison in both red
wine and apple brandy barrels.

Foeders

Rather than expend their effort transferring beer into and out of hundreds of standard-sized barrels, a few American breweries age beers in a much smaller number of vertical oak tanks called *foeders*. This choice has a precedent in Belgium, where a number of Belgian breweries, such as Rodenbach, have been souring their beer in foeders for generations. Foeders are a good choice for adding ingredients that are awkward to pass through the small bunghole of a standard barrel, like dry hops. While larger fermentors reduce the time required for transferring and blending, they also limit the options for experimenting with different base beers, wood types, and microbes. As a result of the higher risk from concentrating batches into larger fermentors, foeders are only a good option for breweries with established souring programs.

All else being equal, the larger an oak fermentor the less oak and oxygen exposure the beers aged in it will receive proportionally. This is a result of the inverse relationship between barrel size and the surface–area-to-volume ratio. The thicker staves required for foeder construction compared with more diminutive barrels further reduce permeability.

The reason that acetic acid production is often higher in foeders is that air is allowed to enter between the staves at the top of the foeder where the beer does not come into contact with the wood. Traditionally, reeds are placed between the staves to ensure they are watertight, and this is another possible explanation of how oxygen is able to permeate into the foeders more rapidly than would be expected. While acetic acid is something American brewers tend to shy away from, it is a classic component of Flemish reds.

New Belgium Brewing Company has the largest fleet of foeders at an American brewery. All of them have been purchased secondhand from wineries, and are constructed of French oak because of its high oxygen permeability compared with American oak. Brewmaster Peter Bouckaert suggests personally inspecting every foeder you purchase, because evaluating the smell and appearance of the wood is so crucial. Foeders are available with stainless steel domes/hats, but New Belgium favors flat tops because they can be filled to the top.[13]

When a new foeder arrives at New Belgium it is washed or scraped (downward with a curved piece of metal) to remove the tartaric crystals that wine has deposited on the wood. Scraping is only done to as high as the brewers can reach while standing in the empty foeder. Heavily coated foeders are power washed to remove the tartaric crystals. The foeders are re-scraped periodically, as brewer Eric Salazar explains, "Scraping only happens when we feel that beer-stone (calcium oxalate) is impeding oxygen uptake through the foeder walls. This is determined by a rigorous tasting schedule and experience with the progress of acidification in each foeder. We try to taste every foeder monthly."[14]

The most important consideration for placement of foeders is whether the floor will support the massive combined weight of wood and beer. A secondary consideration is the microclimate. Despite the large thermal mass of foeders, temperature variations in a location can change the character of the beer produced. New Belgium has noticed that subtle differences in location, like being nearer a heat source, can influence the character of the finished

Partially assembled foeder at Anchorage Brewing in Alaska. Foeders must be disassembled in order to fit through the door of the brewery. (Courtesy of Anchorage Brewing Company)

beer. If the beer in one foeder is not "behaving" they will swap a few barrels (a couple of hectoliters) from it with a better tasting foeder to introduce microbes that produce their desired character.[15]

Gabe Fletcher, at Anchorage Brewing in Alaska, performs the primary fermentation for most of his beers in one of his 60 bbl. (70 hL) temperature-controlled foeders. The fermentation temperature is constrained by chilled glycol running through a dimpled cooling plate in the center of each. Once primary fermentation is complete, the beers are transferred to smaller barrels (e.g., wine, cognac) for aging. For most batches, each oak barrel receives a gallon (3.8 L) of a thin Wyeast *B. bruxellensis* (WY5112) culture from his propagator tank. Sour beers also receive 16 fl. oz. (0.5 L) from the mixed bacteria propagator once the *Brettanomyces* is established, usually after about two months.[16]

After 8 to 18 months, Fletcher blends the barrels back into the foeder for two weeks of dry hopping, or into a stainless steel tank for priming and re-yeasting with wine yeast prior to bottling. To clean his foeders Fletcher runs 180°F (82°C) water through the CIP loop. If the foeder is to be left empty then the wood is dried quickly to prevent mold growth. To do this, Fletcher runs a fan placed in the 3 ft. (0.9 m) opening of the stainless steel lid for a few days.

Tips for Barrel Selection

If you decide that either barrels or foeders are the right choice for your beer, the next step is procuring them. The more recently a barrel has been emptied, the better. A freshly dumped barrel will still be hydrated, which means the wood is swollen, making it watertight and free of unwanted microbial residents.

Visual Inspection
Interior with a flashlight
Accept: lees in wine barrel, or liquor in a liquor barrel
Reject: mold

Exterior, including bottom
Accept: scuffs, marks, or shallow scrapes
Reject: gaps, cracks, or holes

Aromatic Evaluation

Interior

Accept: the previous resident (wine or spirits), toasty, or oaky

Reject: dank, moldy, vinegary, nail polish or otherwise unpleasant

If you are planning to age a sour beer with *Brettanomyces*, any wild yeast that might be present in a wine barrel is not a major concern. Aging a clean beer in a wine barrel is a much more risky proposition.

Barrel Tea

To get an idea of the quality and quantity of the oak character remaining in a barrel, Jeff Stuffings of Jester King Brewery suggests making a barrel tea. He does this by pouring about a gallon of hot water into an empty barrel, inserting a hard bung, and rolling the barrel around. After 10 minutes of sitting, he pours the tea and tastes it. The brewers at Jester King now source their wine barrels locally, which entails more effort and money, but the ability to evaluate each barrel has meant more control of the barrel-character of their finished beers, and less of the undesirable characters that they experienced early on when purchasing barrels sight-unseen from brokers.[17]

Preparing Barrels for First-Use

When you purchase barrels, you should have already brewed, or at a minimum be ready to brew, the beer that will be filling them. This will ensure that the barrel does not dry out or grow bacteria or mold over a prolonged idle period waiting for your beer. This is less critical for spirit barrels, but wine or beer barrels can quickly turn acetic if stored without being rinsed. There will always be another opportunity to procure a barrel—do not buy one until you are prepared to fill it.

When a freshly dumped barrel arrives, you can rack beer into it immediately. However, there is always a chance that the barrel may leak no matter how recently it was emptied. This probability increases the longer the barrel has been empty. The only way to be absolutely sure a barrel is watertight is to fill newly acquired barrels completely with water. If this is not possible, put three to five gallons (around 10–20 L) of water into the barrel and roll it to check for the appearance of damp spots on the exterior. Avoid the risk of contaminating clean areas of the brewery by dumping used water outside that area. Be advised that while a few brewers pressurize partially-filled barrels to check for leaks, this is a risky and potentially deadly practice. Even with less than 14 kPa (just a few psi) of pressure, barrels can and will rupture, causing major injury or loss of life. It is simply safer to use another method.

Even if the barrel was recently emptied, you may still want to rinse it with water to reduce the residual wine or spirit character before filling. You should rinse barrels that were filled with beer or wine immediately after emptying to reduce the opportunity for *Acetobacter* growth, unless you are going to refill them within a day. Ron Jeffries of Jolly Pumpkin offers the following advice:

> *We often clean then fill our "new" barrels with water. This will show us any leaks and often swell the wood to a point where the barrels no longer leak within a few days. Of course you will lose a little of the whiskey flavor, but not too much. If you are very concerned by this you can refresh your barrel by pouring a liter or two of your favorite [spirit] back in the barrel, rolling the barrel a bit, then dumping."*[18]

Flushing a barrel with carbon dioxide also suffices as a short term storage solution.

Dried out wood is not the only cause of leaky barrels. Phil Burton of Barrel Builders in St. Helena, CA says that wood-boring beetles are a pest common to certain regions. Oak barrels left outside during the late spring and early summer will sometimes exhibit the telltale symmetrical hole they create to lay their eggs. While thankfully borers will not spread to filled barrels, having a few holes is enough to transform a new barrel into a messy sieve. There are products that can be applied to the barrel to prevent these pests from attacking, and correctly sized wood spiles can be used to repair their holes, but the best option is to prevent the bugs from gaining access to empty barrels or they will spread.

Rather than going through the effort of rehydrating a barrel, you can instead keep it hydrated. If the timing of pickup and brewing requires your barrel to sit empty for more than a couple of weeks, especially if the humidity is low, consider filling it with water laced with a combination of citric acid and potassium metabisulfite. The citric acid lowers the pH, making the metabisulfite more effective at preventing microbial growth.

For each gallon of water it takes about 0.25 oz (2 g/L) of potassium metabisulfite and 0.15 oz (1 g/L) of citric acid.[19] Dissolve the chemicals in a small amount of warm water, and then fill the barrel part way with cool water. Add the holding solution, and then top-off with more cool water to ensure it is evenly mixed. Test monthly, topping off the barrel with more water and chemicals as needed. The holding solution will leach out oak character from the barrel, so the best option is to keep the barrel filled with beer if you can (unless your intent is to mellow the character of the wood).

The staff at the Lost Abbey swears by burning a sulfur stick/wick inside a barrel.[20] But never burn one in fresh spirit barrels because the alcoholic vapors can combust![21] This method addresses the microbial issue, but does not keep the wood hydrated. To keep the barrel sanitary, a fresh wick must be burned every couple of months. When you are ready to fill the barrel you will still need to rinse it and check for leaks.

Transferring to Barrels

It is important to determine in advance how you are going to empty a barrel before you fill it, because once the barrel is full of beer it becomes much more difficult to move or modify. Unlike other fermentors you do not need to sanitize a barrel with heat or chemicals. Any *Brettanomyces* living in the wood from a previous wine or beer will only add to the unique flavor of the beer aged in that barrel. Barrels can be used for primary fermentation or secondary aging; your choice will depend on your souring method and what sort of flavor you want the finished beer to have. For more information on the choices see Chapter 5.

Moving beer into barrels after primary fermentation is the norm for American brewers, but there is at least one compound, furfurylthiol, created from the interaction of yeast enzymes and components in the wood during primary fermentation, that contributes a flavor likened to roasted coffee.[22] Belgian lambics are fermented entirely in oak, as are many of the American spontaneous fermentation projects currently underway. Anchorage brewing is one of the only American breweries whose beers never ferment in stainless steel. However, in my experience the flavors derived from fermenting with oak (rather than aging) are comparable to standard fermentors.

Cleaning Between Uses

After emptying out the beer, a barrel can be reused immediately to age another batch. While you can simply refill the barrel, cleaning the wood first is generally advisable. The gentle slope of the barrel and rough texture of the wood will cause trub to settle all over its interior. If allowed to build up over multiple batches, the presence of so much yeast can lead to autolysis by-products building up in excess of what *Brettanomyces* benefits from, resulting in off-flavors. There are brewers who suggest that aggressive cleaning with hot water is needed to minimize *Acetobacter*, although these brewers are often allowing their barrels to sit empty for days or weeks between fills. In my experience, if you are draining and refilling the same day, vigorous cleaning is not required. If you do use hot water to clean the barrel, do not worry about killing the microbes responsible for souring the beer, because they can live deep enough into the wood where they are protected.

A quick cool water rinse will do an adequate job of removing trub. Follow that with a few gallons of hot water between 120°F and 130°F (49°C–54°C). Roll it around, dump, and repeat until the water runs mostly clear. Rinse the barrel thoroughly to avoid leaving behind cooked yeast cells (which can contribute off-flavors). Breweries with extensive barrel programs usually invest in a barrel washer, a specialized piece of equipment that sprays hot water around the interior of the barrel to remove more of the buildup. They can be somewhat expensive (hundreds of dollars), and are not necessary for small-scale operations. Large barrel washer models include a rack to hold the inverted barrel for a few minutes while the sprayer ball does its job, whereas others require the user to hold the wand in the barrel. In addition to reducing manual exertion, a barrel washer more effectively removes beerstone, restoring permeability to the wood.

Altering your barrel cleaning regime is one of the techniques at your disposal to produce beers with the desired acid profile. For example, Belgian Flemish reds tend to be aged in foeders that are scraped clean, and that highly permeable surface is part of the reason for their above-threshold acetic acid. Cantillon adds sharp stainless steel chains and hot water to their barrels, using a machine that rotates the barrel like a gyroscope, as well as steam cleaning.[23] Other lambic breweries have different regimes, for example, Brouwerij Boon uses hot water, and 3 Fonteinen employs steam.[24] These different cleaning regimes are one of several factors that determine the acid profile of a lambic. MacGyver-minded homebrewer Levi Funk has rigged his own barrel steamers with a pressure cooker,[25] but a steam cleaner is a simpler option. With the reasonable price of suitable barrels from wineries and distilleries, rather than trying to rejuvenate the interior, I recommend you buy replacement barrels after a few batches if you feel that any lack oak character.

Rather than relying on heat and pressure to clean barrels, some brewers use hydrogen peroxide-based cleaner. The standard rate for peroxide-based cleaner is 12 oz. in 2 gal. (0.36 kg in 8 L) of warm water for a 55 gal. (208 L) barrel. After agitating the barrel to clean it, repeatedly rinse it out with warm water, and then dissolve 6–8 oz. (0.17–0.23 kg) of citric acid in 2 gal. (7.6 L) of water to neutralize the alkaline cleaner. Finally, rinse with clean water to remove the citric acid before filling with beer.

Storage

Choosing where you want to position your barrels is a long-term decision. This is especially so if you do not have a forklift—once you pick a spot for the barrel that is where it is going to stay until it is emptied, so choose wisely. A single 60 gal. (227 L) barrel filled with beer weighs more than 600 lb. (270 kg), so check that your floor is capable of supporting the weight before filling the barrel. Having a floor that will not be affected by minor spills or leaks is smart as well, because it is difficult to clean under barrels.

Commercial barrel racks are available from specialty barrel product retailers and minimize pressure points that could eventually result in cracked staves. Metal barrel racks are generally designed to be stacked, making them a good choice if you have limited space in which you want to fit a large number of barrels. Remember not to stack barrels unless you have a forklift with which to move them around, because once you fill the barrels on top any lower barrels are trapped. Many brewers' stacks only go three or four barrels high, although I have heard of some going as high as six.

You can build an inexpensive barrel rack out of a wooden shipping pallet by removing the slats and cutting curved slots to cradle the barrel. One pallet can comfortably hold two barrels if you cut the slots far enough apart. Just remember that if you plan to siphon the beer out of the barrel you will need to get the barrel a foot or two (about 0.5 m) off the ground. For most small-scale situations, however, the simplest option is ground-level barrels with a pump to transfer the beer.

The most rudimentary configuration is to place a barrel directly on the floor with pieces of wood on either side to prevent it from rolling, but this does put a large amount of pressure on the center staves. If you want to take advantage of vertical space it is possible to stack barrels, pyramid-style, as Cantillon does. Using this arrangement, Cantillon stacks a maximum of two layers of pipes, with a single layer of smaller barrels on top. Four wedges of wood chocks beneath each of the barrels prevent them from shifting and better distributes their weight; it is especially difficult to remove the barrels on the lowest level for draining or cleaning. If you want to stack barrels using chocks, a suggested form is an isosceles triangle with long sides of 5 in., a short side of 3 in., and 2 in. thick (12.7 × 7.6 × 5.1 cm).[26]

Fermentation and Sampling

If you are filling a barrel with beer fermented under pressure, it is helpful to leave 2–3 gal. (8–11 L) of head space initially, because the rough interior surface can cause foaming. If you are performing primary fermentation in the barrel, or adding anything fermentable (e.g., fruit, honey) to the beer at the same time it goes into the barrel, then 5 gal. (18.9 L) of head space should be adequate. In any of these cases, top-off the barrel with reserved beer after the kraeusen recedes.

There is no reason for a freshly emptied barrel when used right away, or one kept hydrated, to leak when it is filled with beer. If you do notice a small leak after filling, the wood should swell to stop the leak in fewer than 48 hours. An application of keg lube can hold the liquid in while the wood takes time to swell, but is generally unnecessary. After the leak stops, clean the area where beer escaped with no-rinse sanitizer to prevent mold from growing. Ron Jeffries gives an honest assessment of running a brewery devoted to barrel aging: "Many of our barrels will seep a bit now and again throughout their life, it seems we are constantly moving little buckets from under one rack to another. A little loss, but not too much. Just part of the fun of barrel aging!"[27] Applying melted paraffin wax is a more extreme measure to consider if the leak does not show signs of stopping after two days. There are even more drastic steps available, such as inserting a wedge of wood, or even coopering to fix the problem.

As a beer ages in a permeable barrel it will slowly evaporate through the wood (the "angel's share" as distillers so eloquently put it). This causes an empty head space to form, which allows the wood at the top of the barrel to dry and open up gaps between the staves, the start of a vicious cycle. There are brewers who see this as a major concern. At a minimum, ensure that your barrel is completely filled initially—starting with a half-filled barrel is asking for serious trouble. Humidity is another thing Jeffries suggests keeping an eye on, although Michigan is not especially dry so he has not invested in humidity control himself,[28] unlike at other breweries (Russian River in California being one example).[29]

Tasting your sour beers as they age is an important practice, but you do not want to be pulling samples every week (although it is tempting). Keep a clipboard next to each barrel to record key pieces of information like fill date, gravity, pH, and tasting notes. This will make it easier to keep track of what flavors the microbes in each barrel contribute, and the length of time it takes for beers aged in them to reach a stable gravity.

To take samples from barrels and carboys, use a wine thief through the bunghole. Always sanitize the thief between samples from barrels or fermentors if you are trying to maintain separate cultures. Pulling samples in this way does introduce a small amount of oxygen and does disrupt the pellicle briefly, but, especially for impermeable fermentors, this is usually not enough to cause problems.

Foeders and some large horizontal barrels come with stainless steel sample ports/cocks. There are several different models, but most operate in a fashion similar to a *zwickel*. Sample ports are available that can be installed in any barrel, but the cost and effort is usually not justified. If you want to install one, avoid the less durable wooden models. If you are installing a sample port in a standard-size wine or spirit barrel, ensure that the spigot does not require a nut be installed on the interior. The spigot can of course be detached and moved to a new barrel should you ever want to get rid of the initial barrel.

At Russian River, Vinnie Cilurzo pioneered the technique of drilling a hole with a 7/64 in. drill bit half to three-quarters of the way from the top of the head (end cap) of each barrel. Such a small hole will not harm the structural integrity of the barrel. Cilurzo warns that it is hard to tell whether the small hole is drilled out all the way until there is beer in the barrel to see if a stream of beer comes out. As a result they have started drilling the hole when the barrel is filled with water to ensure the hole is drilled correctly.

To plug the hole Cilurzo buys two sizes of McMaster-Carr® Type 316 stainless steel nails: the 4D size, 1.5 in. long (product ID #97990A102); and the 6D size, 2 in. long (#97990A104).[30] Cilurzo uses the smaller nail to plug the hole, keeping an extra in his pocket just in case he drops the one removed from the barrel. He keeps the larger nails on hand as insurance in case a hole gets bored out and beer starts leaking around the smaller nail (although this has not happened yet).

Sometimes Cilurzo uses barrel wax (gate tallow) around the nail after pulling a sample, but regrettably they do not sell this wax in homebrew sized quantities.[31] Russian River has not experienced a nail blowing out, because the hole is a snug fit. Anchorage Brewing uses a similar system, but brewer Gabe Fletcher decided to insert a stainless steel screw instead of a nail for added peace of mind.[32]

This technique allows samples to be pulled quickly and sanitarily. Because the bung is not removed it minimizes both the oxygen that enters the barrel and disruption of the pellicle. When beer exits the barrel without a way for air to displace it a partial vacuum is created that can slow or stop the flow. This makes it easier to control the flow by loosening the bung and is a valuable method for breweries with many barrels, separate cultures that they do not want to intermingle, or those with concerns about acetic acid production.

Barrel Aging for Homebrewers

If you do not have the wort production capacity, or the desire to fill an entire standard-sized barrel as a solitary homebrewer, get a group together. Rather than trying to coordinate a brew day, it may be easier if everyone agrees on a recipe to brew in advance and brings their share to fill a barrel on the given day. After aging, everyone participates in bottling and gets to take home the same percentage of the batch that they put in. The hardest part of this is getting a group of passionate homebrewers to agree on a recipe!

Our small group in Washington, DC has had two barrels going for five years. Our strategy has been to give a general framework for the recipe, allowing brewers to select their own brewer's yeast, base malt, and crystal malt. To keep things simple we do not add fruit, spices, or dry hops to the barrel, allowing each member to add extra ingredients to their portion if desired once barrel aging is complete. The work of packaging several hundred bottles of beer in a day is reasonable when you have eight people divided into three teams: one team racks beer out of the barrel, and mixes in yeast and sugar; at the same time the two other teams fill and cap/cork bottles. In the span of about four hours we are able to drain the barrel, bottle 16 or so cases (the rest goes into kegs and carboys), and then refill the barrel with the next batch.

Make sure the terms are clear to everyone involved before getting the barrel and starting the project. What is expected of each member? What happens if someone moves away while the beer is aging? How are replacement members selected? Will beers be screened before going into the barrel?

If you have the space, find a way to get a full-sized barrel. Talk to your local homebrew club or homebrew shop to try to find enough people to join the project. It is safest to plan to have one extra batch brewed (e.g., 13 batches of 5 gal. each for a 60 gal. barrel, or 12 batches of 20 L each for a 220 L barrel), because many homebrewers tend to yield slightly less fermented beer than their target volume.

I realize that not every homebrewer has the space or capacity to fill a barrel this large. For those people who for whatever reason cannot manage a big barrel, there is a huge range of homebrew-sized barrels available, ranging from a few quarts or liters to volumes approaching full size. Nano-distilleries and home winemakers are other possible sources for small used barrels.

Freshly coopered small barrels have the same drawbacks as any brand new barrel, and their higher surface-to-volume ratio only intensifies these issues. As a result, you will need to age several clean beers in a small barrel for short periods of time before a sour beer goes in. Alternatively, you can age a quick succession of sour beers, before moving each of them to a neutral fermentor until they are ready to blend and package.

A high surface-to-volume ratio and thin staves also means that small barrels let in proportionally more oxygen and lose more beer to evaporation than larger barrels. Additional oxygen can lead to both oxidation and acetic acid production, so look for signs of these early. Transfer to an impermeable fermentor if the character threatens to become too intense, or coat the exterior with paraffin wax following homebrewer Levi Funk's advice on his *Funk Factory* blog.[33] For the first few uses, excess oxidation and evaporation may not be an issue because of how quickly oak character will be achieved, but it can become a concern with repeated usage. The smaller the barrel the more this will be a concern, so get the biggest barrel that you can handle. Otherwise, homebrew-sized barrels should be cared for using the same techniques as for full-size barrels.

Emptying Barrels

Once the flavor and final gravity of a barrel-aged beer indicate that it is ready for packaging, the only challenge remaining is transferring it out of the barrel. This is especially challenging if fruit or hops were added directly to the barrel, because of the increased chance of a blockage or inadvertently transferring sediment to the bottling equipment. As a result there are several breweries, such as Cascade Brewing and New Belgium, that wait until the beer has finished barrel aging before blending into a stainless steel tank where other ingredients can be added more easily.

If the barrel is elevated above floor level on a rack, a siphon can empty it. Gravity is especially effective for a solera method barrel, even if it is on the floor, because it is never drained completely. While siphoning is easy and inexpensive, draining 60 gal. (227 L) of beer with a standard 5/16 in. (0.8 cm) interior diameter racking cane will take an hour or more. If you do not have a pump, at least invest in a 5/16 in. (0.8 cm) auto-siphon. The few breweries that rely on siphoning usually lift the barrel to be transferred with a forklift to accelerate the rate of flow.

Most brewers rely on self-priming pumps, which expedite the process and allow for transferring out of floor-level barrels rapidly. March® pumps are the most popular type for small-scale brewers because they are heat and food safe and relatively inexpensive, although they require practice to prime and operate smoothly. Peristaltic pumps can sometimes be obtained inexpensively secondhand from laboratories. Most brewers keep a second pump and tubing exclusively for sour beers because they are not completely confident in their ability to sanitize the interior of the pump.

If removing beer through the bunghole, attach a metal fitting to the end of the tubing that is hanging in the barrel. An L- or U-shape is especially useful for reducing the amount of trub sucked up. When transferring beer out, lower the tubing into the barrel until it starts to capture trub, and then raise it slightly until the beer runs clear. I often rack the first beer pulled from the barrel onto fruit because the trub will have another chance to settle out before packaging. If you work with a lot of barrels, it may be worth investing in a Bulldog Pup, or Rack-it-Teer. These stainless steel contraptions allow you to push the beer out of the barrel with CO_2 pressure, which has the added benefit of minimizing oxidation. Use caution when transferring a fruit beer under pressure to avoid clogging the tubing with fruit, causing the barrel to burst (see also Chapter 2).

At Russian River, rather than use a siphon or pump to remove beer from barrels with fruit in them, the brewers drill a 15/16 in. (2.38 cm) hole in the head of the barrel at the six o'clock position prior to filling with beer. A new, unused Belgian cork (the same ones they insert into their bottles) fits perfectly in the hole while the beer ages. It took practice to master the technique, but the brewers have learned to quickly remove the cork and push the tubing into the hole without losing much beer (it is worth practicing with a water-filled barrel first). The tubing used by Russian River, from McMaster-Carr (#5231K944), has an outside diameter of 15/16 in. (2.38 cm) and inside diameter of 11/16 in. (1.75 cm), which is wide enough to not be clogged by any spent fruit that flows out with the beer. The tubing deposits the beer in a strainer, which catches large chunks of fruit. From there the beer is pumped to the blending tank.[34]

Other Fermentors

If you are not going to age your beer in a barrel, there are several alternative fermentors to consider. Most sour beers need to age for so much longer than standard ales that factors usually of minimal importance, e.g., the amount of oxygen that diffuses through the walls of the vessel, become consequential. The permeability of glass, plastic, and metal are not affected by their hydration (as wood is), so completely filling these fermentors is not essential in the same way it is for barrels. However, the larger the head space, the more oxygen will be allowed in each time you remove the lid or bung to pull a sample.

Stainless Steel

The advantages of stainless steel fermentors are that they are easy to sanitize and impervious to oxygen. With the right cleaning and sanitation regime it is safe to ferment both clean and sour beers in the same tanks, but most brewers are reluctant to tie up a conical for months with a single batch. That is not to say that you cannot perform primary fermentation in them before moving the beer into barrels for extended aging. The few breweries that do produce sour or funky beers fermented completely in stainless steel tend to do so with speedier methods, like 100% *Brettanomyces* fermentation, pre-boil souring, or only for lower gravity beers, like Berliner weisse. While the metal itself is scratch resistant and easy to sanitize, it is best practice to have two sets of fittings to ensure that they do not transfer any souring microbes to a clean beer.

Aging in kegs rather than barrels gives these beers microbial complexity without the added wood notes that accompany their barrel-aged equivalents. This is an easy way to start playing with souring microbes without contaminating the rest of your equipment. For homebrewers, Cornelius ("corny") kegs are a good choice for aging sour beers on fruit or dry hops, thanks to their wide openings and the ease of purging them with CO_2. However, the secondary fermentation under pressure creates carbonation issues, as additional CO_2 generated by the *Brettanomyces* builds up and makes dispensing the kegs difficult. Closely monitor the rise of pressure in the keg to ensure it does not reach a dangerous level.

Glass and Plastic Carboys
The classic glass carboy can hold aging sour beer with good results. Their biggest advantages, compared to other fermentors at the same price point, are that no oxygen can get in and they are easy to sanitize. When you have to move them be especially careful, as no one wants a floor covered with broken glass and year-old sour beer. While there are purpose built products available to reduce the effort and danger of moving carboys, many homebrewers swear by placing each carboy in its own plastic milk crate. While my preference is to avoid glass, I do have several small glass jugs to store 1 gal. (3.8 L) experiments. These allow me the flexibility to sour a smaller amount of beer or try out a new fruit, hop, or spice without risking an entire batch.

Plastic carboys are one of the best options for homebrewers, or commercial brewers looking to run small-scale experiments. One advantage to plastic carboys is they have a much lower likelihood of breaking than glass carboys. They also have a wider opening, which offers greater convenience for getting fruit or hops in and out. They may let a negligible amount of oxygen in, but opening the stopper once will let in more air than months of aging. I age most of my sour beers in plastic carboys because I have been happy with the results. Even after 18 months, I have not tasted oxidation or acetic acid. If you avoid scratching the interior, plastic carboys can ferment both sour and clean beers without cross contamination. However, if you are able to keep two sets of fermentors, doing so is much better.

Plastic Bucket

I have yet to age a sour beer in a high-density polyethylene (HDPE) plastic bucket. The most common concern cited is that the high permeability of the plastic allows in too much oxygen, but I have tasted several homebrewed sour beers aged in them that have not been objectionably acetic. To determine the maximum amount of acetic acid produced in parts per million (ppm), you can multiply the oxygen permeability of your fermentor in cc of oxygen per liter of beer per year (cc/L/y) by 2.7 (this is assuming that all of the oxygen is converted into acetic acid).[35] Raj Apte found that Flemish reds range from 1,500–2,500 ppm acetic acid.[36] According to these numbers you would need to age in a vessel that lets oxygen in at a rate of 239 cc/L/y for three years to reach 2,000 ppm acetic acid. For reference, the plastic of a 5 gal. bucket has a slightly lower oxygen diffusion rate, about 220 cc/L/y.[37]

However, the biggest concern with buckets is not the amount of oxygen that diffuses into the beer through the plastic, but rather the amount that could flow in if the lid is not sealed completely (which is difficult to ensure). An improperly sealed lid will allow the free exchange of gases, which can lead to an exceedingly acetic beer in a short time, a change that can be hard to detect before it is too late.

Buckets are not without advantages, like the wide opening that allows better access to the beer for adding fruit or dry hops. They are also easy to store stacked and they are reasonably priced. They can be used without issue for primary fermentation because the carbon dioxide production purges oxygen, but it is best to avoid them for long-term aging of sour beers (or of any beer for that matter).

Amphora

This ancient style of clay pot is being used experimentally to age a batch of Belgian lambic at Cantillon. Head brewer Jean Van Roy was inspired by Italian winemakers, who were aging their spontaneously fermented wines in similar vessels with excellent results. The amphorae were first soaked in water, and then filled with lambic in 2012. It will take time before anyone knows how the flavors produced by these 53 gal. (200 L) vessels will compare to the well-used barrels that serve as fermentors for most of Cantillon's batches.[38]

In 2012, TRiNiTY Brewing Company (Colorado Springs, CO) collaborated with Black Fox Brewing on Little Death Ride, a Mayan-inspired

Amphorae at Brasserie Cantillon. (© Brasserie Cantillon)

beer that was aged on clay in an attempt to "lend somewhat of a musty and dry character as if it were created in clay pots," according to Jason Yester, TRiNiTY's brewmaster. Additional starches, proteins, flavors, and textures came from corn, beans, and squashes in the grist; further flavors were contributed by later additions of wild cinnamon, cacao nibs, peppers, and annatto seeds. Yester ferments his Farmhouse Series with an evolving blend of saison yeast strains and *Brettanomyces*. For example, a recent pitch consisted of 70% WY3726 (Farmhouse Ale), 20% *Brettanomyces* Drie, and 10% WY3711 (French Saison).[39] TRiNiTY often crops and repitches from mixed fermentations, allowing the blend to evolve. Fermentations are not restrained, and have occasionally run as hot as 118°F (48°C)! Yester says, "A lot of brewers are all about control and precision and I'm all about 'choose good things and put them into the beer' and then let the beer have its own attitude or personality."[40]

Closures and Airlocks

In addition to the oxygen that permeates through the walls of the fermentor, you will also need to consider the permeability and seal of the bung and airlock. The bunghole of most barrels snugly holds a size 10½ Plasticoid Rubber Stopper, but test yours before filling.

For carboys, there is a wide range of bung designs and materials. The high permeability of the Eger Products Plastisol Topper "hood" is the only one that has been shown to let in a truly excessive amount of oxygen, so take care with long-term aging if using these.[41] If you are fermenting in a bucket, where no bung is required, lightly press on the lid to check if the airlock releases the pressure, if it does not then the seal is not airtight.

Smaller production breweries and most homebrewers rely on liquid-filled airlocks to release CO_2 pressure. As long as these remain filled to the indicated line, they are effective. Brewers with larger barrel collections, or those whose souring beers are stored in a hard-to-access location, usually select waterless airlocks.

Once CO_2 production becomes sluggish some brewers switch to a hard bung, but you should be careful not to switch too early or the remaining pressure can eject the bung. This is only a safe idea in a barrel where excess CO_2 can slowly permeate the wood. Lambic producers see the change to a hard bung as an important step in the development of their beer and as a way to encourage the desired microbes to thrive.[42] Gabe Fletcher, of Anchorage Brewing, says that in his experience *Brettanomyces* produces more of its signature aromatics when it works under pressure.[43] He notices this especially during bottle conditioning, but it seems like it could also happen in the barrel with a hard bung.

Russian River uses convertible Alasco bungs. The brewers change these bungs from the waterless airlock setting to solid setting after the initial burst of *Brettanomyces* activity is completed, about three months. Previously, they would switch from vented Ferm-Rite bungs to traditional hard bungs at the same point.[44]

Waterless airlocks can be time-consuming to clean and sanitize if kraeusen foams into them, so Ron Gansberg of Cascade Brewing came up with his own unique solution. He wedges a plastic cotton swab with one end cut off between the bung and the barrel to allow CO_2 out of the barrel. If the ambient temperature falls and a small amount of air is pulled into the barrel, the cotton head of the cotton swab filters out any microbe-carrying dust. The restriction on this technique is that if there is any *Brettanomyces* or *Acetobacter* present in the beer, they will rapidly produce acetic acid when exposed to the oxygen in air.[45]

Aging on Wood

American sour beers often exhibit flavors contributed by the toasted oak of the barrel. However, I realize that barrel aging is not an option for every brewer on every batch, so if you use one of the other fermentors discussed above, consider aging on oak. Barrel alternatives are placed directly into the beer, so the amount and treatment of the wood can be customized to fit your goal for the specific beer. They are also much less expensive than even a secondhand barrel, and far simpler to use.

Oak Options

Chips. Oak chips have a high surface area and tend to contribute their character quickly. This can result in a beer going from no oak flavor to too much in a matter of weeks. They also tend to lend less complexity than other oak products. Oak dust is even worse, relinquishing its flavor in a matter of days. Your goal should be the slow release of flavors, unless you are attempting to boost the oak character quickly before packaging.

Cubes. Oak cubes (sometimes called beans) have a lower surface area, which slows the rate at which they impart their flavor. Their uneven toasting also tends to give a more complex oak character that is similar to a barrel. Around 0.2 oz. cubes per gallon (1.5 g/L) is a good place to start for a mild oak flavor in a long-aged sour beer. Boil or steam the cubes for five minutes to remove the harsh fresh oak flavors that would usually be stripped by whatever was aged in a barrel before the beer. Additional oak can be added after a few months if the wood character is not assertive enough.

Spirals and staves. Oak spirals and staves have many of the same advantages of cubes, such as slow release of flavor and high quality toast-ing, though homebrewers may find them more difficult to cope with on a small scale. Boiling spirals requires a larger pot and more water, and soaking them in a spirit requires more to cover them. For professional brewers the situation is often reversed, dealing with a few spirals is often much easier than hundreds of oak cubes. Ithaca Beer Company ages Brute on lightly toasted French oak spirals with excellent results.

Some homebrewers claim success with a technique pioneered by Raj Apte that uses a toasted oak chair leg wrapped in Teflon tape that is extended through the neck of the carboy into the aging beer.[46] The idea is that the wood allows the right amount of air into the beer to mimic the micro-oxygenation of barrel aging, and that the oak replaces the flavor from the barrel. It seems like an ideal method, but there are a few practical issues. If carbon dioxide pressure increases more rapidly than it can diffuse, the result is wort being forced out through the wood, and swelling that can crack the glass.

If you are interested in trying this technique, insert a toasted oak dowel through a rubber stopper to prevent the neck of your carboy from cracking as the wood swells. Carbon dioxide pressure will still build, so you may want to drill an extra hole in the stopper for an airlock.

There are several other schemes for getting additional oxygen into sour beers aged in impermeable fermentors, but I do not subscribe to them because there is a much larger risk of ruining a beer with too much oxygen than too little. If you have the capacity, consider aging the same beer in an oak barrel and on oak in one of your other fermentors to see which one makes the most sense for your situation and palate.

To mimic wine, bourbon, port, or brandy barrel aging, soak the oak in the alcohol of your choice for weeks or months before adding it to a beer. Avoid boiling or steaming the oak after soaking, which would remove the spirit character. Try to match the type of wood to the spirit, for example, heavy-toast American oak for bourbon, and medium-toast French oak for red wine.

For beers containing 6% ABV or higher, TTB allows up to 1.5% of the alcohol to come from "flavors and other nonbeverage ingredients containing alcohol."[47] For beers below 6% ABV, up to 49% of the alcohol content can be obtained from nonbeverage flavoring.[48] As these are "nonbeverage" the TTB is not talking about adding bourbon or tequila to your beer, but flavorings that use alcohol as an extracting agent, such as vanilla extract. If these nonbeverage ingredients provide more than the amount of alcohol permitted by TTB regulations, or you fortify your beer with a distilled alcoholic beverage, then you are required to the have the applicable federal and state licenses as a distiller or rectifier and pay the substantially higher tax rate for producing distilled spirits ($13.50 per proof gallon). Please check the current TTB regulations for current guidelines, restrictions, and information on labeling barrels with a required unique identifier.

Woods Other than Oak

While oak is the wood of choice for nearly all barrels, it is not the only option available. There are still chestnut wood barrels fermenting spontaneously fermented beer, but these are rare and like the oak barrels they are well used and do not contribute much character. Resiny palo santo wood, from which Dogfish Head had a custom-built foeder made to age Palo Santo Marron, is a nice counterpoint to darker flavors.

There are many woods that add interesting flavors, but do not have the structural properties to be turned into reliable barrels. Fruit woods, like apple and cherry, tend to add more spicy and fruity sweetness and less tannin. Maple is another option a few breweries are exploring for its sweet lumber-like flavor. One such example is Ommegang Biere D'Hougoumont, although this should not be confused with beers like Founder's Canadian Breakfast Stout, which is aged in oak barrels that previously held maple syrup.

Cigar City Brewing and the Bruery collaborated in 2011 to brew Dos Costas Oeste (Two West Coasts), a spiced saison that showcased Spanish cedar (*Cedrela odorata*), the aromatic wood that cigar boxes are traditionally constructed from. Cigar City has aged numerous beers on this wood for their Humidor series. Spanish cedar imparts an earthy-spicy flavor that head brewer Wayne Wambles describes as "white grapefruit, sandalwood, white pepper, and hints of clove." The second version of Dos Costas Oeste used grapefruit wood, which imparted a light tartness and citrus aromatics.[49] The third version was aged on lemon wood. All three versions of Dos Costas Oeste were aged in stainless steel on wood spirals.

Jester King produced the wonderfully aromatic El Cedro by taking a golden 8.0% ABV beer that had been fermented with their house saison strain and aging it with Citra dry hops and Spanish cedar spirals. After bottle conditioning with *Brettanomyces*, the result was an aroma filled with pineapple, citrus, and cedar spice.

The best option to ensure the wood is food safe is to purchase from grill and barbecue stores, which carry many interesting woods, especially online. Before you buy wood that is intended for carpentry, talk to someone knowledgeable to ensure it has not been pressure treated or doused with chemicals. If you have time, allow freshly cut wood to age for two months or more to allow volatile chemical components to escape.

These alternative woods can be used raw or toasted for adding to beer. If you want darker, toastier wood flavors, heat the raw wood in an oven or gas grill at 300°F–350°F (149°C–177°C) until the desired color and aroma are reached. The longer the wood is toasted the more of its delicate varietal aromatics will be driven off. Do not worry if the toast is uneven, as the gradation will give additional complexity. Toasting will sanitize the wood, so it can be added to the beer while still hot. Baking the wood in a low oven at 180°F–200°F (82°C–93°C) for 30 minutes is a way of heat sanitizing the wood without significantly changing its character. Boiling or steaming the wood to sanitize it will remove some of the flavor. The toast level, amount of wood, extraction temperature, and time it takes to get the ideal flavor contribution will vary with the wood and beer. Getting it right takes experimentation, but the flavors non-traditional woods can impart are well worth the investment in time. Serving a beer with wood in a corny keg is a good way to observe how the flavors evolve over time. Try small-scale experiments before deciding on a program for an entire batch.

References

1. Mario Stanga, *Sanitation: Cleaning and Disinfection in the Food Industry*.
2. Thomas Henick-Kling et al., "*Brettanomyces* in wine." 2000.
3. Chris D. Curtin et al., *FEMS Yeast Research* 7(3): 471.
4. Bruce Zoecklein and Lisa Van de Water, "Practical Monitoring and Management of *Brettanomyces*," presentation.
5. Jamie Goode, *The Science of Wine: From Vine to Glass*.
6. Adam Nason, "Odell Brewing founder on Woodcut Series and barrel-aging," quoting an interview on BeerPulse.com, June 15, 2012. http://beerpulse.com/2012/06/odell-brewing-founder-on-woodcut-series-and-barrel-aging/.
7. Lee Williams "Behind the Scenes at Odell Brewing Company, Fort Collins, CO," *Serious Eats: Drinks* blog, January 24, 2012, http://drinks.staging-seriouseats.com/2012/01/behind-the-scenes-brewery-tour-odell-brewing-fort-collins-colorado.html.
8. "Hair of the Dog Brewing Co.," Alan Sprints interview on "The Sunday Session," MP3 audio podcast, *Brewing Network*, July 31, 2011, http://thebrewingnetwork.com/shows/778.

9. "Class and Type Designation," in *The Beverage Alcohol Manual: A Practical Guide. Basic Mandatory Labeling Information for Distilled Spirits* (Washington, D.C.: Alcohol and Tobacco Tax and Trade Bureau, 2007), vol. 2, 2–5.

10. Jason Perkins, personal communication with author, October 7, 2011.

11. Terry Hawbaker, personal communication with author, September 16, 2009.

12. "Lost Abbey to Release Veritas 009," May 23, 2011, *Lost Abbey* blog, Accessed April 25, 2013. http://www.lostabbey.com/2011/05/23/lost-abbey-to-release-veritas-009/.

13. Lauren Salazar, personal communication with author, October 19, 2011.

14. Eric Salazar, personal communication with author, January 18, 2012.

15. Lauren Salazar, pers. comm., October 19, 2011.

16. Gabe Fletcher, personal communication with author, February 18, 2012.

17. Jeff Stuffings, personal communications with author, October 30, 2012.

18. Greenbrewmonkey [Ron Jeffries], August 31, 2007 (7:08 a.m.), comment on Rosie, "Oak Barrel - Is it Wet?" *ProBewer.com* message forum, August 31, 2007, http://discussions.probrewer.com/showthread.php?8835-Oak-Barrel-Is-it-Wet.

19. Daniel Pambianchi, "Solving the Sulfite Puzzle," *WineMaker*, Winter 2000, http://winemakermag.com/634-solving-the-sulfite-puzzle.

20. Tomme Arthur, personal communication with author, June 2, 2013.

21. Gordon Strong, *Brewing Better Beer: Master Lessons for Advanced Homebrewers*.

22. Harold McGee, *On Food and Cooking: The Science and Lore of the Kitchen*.

23. "Brouwerij De Keyzer," Rob Hurvitz, *roblog – Official Blog of Rob Hurvitz*, May 28, 2011, http://www.dubman.com/spooky/me/default.asp?show=1105.

24. Jef Van den Steen, *Geuze & Kriek: The Secret of Lambic*.

25. Levi Funk, "Steam Cleaning a Barrel (part 3)," *Funk Factory* blog, January 22, 2012, http://www.funkfactorygeuzeria.com/2012/01/steam-cleaning-barrel-part-3.html.

26. *WineMaker*, Wine Wizard, Feb/Mar 2005.

27. Greenbrewmonkey [Ron Jeffries], August 31, 2007 (7:08 a.m.).

28. Ron Jeffries, personal communication with author, September 26, 2011.

29. Vinnie Cilurzo, personal communication with author, June 7, 2013.

30. Vinnie Cilurzo, quoted in comment, jmg, December 24, 2011 (8:37 p.m.), comment on Woolsocks, "Hole for 'Vinnie Nail'," *ProBrewer .com* message forum, December 23, 2011, http://discussions .probrewer.com/showthread.php?23357-Hole-for-quot-Vinnie-Nail -quot&p=74332#post74332.

31. *Barrel Builders, Inc.*, website homepage, last accessed March 17, 2013, http://www.barrelbuilders.com/.

32. Gabe Fletcher, pers. comm., February 18, 2012.

33. Levi Funk, personal communication with author, October 31, 2012; "Paraffin waxing a barrel," *Funk Factory* blog, February 21, 2012, http://www.funkfactorygeuzeria.com/2012/02/paraffin-waxing -barrel.html.

34. Cilurzo, quoted in comment, jmg, December 24, 2011 (8:37 p.m.), comment on "Hole for 'Vinnie Nail'," *ProBrewer.com.*

35. Inspired by a post by "Baums" on the *Burgundian Babble Belt*:
    O_2 = 32 g/mol
    Acetic acid = 60 g/mol
    It takes one molecule of O_2 to produce one molecule of acetic acid, therefore,
    $60 \div 32$ = 1.875 g of acetic acid per 1 g O_2.
    1 cc of O_2 weighs 0.00143 mg
    0.00143×1.875 = 2.68 mg acetic acid
    2.68 mg/L = 2.68 ppm.

36. Jeff Sparrow, *Wild Brews: Beer Beyond the Influence of Brewer's Yeast.*

37. Ibid.

38. "Back to the Future," *Cantillon*, last accessed April 25, 2013, http:// www.cantillon.be/br/3_22.

39. "Catching Up with Trinity Brewing - An Interview About All the Upcoming Plans and Releases," Eric Steen, *Focus on the Beer* blog, interview, June 11, 2012, http://www.focusonthebeer.com/2012/06 /catching-up-with-trinity-brewing.html.

40. Jason Yester, interview with Michael Tonsmeire and James Spencer on "Sour GABF," MP3 audio, *Basic Brewing Radio*, October 18, 2012, http://traffic.libsyn.com/basicbrewing/bbr10-18-12sourgabf.mp3; "Trinity Brewing Co.," Jason Yester interview on "The Sunday Session," audio podcast, July 17, 2011, http://thebrewingnetwork.com /shows/775.

41. Erich Gibbs, "Measurement of Oxygen Transfer Rates for Carboy Closures and Air Locks," (BetterBottle, a division of High-Q, Inc.), November 10, 2011, http://www.mocon.com/pdf/optech/Closures%20-%20Oxygen%20Passage%20Study.pdf.

42. Vinnie Cilurzo, Yvan de Baets, and Jean Van Roy, "Barrel-Aged Sour Beers from Two Belgian's Perspectives," panel interview, 2011.

43. Gabe Fletcher, pers. comm., February 18, 2012.

44. Vinnie Cilurzo, personal communication with author, February 22, 2012.

45. Ron Gansberg, personal communication with author, June 13, 2011.

46. Raj Apte, *Lactic Acid Beverages: sour beer, (milk), and soda.* Accessed March 17, 2013. http://www2.parc.com/emdl/members/apte/GingerBeer.pdf.

47. Use of ingredients containing alcohol in malt beverages; processing of malt beverages, 27 C.F.R. § 7.11(a)(2) (Jan. 3, 2005).

48. The TTB regulations give an example: "A finished malt beverage that contains 5.0% alcohol by volume must derive a minimum of 2.55% alcohol by volume from the fermentation of barley malt and other materials and may derive not more than 2.45% alcohol by volume from the addition of flavors and other nonbeverage ingredients containing alcohol." Use of ingredients containing alcohol in malt beverages; processing of malt beverages, 27 C.F.R. § 7.11(a)(1) (Jan. 3, 2005).

49. Joey Redner, Wayne Wambles, Patrick Rue, Tyler King, "Califlorida: A Tale of East Coast/West Coast Collaboration," presentation at SAVOR, Washington, DC, 2011, *Craft Beer Radio*, MP3 audio, 2011, http://www.craftbeerradio.com/savor/savor2011.html.

ADDING FRUITS AND VEGETABLES

10

The sensation of biting into a piece of ripe fruit is one of my favorite things about summer. Naturally bright, acidic flavors and complex aromas express the season in taste and smell. Fruit enhances complexity and should complement, rather than conceal, the aromatics produced in the souring process. Conversely, adding unappealing or mediocre quality fruit will not improve the flavor of your beer.

Vegetables have an equally long history of use in brewing, but not the same natural affinity with sour beers. Most vegetables are not characteristically sour, so their flavors do not mesh as seamlessly with acidity. There are a couple of exceptions, like rhubarb, but for the most part vegetables are at their best when they play a supporting role. On the other hand, many vegetables contain complex carbohydrates that can provide sustained nourishment for the souring microbes, rather than the quick sugar rush received from fruit.

Fruits

Crusading American brewers are benefiting from and expanding on the lead of their Belgian counterparts. Adventurous American artisans have not been constrained either by classic styles or by the traditionally limited range of fruits used in Belgian lambics. The resulting delicious sours feature a wide array of base beers and fruits: a few of my favorites include Russian

River's Consecration (Belgian dark strong with dried Zante currants), Captain Lawrence's Rosso e Marrone (dubbel with Zinfandel and Merlot wine grapes), and New Glarus Brewing's Enigma (a tart brown with sour cherries and elusive warming spice).

Most fruits will work well when paired with the right beer, but berries (e.g., blackberries and raspberry) and stone fruits (e.g., sour cherry, apricot, and peach) are the most versatile and reliable. Wine grapes (e.g., Muscat and Cabernet Franc) are especially interesting, because the aromatics

A glass of homebrewed sour ale aged on Cabernet sauvignon wine grapes.

that grapes impart to beer are lighter and fresher than their undiluted profile in wine. All of these fruits offer a good balance of acidity and sweetness, as well as persistent aromatic compounds. In contrast, the character imparted by the flesh or juice of certain fruits, especially oranges, is changed by fermentation, making them taste stale and unpleasant in large amounts.

The specific fruit variety will have a large impact on the flavor and color of the finished beer. The results can be unexpected at times, for example, Allagash Brewing Company found that even 2 lb./gal. (0.24 kg/L) of pale-fleshed Montmorency sour cherries did not turn their Coolship base beer into the expected shade of bright red.[1] Sour cherries (often sold as pie cherries) are favored because of their bolder flavor compared to dark sweet cherries. A few brewers blend the two in an attempt to approximate the flavor and color contributed by the Schaerbeek cherries traditionally added to kriek (cherry lambic). Dave and Becky Pyle have found that the color of fruit beers is far too important to many homebrew judges, to the point that they have added a touch of red food coloring to their kriek and saw a marked increase in judges' perceptions of fruit flavor.

Other fruits may take more trial and error. Many brewers seem to believe that the flavor of peaches does not come through in beer, but the Lost Abbey's mythically delicious Yellow Bus was aged on just 1 lb./gal. (0.12 kg/L) of heirloom white peaches grown by one of their

Bottles of Cascade Brewing Blueberry. (Courtesy of Cascade Brewing Company)

employees.[2] Picking fruits that are particularly aromatic and flavorful is a good rule, so, if possible, sample the fruit before you buy.

Local fruit is usually the best choice, because it is allowed to ripen on the plant. I am partial to blueberries, which are native to North America, and have such a distinct flavor. Blueberry-flavored sour beers are rapidly gaining popularity: Cascade Brewing's Blueberry, Upland Brewing Co.'s Blueberry Lambic, and Ithaca Beer Co.'s LeBleu are a few of the commercial examples. With a rate of just 0.8 lb. blueberries/gal. (0.1 kg/L), LeBleu has a spicy and woodsy flavor that does not bear much resemblance to the flavor of fresh blueberries.[3] Upland uses a higher ratio of fruit to beer than most other breweries; three months spent on 3–5 lb. whole fruit/gal. (0.4–0.6 kg/L) infuses their lambics with a prominent fresh fruit flavor (blueberries fall near the middle of that range).[4] Cantillon's Blåbær Lambik is not brewed with what we refer to as blueberries here in America; instead Cantillon added the European native bilberry at a rate of 1.9 lb./gal. (0.2 kg/L) for their first batch, enough to impart an intense fruit flavor.[5]

If you really want to get local, you can forage for wild fruit native to your area. In addition to the lure of gleaning free produce, indigenous fruit adds to the *terroir* of the beer. Persimmons are commonly found in moderate climates and make an interesting choice, but many have skins that are exceedingly tannic (especially before the first frost) so be careful how you use them. Upland adds about 5 lb./gal. (0.6 kg/L) of locally foraged Indiana persimmons to their Persimmon Lambic.[6] The result is a well-integrated, sweet, citrusy fruitiness that does not overwhelm the base beer. Wineberries, huckleberries, mulberries, rose hips, beach plums, crab apples, and paw paws are all options, as are wild versions of more commonly cultivated fruits. On a commercial scale, sourcing an adequate supply of foraged fruits is tricky. Gabe Fletcher, of Anchorage Brewing, initially planned to add several hundred pounds of salmonberries to a batch of funky dark ale, but when the supplier fell through he decided to add lactic acid bacteria and extend the aging to replace the tartness of the berries, creating Anadromous.[7] Wherever you live, take a walk and get to know what is growing in your neighborhood, but remember to check with the landowner before picking fruit from their property.

Fresh orange, lemon, grapefruit, and lime zest all work well. Before harvesting, clean the skin with warm water to remove dirt and wax. Rasp style graters/zesters, like those from Microplane®, are the best tools for removing the essential-oil-rich colored zest while leaving the bitter white pith beneath. Hill Farmstead Brewery added orange zest at a rate of 0.07 oz./gal. (0.5 g/L) to a beer fermented by *Brettanomyces claussenii* that resembled a tripel, to create Mimosa.[8] The Lost Abbey steeped lemon slices and black tea in a low-alcohol pale sour to create Veritas 008. Adding only the zest of citrus fruits is an effective approach to enhance the brightness of other fruit beers, or contribute complexity to an otherwise bland batch. The Lost Abbey includes orange peel in Red Barn Ale, which serves as a component of several of their sour beers.

On the other end of the local spectrum, for most of us, are tropical and subtropical fruits. There are only a few sour beers that feature exotic varieties. In the Jolly Pumpkin–Maui Brewing collaboration, Sobrehumano Palena 'Ole, the tropical notes from yellow lilikoi (passion fruit) were balanced nicely by the underlying graininess of the malt and earthiness of the *Brettanomyces*; the fruit was a seasoning rather than the star, as Jolly Pumpkin's use of flavorings usually are. Upland adds about 5 lb./gal. (0.6 kg/L) of peeled kiwi fruit to their Kiwi Lambic; kiwi fruit's indistinct fruitiness requires adding more fruit than for most of Upland's other sour beers, and even at this high level

Jolly Pumpkin–Maui Brewing collaboration Sobrehumano Palena 'Ole. (© Irene Tomoko Sugiura)

the fruity complexity it adds is only subtle. Guava (as used in the Bruery's Otiose), mango, or papaya would be good choices as well.

With Florida's hot climate and prodigious local fruit growers, it is no surprise that fruit-forward Berliner weisse has become a local specialty, the so-called "Florida weisse." The style is usually traced back all the way to the first batch of Passionfruit and Dragonfruit Berliner Weisse that Jonathan Wakefield brewed on Cigar City Brewing's pilot system in 2011. The neon purple color and saturated fruit flavor helped launch both J. Wakefield Brewing and the annual Berliner Bash on the Bay event.

Cambridge Brewing Company's Double Happiness was created by brewmaster Will Meyers in celebration of his own wedding. It started as a strong blonde ale aged in French oak Chardonnay barrels with *Brettanomyces*.[9] Halfway through a year of aging, Meyers added whole lychee fruit. New Belgium Brewing also uses this subtropical Chinese fruit in Tart Lychee (a blend of Felix, strong golden lager, and lychee juice), which is also lightly spiced with Vietnamese cinnamon before packaging. New Belgium pasteurizes the beer before adding the fruit, but subsequently adds lager yeast to reduce the simple sugars contributed by the fruit before bottling.[10]

Fresh exotic fruits are not always available, and when they are they may be of questionable quality. Lack of fresh specimens is not always a negative. Homebrewer Sebastian Padilla, living in Arizona, told me that he tried everything he could to brew a great sour beer with fresh prickly pear cactus fruit (*tuna*), but each time the beer had a "green vegetable" flavor. He was not happy with the results until he added prickly pear concentrate. Padilla suggests adding 2.5% of the concentrate by volume for subtle results.[11]

San Antonio based Freetail Brewing Company's Fortuna Roja, a sour made with prickly pear, has a huge fruit-forward flavor right after release. Head brewer Jason Davis says the key to getting good flavor from the prickly pears is to blanch and then peel them to remove the "green/pickly/vegetal flavor." Fortuna Roja is aged in wine barrels with a little more than a pound of Texas prickly pears per gallon (0.12 kg/L).[12]

In addition to the flavor advantages, removing the peel is essential for another reason according to Peter Felker, a cactus scientist with D'Arrigo Bros. "There are mucilage ducts and mucilage in the peel. When fermented, methanol can be produced which evidently arises from the 6-methoxy on the glucuronic acid of the pectin/(mucilage)."[13] Methanol is extremely hazardous, so if you choose to add prickly pears, they must be blanched and peeled first.

New fruit hybrids are released onto the market by horticulturists each year. For example, Russian River's Compunction is aged on 0.5–1.0 lb. pluots (a plum-apricot hybrid) per gallon (0.06–0.12 kg/L) for nine months to a year.[14] After trying several varieties of plum-apricot hybrids, brewmaster Vinnie Cilurzo noticed that a higher percentage of apricot parentage had a direct correlation to the tartness of the resulting beer. This is not surprising considering Cantillon's Fou' Foune (lambic aged on 3.3 lb./gal. [0.4 kg/L] of apricots)[15] is consistently one of the most acidic beers available.

Rather than waiting for the development of a hybrid of your two favorite fruits, you can simply add a blend of fruits to your beer. Multiple fruits should be employed for a variety of situations: to soften the character of a "loud" fruit like raspberries, to make an expensive fruit go further, to add color, or to contribute aromatic nuance. Cherries and raspberries are a classic duo (e.g., 3 Fonteinen's Hommage and the original version of Cantillon's Rosé de Gambrinus), but any combination that works well in a pie or smoothie is fair game.

Dried Fruits

Dried fruits can be overlooked by brewers, but there are several excellent sour beers that include raisins, dates, or figs. Flavors imparted by the most common dried fruits tend to meld best with strong, dark base beers that contain similar flavors from specialty malts or dark sugars. Cambridge Brewing's Benevolence (raisins and dates), the Cigar City–Bruery collaboration ISO:FT (dates and fresh guava), and Lost Abbey's Cuvée de Tomme (raisins and fresh sour cherries) are dark sour beers that use dried fruit to admirable effect.

Russian River employs less common dried fruits, sour cherries and Zante currants, in two of its mainstay barrel-aged beers, Supplication and Consecration, respectively. They buy the fruit in 25 to 30 lb. (11.3–13.6 kg) blocks, breaking them apart with a (clean) cement mixer before adding the fruit to the barrels by hand.[16] Dried fruit has several advantages over fresh: it is of consistent quality, easy to store, and does not contain as much diluting water. When buying dried fruit, pay attention to whether oil is listed as an ingredient. The 0.4 lb./gal. (0.05 kg/L) of dried sour cherries in Russian River's Supplication contribute their characteristic flavor, but the small amount of oil sprayed onto them reduces head retention. Fortunately, Russian River was able to find a supplier of oil-free currants for Consecration. If your only option for dried fruit is one that contains oil, give it a spray with Star San solution or fruit wash, followed by a quick rinse in chlorine-free water.

Vegetables

Sour beers flavored with vegetables are far less common than those flavored with fruit, but several excellent examples have been produced. For their Zwanze 2008, Cantillon aged their two-year-old lambic on 2.5 lb. rhubarb/gal. (0.3 kg/L).[17] They recreated the beer for Zwanze 2012, which had a bright fruity snap provided by the rhubarb. The flavor was much more delicate than you would expect from a similar amount of fruit. According to the brewer, Jean Van Roy, the flavors contributed by the rhubarb fade fairly quickly as well.[18]

Jolly Pumpkin has added several different vegetables to their limited release beers. For example, kale was added to the mash of Biere de Goord, and Living Stones Wheatgrass IPA received about a half-gallon (1.9 L) of wheatgrass juice along with the aroma hop addition.[19]

There are several plants that while botanically fruits (i.e., seed-bearing) are considered vegetables in culinary terms. Pumpkin is the most common of these added to sour beer, including those by Allagash (Ghoulschip), Alpine Beer Company (Ichabod 2007 and 2009), New Belgium (Kick, which also included cranberries), Jolly Pumpkin (La Parcela), among others. The 2007 batch of Alpine Beer Company's Ichabod had 100 lb. (45 kg) of halved and roasted pumpkins added to the mash for the 12 bbl. (14.1 hL) batch. It was fermented with a custom blend of abbey ale yeast, *Pediococcus, Lactobacillus,* and *B. lambicus.* This was followed with three 29 oz. (0.82 kg) cans of pureed pumpkin added to each freshly drained wine barrel along with ground spices (13 sticks of cinnamon and 7 nutmeg seeds). As the beer aged in the wine barrels the pumpkin was stirred a few times with a wine thief to improve extraction—by the time it was ready to bottle the puree had settled. The 2009 batch of Ichabod was more pumpkin-forward with twice as much pumpkin added, but brewmaster Pat Mcilhenney said that he plans to double that amount again the next time he brews a sour pumpkin beer.[20]

Pumpkin is not the only squash added to sour beer. Other winter gourds intended for cooking instead of carving are more flavorful alternatives. Root vegetables are another option, such as sweet potato, as used by the Bruery in their 100% *Brettanomyces* Autumn Maple. Baking these starchy vegetables to caramelize their sugars and soften their flesh before adding to the beer will deepen flavors and make them easier to work with.

Starch-containing adjuncts are sometimes added to the mash to give the enzymes from the malt an opportunity to convert them into fermentable sugars. For sour beers, however, adding starchy plants to the boil is a good way to contribute unfermentable carbohydrates to the wort that will feed the souring microbes in the long term. You can even add the cooked (baked or steamed) and pureed vegetable to the aging beer, as Alpine Beer Company did for Ichabod over the course of three months for their 2007 release, and over eighteen months for 2009.[21]

Chile peppers are another culinary vegetable (it is technically a fruit) whose addition to sour beer has not been well explored. Ithaca created Hot and Sour Szechuan Ale by blending their pale sour Brute with a Tabasco® sauce, barrel-aged smoked porter named "Tastes Like Burning (Ralph Wiggums Revenge)". Reviews describe it as extremely spicy, a character that some people enjoyed and others detested.[22]

A subtle addition of chile peppers can work well in the right beer, after all, tartness and heat are at the heart of both Mexican and Thai cuisine. Homebrewer Dan Fogg shared a wonderful 100% *B. claussenii* fermented pale that he flavored with mango and dried chipotle peppers. The fruitiness from the fermentation and added fruit really popped when combined with the heat of the smoked and dried jalapenos.[23] Dark beers may benefit from the subtle fruitiness of dried peppers like ancho and guajillo, which typically have a low Scoville rating. Remember that dried chilies are often coated with a film of oil, which is disruptive to head retention. Like spices, toasting in a dry pan blooms the flavor of dried chilies.

Fresh chilies are an option as well. Upright Brewing created a version of their light, tart year-round beer Four, called Fatali Four, which is aged with *Brettanomyces* and *Lactobacillus* in a variety of barrels (including gin and Pinot noir) and infused with locally grown fatali chile peppers. Founder and brewer Alex Ganum praised this African variety for its "fruity/tropical" flavors, subtle heat, and lack of vegetal character. Each 59 gal. (223 L) barrel ages with 0.5–3.0 oz. (14–85 g) of fresh, ripe, chopped peppers for a couple of months,[24] providing a clean heat and complementary burn that only lasts momentarily.

Choosing the Right Beer

Any type of sour beer is a good candidate for fruit—the dilemma is determining which fruit best suits a particular beer. Fruit tends to be most beneficial for batches that are not adequately acidic or complex. If a beer tastes terrific on its own, I generally skip the fruit addition and package it as is. Adding fruit is not a remedy for an off batch, because the cost of fruit often equals or exceeds that of all the other ingredients combined. In fact, if the off-flavor is derived from your fermentation, the sugars in the fruit may intensify the problem by feeding the offending microbes.

The easiest way to select fruit is to taste a beer to assess the fruit character already provided by the fermentation. For example, many sour red beers start with hints of cherry from the caramel malt, so it takes only a small dose of actual cherries to boost this impression. If your beer was aged in a wine barrel, add wine grapes to enhance those notes, as Captain Lawrence does with 1 lb./gal. (0.12 kg/L) of Muscat grapes in Cuvee de Castleton.[25] Dark beers, especially those with Special "B," often have flavors reminiscent of raisins, which are enhanced with the addition of dried fruit. A root vegetable can complement a beer that has earthy aromatics from *Brettanomyces.* Brighter pale sours work best with delicate fruits like apricots, peaches, citrus, or melons.

Another approach is to add a fruit that balances the character of the base beer. In addition to dates, the Bruery–Cigar City collaboration ISO:FT was aged on guava. The slight tropical note added by the guava brightened the beer, making it more drinkable without dominating the flavor. Finding favorable pairings requires imagination, but drinking the base beer while smelling and tasting a variety of fruits is often enlightening.

If you are stuck, consider how fruits are added to cuisine and pair them with a beer that mirrors those flavors. Let your palate, not tradition, guide your experimentation when it comes to selecting which fruit or vegetable to add. At the same time you are selecting your fruit variety, you should also be determining the desired flavor intensity.

Appendix A contains a chart with suggestions for the sorts of beer that meld with many types of fruits and vegetables. The chart also contains suggested amounts, commercial examples, and the approximate sugar content.

Adjusting for Processing and Quality

During the growing season, local fruit from a farmers' market, roadside stand, or a pick-your-own is your best choice for both eating and brewing. Almanac Beer Co. in San Francisco, California has reimagined the farm-to-table restaurant concept to create "farm-to-barrel" beers for their Farmer's Reserve series. The label for each release highlights the varieties (e.g., Cara Cara oranges, Crimson Baby nectarines) and the local farms where they were sourced.[26]

High-quality ripe fruit offers the best flavor, especially for subtler fruits like peaches and nectarines. Adding (or freezing) fruit at the peak of ripeness is fundamental to getting good fruit flavor into a beer. Ideally, the fruit added to beer should be slightly overripe, when the sugars and aromatics will be at their highest levels. Signs to look for include slightly wrinkled skin, soft flesh, and strong fruity aroma. As an added bonus, fruit that is about to turn is often inexpensive, but be sure to either add it to a beer or freeze it immediately.

In the past, fresh fruit was routine for Belgium's best lambic brewers, but this restriction created issues with production when fruit beers comprise a major part of output. With fresh fruit only available for a small part of the year, brewers were forced into compressed schedules each fall. As a result, even the purists, like Cantillon, now often rely on high-quality fruit that arrives frozen. Freezing does not damage the delicate aromatics, and ice crystals rupture the cell walls of the fruit to allow yeast and bacteria easy access to the sugars within. It is best to either allow the fruit to thaw before mixing with the beer, or have a way to warm the beer to prevent its temperature from dropping far enough to shock the microbes.

When fresh or frozen fruit is not an option, good quality pureed, juiced, concentrated, or dried fruit can work in a sour beer, either alone or in combination. The flavors of these processed options tend to be slightly less robust, but the complexity inherent in the sour beer itself can compensate for any shortfall. Choose products that contain only your target fruit. Highly processed fruit forms (e.g., preserves and marmalade) only lend themselves to already flavorful beers where a restrained fruit flavor is the goal. For instance, raspberry preserves give a singular cooked character that works particularly well in roasty beers.

Because of its higher surface area, less puree is required than whole fruit to get the same degree of fruit flavor. On the other hand, more juice is generally needed than whole fruit because the flavorful skins have been removed. Concentrated juices often list the dilution required to reconstitute them; use this information to judge how much to add. Cambridge Brewing Company has had good results with sour cherry concentrate in Cerise Cassée.[27] Similarly, dried fruits tend to be added in smaller quantities as their flavor is intensified by the removal of water. For processed fruit that has had the seeds or pits removed, remember to account for the higher amount of flavorful flesh or juice by unit weight when compared with the whole fruit.

Some brewers treasure the character that cherry pits add to beer, often described as being woody or almond-like. To replace the pits removed from processed cherries, some brewers add a small amount of crushed sour cherry pits (sold as mahlab for Middle Eastern cooking). Dogfish Head Brewery added mahlab to Midas Touchstone (they suggest 0.2 oz./gal. [1.5 g/L]), a sour cherry variation on Midas Touch.[28] Be careful of this, however, as the TTB has set a limit of 1 ppm of cyanide, a compound which cherry pits contain naturally.

Cherries are not the only fruit with a flavorful pit; Cascade Brewing creates Noyaux by aging a blonde quadrupel on toasted noyaux nuts (apricot kernels) and raspberries in a white port barrel. Cascade has also released the more nut-focused Marzipan, created by aging a single oak barrel of "Northwest style" sour tripel on 4.5 lb. (2 kg) of toasted and crushed noyaux nuts for a month.[29]

Fresh vegetables tend to be more consistent because ripeness is less of a factor in their flavor. For La Parcela, Jolly Pumpkin adds 5% pumpkin to the mash. Canned pumpkin can work well and has a more prominent squash flavor than fresh pumpkins.

The ideal amount of fruit to add depends on several factors: first, the variety, quality, and ripeness of the fruit; second is the base beer itself and the amount of flavor desired in the final product. The stronger and darker a beer is the higher the ratio of fruit to beer required to achieve the same flavor impact. If unsure about how much fruit flavor you want in a batch, a good option is to produce a concentrated fruit beer from a portion of your base beer, using a high ratio of fruit to beer. Once you are ready to package, create measured blends of the fruited beer and the plain base beer. Select your favorite ratio and scale to determine which component is the limiting factor. Leftover beer can be bottled as is, or saved for a future blending session.

Avoid any temptation to flavor your beer with fruit extract. When you consider the amount of time that goes into making a sour beer, it is not worth compromising quality to save a couple of dollars or a little effort. Extracts tend to provide only a single note out of the complex symphony of flavors available from real fruit. Artificial fruit flavor is fine if you are satisfied with a gimmicky beer, but do not waste a base beer that has spent years aging.

Adding Fruit to Beer

Most of the traditional lambic producers wait until a beer has been fermenting for at least a year before adding fruit. This schedule allows the brewer or blender to taste and pick barrels that would benefit from the addition of a given fruit, and leave those that would be better consumed as straight lambic or blended into gueuze. Because few American brewers or homebrewers can afford the time and space to simultaneously age a large number of sour beers, many add fruit to a beer at the same time it is transferred to the secondary fermentor or barrel. Instead of making a single base beer that is flavored in various ways, most American brewers choose to sour several different beers, some that always have fruit added and others that are left plain.

Fruit can be added at various points throughout brewing and fermentation, but, as a general rule, the later you add fruit the more of the fresh aromatics will carry through into the finished beer. Many of the esters in the fruit will be changed if exposed to the heat of the boil, yielding a cooked flavor. Anything that remains is then volatilized by escaping CO_2 during primary fermentation. The Lost Abbey includes grapes in the base beers of two sour beers (Framboise de Amorosa and Cuvée de Tomme), but for the raisins added to Ten Commandments they apply high heat to contribute another layer of flavor. Originally, the raisins were blackened in a large pot over a turkey fryer and then deglazed with wort before being pureed with an industrial stick blender.[30] Increased production now calls for a propane-fueled blowtorch to singe the raisins before they are steeped in hot wort.[31] Adding dried fruits to the boil works well for subtle flavor additions that may not be immediately identifiable. For more assertive additions using dried fruit, add it directly to the aging beer later in the process, as Russian River does when transferring their beers into barrels.

Adding fruit to already soured beer ensures that the wild yeast and bacteria will be the dominant organisms. This allows them to consume the greatest portion of the fruit sugars, resulting in greater acid and ester production. After a beer has aged for six months to a year it should taste at least mildly sour, which indicates that the lactic acid bacteria are hard at work. For their fruited beers, Captain Lawrence often waits until they have already been in the barrel for close to a year before adding fruit.[32] While this is an advantageous time to add fruit flavor-wise, the low pH results in the microbes taking two to three months to consume the included sugars.

Barrels are a popular choice for combining fruit and beer, because they allow the beer to keep extracting oak character as the microbes work on the fruit, but there is more mess involved in getting the fruit in and later reclaiming the beer and cleaning the barrel. If you are adding the fruit to a fermentor with a small opening, like a carboy or barrel, a wide-mouthed funnel makes the job easier.

In the case of larger batches, rather than dealing with fruit in multiple barrels, the brewers at Cascade Brewing transfer soured beer out of barrels and into a large stainless steel tank where fruit can be easily added and subsequently removed through the manway.[33] If you follow this method, taste all the components before blending to avoid accidentally including a heavily acetic or otherwise off-tasting beer. For a homebrewer, a

The staff at Upright Brewing adding peaches to barrels of Fantasia. (Courtesy of Jeff Freeman, Upright Brewing Company)

Cornelius (corny) keg would be a good alternative because it has a large opening that allows easy access to the beer.

For berries and other fruits small enough to fit through the neck of a carboy or bunghole of a barrel, you should remove the stems then wash, freeze, and vacuum pack the fruit in plastic bags until a beer is ready for it. It is essential to freeze before vacuum packing, because the vacuum packer starts to squeeze the juice out of the ripe fruit before it seals. When the beer is ready, I let the fruit thaw in a sanitized fermentor for a couple of hours to avoid causing thermal shock to the microbes, before racking the beer on top of the fruit.

Slice large fruits when fresh (or prior to freezing), removing the pit or stone, then muddle with a sanitized spoon or paddle before transferring beer onto them. Leave on edible skins to provide additional flavor as well as tannins, which enhance the mouthfeel. Leaving the skins on also saves some effort and avoids the loss of fruit flesh incurred in removal. Remember to thoroughly wash the fruit to remove dirt, pesticides, and wax.

When brewing a clean fruit beer, many brewers worry about adding unpasteurized fruit on the cool side because of the presence of wild microbes living on the fruit. However, this is not a major concern with sour beer because various non-*Saccharomyces* microbes are already at work. The sugar loving yeast and bacteria present on the fruit skins may even prove to be beneficial for some beers. In fact, there are breweries that add fruit to the beer at the same time the cultures are pitched to allow the wild microbes living on the skin the best chance to contribute to the fermentation. Upright added 100 lb. (45 kg) of local peaches to each wine barrel of Fantasia along with the saison yeast, *Lactobacillus*, and *Brettanomyces*.[34]

It is important to leave the beer on the fruit for at least two months due to slow fermentation. While there is a minimum, there is no maximum time a sour beer can sit on fruit; I have gone as long as a year without issue. However, the fruit flavor will begin to slowly fade around six months, so bottle as soon as the gravity stabilizes. Contrary to brewhouse lore, I have never witnessed the entire flesh (let alone the pit) of a fruit dissolve during aging.

Correcting Flavor Intensity

After aging, there is the opportunity to add more fruit if the flavor is not potent enough for your tastes. The Lost Abbey created Framboise de Amorosa from their dubbel, Lost and Found, brewed with American two-row, wheat, medium and dark English crystal, Special "B," chocolate malt, dextrose, and raisins to 1.065 OG (16°P).[35] The brewers' goal for the original batch of Framboise de Amorosa was to infuse a beer with enough raspberries so that the flavor met the expectation created by the aroma (overcoming a common complaint about raspberry beers). The flavor of raspberries tends to fade quickly, so the Lost and Found base beer spent six months aging in red wine barrels, before the brewers added more than 1 lb. raspberries/gal. (0.1 kg/L). After three more months of aging they added more raspberries, and at packaging they added a final dose of 100% raspberry concentrate.[36] For subsequent batches, the brewers took a simpler route by making a single addition of fruit and fruit concentrate to the aging beer.[37]

On the other hand, if the fruit flavor is slightly too strong, you may choose to separate the beer from the remaining fruit flesh and allow it to age further, either in a fermentor or bottles. Alternatively, you can blend with a similar beer (or ideally the same) that was not aged on fruit. New Belgium produces many of their fruit beers by blending clean fruit beers with one of their two strongly acidic wood-aged beers to achieve the desired balance. For example, Dark Kriek was a blend of 35% Felix (their pale sour base beer) and 65% dark clean beer aged on cherries.[38] This approach retains sweetness, but requires that the souring microbes be killed (New Belgium accomplishes this with flash pasteurization). Blending and kegging unpasteurized beer can produce a reasonable facsimile, but the result needs to be kept cold and consumed quickly. New Belgium also blends with a beer purchased from another brewery; Transatlantique Kriek is a combination of equal amounts of Brouwerij Boon Kriek and a golden lager brewed at New Belgium.[39]

Bullfrog Brewing Co.'s Black Cherry Bomb started as their house stout aged in a bourbon barrel with cherry puree. When the beer was ready, head brewer Terry Hawbaker kegged a portion of the beer to serve and replaced that volume with a combination of fresh stout and cherry juice.[40] This simple version of a solera allowed the brewpub to serve a small amount of their sour fruit beer on a more regular basis.

Many brewers add fruit to a portion of a batch while leaving the remainder without. This practice yields two beers for the effort of one and provides an opportunity for interesting comparisons or blends. The easiest technique is to wait until the beer is ready to package, then just the right amount can be transferred onto fruit so that the fermentor is completely filled. Sometimes the fruited half is preferable, other times the plain half, but either way it allows the brewer to learn which beers benefit most from fruit additions.

The acids found in fruit are different from the lactic and acetic acid that is produced by *Lactobacillus*, *Pediococcus*, and *Acetobacter*. The two most prominent types of acid found in fruit are malic and citric, both of which can give a sharper impression of acidity than lactic acid (although not as sharp as acetic). Like the malolactic bacteria *Oenococcus oeni*, many lactic acid bacteria have the ability to convert malic acid into lactic acid and CO_2, but they also produce additional lactic acid from the sugars in the fruit; the *Oenococcus*, however, does not.

Impact of Fruit on Alcohol Content

One of the biggest misconceptions about adding fruit is that it always raises the alcohol content of the beer. In fact, fruit rarely increases potency significantly, and for strong beers it often reduces the final alcohol content compared to the base beer.

Many people mistakenly assume that the amount of sugar alone determines how much gravity the fruit will add. In practice, the fruit also contains water, which dilutes both the alcohol and sugar already in the beer. In fact, most minimally processed fruits have a similar sugar content to standard density wort, between 1.040–1.060 SG (10°P–15°P). This does not apply to concentrated juice and dried fruit, because most of their water content is removed during processing. An exception is wine grapes, which often have a sugar content of 1.092 SG (22°P) or higher. (Note that winemakers generally measure sugar content with the Brix scale, which is essentially equivalent to Plato.)

If you are interested in calculating the change in a beer's alcohol after the addition of fruit, see the calculation presented in Appendix B.

Final Thoughts

Adding fruit will not fix a sour beer with off-flavors or provide balance to excessive sourness, but it can improve a beer that has not soured enough or is lacking aromatics. Acids in the fruit will lower the pH, while simple sugars will feed the lactic acid bacteria, causing them to produce more acids. *Brettanomyces*, if present, will ferment some of the added sugars and create alcohol, CO_2, and flavorful by-products. Even when brewing a clean fruit beer, consider increasing the acidity by souring part of the mash, or adding winemaker's acid blend to taste at packaging.

Adding fruit to sour beers has produced several of my best batches of homebrew and a few of my favorite commercial beers. By following the advice in this chapter you will be able to produce beers that can quench your thirst on a warm summer day, or store a little piece of summer to brighten a cold winter night when you are weary of drinking imperial stouts and barleywines.

References

1. Jason Perkins, personal communication with author, October 7, 2011.
2. "Brew Stories - Lost Abbey - Yellow Bus with Tomme Arthur," interview by Dan Sullivan, posted by Brewdies, YouTube video (5:01), September 2, 2010, http://www.youtube.com/watch?v=lHKFEc_lr3c.
3. Jeff O'Neil, personal communication with author, December 21, 2011.
4. Caleb Stanton, personal communication with author, October 4, 2012.
5. Geerts Filip. "Cantillon Blåbær Lambik," *Belgian Beer Board*, March 9, 2007, Accessed December 15, 2013, http://belgianbeerboard.com /index.php?option=com_content&task=view&id=137&Itemid=88888994.

6. Stanton, pers. comm., October 4, 2012.

7. Gabe Fletcher, personal communication with author, February 18, 2012.

8. "ICU Measurements . . . Advice From Hill Farmstead," Shaun Hill, interview by Brandon Jones, *Embrace the Funk* blog, May 14, 2012, http://embracethefunk.com/2012/05/14/icu-measurements-advice-from-hill-farmstead.

9. "Double Happiness: Barrel aged wild ale with lychee fruit," archive page, *Cambridge Brewing Co.*, last accessed March 18, 2013, http://cambridgebrewing.com/beer/description/double-happiness.

10. Eric Salazar, personal communication with author, January 18, 2012.

11. Sebastian Padilla, personal communication with author, July 29, 2010.

12. Jason Davis, personal communication with author, June 14, 2012.

13. Peter Felker email message to Jason Davis, communicated to author, September 19, 2012.

14. Vinnie Cilurzo, personal communication with author, June 28, 2008.

15. "Fou' Foune," *Cantillon,* last accessed March 17, 2013, http://www.cantillon.be/br/3_107.

16. Vinnie Cilurzo, Keynote presentation at National Homebrewers Conference 2007, *Brewing Network*, MP3 audio, July 7, 2007.

17. "Cantillon Zwanze 2008," Aschwin de Wolf, *Lambic and Wild Ale* blog, May 27, 1010, http://lambicandwildale.com/2010/05/27/cantillon-zwanze-2008.

18. "Brasserie Cantillon," Jean Van Roy interview on "The Sunday Session," *Brewing Network* audio podcast, May 8, 2011, http://thebrewing network.com/shows/751.

19. "Wheatgrass IPA," [featuring Ron Jeffries] YouTube video (01:50), posted online, ChiefLiaison, February 14, 2012. https://www.youtube.com/watch?v=a4IVMHqSYww.

20. Pat McIlhenney, personal communication with author, December 5, 2011.

21. Ibid.

22. "Ithaca Hot and Sour Szechuan Ale," *RateBeer,* last accessed December 15, 2013, http://www.ratebeer.com/beer/ithaca-hot-and-sour-szechuan-ale/118917.

23. "Time to Spice it Up!" Daniel Fogg, *City Brewer* blog, May 13, 2009, http://citybrewer.blogspot.com/2009/05/time-to-spice-it-up.html.

24. Alex Ganum, personal communication with author, September 19, 2012.

25. Scott Vaccaro, personal communication with author, June 13, 2011.

26. "Introducing Farmer's Reserve No 3 & 4," *Almanac Beer Company* blog, May 3, 2013, accessed December 15, 2013, http://www .almanacbeer.com/2013/05/introducing-farmers-reserve-no-3-4.

27. Will Meyers, personal communication with author, November 14, 2011.

28. Sam Calagione, *Extreme Brewing: An Introduction to Brewing Craft Beer at Home.*

29. "Cascade update: Noyaux, Cerise Nouveau, Smashed Pumpkin Rum Barrel Sour Pumpkin," Adam Nason, *Beerpulse.com*, October 30, 2012, http://beerpulse.com/2012/10/cascade-update-noyaux-cerise -nouveau-smashed-pumpkin-rum-barrel-sour-pumpkin.

30. Tomme Arthur, "San Diego in Da House—Tomme Arthur," presentation, Washington, DC, June 19, 2007.

31. Lost Abbey and Port Brewing, "The Making of Ten Commandments Ale," YouTube video (03:34) posted online July 18, 2011, http://www .youtube.com/watch?v=3a4rLxUZlL4.

32. Scott Vaccaro, interview on "The Sunday Session," audio podcast, August 31, 2008.

33. Ron Gansberg, personal communication with author, June 13, 2011.

34. Upright Brewing, "Fantasia & Blend Love."

35. "Lost and Found Abbey Ale," *The Lost Abbey* blog, last accessed April 25, 2013, http://lostabbey.com/beer/lost-and-found-abbey-ale.

36. Tomme Arthur, quoted by Sage Osterfeld (media liaison, Lost Abbey), in discussion with author, December 12, 2011.

37. Tomme Arthur, personal communication with author, June 1, 2013.

38. "Dark Kriek," New Belgium Brewing, beer bottle label, 2009.

39. "Transatlantique Kriek," *New Belgium Brewing*, last accessed March 18, 2013, http://www.newbelgium.com/beer/detail.aspx?id=fc099739 -4419-4714-86db-5aafc83e56e0.

40. Terry Hawbaker, personal communication with author, September 16, 2009.

41. Dave and Becky Pyle, personal communication with author, April 18, 2010.

42. "At Logsdon, Ales For Every Seizoen," *Hood River News*, February 18, 2012.

AGING AND BLENDING

11

Traditional sour beer production is largely spent waiting for the microbes to complete acidification and esterification, punctuated by a couple of key decision and action points. Once the wort is brewed and all of the microbes have been pitched, your next task is to provide your microscopic comrades with tranquil working conditions. You will need to check their progress only occasionally, deciding when the beer in each fermentor is ready to be blended with other batches or if it would best be packaged unmingled. While tools like hydrometers and pH meters are valuable for recording objective measurements, a trained palate is just as essential.

The Long, Slow Fermentation

Sour beers brewed with most production methods will continue to improve the longer they are allowed to age in the fermentor, up to a point. As an exception, extended aging does not dramatically improve most beers brewed with quicker methods, such as sour mashing, sour worting, and 100% *Brettanomyces* fermentations. For mixed-fermentation sour beers, under ideal conditions, acidity and complexity will continue to increase for the majority of the aging process, usually for several years. At a minimum you should wait until the gravity is stable before bottling, but aging beyond this point can be beneficial.

The ambient temperature is the most important factor to consider. The cooler end of "room temperature" is best, anywhere from 60°F (16°C) to 75°F (24°C). Even some gueuze producers are turning to temperature control for their barrel stores, for example, 66°F (19°C) is the peak aging temperature at the Gueuzerie Tilquin.[1] The higher end of the range will encourage more rapid souring and higher acetic acid production, while lower temperatures will lead to less aggressive sourness and heftier *Brettanomyces* aromatics. If you go below the low end of the range souring will progress extremely slowly, while above the high end encourages excessive acetic acid formation if any oxygen is available. These are general rules, and you will need to experiment to determine how the specific strains of yeast and bacteria in your beers respond to temperature given your choice of fermentors.

Gradual temperature fluctuations throughout the year within the suggested range is not a major concern, but you should avoid aging sour beers where they will be exposed to large daily swings. More erratic temperatures are of less concern with larger fermentors, because the thermal mass cushions the temperature swings that the beer experiences. Brewing sour beer forces you to accept many uncontrollable variables which influence the results, so it is worth addressing those that can be controlled.

The only issue with lowering the ambient temperature with air conditioning is that it also reduces the humidity. The less moisture there is in the air, the faster the rate of evaporation from barrels and airlocks. To counter this, a few breweries have installed systems that control the humidity of their barrel storage. Humidity close to 100% will effectively halt evaporation of water, but can lead to mold growth. A good balance is struck at around 70% humidity.[2]

If you allow the ambient temperature to fluctuate, a drop in temperature will cause the gas in the fermentor to contract and suck the liquid in a liquid-filled airlock into the beer. Check the liquid level in your airlocks at least once a month, and as soon as possible after large temperature drops, to ensure that they are filled to the line. Empty or under-filled airlocks are one of the primary ways that excessive oxygen gets into aging beers. If you are storing the aging beer somewhere with frequent temperature swings or where it cannot be checked regularly, then an airlock that does not rely on liquid is your best option.

The pellicle on a sour beer aging in an apple brandy barrel.

Even though sour beers are rarely highly hopped, it is still safest to minimize the amount of light to which they are exposed. Unless they are stored in a perpetually dark room, place glass and clear plastic fermentors back in the boxes they came in or cover each with a pillowcase. Opaque fermentors, like wood and stainless steel, block light and thus can be stored in direct sunlight without issue. Aging sour beers somewhere out of sight and out of mind can make it less tempting to harass them, as long as you remember to refill the airlock occasionally.

As the successive waves of microbes work, they will sometimes develop a rather unappetizing skin on the surface of the beer called a pellicle, the appearance of which is not something to worry about (unless of course your goal was to produce a clean beer). Pellicles range in appearance from slimy, to powdery, to waxy. Certain species and strains produce more substantial pellicles than others, but the presence or complete absence of any pellicle is not a sign that the flavor of the resulting beer will be better or worse. All else being equal, a thicker pellicle is a sign that there is more oxygen entering the head space. I have had fantastically sour and funky batches that only grew a light powdery covering, and terrible beers that grew huge pellicles because too much oxygen was getting into the fermentor. The pellicle does provide a measure of protection against *Acetobacter*,[3] so store your aging beer somewhere with minimal vibrations to avoid disrupting the pellicle and thus the protection.

The one type of pellicle you should be concerned about is the emergence of one that displays color other than white or beige. Black, green, and other vibrant colors are signs of mold or other undesirable microbes (unless you added fruit or dry hops, when in some cases it is apparent they are responsible for the color).

Topping-Off

One of the primary disadvantages of barrel aging is that the wood allows the evaporation of both water and alcohol from the beer. This is a particular concern if barrels are stored where there is a combination of high temperature and low humidity. As evaporation reduces the volume of beer, the head space becomes larger and allows the wood at the top of the barrel to dry, creating a larger surface area for oxygen to come into contact with the beer, which in turn spurs acetic acid production. In most cases replacing the beer lost to evaporation is not necessary, but if acetic acid production is higher than desired it is worth considering.

Try to strike a balance between the frequency and the volume of top-offs. Replenishing too often will only serve to expose your beer to more oxygen when you remove the bung. A rule of thumb is to top-off when the barrel is either more than 5%–10% empty or every two to four months, whichever is less frequent. If you complete the primary fermentation in the barrel, an initial top-off after the kraeusen settles is usually required. Cantillon started topping-off at this point in their process a few years ago and their acidity has become much softer as a result.[4]

The ideal liquid for topping-off is more of the same beer that is already in the barrel. The easiest way to accomplish this is to sour extra beer in carboys or kegs until it is needed. If you inoculated your topping-off beer with the same microbes it will not have additional sugars, which will save you one extra consideration when determining the amount of priming sugar to add. Using the same beer is not always an option, so many brewers keep a low finished gravity, neutral beer on hand to top off all of their beers. For example, Russian River will sometimes use their 100% *Brettanomyces* fermented Sanctification for this purpose, and the Lost Abbey often uses Mellow Yellow, a soured version of their pale Amigo Lager.

The best way to top-off a beer is to siphon or pump the additional beer into the barrel to minimize oxidation and disruption of the pellicle. You may want to experiment on different barrels to see if the time and effort expended is worth it for your situation. The brewers I talked to were split on whether or not they topped-off, although none mentioned any benefits to skipping it other than the effort saved.

Monitoring

The flavor of sour beers can change drastically, even years into aging. Once you are happy with the way the beer tastes, you can start checking the gravity of the beer once a month. In most cases, you should not bottle if there has been any month-to-month drop. A stable gravity is enough confirmation that CO_2 production has ceased, even with a pellicle present, but be wary of bottling a sour beer with a gravity above 1.012 SG (3°P), unless it has a high alcohol content or other extenuating circumstances.

In general, if a sour beer does not taste good then give it more time. Terry Hawbaker, then at Bullfrog Brewery, was about to dump a batch of soured honey saison, before it turned the corner after more than two years in the barrel; it became the 2008 Great American Beer Festival® (GABF) gold medal-winning Beekeeper in the Wood- and Barrel-Aged Sour Beer category.[5] With that said, many brewers encounter a batch that never turns that corner. Subtle changes can happen after packaging, but taking the beer away from oak and oxygen reduces the rate of change.

You may choose to keep a pH log as well. It is difficult to remember exactly how sour a beer is from sample to sample by taste alone. Keeping track of the pH will allow you to judge if the acidity has leveled off, possibly requiring feeding the microbes with new fermentables if the sourness is not as assertive as you would like, or letting you know in advance that blending with a more acidic beer will be necessary.

Blending

Blending is one of the most important steps in sour beer production. It is also the only skill that can ensure consistently high quality results. Unfortunately, it is also one of the most challenging skills to learn, especially from a book.

At its most basic, blending is combining multiple fermentors of the same batch of beer. This removes barrel-to-barrel or batch-to-batch variation and makes for a more uniform product. If this is all you want to do, taste all of the barrels and eliminate any that have an unpleasant flavor that cannot be blended out. For example, a beer that is too oaky can be included because the beer from other less-characterful barrels will dilute its oak character. Other problems that can be overcome with blending include: too much or too little spice, dark malt, or bitterness. However, microbes that produce an off-flavor in one barrel often produce more of that same flavor in the bottle. Do not try to blend out negative fermentation characteristics without first killing the microbes that are causing the problem.

Many brewers who do not have a complex blending procedure still produce excellent beers. However, many will also taste the blend to determine whether the acidity should be adjusted. If the acidity needs to be increased, most brewers keep on hand an "acid beer" (a particularly sour batch or barrel) to add. Similarly, some breweries add a dry *Brettanomyces*-inoculated beer to mellow acidity or soften other flavors.

Sour beer production is a craft. The steps are mostly mechanical, and as long as you understand a few basic cause-and-effect relationships you can produce solid beers with occasionally wondrous results. The true art is in the complex and artistic blending of the results. Rather than simply tweaking or standardizing, blending can be undertaken to radically change the balance and flavors of a beer. Going beyond blending batches or barrels of the same beer for consistency, there are breweries that combine a number of different beers treated in different ways to produce a unique end product that is impossible to create from a single fermentation.

The first step to blending several different beers is to coordinate several batches so they are ready to package at the same time. It continues with regular tasting of the beers to determine when they are at their peak. On blending day, decide what you are trying to create and then optimize both the quality and quantity of beer to be packaged. This is far more difficult and requires greater planning and vision than other types of blending. A good deal of the skill of blending cannot be taught. Practice every chance you get, blend bottled beers in the glass, blend your beers with those from other brewers, and try to attend blending sessions with brewers whom you respect.

Ideally, the beers available for blending will have a range of characters in terms of acidity, malt, oak, funk, and mouthfeel, amongst others. By diversifying your methods, microbes, barrel sources, or malt bills, you can ensure a variety of beers will be available to broaden your blending options. One of the advantages Belgian gueuze blenders, like De Cam Geuzestekerij and Gueuzerie Tilquin, have is that they buy wort from several breweries, which gives them a range of characters to pick and choose from when creating a blend. In addition to the hype that the collaborative American sour Isabelle Proximus generated, it was a successful beer because it was aged in barrels containing the different house microbes from each of the five breweries involved.[6] This gave more depth than would have been possible aging in barrels with microbes from any one of the breweries alone.

There are a few American brewers who are particularly skilled at the art of blending. While most of Russian River's beers are only adjusted for pH after blending barrels of the same base beer, they have released a handful of more experimental blends. Deviation IX, released for Bottleworks' ninth anniversary, was a blend of Beatification PH1 (Redemption aged in barrels previously used by New Belgium Brewing), spontaneously fermented Sonambic, Sanctification, and barrels left over from previous blending sessions (Russian River's "orphan" ale). Deviation IX was bottle conditioned with a fresh dose of *Brettanomyces.*[7]

Tomme Arthur of the Lost Abbey states only that his goal in blending is to produce the best blend regardless of the quantity. Arthur says that "less is more"—fewer barrels can often yield a better character than blending in more to boost quantity. "Always blend to taste and not to volume," says Arthur, who states that his blending process "always starts with a very well defined idea." The Lost Abbey has beer brewed and put into barrels specifically for their regular production sour beers, but smaller releases often start with a favorite barrel or two and then other beers are sought out from their extensive collection to add character. Leftovers from previous blending sessions, and also one-off projects, are often included in the Lost Abbey Veritas series.[8]

At the Bruery, blending sessions for production beers start with a review of the targeted volume to be produced. The brewers start by checking the barrel log to see what is available that is of sufficient age, and then build a list of samples to be pulled. At a minimum, both head brewer Tyler King and founder Patrick Rue are involved in blending, but as King puts it, "The more taste buds involved, the better the result will be." Depending on how much beer King and Rue are trying to blend, sometimes they will pre-mix the samples pulled from all of the different barrels from individual batches of the same beer to reduce the number of components they need to work with. Having a large number of components is one of the downsides of aging beer in hundreds of barrels, and it is one of the reasons a few breweries have turned to foeders as their production grows. King and Rue start by tasting all of the samples, moving out any that have off-flavors or are not ready. They then blend the remaining beers in equal proportions to provide a starting point. This has never resulted in the final blend, so they experiment with removing certain beers that they were not as excited about until they find their favorite combination. Beers that did not taste ready are saved for the next release, but those with a strong acetic character are thrown out along with the barrels they came from.[9]

Lauren Salazar has been in charge of the blending program at New Belgium for many years. When she first started blending La Folie, New Belgium's iconic sour brown, she would taste the beer from each foeder and write out the chemical compounds she sensed, but this turned out to be unhelpful when it came time to actually select what to blend. She decided it was more important to take actionable notes about whether or not the barrel should be included. Her current process starts with tasting all of the foeders of Oscar, the base beer for La Folie, regardless of their age. She assigns each with a letter: U ("Users," these are the best barrels), B ("Blenders," barrels with nice sour and interesting notes, great to build complexity), or W ("Waiters," these need more time and are not used). Each barrel also gets a "smiley face" (happy, sideways, or sad), which indicates how interested and excited she is about the flavors.[10]

Lauren Salazar's favorite beers receive exclamation marks, and a rare heart symbol indicates a foeder that is good enough to keg and serve as is. These unblended releases are sold as NBB Love, with the few kegs that escape from the brewery going to beer bars such as Falling Rock Taphouse in Denver, Colorado, and perhaps farther as production increases. With their ever-expanding wood cellar, New Belgium promises that NBB Love will be making more frequent appearances outside their home state. New Belgium has also released a version of NBB Love that faced a few months of additional aging in fruit whiskey barrels. These were used bourbon barrels that previously aged a mixture of fruit juice (blackberry, peach,

Leopold Bros barrels at New Belgium Brewing Company. (Courtesy of New Belgium Brewing Company)

or apple) and whiskey at Leopold Bros. in Denver. The apple is especially distinct, but Lauren Salazar prefers to focus on Oscar that was aged for one to three months in the blackberry whiskey barrels, a combination she describes as, "Char, the blackberry, that lovely vanilla, and then the weird granny smith apple, plum, cherry, that kind of mélange, that's it for me!"[11] New Belgium has more of these barrels aging a variety of experimental batches. After the first use theses barrels have contributed all of their residual fruit character, and are passed onto other local brewers such as Funkwerks (Fort Collins, CO) and Crooked Stave.

When Lauren Salazar blends, she starts by tasting all of the barrels with Eric and takes notes. Each of them combines samples, trying their best to keep track of what works. Once they find good combinations they share them with each other. Eric and Lauren do not base their blends on the analytical measures of the various concentrations of flavorful molecules; instead they rely solely on flavor.[12]

Russian River's Vinnie Cilurzo articulated the main problem facing homebrewers who do not have access to hundreds of barrels:

Blending is tough for the homebrewer because you need lots of beer to pull from. In our case at the brewery we have usually 60 wine barrels from each batch, so making a blend is easy. If you only have one wine barrel you really have nothing to blend. One thing to suggest is to make the beer in the barrel a little sourer than you actually want and you can blend un-soured/non-barrel beer to the beer to create what you want.[13]

You can build a blending cellar by saving parts of each batch in glass jugs or kegs. There are ways you can increase the number of beers available for blending: splitting batches, partnering with other brewers, including older batches that have already been bottled, and beers from other commercial breweries. Having more beers is like giving a painter more colors—if you have red and blue you can blend many shades of purple, but no matter what ratios you try it will be impossible to make green without starting with some yellow.

Blending tips:

- Taste all of the beers alone before you start blending. Evaluate the flavor and relative level of acidity for each. The best blenders are not necessarily the ones capable of doing it quickly. These beers took months or years to ferment, so work deliberately.

- Form an idea of what you are trying to accomplish before you start mixing beers. What flavor are you trying to enhance or balance? Do not expect new flavors to appear that are not found in the beers you are blending. Sometimes the combination of certain flavors and aromas will produce a unique sensation, but this is hard to predict.

- If your goal is to blend something similar to a particular commercial beer, established style, or previous batch, then it is best to have a representative example on hand to compare. For example, if you are blending something similar to a gueuze, have one of your favorites to hand as a reference while you blend. If you are trying to recreate a favorite blend, sample the original as you work. If you are drinking a beer that has been in the bottle awhile remember that its flavor has changed since it was blended (this is where good notes are invaluable).

- Blend and sample the beer at the temperature you plan to drink the finished beer. This will give you a more accurate impression of what the flavors and aromas will actually be.

- Clean your palate between samples. Water is a must, but unsalted crackers or popcorn are especially effective for cleaning the taste out of your mouth when blending sour beers.

- The easiest method is to pick your favorite beer to be the base, which will make up at least half of the blend. This allows you to focus on this beer, picking out the flavors you would like to add, enhance, or reduce.

- Start by blending two beers together and tasting the result. Evaluate a blend at each step and adjust that balance rather than trying to manipulate multiple variables simultaneously.

- Blend measured amounts of the beers together and take good notes. Once you have the ideal blend in your glass you will need to know its composition to be able to create it on a larger scale. It is easier to keep a good record when you start over with an empty glass rather than taking a sip and then adjusting.

- Use a graduated cylinder for the blending (the narrow diameter makes for more accurate volume readings); alternatively, measure by weight. A 50 g or 100 g blend is a manageable sample size and makes determining the percentages in the blend simple.

- Do not mix a younger sweeter beer with an old sour without being ready to account for the effect this will have on carbonation. Generating carbonation from blending adds an exponentially more difficult layer of complexity to blending with only minimal benefits. Skip this until you have mastered getting the flavor of your blends exactly where you want them, but if you are interested there are instructions for predicting carbonation from blending in Chapter 12.

- Be prepared to adjust the acidity of the blend by having a strongly acidic beer on hand. If you do not have an acid beer, food grade lactic acid can fill this role. In my experience, it does not add an off-flavor when a small amount is added to boost the sourness of a beer that is already tart and funky, or has other distinct flavors. Some brewers maintain a bio-reactor to produce sour wort for acidifying the mash or boil. This tart beer can also be blended into fermented beers, usually at packaging, to increase acidity.[14] In a bio-reactor, diluted wort is inoculated with a pure culture of *Lactobacillus* and allowed to ferment in its optimal temperature range. Soured wort is taken from the fermentor, which is then replenished with fresh wort on a regular basis. This method is probably impractical for most homebrewers, but the spent liquid from a *Lactobacillus* starter can be bottled and saved for the same purpose.

- Adding vinegar is an option if you want to add sharpness to the acidity. You can create your own malt vinegar (see Chapter 13), or add the commercial vinegar of your choice. In the bottle without oxygen the increase in acetic acid from the *Acetobacter* in unpasteurized vinegar will be minimal, but it is safest to pasteurize the vinegar before blending. Although, even with no live *Acetobacter*, *Brettanomyces* can still produce ethyl acetate, which some people find unpleasant even at relatively low concentrations. Acid blend (a powdered combination of malic and citric tartaric acids) works well to add brightness to fruit beers.

- When you get close to your ideal blend you may want to craft several similar blends to taste side-by-side. Tasting similar beers next to each other highlights the differences. You can also carbonate the samples with a carbonator cap. Dissolved CO_2 will change the perception of the body, acidity, and the aromatic potency. Adding carbonation reduces the amount of imagination needed to envision the finished beer.

- If it is practical, decide upon your favorite blend one day, but wait until the next to blend and package. This avoids the issues associated with over-sampling and then making a mistake, and it gives you a chance to drink the winning blend again on a fresh palate before proceeding.

- On a commercial scale, using pumps to blend by volume is the only reasonable option. For homebrewers, it is easiest to blend by weight if you have a scale with a high enough capacity. An auto-siphon is also a must for homebrewers. Hold the end of the tubing above the blend until the air has cleared out the line and the beer starts to flow (otherwise you will be oxidizing the beer as air bubbles out of the line). In either case, flush the blending vessel with CO_2 to minimize oxidation.

- Do not use an entire batch when blending for packaging. Reserve 5% of each component beer, then taste the blend and adjust the ratio as needed before packaging.

Blending can produce fantastic results, but reserve at least a small portion of each beer to bottle unblended. It is interesting to drink the blended and unblended samples next to each other. Learning how the flavors continue to evolve as the beer ages in the bottle or keg is a lifelong pursuit. The fact that highly experienced blenders can taste one of their beers at bottling and predict how much time it will need to reach its peak flavor is astonishing. If you take one thing away from this book, let it be the importance of brewing with blending in mind.

Solera Method

The solera blending method is most closely associated with traditional balsamic vinegar and Jerez sherry production. Rather than blending to taste at bottling, the solera method relies on blending during aging. A solera is a blend of liquids of various ages that is matured in either a single vessel or multiple sets of vessels. Regardless of what is being produced, nearly every commercial solera is aged in barrels, but other types of fermentors can serve the same function. The benefit of a solera is that it facilitates the regular packaging of a consistent blended product without the complexity of blending from multiple fermentors of varying ages.

When beer in the barrel is ready, a portion of it is transferred out for packaging, and then the empty space is filled with a younger beer. Traditionally, the solera is a multilayered process: older barrels are replenished with a blend of beer from younger barrels and freshly brewed beer refills the younger barrels. Technically the word "solera" only refers to the oldest barrels, the *criadera* (nursery) are the younger barrels whose content is waiting to move into the solera. In certain cases, most notably traditional balsamic vinegar, each older set consists of successively smaller barrels to account for evaporation. If you do not have room for multiple levels, a single barrel (or set of barrels) can be packaged from and then refilled with fresh beer.

Whether one barrel or many, the method creates a blend that has already aged together. This is a more organic way to blend, but it takes away control from the brewer. As a result, it may not produce beer as perfectly balanced as traditional blending, but it is much easier and allows for a more constant stream of production. From a practicality standpoint, especially for homebrewers, the solera method also means that you do not have to deal with completely empty barrels.

The average age of the blend in years will converge on the inverse of the fraction of the beer that is added each year. So, for example, if you replace half of the beer each year, the average age of the blend will eventually converge on two years. The same is true if you replace one quarter of the beer twice a year; what matters is the total amount replaced within a set period, not the timing of individual refills. The amount replaced also includes the portion lost to the angel's share. Ultimately, the amount to pay attention to for this calculation is the volume of beer added to the fermentor, not what is removed. I created a spreadsheet that calculates the age of a solera that is available to download.[15]

My friend Nathan Zeender and I share two solera barrels producing sour beer. The red wine barrel holds a pale lambic-inspired beer and the apple brandy barrel holds an orange-hued beer whose malty character is reminiscent of a Flemish red. The primary sets of microbes working in each barrel are cultures of Bugfarm from East Coast Yeast. Solera appealed to us because neither of us had a need for 30 gal. (114 L) of sour beer each year in addition to our other batches. We pull out 20 gal. (76 L) about once a year, replacing it with 22–25 gal. (83–95 L) of wort or beer to account for evaporation; eventually this will yield a blend with an average age at bottling approaching two-and-a-half years. We usually bottle 5 gal. (18.9 L) of each pull as is, and use the rest to experiment with fruits, spices, flowers, dry hops, and blending.

As your solera continues you may need to adjust its character by altering what goes into the barrel. In our case, the apple brandy barrel-aged beer was close to too sour at the first pull, so we fermented the replacement beer with brewer's yeast first, rather than refilling with wort, to reduce the carbohydrates available to the lactic acid bacteria. Alternatively, if the beer had been not sour enough, we would have used wort high in complex carbohydrates to give the microbes more to eat. If you let the beer age more than a year between pulls and plan to refill with unfermented wort, you will need to pitch fresh brewer's yeast to ensure there are enough viable cells to complete the initial fermentation.

A few of the breweries that age their sour beers in foeders, such as New Belgium, rarely drain them completely. While this process could technically be considered a solera, the real purpose is to ensure a healthy microbial culture (additional blending at packaging is still carried out).

Will Meyers, of Cambridge Brewing Company, was the first to create a beer, Cerise Cassée, using a true multi-level solera. Specifics on how this beer is brewed are found in Chapter 5.

After five years of using the same barrels to continuously ferment Cerise Cassée, Meyers started to worry about growing amounts of acetic acid and autolysis flavors. As a result of the way he initially stacked the barrels, he had been unable to remove them for cleaning. Meyers suggested that the accumulation of beerstone (calcium oxalate) on the wood over time had reduced the permeability of the oak and eventually killed aerobic microbes such as *Brettanomyces*. To remedy the problem, Meyers hit the reset button on production, packaging most of the solera-level beer after blending with 8.5%ABV clean fermented beer to reduce the acidity and boost the sweetness. He moved the beer in the criadera to a tank to allow him to clean all of the barrels, and rearrange them to facilitate individually cleaning or replacing them in the future. Meyers then refilled the solera barrels with the beer taken from the criadera, and finally refilled the criadera with fresh wort.

The production method for Cerise Cassée also causes a slow buildup of trub in the barrels, which contributes to autolysis. Using filtered or fined beer to refill the barrels, as New Belgium does, would greatly extend the time you can go between cleanings. If your equipment or target flavor requires a primary fermentation in the barrel, try sucking the dead yeast out of the barrel when pulling beer out. This is difficult, however, because the wood's gentle slope and rough texture fail to gather the trub into a neat pile at the center.

The solera method is well worth a try for those commercial brewers and homebrewers without the space or capacity to maintain multiple barrels. After the initial effort to fill the barrel, it is easy to brew enough beer for refills. You do not even need to refill the solera with the same beer each time; using a keg or carboy, homebrewers can produce evolving blends from leftover beers. Say you have extra beer from a blending session, simply combine them and let them age, pulling and replacing the next time you have surplus beer you think would mesh with the current flavor profile.

Barrels aging Cerise Cassée at Cambridge Brewing Company. (Courtesy of Will Meyers, Cambridge Brewing Company)

Creativity after Brew Day

Look at brew day as representing just one step in your creative process. The best brewers are the ones who are able to take whatever the microbes give them and make adjustments to turn out delectable finished beer. Blending takes time and patience to master, but you are not required to be a supertaster or know the name and characteristics of every flavor-active chemical to get there. Practice and passion are critical. Remember that a single batch of wort can contribute to more than one packaged beer: blend, or solera portions of the same beer, and then taste the different permutations side-by-side to judge which treatment worked best. Do not forget to take notes of the process; the last thing you want is to blend a new favorite beer and forget the path that got you there.

References

1. Jef Van den Steen, *Geuze & Kriek: The Secret of Lambic*.
2. Ibid.
3. Jeff Sparrow, *Wild Brews: Beer Beyond the Influence of Brewer's Yeast*.
4. Vinnie Cilurzo, Yvan de Baets, Jean Van Roy, "Barrel-Aged Sour Beers from Two Belgian's Perspectives," panel interview, 2011.
5. Terry Hawbaker, personal communication with author, September 16, 2009.
6. "Isabelle Proximus is Coming," *The Lost Abbey* blog, last accessed December 15, 2013, http://lostabbey.com/isabelle-proximus-is -coming.
7. "Bottle Logs," hyperlink via "Brews", Russian River Brewing Company, last accessed February 5, 2014, http://russianriverbrewing .com/bottle-logs/.
8. Tomme Arthur, personal communication with author, December 12, 2011; ibid., quoted by Sage Osterfeld (media relations, Lost Abbey), in discussion with author, December 12, 2011.
9. Tyler King, personal communication with author, October 19, 2011.
10. Vinnie Cilurzo, personal communication with author, June 11, 2011.
11. Lauren Salazar, personal communication with author, October 19, 2011.
12. "Interview with New Belgium's Lauren Salazar," interview by Luis Tovar, *Hooked on Hops*, March 15, 2013, http://hookedonhops .com/2013/03/15/interview-with-new-belgiums-lauren-salazar.
13. Lauren Salazar, "NHC: Tips and Tasting," *Basic Brewing Radio* MP3 audio, July 19, 2007.
14. Ken Belau, "Acidification in the Brewhouse," presentation archive, January 14, 2011.
15. Michael Tonsmeire, "Solera Aging Spreadsheet," Excel® spreadsheet (last updated March 23, 2013 [file name SoleraAging _Update_03232013.xlsx]), *Internet Archive*, December 5, 2010, http://archive.org/details/SoleraAgingSpreadsheet.

PACKAGING

12

After all of the time and effort spent designing, brewing, fermenting, and blending a sour beer, you should be prepared to invest that same level of care and thought when it comes to packaging. As with many of the other steps that go into producing a sour beer, there are new packaging techniques to challenge traditional approaches. As you might expect, the new ways are neither inherently better or worse.

Carbonation

If you choose to bottle condition, picking the right carbonation level is a difficult decision. Taste the beer and consider how bubbly you want it to be. Carbonation will lift aromatics, enhance the acidity, and change the mouthfeel. Despite the perception that CO_2 bubbles cause the tingle when you drink a beer, this sensation is actually created by carbonic acid from the dissolved CO_2 interacting with an enzyme (carbonic anhydrase 4) attached to sour-sensing taste buds.[1] Achieving the target level of carbonation is more challenging than in most other types of beer because of the age and range of microbes involved. Force carbonation removes the tension of selecting the target amount of carbonation in advance, by allowing you to dial in the level that most complements your beer. However, for several reasons noted below, it is not as popular with sour beers as it is with other beers.

Two classic sour beer styles, gueuze and Berliner weisse, have the highest carbonation levels of any beers (often approaching 4 volumes). High carbonation tends to increase the perception of acidity (because the dissolved CO_2 contributes carbonic acid) and gives the impression of body in otherwise thin beers. This sharp carbonation also masks complexity, however, by cleaning off the tongue before the flavors are savored. The classic styles that retain a modicum of body and sweetness, Flemish red and oud bruin, generally receive moderate carbonation. Too much carbonation can make a fuller beer taste thin and "spritzy," making them less enjoyable.

If you love the way samples of a beer taste, there is no requirement to add carbonation at bottling; there are a few brewers who leave especially long-aged sour beers still. Brasserie Cantillon Brouwerij and 3 Fonteinen each produce uncarbonated lambic (Bruocsella 1900 Grand Cru and Doesjel, respectively), while De Struise Brouwers makes an uncarbonated Flemish brown (Aardmonnik/Earthmonk). Skipping carbonation is a good option for sour beers that are especially acidic or complex, allowing the full flavor of the beer to be expressed. However, without carbonation the aroma will be more subdued, and can leave the wrong beer tasting thin and lifeless.

For most of my beers I aim for low-to-moderate carbonation (2.1–2.3 volumes) because that is the way I enjoy them. For higher alcohol sour beers, especially those with residual sweetness, I tend to go slightly lower than that. For pale, dry sour beers I will venture higher, but rarely do I aim for the intense levels of many commercial examples. Choosing the carbonation level is all about enhancing a beer's best assets, and diminishing those that are less flattering.

Bottle Conditioning

Most American sour beers are bottle conditioned, although the choice is not necessarily made solely because it produces better beer. The practical reason so many breweries bottle condition is that it isolates the microbes in the sour beer from the high-tech bottling line that packages their clean beers. For homebrewers, keeping these microbes out of your kegs and tap lines might be motivation as well. One of the most significant advantages of bottling is that the beer can be gradually sampled as it continues to evolve. It allows for greater levels of carbonation, and more complexity from the conditioning the beer receives from the mixed microbial culture. Compared with bottle conditioning a clean beer, the process for sour beers can take longer, and often requires additional aging even after carbonation is generated.

Bottles of Allagash Brewing's Coolship series conditioning.

To reach your desired level of carbonation you will need to add a fermentable sugar at packaging that the yeast will convert into CO_2. The most common way to prime a bottle-conditioned beer is with sugar. There are all sorts of sugars available for priming, but I usually opt for refined sucrose (cane, beet, table, or white sugar) because it is consistent, the least expensive, and does not impart a flavor of its own. Clear candi sugar and corn sugar (dextrose) are equally good choices, but they tend to be more expensive. Agricultural products like honey, maple syrup, and molasses are composed of many different sugars (and other compounds besides), and this means it is difficult to predict the exact amount of carbonation that a given amount will stimulate. If you want the flavor of an unrefined sugar, I recommend that you add it to the fermentor and wait for it to ferment out before priming with a pure source of sugar prior to bottling. Similarly, do not add malt-based fermentables (e.g., wort, malt extract) to carbonate sour beers. The microbes will slowly consume the dextrins provided by malt, eventually resulting in more carbonation than formulas predict. Adding a smaller amount of wort or malt extract can compensate, but will cause a long delay between bottling and full carbonation.

Fruit juice and concentrate are capable of priming a beer for natural carbonation. The same formula for priming presented later in this chapter can be utilized for fruit juice as well, but remember that most of the gravity contributed by fruit is from fully fermentable simple sugars. For several of their fruit beers, the Lost Abbey adds a small amount of 100% fruit concentrate at bottling in addition to the fruit added in the barrel. This final dose traps the more volatile fruit aromatics, which are normally driven off by fermentation.[2]

I sampled a homebrewed kriek from Dave and Becky Pyle (NHC Homebrewer of the Year 2005 winners) that got all of its cherry character from priming with 100% cherry juice; it was excellent, but had a relatively subtle fruit flavor and was on the high end for carbonation.[3] The amount of fruit juice required for carbonation is well below the amount needed to contribute a strong fruit character, so it is a technique more often used to boost the existing flavor of a fruited beer at packaging. Dave Logsdon, the founder of Wyeast Laboratories, primes both his saisons and his wits at Logsdon Farmhouse Ales (Hood River, OR) with pear juice for a subtly fruity house character.[4]

Sweetening sour beer with an unfermentable artificial sweetener has been done in Europe for decades. An example is the saccharin added to the Dutch version of Mestreechs Aajt by Gulpener Bierbrouwerij[5] (the version exported to America does not contain artificial sweetener). If you want to sweeten your beer in this way, be aware that the most common packaging method involves diluting the chemical, which is usually 200–500 times sweeter than sucrose, with a small amount of dextrose and maltodextrin. Dextrose (glucose) is fermentable by pretty much all of the microbes used to ferment both clean and sour beers. Maltodextrin is unfermentable by ale and lager yeast, but most of the souring microbes (other than certain strains of *Lactobacillus*) produce the enzymes needed to break it apart into its component sugar molecules. The amount of these fermentables is large enough that, if adding at bottling, you may need to adjust your priming rate accordingly. A better option is the artificial sweeteners that use water for dilution.

Once you pick a sugar source, use a priming sugar calculator that takes into account the actual amount of beer to be packaged, the peak temperature the beer reached, and a target amount of carbonation. Weigh your sugar with a scale, rather than using volume, for added accuracy. I repeat, do not simply dump in an entire prepackaged baggie of priming sugar from the homebrewing store! Pre-measured carbonation drops (conditioning tabs) are handy if you are only bottling a small batch, but I like the control afforded by batch priming.

When it comes time to bottle, sour beer aged in barrels, or in a carboy with an oak dowel or peg inserted through the neck (see discussion of this technique in Chapter 9), contains about half of the residual carbonation when compared with beer aged in metal, glass, or plastic fermentors which is usually assumed to be holding 0.5–0.8 volumes of CO_2, depending on the highest temperature it experienced after fermentation finished. As a result, if your beer tastes "wine flat" (still), consider adjusting your calculations and adding more priming sugar (or be willing to accept a lower carbonation level than the calculator predicts). For my barrel-aged sours I assume 0.3–0.4 volumes of residual CO_2. Using this estimate has yielded the expected amount of carbonation in all of the beers from the group barrels I have participated in. Using a hard bung on a barrel will cause more CO_2 to be retained by the beer in the short term, but because the wood is porous the saturation will drop to a similar level over the long term. Remember that if you add fruit or other fermentables close to packaging, the renewed fermentation will saturate the beer with CO_2, bringing it back to the usual expected level.

Re-yeasting

With the long aging period and low pH of a sour beer, the yeast cells remaining will not have a high viability. In most cases, the yeast in sour beers aged less than 18 months will be able to ferment the priming sugar without assistance. However, because *Brettanomyces* is the dominant yeast at this stage, conditioning will usually take several months. To reduce this wait, many brewers choose to introduce a culture of fresh yeast along with the priming sugar.

A low pH can slow the yeast, so give the beer extra time before you start checking the carbonation level. Wine strains (including Champagne) have the advantage of being selected for both acid and alcohol tolerance, so they are the best choice for particularly strong or acidic beers. Wine yeast has adapted to fermenting only relatively simple sugars, so there is less concern that it will dry out the beer in the bottle after the priming sugar is consumed. White Lab's Neva Parker confirms that no matter what species or strain of yeast consumes the sugar, the same amount of CO_2 will be produced.[6] This is because the metabolic process that generates energy for any yeast cell involves the same basic chemical equation. This is also the reason that you can use the standard formula to calculate the alcohol in a sour beer.[7] A final consideration is picking a strain that is highly flocculant, because this will make leaving the yeast sediment in the bottle easier when you pour.

Russian River's sour beers have always been re-yeasted for bottle conditioning with either *Brettanomyces* or a wine yeast strain. Early batches used the William Selyem wine strain, which was a wild *Saccharomyces* isolated from Zinfandel grapes at Martinelli Winery in Sonoma County. Liquid cultures can only be obtained from White Labs by special order. Russian River liked the strain because it deals well with high-temperature bottle conditioning, 75°F–85°F (24°C–29°C). Because the culture was in liquid format only, it made scheduling bottling difficult. Eventually they switched to the Rockpile strain, which was isolated in Sonoma as well, but comes in an easier to maintain dried form as Enoferm RP-15. Brewmaster Vinnie Cilurzo reported that this strain added a slightly minerally extra dimension to his sour beers.[8] Over time though, Cilurzo continued experimenting, and found another dry wine yeast called DV-10 that he liked better. To guarantee carbonation, Russian River repitches at about 2–2.5 million cells per milliliter (double the repitching rate for their clean beers).[9] Recently, a few Russian River batches have been conditioned with a blend of wine yeast and *Brettanomyces*. The brewers usually see the target amount of carbonation after four to six weeks, but they hold the bottles warm a few weeks longer to ensure it is stable.

My standard rate for a 5 gal. (18.9 L) batch is 0.07 oz. (2 g) of dry yeast rehydrated in 90°F–100°F (32°C–38°C) water. An alternative is to aim for a standard target of two billion viable yeast cells per gallon (0.5 billion cells/L). The only risk of adding too many yeast cells is that more sediment in the bottle can result in the production of additional carbonation as the *Saccharomyces* cells undergo autolysis.

Once the beer is in bottles, leave it at 68°F–74°F (20°C–23°C) until carbonation is stable and the yeast have cleaned up any unpleasant by-products. My pale sour beers (especially those brewed with wheat or rye) often develop an odd cereal finish after bottling that was not present before, which lingers for a few months. This Cheerios® flavor fades with time, but it is worrying if you have never experienced it before.

If the strain of *Pediococcus* you pitch goes through a phase of "sickness" in the fermentor due to increased exopolysaccharide synthesis (see Chapter 4), odds are it might happen again in the bottle. This is because *Pediococcus* tends to get sick, or "ropy," in the presence of simple sugars (the presence of glucose increases production of the mucous-laden exopolysaccharides).[10] If you do experience sickness in the bottle, leave the packaged beer somewhere warm and wait until the *Brettanomyces* removes the ropiness before drinking. At one time, Russian River's sour beers became sick a second time in the bottle. When this happened they would hold the bottles a few additional months, necessitating additional warehouse capacity.[11] If this is a concern, you should consider blending with young beer to provide the carbohydrates for bottle refermentation as discussed later in this chapter.

Finishing with *Brettanomyces*

Adding a fresh culture of *Brettanomyces* is another way to add complexity, especially if your beer is lacking funk. Adding extra *Brettanomyces* may not be necessary though, as Gabe Fletcher of Anchorage Brewing notices an increase in *Brettanomyces* character during bottle conditioning even when re-yeasting with *Saccharomyces*.[12] Using *Brettanomyces* to bottle condition requires similar pitching rates to *Saccharomyces*, about 10% of what you would pitch for a primary fermentation. *Brettanomyces* will not ferment as quickly as *Saccharomyces*, but it is acid and alcohol tolerant and will eventually carbonate the beer. According to Chad Yakobson, ester production by *Brettanomyces* is independent of fermentation.[13]

Some breweries add *Brettanomyces* to otherwise clean beers at bottling, such as Orval from Brasserie d'Orval and Brewery Ommegang's Ommegeddon. In theory this is a brilliant idea for adding funky complexity without tying up fermentor space or risking contamination, but in practice it is problematic. If the beer still has residual carbohydrates in addition to the priming sugar, the *Brettanomyces* will slowly ferment these dextrins, leading to overcarbonation. It only takes a drop of 0.002–0.004 SG (0.5°P–1°P) to fully carbonate a beer, so it does not take much to cause substantial overcarbonation.

If you want to try adding *Brettanomyces* to a clean beer, you need to start with a beer that is already dry and packaged in heavy-gauge bottles that can handle high pressure. For beers that are not suitably dry for bottling with *Brettanomyces*, the yeast should be added to the fermentor and allowed to ferment until the gravity is stable. You will learn at what gravity it is safe to bottle future batches, assuming consistent recipe and process. If you are going to keg a beer, to create just a hint of *Brettanomyces* character you can pitch an active culture at the same time as you add dry hops, but not give the beer any extra time. Early on, Russian River bottled a *Brettanomyces* finished beer to release the first batch of Redemption. Redemption was inspired by the Belgian singles that Vinnie and Natalie Cilurzo sampled on a trip to Belgium. The beer had been brewed a few times to serve on draft at the pub, and involved a grist that included small percentages of wheat malt, Vienna, and acid malt, in addition to base malt. For the first bottling they wanted to do something special, so they dosed the beer with *Brettanomyces*. Vinnie Cilurzo has described the aged bottles as one of the best beers he has brewed, but the *Brettanomyces* has also continued to attenuate, causing overcarbonation.[14] Subsequent bottlings of Redemption have not included *Brettanomyces*. In 2012, Cilurzo collaborated with Sierra Nevada Brewing Co. to produce Brux Domesticated Wild Ale, a strong Belgian ale into which they injected a slurry of *B. bruxellensis* in each bottle.[15]

Brettanomyces often adds a rustic charm to saison. Depending on the strain, it can add flavors that include cherry, lemon peel, wet hay, leather, and barnyard. Many American breweries, including the Bruery, Ommegang, and Boulevard, brew delicious saisons with *Brettanomyces* character. While only a handful of modern saisons are truly sour, historically most of them were. Any of the commercially available *Brettanomyces* strains can work well in a saison. Strains marketed as *B. bruxellensis* are especially well suited to hoppy saisons because of their earthy counterpoint to bright fresh hops. One favorite is White Labs' *B. claussenii* (WLP645), which contributes a subtle fruity, funky flavor that builds complexity without obscuring the flavors produced by the primary saison strain. You can pitch *Brettanomyces* at any time, but the earlier you add it, and the more healthy cells you pitch, the quicker you will get a noticeable character.

The Bruery's saisons, Rue and de Lente, get their light earthy funk from the addition of *Brettanomyces* as they age (for de Lente it is *B. bruxellensis*). Saison Rue is primarily American two-row malt with 35% rye malt, a small percentage of brown malt to add bread crust flavors, and dextrose to boost fermentability. It is hopped with Magnum and Sterling, and receives subtle spicing. After primary fermentation, *Brettanomyces* is added for bottle conditioning. Tyler King, the head brewer, says *Brettanomyces* only drops their saisons an extra 0.002 SG (0.5°P) after bottling.[16] Due to the possibility of hyperattenuation, be wary of adding *Brettanomyces* at bottling unless the beer already has a low final gravity.

Before moving on to work at Cabinet Artisanal and then Pizza Boy Brewing Co., Terry Hawbaker earned his reputation for saisons at Bullfrog Brewing. His Busted Lawnmower Saison was one of my favorite American examples of the style, bright and crisp with a bright, fruity funk. Hawbaker fermented it with a house culture that combined *B. claussenii* and the Dupont saison strain, a blend he pitched for all of his saisons. The fermentation was warmed to 94°F (34°C), where these two strains provided a combination of flavor and attenuation. In addition to the *B. claussenii* in the primary fermentor, Hawbaker pitched *B. bruxellensis* into some kegs for even more funk. Hawbaker's experiments with wild yeast and barrel aging garnered him a 2008 GABF gold medal in the Wood- and Barrel-Aged Sour category for Beekeeper, a buckwheat honey-spiked saison (Beesting) that spent well over two years in Cabernet Sauvignon barrels before it was released.[17]

At both the Lost Abbey (Ten Commandments) and Pizza Port (SPF 8), Tomme Arthur has brewed strong, dark, spiced saisons. Arthur is known for his complex recipes; in addition to seven malts (Pilsner malt, roasted wheat, flaked barley, Weyermann caramel malt, Weyermann melanoidin malt, Special "B," and debittered black malt) and three hops (Amarillo, First Gold, and Tettnang), he added caramelized raisins, orange zest, rosemary, and buckwheat honey to create SPF 8. At Pizza Port, Arthur would pitch a blend of yeasts, including the Dupont strain for flavor and an American ale strain for attenuation. The Lost Abbey version (Ten Commandments) receives the house *Brettanomyces* for added complexity.[18]

Bottle Conditioning with Young Beer

Before refined sugars were inexpensive and widely available, one of the original ways to stimulate carbonation in beer was to blend in a younger, sweeter beer and allow the yeast to ferment the remaining carbohydrates. Young beer also has the advantage of containing fresh yeast cells to create CO_2. This is still done by many German brewers, who still adhere to the

Reinheitsgebot, where they add either young beer or wort so as to avoid the addition of refined sugars and artificially produced CO_2.

For sour beers, blending old and young batches to generate carbonation is closely associated with the production of gueuze, the brewers and blenders of which maintain huge cellars of bottle-conditioning beers. This method adds a further constraint to blending in addition to having to target flavors. Attempting this method is not a good option unless you have the knowledge and confidence to predict the final gravity of your beer, and you are willing to wait six months to a year for conditioning to complete. It relies on the slow fermentation of dextrins in the young beer by *Brettanomyces*, which is why reaching the target carbonation level takes so long. If you underestimate the fermentables remaining in the young beer, the blend will eventually overcarbonate; overestimate them and you will produce flat beer.

One major advantage of blending in young beer that has already passed through a period of *Pediococcus* sickness once, is that the beer will not normally become sick again in the bottle,[19] although some counterexamples have been seen in gueuze bottles. Avoiding bottle sickness could quicken your production cycle by a couple of months, but because of how slowly this blending method produces carbonation these savings are difficult to realize.

Beers in the Allagash Coolship series are carbonated by the fermentation of carbohydrates and yeast provided by young beer. However, depending on choices made for the flavor of the blend, the brewers sometimes also need to add a small amount of refined sugar. Brewmaster Jason Perkins relies on a standard formula to determine how much CO_2 will be produced from every gravity point of fermentation. The difficulty is predicting how big the drop will be with any certainty, even when using beers brewed on their precisely controlled commercial brewhouse. Perkins told me that assuming the blend will attenuate to the same final gravity as the driest component is a good rule of thumb, but only if your wort production method and recipe are consistent.[20] It has taken a couple of years of experimentation with different blends to figure out what works for their beers. Since a reduction of 0.002–0.004 SG (0.5°P–1°P) is all it takes to carbonate a beer, if your blend is substantially denser than its driest component you will need to place it in a fermentor and wait for the gravity to drop.

If this is something you are interested in, the easiest way to deal with the problem is to blend to taste and then determine how much additional sugar is needed to reach your target carbonation. The formulas below were adapted from those provided by Kai Troester on his excellent website *Braukaiser.com*.[21]

Using US standard units:

C_Y: The carbonation provided by the young beer in volumes CO_2.
V_Y: Young beer volume in quarts.
V_O: Old beer volume in quarts.
GU_Y: The current gravity units (points) of the young beer.
GU_O: The current gravity units of the old beer. This is taken from a hydrometer reading and assumes that the old beer has completed fermentation.

To solve for the amount of carbonation from a given amount of young beer:

$$C_Y = \frac{.51 \times V_Y(GU_Y - GU_O)}{V_Y + V_O}$$

To solve for the amount of young beer for a given amount of carbonation:

$$V_Y = \frac{C_Y \times V_O}{.51(GU_Y - GU_O) - C_Y}$$

To determine the additional sugar needed:

M_S: Sugar weight in ounces.
C_S: Carbonation that needs to be created from the sugar in volumes CO_2.
A: The sugar's fermentability factor (1.0 for table sugar, 0.92 for corn sugar).*

$$M_S = \frac{.14 \times C_S \times V_T}{A}$$

Using metric units:
C_Y: The carbonation provided by the young beer in g/L CO_2.
V_Y: Young beer volume in liters.
V_O: Old beer volume in liters.
AE_Y: The current apparent extract of the young beer in degrees Plato.
AE_O: The current apparent extract of the old beer. This is taken from a hydrometer reading and assumes that the old beer has completed fermentation.

To solve for the amount of carbonation from a given amount of young beer:

$$C_Y = \frac{4.17 \times V_Y(AE_Y - AE_O)}{V_Y + V_O}$$

To solve for the amount of young beer for a given amount of carbonation:

$$V_Y = \frac{C_Y \times V_O}{4.17(AE_Y - AE_O) - C_Y}$$

To determine the additional sugar needed:
M_S: Sugar weight in grams.
C_S: Carbonation that needs to be created from the sugar in g/L CO_2.
A: The sugar's fermentability factor (1.0 for table sugar, 0.92 for corn sugar).[*]

$$M_S = \frac{2 \times C_S \times V_T}{A}$$

Even if you do not want to get your carbonation from the sugars remaining in a young beer, you may choose to blend in a small amount (say 3%–5%) of a young batch to provide active cells for carbonation rather than re-yeasting with a clean strain. Measure how much gravity the young beer adds to the blend, as you may need to lower the amount of priming sugar accordingly.

---

[*] John Palmer (2006), *How to Brew*.

Large format bottles sealed with champagne corks.

Bottles

Glass bottles are the most common packaging for sour beers for both practical and aesthetic reasons. While many breweries close their bottles with corks and cages, regular crown caps are a reliable option. The practical argument for the heavy-gauge corkable bottles over the more common 12 oz. (355 mL) kind is their ability to safely contain higher levels of carbonation.

If you want to cork bottles, check that you have the correct size of corks and a corker capable of accepting your bottles. Champagne corks are difficult to remove without the huge pressure that those sparkling wines develop; Belgian corks are a better choice for most bottles, but remember that they come in multiple sizes. Sink the cork in deep enough that you are able to secure the cage over it. If your corker does not have an adjustable nut that allows you to set the depth of the cork, place a drilled stopper onto the plunger to mark the desired depth. There are people who claim that you do not need to sanitize the corks, but a quick steaming is traditional. Alternatively, I find a quick dip in Star San has the added benefit of making it easier for corks to slide into bottles.

The most common size of corked bottle is 750 mL, but the 375 mL ones will take the same size corks. If you are using a Ferrari floor corker, bottles smaller than 375 mL will not be tall enough to reach the plunger. A friend and I have bottled collaborative blends in 1.5 L magnum bottles that his Ferrari was barely able to accommodate (requiring one person holding the bottle at an angle while the other depresses the lever). For bottles that do not fit the corker, or if you do not want to invest in a corker, then the easiest option is plastic Champagne corks, which are knocked into the bottle with a rubber mallet.

If you only have a corker capable of inserting wine corks, follow the lead of several Belgian breweries (e.g., Fantôme, and Cantillon) and place a cap over them (usually these bottles require larger 29 mm caps). The cap prevents the cork from escaping, taking the place of the cage. I am not especially fond of this method because I have bought a couple of bottles where the beer leaked past the cork, resulting in mold growing under the cap.

For my own consumption, I package most of my sour beers in regular capped, long neck 12 oz. (355 mL) bottles. These are the bottles I have the most of and it enables me to space out my consumption more, allowing me to see how a beer changes as time passes. I usually buy oxygen-absorbing caps, although I have not done a real side-by-side comparison with regular ones; for a few extra dollars these caps buy me a little peace of mind. I save the heavier corkable bottles for beers that will be carbonated above 3.5 volumes, those beers I am worried still have residual fermentables, and also beer that is receiving *Brettanomyces* for the first time at bottling.

While most brewers sanitize their bottles with chemicals or heat just as they would for any other beer, the truth is that the odds of an off-flavor developing in a sour beer are extremely low at this point. The most common beer spoilage microbes have already been added to the beer, and the alcohol, acidity, and low oxygen create an inhospitable environment. Dave Pyle told me that he uses bottles that are simply rinsed, but not sanitized, to save time.[22] For me, normal sanitation is worth the extra time, even if it is just so I feel better.

If you do not want to invest money and effort into corking bottles there are still a few options that will make capped bottles look extraordinary. Covering the cap and neck with colored bottling wax adds visual appeal (and extra work opening the bottle). Bottling wax has a thicker plastic-like texture that coats a bottle much more nicely than paraffin wax. I have an old coffee mug that I have sacrificed to waxing. I fill it halfway with wax beads and microwave at 50% power until they are barely melted. Placing the wax beads in a coffee can that is sitting in a pot of simmering water works equally well. It often takes two or three coatings for the thickness to approach what you see on most commercial beers. If the wax cools too much, I put it back into the microwave for a few seconds. On a commercial scale, wax blocks and a small crock-pot are more practical (just remember to clean out the pot while the wax is still liquid if you plan on using it for multiple colors). Another option is to affix shrink-wrap neck wrappers, which are less messy to apply and remove, but they do not look quite as classy. If you plan on putting anything over the cap, check that the exterior of the bottle is completely dry or the cap will begin to slowly rust.

For a long time I was suspicious of the claim that dipping the neck of a bottle in wax reduces oxidation, because it seemed impossible for oxygen to enter with all of that CO_2 pushing out. That was, however, until I read that Fick's laws of diffusion state that the rate of diffusion is influenced only by the concentration of each individual gas. That is to say, in the case of a bottle of beer, a higher concentration of oxygen outside the bottle than inside will cause oxygen to slowly diffuse into the beer regardless of how much CO_2 pressure there is inside the bottle pushing out. Oxygen barrier caps are available which slow the diffusion of oxygen, certainly a more practical option than wax if oxygen protection is your only goal. The rate of diffusion is also influenced by the bottle design, which is why a number of craft brewers (like Sierra Nevada) have switched from screw-off to pry-off bottles, which give a wider area of contact between the lip and the cap.[23]

Microbial Stabilization

If your goal is a beer that retains residual sweetness, you may need to stabilize the microbes before packaging. While there are only a few American breweries that sell pasteurized sour beer at the time of writing, it is fairly common among larger Belgian producers of fruit lambic and Flemish red. Some beer drinkers feel that the sweetness balances the acidity, although in most cases the sugariness also obscures subtle flavors developed by the mixed fermentation.

Situations where having viable wild yeast or bacteria in your packaged beer can cause problems include: back-sweetening with sugar, fruit juice, or fruit syrup; blending with a large volume of young sour beer or clean beer at packaging; halting fermentation before the attenuation limit is reached; and packaging before fermentation is complete. In any of these cases, live microbes will continue to ferment the residual sugars and dextrins in the bottled beer, eventually leading to overcarbonation. To prevent this, there are three options discussed below: chemical, heat (pasteurization), and filtration. If you do decide to kill the microbes, it will also influence other choices, like whether to force carbonate or naturally condition. If you choose the latter, fresh yeast must be pitched to consume the priming sugar.

If these choices seem too drastic, then keg the unpasteurized beer and serve it hastily. Chill the beers as close to freezing as possible before blending or sweetening and then hold there to slow the activity of the microbes. If you serve the kegged beer over the span of a month or two, you will be able to enjoy it before the microbes dry it out completely. Kegging also provides the protection of a pressure release valve to vent excess carbonation.

If you want to sweeten or blend only a small amount of the beer, then the easiest option is to wait until the beer is served; more information on blending in the glass is found later in this chapter.

Chemical

Homebrewers have had good success stabilizing sour beers with chemicals marketed primarily to wine and cider makers. The first step is to crash chill the beer and fine it with gelatin or isinglass (or another positively charged fining) to remove most of the yeast and bacteria cells from suspension. Follow the instructions for the fining, and after a week transfer the clear beer off the trub and into a sanitized fermentor, or dump the trub if you are using a conical.

Stir in one crushed Campden tablet, or 0.015 oz. of potassium metabisulfite, for each gallon of clear beer (0.11 g per L). In a couple of days the free sulfur dioxide (SO_2) will have done its work, leaving the beer completely free of microbes. It is important to do this step in a well-ventilated area. If you want to naturally carbonate the beer, then pitch wine yeast, which are selected for sulfite tolerance. I utilized this method to stabilize a Russian imperial stout with *B. anomalus* when it reached 1.020 FG (5°P); in the six years since bottling it has not become overcarbonated. Sulfite is also a powerful antioxidant, which is one of the reasons wines age so gracefully.

Chemical stabilization along with natural carbonation will not allow you to sweeten with sugar or fruit, but it does allow you to blend a sour beer with a fully fermented clean beer. If you want a sweet Lindemans-style fruit lambic (blended with fruit syrup and sweeteners) you can follow these same steps to stabilize the beer, but then force carbonate. For long-term storage it is safest to add potassium sorbate as well to ensure that any microbes that enter during packaging are unable to thrive on the easily fermentable fruit sugars (the amount required decreases as the alcohol rises and the pH of the solution drops).

Using chemicals is simple, inexpensive, and causes no detriment to the final flavor of the beer. The main drawback is that there are people who have sulfite allergies. If you have one, or are planning to share your beer with someone who does, select one of the other methods. For professional brewers these chemicals are not an option, because the TTB puts a limit of 10 ppm SO_2 and 0.1% potassium sorbate in packaged beer,[25] which is too low a concentration for killing yeast and bacteria.

Pasteurization

For commercial brewers and homebrewers who want to avoid adding chemicals to their beer, unwanted microbes can be killed with pasteurization. There are three pasteurization techniques: bulk, bottle, and flash.

Flash pasteurization. Flash pasteurization is solely the realm of commercial breweries. New Belgium pumps their blended sour beers through a narrow stainless steel tube which quickly heats and then cools the beer to kill the yeast and bacteria. New Belgium's equipment allows them to flash pasteurize 85 bbl. (100 hL) of beer per hour. From there, the sterile beer is partially force carbonated before it is primed and re-yeasted.[26] This process allows the brewers to reliably hit their target amount of carbonation regardless of residual carbohydrates and without a large dose of priming sugar. New Belgium's process also extends the shelf life beyond what pure force carbonation would achieve, because the yeast will scavenge some oxygen, thus partially reducing oxidation.

Bulk pasteurization. To bulk pasteurize, transfer the beer to your kettle and slowly heat it to 150°F (66°C). Ethanol does not boil until it reaches 172°F (78°C), but molecules will begin to evaporate before this temperature is reached (in the same way that an uncovered bowl of water will slowly evaporate without coming to a boil). Work in a well-ventilated area to eliminate the risk of the alcohol vapor igniting. As the beer heats you will notice foaming, because the warmer it is the lower the saturation point for CO_2 will become. After 30 minutes at 150°F (66°C), force chill the beer to room temperature.

After pasteurization your beer is stable, but be careful to keep it that way. To bottle condition add yeast and priming sugar, or force carbonate at your leisure. For bottle conditioning following pasteurization, remember that the amount of CO_2 usually assumed to be dissolved in the beer will not be present; when calculating your sugar addition, assume 0.0 volumes of CO_2. If you choose to force carbonate, you have the option of sweetening the beer with fruit juice or sugar at the same time you pasteurize.

Bottle pasteurization. If you only have a small amount of beer, for example, part of a batch or an experimental blend, you may not want to deal with all of the transferring that bulk pasteurization requires. To bottle pasteurize, prime and fill your bottles, accounting for the reduction in dissolved CO_2 (see bulk pasteurization above). Place as many uncapped bottles as will fit into a pot and then fill it with room temperature water to the shoulders of the bottles. Heat the pot slowly, checking until the temperature of the beer reaches 150°F (66°C). At that point, turn off the heat, cap the bottles (being careful not to burn yourself), and allow them to sit in the pot with the heat off for an additional 30 minutes before removing. Once the bottles have cooled completely, open each and add a fresh yeast culture before recapping. If you have more bottles than will fit in the pot, start subsequent batches in room temperature water to minimize the thermal shock to the glass.

Heat is an inexpensive and robust method of killing microbes. On the homebrew scale it requires no special equipment. The disadvantage is that it can deaden the flavor of a beer, and as a result is ill suited to light or fresh tasting batches.

Filtration

Sterile filtration is more common in commercial breweries, but it is possible at home with the right equipment. You would need to get an absolute 0.45 micron filter to remove both yeast and bacteria,[27] which is a tighter specification than most fine/finishing filters. A filter fine enough to remove bacteria will also strip out flavor and aroma compounds, making it a poor option for beers known for their complexity. Similar to the other two methods, if you want to naturally carbonate a sterile filtered beer you cannot create a sugary beer, but if you force carbonate you can sweeten with any sugar source you want.

Even if your goal is not to sterilize the beer through filtration, there are reasons to pass your beer through a coarser filter. There are brewers who worry about leaving a souring beer in contact with a large amount of brewer's yeast. As yeast cells die they can impart goat-like aromas from the caproic, caprylic, and capric acids that are released from their cell walls. *Brettanomyces* is capable of turning those acids into delicious fruity esters, but this takes time and is unpredictable (and at a minimum will alter the flavor of the beer after it is bottled). According to Chad Yakobson, having excess brewer's yeast in the bottle can also lead to overcarbonation, because as the *Saccharomyces* cells undergo autolysis they release trehalose (a sugar that can be fermented by *Brettanomyces*).[28] Russian River filters their beers at 20 microns to remove any flecks of pellicle or fruit. Far from this being untraditional, Cantillon uses a coarse five-plate cellulose filter to accomplish a similar objective.[29]

Brouwerij Verhaeghe, located in West Flanders and makers of Duchesse du Bourgogne, do a rough filtration to slow the reduction of the sweetness they introduced by blending in a younger beer, giving them a relatively stable bottled product that has not been completely stripped.[30] Rough filtration may also be required after aging a beer on fruit puree, which is challenging to separate from the beer.

Kegging and Force Carbonation

If dealing with the inherently unpredictable nature of natural carbonation is too large of a risk for something you have spent so much time on, you can opt to force carbonate. This is accomplished in the same way as force carbonating a clean beer. Once the desired level of fizz is reached, either enjoy it on tap or bottle the bright beer. It may be difficult to serve highly carbonated styles like gueuze at the pressure required, but it is possible with the right equipment.

The few people in the American craft beer industry who advocate stabilizing and then force carbonating sour beers, including Lauren Salazar and Chad Yakobson, do so because it allows the profile of the beer to be stabilized, eliminating the risk of changes that may occur during bottle conditioning.[31] When you add fermentables at bottling the flavor profile can change as the microbes consume them and produce by-products in addition to CO_2 and alcohol. If you are doing an intensive blending session to achieve a specific flavor profile, this is something to consider. Force carbonation is often combined with a method that kills the microbes for even greater flavor stability.

In the case of New Belgium, after flash pasteurizing, the blended beer is then force carbonated to a known level before *Saccharomyces* is added along with enough sugar to increase the carbonation to the desired level. This is a relatively common practice among large craft brewers.[32] Live yeast extends the shelf life of bottled beers by scavenging about 30% of the available oxygen.[33] The downside is that, without the extended oxygen-scavenging activity of *Brettanomyces*, and the autolysis of yeast cells, aging will not be as dynamic. For me this is part of the joy of drinking sour beers—watching flavors evolve. Homebrewer Remi Bonnart has had good results from bottling unfiltered sour beer from a keg with a counter-pressure bottler. This technique allows the carbonation to be set, but still allows for oxygen scavenging *Brettanomyces* to improve long-term flavor development.[34]

Kegging is especially well suited to sour beers that you are not planning to age, like those with dry hops. Kegs are also a simple choice for special blends intended for a party or festival, because something that you are planning to consume rapidly does not justify the time and risk that bottle conditioning demands. If you allow the beer to ferment and sour in a keg, excess carbonation may be produced. Pizza Boy's Terry Hawbaker suggests using flow control faucets to prevent excessively foamy pours.[35]

From a practical standpoint, kegging is not without its drawbacks. It is best to have dedicated kegs, connectors, beer lines, shanks, and faucets for your sour beers, because there are too many places capable of harboring microbes. I keep a dedicated keg for sour and funky beers that I run on a picnic/party tap in my kegerator so I do not accidentally attach it to one of the clean taps. Some homebrewers who use ball-lock Cornelius kegs for their clean beers will buy a set of pin-lock kegs for their sours to prevent mistakes. At a minimum, mark the kegs you devote to sour beers in the same way you mark the rest of your equipment.

Some breweries, like Cambridge Brewing Company and San Diego's Modern Times Beer, use the same kegs for both clean and sour beers. In both cases, to ensure that none of the microbes survive, the brewers will run any keg that previously contained sour beer through their standard cleaning/sanitation regime twice before it is refilled with clean beer.[36]

Other Options

There is a history of serving young lambics on cask in Belgium, but few American sours are served this way except for tiny releases served at tasting rooms or brewpubs. The Bruery occasionally releases cask-conditioned test batches at their taproom. The practical benefit of serving a sour beer on cask is that it keeps the microbes away from your draft lines. The oxidation associated with serving on cask has the risk of turning a beer with an acetic character into malt vinegar after only a few days, so either quick consumption or a cask breather is recommended.

Beer gas, a blend of nitrogen and CO_2, is another choice for dispensing sour beers, although rare. This serving method, which many people associate with Guinness® Draught, mellows rough edges and boosts the perception of body. The main drawback of nitrogen is that its low solubility means it is not effective at liberating aromatic molecules from the beer up to your nose in the way CO_2 does. If you have a batch that is too thin or harsh, beer gas may be worth trying, but only if you are willing to either dedicate your stout faucet to sour beers or take it apart afterward for a thorough sanitizing.

In Belgium, Rodenbach Classic is available in cans, but while canned craft beers are an exploding part of the market in America, their down-market image is a hard sell for domestic sour ales. Cans send the opposite message of corked and caged bottles, but as sour beers gain acceptance I could certainly see brewers of light and refreshing sour beers opting for cans. In 2012, Brewery Vivant became the first American brewery to can a beer intentionally containing *Brettanomyces* with Escoffier, a firmly funky, strong, dark ale brewed in collaboration with New Belgium.

Waiting for Carbonation

With your precious beer safely stored in bottles, kegs, or casks, all there is left to do before enjoying it is to wait for carbonation. Some breweries use pressure gauges from Barby Kuhner, which they affix to flip-top bottles filled on their packaging line. The gauge allows the brewers to monitor the carbonation levels without opening a bottle each time they check. If you don't have one of these, open a bottle after a few weeks to ensure the beer is starting to carbonate (and is not becoming overcarbonated). Once you see that the yeast has started to produce carbonation, try to ignore the beer as much as you can for a couple of months.

Bottle Aging

Once the beer is carbonated it is ready to be consumed, technically. Most bottle-conditioned sour beers benefit from a few months or years of aging in the bottle, while a select few can age gracefully for a decade or longer. Unlike clean beers, the microbes responsible for a traditionally brewed and carbonated sour beer will continue to change the beer's character over several years. The only categories of sour beer that do not benefit from additional aging are those that are dry hopped or otherwise flavored with fresh botanicals shortly before packaging. As fresh aromatics fade, however, you may still enjoy the character of the underlying beer.

The rules for aging sour beers are similar to most other types of beer. Ideally, you would have a place with a consistently cool temperature, 45°F–55°F (7°C–13°C), minimal light, and no vibrations (although that factor is the least important). Lower temperatures will produce more gradual aging; warmer temperatures will induce more rapid changes to the flavor. This is because heat increases both the metabolism of the microbes and the rate of abiotic chemical reactions. Another factor that should be considered is ambient aromatics. A friend stored beers in an old steamer trunk whose pungent musty aroma permeated the crown liners and infused into the beers, something I probably would not have believed if I had not smelled both the trunk itself and several beers stored within.

I have been lucky enough to taste a handful of bottled commercial gueuze that were more than a decade old, each of which has been out-standing. Acidity softens slowly as *Brettanomyces* and time create esters by combining acids with alcohol. That sort of longevity will not be the case for every sour beer, but good storage and handling will raise the odds of having a delicious result. Remember, not all sour beers mature equally well; stronger and darker beers tend to resist the negative effects of oxidation and as a result improve more with age. Fruit also contains powerful antioxidant compounds, but for better or worse fruit beers lose their fresh fruit flavor as they age.

It is not a requirement to age corked beers on their sides to keep the cork wet like wines. This is because the corks used for beer bottles hold pressure, ensuring that there is enough humidity in the head space to keep the cork supple. Several homebrewers and professional brewers, like Brian Strumke of Stillwater Artisan Ales, swear by aging bottles on their sides to allow for more surface area between the beer and the head space. Aging bottles on their sides also prevents a pellicle from leaving an unsightly ring around the neck of the bottle. It is also the standard practice in Belgium for bottle-conditioning gueuze to be stored this way. If you want to try it, a wine rack is the simplest choice, but a less expensive option is to stack the bottles either on a shelf or in a box placed on its side. Remember to plan ahead and turn the bottles upright at least a week before serving to give the sediment enough time to settle.

Drinking

Once your beer is carbonated the only thing left to do is enjoy it! The first taste of a batch is one of the things I anticipate and dread most about the brewing process. That sip is the culmination of countless hours, usually spread over more than a year. Even though I have an idea of how it will taste from samples pulled during fermentation, there is still something special about that first taste of cooled and carbonated sour beer after months of warm and flat previews.

With the time and effort devoted to brewing, blending, and aging a sour beer, please do not pull one out of the fridge and drink it from the bottle. Like all beers, the flavor and especially the aroma of a sour beer benefit from drinking at a moderate temperature and out of a glass. Traditionally, Belgian lambics are served from straight-walled tumblers, but these days many brewers advise using a stemmed tulip or snifter. For me, it depends on the beer. A fruited sour beer tends to look best in a narrow flute or Pilsner glass that shows off the color and clarity of the beer, while a strong dark sour benefits from a snifter that curves inward to catch and concentrate the intense aromatics. For most other sour beers, I use a wine glass.

Reward your patience and effort by taking time to enjoy and evaluate your beer.

Ensure that the glass is clean before you open the beer. Extremely carbonated beers may start to slowly foam after they are opened, so you should be prepared to pour immediately. If you are anticipating an over-carbonated beer, rinse the glass with filtered water to minimize the foaming by removing the nucleation sites provided by dust. Chilling the beer close to freezing will also minimize foaming by increasing the liquid's ability to hold the dissolved gas.

Serving temperature is a matter of personal preference. I like drinking simple, low alcohol sour beers at a temperature between 40°F and 45°F (4.5°C–7.5°C), while stronger, darker sour beers are at their best from 59°F to 63°F (15°C–17°C). In general, it is safest to pour the beer a little too cold and allow it to warm as you drink it. My preference also varies with the season, since when it is hot out I tend to enjoy beers served a few degrees cooler.

Pour a beer deliberately. A vigorous pour will boost head formation and release aromatics. I usually opt for a forceful pour because most sour beers do not have durable heads. The high carbonation, long bottle aging, and variety of yeasts and bacteria often cause sour beers to have loose or powdery yeast sediment. As a result, it is best to try to pour the entire bottle without tilting it back and forth. A wicker or wire Belgian lambic basket is an elegant way to hold a sour beer when you are not going to pour the entire 750 mL bottle at once. The basket cradles the bottle at about a 30° angle, which prevents the sediment from being disturbed on each pour. The authentic versions are hard to procure outside of Belgium, but it is much easier to find nearly identical versions marketed as "wine baskets." A basket also allows a beer that is being stored horizontally to be served without disturbing the sediment.

A lambic basket, with a bottle of Hanssens Oude Gueuze. (©Brian Rous)

Critical Evaluation

Of course, there are times to just enjoy a glass of sour beer while talking with friends or eating dinner, but there should also be times when evaluating the beer is your focus. When you sit down to seriously evaluate a beer, try to identify the elements of it that you enjoy and what you would like to change. You must translate these desired alterations to the aroma, appearance, flavor, and mouthfeel into adjustments to your process and recipe. Compiling written tasting notes for a batch over time will allow you to track the progression of the beer, assessing when it has peaked.

Lauren Salazar, New Belgium's long time sensory guru, suggests that you pay close attention right before and after the pour. Start by smelling the empty glass to ensure it does not have an off-aroma. Fill the glass no more than halfway to allow room for swirling. If the head retention is worse than expected, this may indicate that the glass was not cleaned thoroughly. Volatile aromatic molecules dissipate quickly, so Lauren Salazar starts with short sniffs while wafting the more delicate aromas. Swirl the beer to increase the intensity of the aroma, and then put your nose into the glass.[37]

Try not to nitpick or jump to conclusions. Take a minute to savor the overall impression of the beer before you start teasing out the individual flavors. The natural human drinking motion works for an overall impression, but fails to highlight subtler characters. There are three ways to alter the way you naturally drink that will emphasize certain types of flavors. Take a sip, swallow, and breathe out through your nose (retro-olfaction)—this emphasizes *Brettanomyces* aromatics. Allow the beer to warm in your mouth, which Lauren Salazar recommends for bringing out fatty acids.[38] Finally, aerating the beer by slurping it stresses the bright flavors, which is particularly valuable for fruit beers.

While you drink, think about what the beer is supposed to be and identify the differences between what you taste and smell and what you were expecting. If there is a significant flaw, determine if it is something that will age out (see also Troubleshooting in Chapter 13). Try drinking the beer a few degrees colder to diminish the off-flavor.

Lauren Salazar advocates sensory evaluation as a job for everyone in the brewery; the more people she can recruit for tasting panels the better for motivating employees and improving the statistical significance of her analysis. A few of her key principles behind running a sensory panel: have the same group of people every time; people need to be objective (a ballot can help); standardize the procedure so it is done the same way every time; and do not screen people based on whether they are supertasters or not, because their passion and commitment are more important than their number of taste buds. Calibrate people, try to find commonalities in the terms people use, and be as specific as possible in how you describe the character.

For those of us without a staff, rope your friends into the evaluation process. Try to avoid telling them much about the beer. Have people remain quiet as they first start drinking to avoid undue influence from more experienced (or louder) tasters.

You may also want to get completely unbiased feedback by entering your beer into a competition. Sour beers tend to be judged more subjectively than other styles because each one has such a broad range of flavors. Other than the categories for the classic sour beer styles of Europe, many competitions also have other categories that can accommodate sour beers. For Beer Judge Certification Program sanctioned competitions these currently include: Belgian Specialty Ales, Specialty Beers, Barrel and Wood Aged Beers, and Fruit Beers.[39] For the GABF: American-Style Sour Ale, American-Style Brett Ale, Wood- and Barrel-Aged Sour Beer, Other Belgian-Style Sour Ale, Experimental Beers, and French- and Belgian-Style Saison.[40] Part of the key to winning in styles that require you to include a description is to be accurate as to what the beer tastes like and not how it was brewed. Most beer judges want to clearly taste every ingredient that you specify as having included.

Blending and Sweetening in the Glass

If your goal is to produce a sweet beer, or a blend of a sour and a clean beer, and you do not want to deal with the methods described earlier in this chapter, there is no shame in blending or sweetening a beer in the glass. Blending to taste at serving can help introduce someone to drinking sour beers; cut in a young malty beer to reduce the acidity and raise the sweetness.

While blending multiple batches together before bottling would adjust the entire batch, I often enjoy the ease and freedom of blending beer by the glass. There is no risk of oxidizing the beer or creating excessive carbonation, and you are only committing to one glass of the concoction, not an entire batch. Blending can be either as simple as adding a splash of saison to temper the sourness of a sharp lambic or as complex as creating a new style. One of my favorite discoveries is Flemish imperial stout (made by blending Flemish red and Russian imperial stout). You can also blend sour beers of different ages to sample a combination that was not possible at packaging. Play with different flavor combinations to get ideas for which blends you may or may not want to try on a larger scale.

If you want pure sweetness, adding refined sugar in the form of simple syrup is the easiest option. For simple syrup, boil equal parts (by weight) filtered water and table sugar for five minutes, and then allow it to cool. The finished syrup can be stored covered in the refrigerator for a couple of months. The supersaturated sugar syrup is much easier to incorporate into a cold beer than crystallized sugar. Having simple syrup on hand when trying sour beer allows the drinker to control the level of sour and sweet for themselves.

Adding sugar to sour beer at service is not a new concept; before pasteurization and artificial sweeteners were discovered, customers in Belgian cafés had the option to sweeten their lambics with sugar cubes and a small paddle if it was too sour for their tastes. Faro was produced either by suspending a lump of candi sugar in the cask or mixing in a liquid sugar.[41] In either case, it would need to be used up quickly before the microbes in the beer consumed the sugar.

Fruit juice is another option if you want flavor in addition to sweetness. This is particularly helpful if you are serving beer to someone who likes the sweeter fruit lambics, because this method imparts a fresh fruit flavor and mellows the sourness of the beer. As with adding juice earlier in the process, only add those you enjoy drinking straight. Citrus juice works especially well in this application, because if used during fermentation instead its flavor changes for the worse. At the Selin's Grove brewpub in Pennsylvania, their highly regarded fruit beers (Phoenix Kriek, Saison de Peche, and Framboise) are produced by adding a large volume of high quality fruit juice directly to cold kegs of clean beer.[42]

While frowned upon by traditionalists, there are a large number of other beverages that you can try blending into sour beer. You can impart interesting flavors by mixing in other alcoholic beverages (just please do not call it a beertail). For example, mead or a biodynamic white wine adds fruity balance to a funky pale sour. Red wine, port, or a characterful spirit adds a layer of complexity to a strong dark sour beer. Adding ice tea, lemonade, or soda creates a refreshing summer shandy/*Radler*, although adding a sugary beverage also mutes the complex flavors that took so much effort to create.

In the tradition of Berliner weisse you can try adding a sweetened fruit, herbal, or soda syrup in the glass to taste. In fact, this convention is so strong in Germany that my wife was refused a glass of Berliner weisse when she requested it without syrup![43] While the classic neon-red (raspberry) and green (woodruff) syrups are available at German specialty shops and online, I find making my own syrups to be more satisfying. For fruit, you can follow the recipe below, but there are also hundreds of recipes for soda syrups that would benefit from the acidity provided by a sour beer.

Several brewpubs produce seasonal syrups of their own to add to their house Berliner weisse. For their annual Great Pumpkin Festival, Cambridge Brewing Company creates a fresh pumpkin and spice-infused simple syrup that transforms their Berliner Kendall into Ich Bin Ein Kürbisweisse.[44] The kitchen at Peekskill Brewery has created several syrups to add to Zeitgeist Berliner Weisse, including a plum–ginger syrup that is brewmaster Jeff O'Neil's favorite.[45] For a commercial brewer this is a fun way to add a few additional beers to a draft list without much additional effort.

Blueberry Syrup[46]

Ingredients
- 20 oz. (0.6 kg) blueberries
- 2 cups (0.5 L) water
- 4 oz. (0.12 kg) sugar
- 1 tbsp (15 mL) lime or lemon juice

Instructions
Simmer the blueberries in the water for 15 minutes. Strain the mixture into a bowl through a cheesecloth-lined colander. When the berries are cool enough to touch, squeeze the cheesecloth to extract the remaining liquid. Return the blueberry juice to the pot, adding the sugar and citrus juice. Stir to prevent scorching. Bring back to a simmer for two minutes. Once it is cooled it can be added to a beer immediately or stored up to a month in the refrigerator.

Substitute another fruit if you would prefer, but based on the fruit's acidity and sugar level, you may also need to adjust the amounts of sugar and citrus juice in the recipe.

References

1. Jayaram Chandrashekar, et al., *Science* 326(5951):443.
2. Tomme Arthur, quoted by Sage Osterfeld (media liaison, Lost Abbey), in discussion with author, December 12, 2011.
3. Dave and Becky Pyle, personal communication with author, April 18, 2010.
4. "At Logsdon, Ales For Every Seizoen," *Hood River News,* February 18, 2012.
5. Jeff Sparrow, *Wild Brews: Beer Beyond the Influence of Brewer's Yeast.*
6. Neva Parker, personal communication with author, November 14, 2011.
7. "Calculating ABV for Sour Beers," Michael Tonsmeire, *Mad Fermentationist,* November 26, 2013, http://www.themadfermentationist .com/2013/11/calculating-abv-for-sour-beers.html.
8. Tomme Arthur and Vinnie Cilurzo, "Cult Beers of California," *Craft Beer Radio,* MP3 audio, 2009.
9. Peter Bouckaert, Ron Gansberg, Tomme Arthur, Tyler King and Vinnie Cilurzo, "A Comprehensive Look at Sour Ale Production," panel interview, Craft Brewers Conference, San Diego, May 4, 2012.
10. Maite Dueñas, et al., *International Journal of Food Microbiology* 87(1–2):113.
11. Vinnie Cilurzo, "Meltdown and Sour Beers," Keynote presentation at National Homebrewers Conference 2007, *Brewing Network,* MP3 audio, July 7, 2007.
12. Gabe Fletcher, personal communication with author, February 18, 2012.
13. Chad Yakobson, personal communication with author, December 3, 2011.
14. Vinnie Cilurzo, "The Sunday Session: Vinnie Returns to the Session," *Brewing Network,* MP3 audio podcast, January 17, 2010, http:// thebrewingnetwork.com/shows/596.
15. Oskar Blues Brewery, "Brian Grossman and Vinnie Cirluzio[*sic*] introduce 'Brux'," YouTube video (11:22), June 3, 2012, http://www .youtube.com/watch?v=jF41bGkhWx0.
16. Tyler King, personal communication with author, October 19, 2011.
17. Terry Hawbaker, personal communication with author, September 16, 2009.
18. Phil Markowski, *Farmhouse Ales: Culture and Craftsmanship in the Belgian Tradition.*

19. Cilurzo, "Meltdown and Sour Beers," July 7, 2007.

20. Jason Perkins, personal communication with author, October 7, 2011.

21. Kai Troester, "Krausening," *Braukaiser.com*, January 2, 2010, http://braukaiser.com/wiki/index.php?title=Kraeusening.

22. Pyle, pers. comm., April 18, 2010.

23. salad [user], quoting Sierra Nevada letter in forum post, "Sierra Nevada goes to pry-offs," *SuperTopo*, June 6, 2007 (03:29 p.m. PT), http://www.supertopo.com/climbing/thread.php?topic_id=394023.

24. "Lauren Salazar of New Belgium Q & A," interview by Brandon Jones, *Embrace the Funk* blog, July 26, 2012.

25. Alcohol and Tobacco Tax and Trade Bureau, *Flavoring Substances and Adjuvants Subject to Limitation or Restriction*, last modified September 4, 2012.

26. Lauren Salazar, personal communication with author, October 19, 2011.

27. *Oxford Companion to Beer*, editor Garrett Oliver (New York: Oxford University Press, Inc., 2012), s.v. "filtration."

28. Yakobson, pers. comm., December 3, 2011.

29. Vinnie Cilurzo, Yvan de Baets, Jean Van Roy. "Barrel-Aged Sour Beers from Two Belgian's Perspectives," panel interview, 2011.

30. "How to Make Sour Ale: an inquiry," Raj B. Apte, archived website, November 2004, *Internet Archive: Wayback Machine*, last accessed April 25, 2013, http://web.archive.org/web/20080209170719/http://www2.parc.com/emdl/members/apte/flemishredale.shtml.

31. Lauren Salazar, interview, *Embrace the Funk*, July 26, 2012; Yakobson, pers. comm., December 3, 2011.

32. Salazar, pers. comm., October 19, 2011.

33. Guy Derdelinckx, [in French] *Cerevisia* 1987, 12(3):153.

34. Remi Bonnart, personal communication with author, February 22, 2012.

35. Hawbaker, pers. comm., September 16, 2009.

36. Caleb Staton, "Exploring the American Sour Niche," *The New Brewer*, July/August 2010.

37. Salazar, pers. comm., October 19, 2011; ibid., "NHC: Tips and Tasting," *Basic Brewing Radio* MP3 audio, July 19, 2007.

38. Ibid.

39. *BJCP Style Guidelines for Beer, Mead, & Cider*, 2008 edition.

40. "Beer Styles," Great American Beer Festival, last accessed December 13, 2013.
41. Sparrow, *Wild Brews*.
42. Steve Leason, personal communication with author, October 17, 2009.
43. Audrey Flake, personal communication with author, December 5, 2009.
44. Will Meyers, personal communication with author, November 14, 2011.
45. Jeff O'Neil, personal communication with author, December 21, 2011.
46. Recipe based on: "Blueberry Soda," Alton Brown, published on *FoodNetwork.com*, last accessed December 15, 2013, http://www.foodnetwork.com/recipes/alton-brown/blueberry-soda-recipe/index.html.

TROUBLESHOOTING GUIDE

13

Despite all of the information in this book and your best efforts, not every batch of sour beer will come out exactly the way you envisioned. There are techniques to remedy many of these problems; others can be blended away, but in some cases there will be unpleasant flavors that you cannot rectify this way. You will have to learn to ignore these off-flavors or, more likely, jettison a batch or two. All but a couple of the brewers that I interviewed mentioned having to occasionally dump barrels; there is no shame in it.

Fermentation Did Not Start

Fermentation should start within 24 hours of pitching with every production method covered in this book, other than spontaneous fermentation. If there is no CO_2 production, pH drop, or kraeusen formation after a day, check the wort temperature and reevaluate your procedure. If the wort temperature is below the ideal range for your yeast strain, either warm the wort or pitch a brewer's yeast strain suited for the cool temperature. It is good insurance to keep several strains of dried yeast on hand for this situation.

Depending on your technique, local microflora, and temperature, most spontaneous fermentations show activity within the first three to five days, although it can take longer. If you do not see any action after a week, try to increase the temperature if the wort is too cold, or aerate the wort and pitch brewer's yeast.

Too Much Lactic Sourness

Historic brewing guides and recipes called for neutralizing acidity with egg shells, chalk, or baking soda. These ingredients can raise the pH, but can also cause the beer to taste chalky or salty, and as a result should only be an option of last resort. A better option is to blend with another batch to balance the acidity. If your beer has slightly too much lactic acid sourness, blend it with a dry beer that lacks acidity (if the beer you are blending in has *Brettanomyces* character, all the better). If the beer is much too sour, you will need to kill the microbes using heat, chemicals, or filtration (see Chapter 12) and blend it to taste with a sweet beer. Alternatively, you can reserve highly lactic acid batches as acid beer to blend into insufficiently sour beers.

Vinegar or Nail Polish Remover Aroma

A vinegary aroma, or one reminiscent of nail polish remover, is a sign that too much oxygen has been getting into the aging beer, causing *Brettanomyces* or *Acetobacter* to create acetic acid. If the flavor is light, you may be able to rescue the batch by preventing further contact with oxygen. If the beer is in a wood or plastic fermentor, move it to an impermeable glass or stainless steel fermentor. If the batch is already in an impermeable fermentor, inspect seals, gaskets, stoppers, airlocks, or other routes that air may be taking into the fermentor. If the acetic acid is already too aggressive, reserve the beer for blending, where it can contribute sharper vinegar acidity to softer beers. If it is too potent even to be blended, turn the batch into beer vinegar.

Beer Vinegar

If a batch of beer is excessively acetic and overly vinegar-like, instead of dumping it, embrace the flaw and turn it into beer vinegar. Put a gallon of the beer into a glass jug (leaving a few inches (5 cm) of head space) and secure a piece of cheesecloth or paper towel over the mouth with a rubber band. Place the beer in a dark spot, leaving it alone for a few months. As the beer ages, *Acetobacter* will take oxygen from the air and convert the ethanol in the beer into additional acetic acid. If the beer does not get vinegary enough, you can shorten the process by adding mother of vinegar (*Acetobacter* colony) or a small amount of unpasteurized vinegar (it does not need to be malt vinegar to work). It is somewhat cathartic to do something intentionally that you have spent so much effort avoiding.

When your beer vinegar is sour enough for your taste, bottle it. Spritz the finished vinegar onto fish and chips, include in homemade mustard, or make vinaigrette. In addition to using the beer vinegar on food, you can blend it into other beers that need a sharper acidity.

Not Enough Sourness

Take a gravity reading. If it is still above 1.006 SG (1.5°P), you can either continue to wait or pitch additional lactic acid bacteria. If the gravity is lower than that, feed the beer maltodextrin, fruit, or wort to try to provide the microbes with a new source of carbohydrates. Fruit is especially effective because it adds malic or citric acid in addition to sugars. My first batch of Flemish red was not as sour as I wanted, but 2 lb./gal. (0.24 kg/L) of blackberries improved the balance immensely. Blending with an acidic beer is another option. This highly acidic beer can either be created expressly for the purpose or reserved from particularly sour batches. When faced with the need for additional acidification without a secondary sour beer source, some homebrewers have resorted to the use of pure lactic acid. While far from ideal, and certainly less noble, food grade lactic acid has been used for this purpose. Although pure lactic acid gives an odd salty chemical flavor when added as the only souring agent, in my experience a small amount can boost the acidity of an already soured beer without contributing off-flavors.

Not Enough Funk

If you have enough acidity but the *Brettanomyces* has not produced enough funky flavors for your tastes, you have several options. In many cases *Brettanomyces* continues to produce its by-products after bottling, so you may not need to do anything. If the beer is less than 18 months old and has a subtle funk, consider aging it longer. If the beer has no funk after extensive aging, pitch an active culture of *Brettanomyces*. If the gravity is already below 1.006 SG (1.5°P), add a carbohydrate source, such as dextrinous wort or maltodextrin. *Brettanomyces* seems to operate better in low nutrient environments than *Lactobacillus* or *Pediococcus* do, but additional fermentables accelerate its production of esters and phenols. Blending is also a good option, especially if you have a batch that is funky but not sour enough.

Final Gravity Too High

In a situation where the final gravity is too high, the concern is that the beer may continue to slowly attenuate after packaging. How much residual gravity is too much will depend on the souring method you are using, and particularly whether *Brettanomyces* is present. The safest option is to keg the beer rather than bottle it. The pressure release valve on the keg should be pulled to vent the head space if excess CO_2 pressure is generated.

Most standard mixed-fermentation beers will fall below 1.010 FG (2.5°P). Allowing the *Brettanomyces* additional time to continue working is the easiest method to reduce higher final gravities. If your beer is adequately sour and funky, consider pitching a highly attenuative brewer's yeast strain to lower the residual gravity without drastically impacting the flavor. A high alcohol, low pH environment is tough on yeast cells, so if you choose this option, pitch an actively fermenting culture.

If you soured the beer before primary fermentation, the pH might have been too low for the *Saccharomyces*. In this case it is only a flavor consideration, because there is no *Brettanomyces* present to ferment the residual sugars. If it is too sweet, pitch an active starter of an attenuative acid-tolerant *Saccharomyces* strain, such as WY3711 French Saison.

Unusual Appearance

The microbes at work often cause souring beers to take on peculiar appearances, but most of the time this is nothing to worry about. Healthy pellicles can range from thin and spotty to thick and full, but the color will range between white and beige. Bold colors, especially green and black, are a sign that mold or other invasive microbes are at work. Mold requires oxygen to thrive, so first ensure that no air is able to enter the fermentor. Mold growth is especially common in fruit beers where the fruit floats on the surface of the beer, although it is also easy to confuse yeast and bacteria strains growing on the fruit for mold growth. If the beer is aging in a barrel, get rid of the barrel unless you have the ability to steam sanitize.

If the beer is viscous or ropy, this is a natural part of the aging process caused by *Pediococcus*, commonly referred to as being "sick." Leave the beer to age for two to four months to allow the *Brettanomyces* to break apart the offending polysaccharides. If this stage has not passed after four months, add an active starter of *Brettanomyces* and allow it to work until the viscosity returns to normal.

Too Much Oak

If your beer has taken on too much oak flavor or tannins, the first step is to remove any oak cubes or spirals, or transfer the beer out of the barrel. Extended aging in glass (including bottles), plastic, or stainless steel can allow oak flavor and tannins to mellow. This can take a couple of years, but with a sour beer it may be worth the time investment. In fact, many winemakers intentionally over-oak their red wines before bottling so that the wood will fade to the desired level after several years of aging, when other attributes of the wine have also mellowed. As with many other issues, blending is a good option, especially if you have a similar beer that is lacking in oak character.

Sulfur Aroma

The aromas of rotten egg, flatulence, or burnt matches are all signs that there are sulfur compounds present in the beer. These are usually produced during the active phase of fermentation, especially in cases where the yeast cells are stressed by low temperature or low pH. In most cases, when the gaseous sulfur compounds are allowed to escape, this defect will pass with additional aging. If your beer is being stored under pressure, change vessels or closures to allow the CO_2 to escape, which will carry the sulfur compounds with it.

Other Off-Flavors

During fermentation and aging of mixed-culture beers, you may detect many other strange and unpleasant flavors and aromas. The most common of these, like diacetyl and acetaldehyde, are intermediary by-products of the fermentation process that will pass if given more time. *Brettanomyces* in particular is a master at reducing a variety of off-flavor compounds produced by other microbes. However, there are a number of other flavors, such as an overpowering sherry or cardboard aroma from oxidation, and overly funky flavors produced by certain strains of *Brettanomyces*, that will not pass. Do not dump a beer immediately because of the presence of oxidation, but if that flavor lasts for more than six months, the chances of it going away are minimal.

Bottled Beer is Undercarbonated

If you are worried about undercarbonation and your beer is less than a month old, especially if it was not re-yeasted, turn each bottle upside down and swirl to rouse the yeast. Moving the bottles to a warmer location also encourages the yeast to carbonate the beer more rapidly. If the beer still does not carbonate you need to determine why, so take a gravity reading. If the specific gravity is still above what it was at bottling then you need to add fresh yeast to each bottle. Using an eyedropper or pipette to dose with a consistent amount of rehydrated wine yeast is the best option. If the gravity is at the same level it was at bottling, the problem is that you did not add enough priming sugar. In this case, carbonation drops or a carefully measured amount of priming solution are the best options. Once the fresh yeast or sugar is added allow a few weeks for carbonation.

Bottled Beer is Overcarbonated

If a batch becomes overcarbonated in the bottle, the first thing to do is cool the bottles close to freezing. Cold slows the metabolism of the yeast and bacteria to stabilize the carbonation, but even near-freezing temperatures will not halt this completely. Take a gravity reading to determine if the specific gravity has gone below what it was at packaging. A low reading at this stage will indicate that you bottled too soon, whereas a reading that matches the specific gravity at bottling indicates you added too much priming sugar.

There is no good solution to overcarbonated bottled beer. Uncapping the bottles to vent them will release a small amount of carbonation, but if there is enough carbonation to cause the beer to gush this must be repeated many times to significantly reduce the carbonation. A more radical solution is to pour the bottles back into a fermentor or keg to allow it to degas, before priming and rebottling (this risks oxidation and is a nuisance).

Wheaty Flavor in Bottle-Conditioned Beer

I have tasted a strange grainy flavor in young sour beers I have brewed myself and in several that commercial brewers have produced. I often describe it as Cheerios®, but I know several homebrewers who have other terms to describe the same flavor in their own beers (including some who think it is diacetyl). It is a result of intermediary by-products created as the yeast and bacteria ferment the priming sugar. Luckily, the flavor will pass if the beer is stored between cellar and room temperature, but this process can take several months.

RECIPES

14

While the general guidelines for grain and hop selection discussed in Chapter 4 are exceedingly important, the majority of a sour beer's character comes from the fermentation, aging, wood, fruit, and blending choices. With so many available combinations, I realize that complete recipes would be helpful.

While there are hints and suggestions for recreating commercial recipes throughout the book, I was uncomfortable providing complete recipes that I had not brewed myself. The vast majority of the recipes included below are presented exactly as I brewed them. In a few cases, however, I included minor adjustments that I would make if I were to re-brew. Several of my early batches were more complex than I would design them today, but the results were good enough that I have left the recipes as brewed.

All fermentables are given by percentage to allow for easy adjustment for desired volume and system efficiency. Sugars are listed as a percentage by extract, while grains are given as a percentage by weight. I have never brewed a sour beer that relied on malt extract for the bulk of its fermentables (although I have added it to boost the gravity of strong sour beers). You can convert any of these recipes to suit the limitations of your system, but be warned that the fermentability of the extract may mean that your results differ significantly from the target. Swap out some or all of the base malt for an equivalent extract, and steep or mini-mash the remaining grains.

Hop additions are given by the number of IBUs contributed based on the Tinseth formula; adjust by the volume of beer, as well as the alpha acid percentage (AA%) and processing of the hops you are using. For most recipes the variety of hop selected is not particularly important; because it is only a small amount added early in the boil, substituting a similar variety should yield equally good results. The few recipes that include late boil or dry hop additions are given by weight, because their contribution to the aroma of the beer is more important than their bitterness.

All spices, herbs, and other ingredients given by weight or volume, are per gallon for standard and per liter for metric unless otherwise noted.

I add yeast nutrient to most of my beers, including sour beers. I add a Whirlfloc® tablet (kettle fining) to most of my clean and 100% *Brettanomyces* beers, but for long-aged sour and *Brettanomyces* beers I tend to skip it because I allow the microbes enough time to clear the beer on their own. Do what makes the most sense for you and your system.

The alcohol by volume (ABV) is given by the standard formula. In truth, for sour beers this is an estimate, because the complex fermentation produces a significant amount of by-products other than alcohol and carbon dioxide. The evaporation that occurs during barrel aging may also change the percentage of alcohol in the beer. As a result, the only way to know for sure exactly how much alcohol a beer contains is through direct laboratory analysis of a sample.

While many recipes are written with a particular fermentation method in mind, most can be adapted to be fermented with any of the methods covered in this book. For fermentations other than 100% *Brettanomyces* and spontaneous, pitch a healthy culture of *Saccharomyces* (as much as you would pitch for a similar gravity and volume of clean beer) along with or followed by your other microbes. The actual amount and timing of *Brettanomyces*, *Lactobacillus*, and *Pediococcus* pitched will be determined by the souring method, but the exact pitching rate is far less important because these microbes are not responsible for the initial fermentation.

Each recipe includes variations. I often split batches, adding fruit, dry hops, or spices to half while leaving the remainder as is. Most of the variations have been tested, but there are times when I tried an addition on one recipe that seemed like it would be a good fit for another as well.

CLASSIC INSPIRATION

The European sour beer "styles" that inspired many American brewers in the first place are still very popular to brew. While many brewers leave them as is, others use them as a base for unique treatments with barrels, spices, fruit, or dry hops.

No-Boil Berliner Weisse

The perfect sour beer for the summer: tart and refreshing, with doughy wheat and a touch of fruity funk. This is a quick beer to brew because it is not boiled, and the fermentation is much shorter than most other sour beers. People argue over whether *Brettanomyces* is appropriate in the style, but I find that its hint of funk covers the slightly off aroma that *Lactobacillus* can produce.

Ingredients
· 66.7% German Pilsner malt
· 33.3% wheat malt
· 2 IBUs Fuggles (mash)
· Safale US-05 Ale Yeast
· Wyeast 5335 *Lactobacillus*

Boil time:	0 minutes
Original gravity:	1.032 (8°P)
Final gravity:	1.002 (0.5°P)
ABV:	3.8%
IBU:	2
SRM:	3

Directions
Mash in at 125°F (52°C). After 10 minutes, pull a decoction big enough to bring the mash to 146°F (63°C) when it is returned; add the hops to the decoction. After returning the decoction leave to convert for 45 minutes, before raising to 158°F (68°C) to finish.

Heat until the first few bubbles of the boil emerge, and then chill immediately to 70°F (21°C). Ferment around 65°F (18°C).

Allow to ferment until the gravity is stable, then carbonate to 3.8 volumes of CO_2.

Variations
Add a pure culture of *Brettanomyces,* or bottle dregs, for a more complex character. A bright fruit would be a good addition, but, honestly, it does not need it.

Belgian Lambic/Gueuze

The most emblematic sour beer style, its character is less about recipe and more about technique. A simple grist and hopping schedule, but a long mash and boil that sets the stage for a long fermentation. Develops a classic minerally lemon rind character as it ages.

Ingredients
- 66% German Pilsner malt
- 34% unmalted wheat berries
- 13 IBUs of Hallertau Select (300 min.)
- Wyeast 3763 Roeselare Blend
- Additional slurry from previous lambic batch

Boil time:	330 minutes
Original gravity:	1.048 (11.9°P)
Final gravity:	1.002 (0.5°P)
ABV:	6.0%
IBU:	13
SRM:	4

Directions
Turbid mash (See Chapter 3).

Ferment with Wyeast 3763 Roeselare Blend, plus a cup of slurry from a previous batch of lambic, at around 65°F (18°C). Add 0.25 oz./gal. (2 g/L) boiled and drained house toast Hungarian oak cubes to the primary fermentor (or ferment in a neutral oak barrel).

Carbonate to 3.0 volumes CO_2.

Variations
Blend multiple vintages of this recipe to create a gueuze. Try spontaneous fermentation (replacing the Hallertau Select with 0.8 oz./gal. (6 g/L) of a three-year-old low alpha acid variety). After the beer has aged for a year, add a fruit such as apricot, cherry, raspberry, or currant.

Wine Barrel Flemish Red

This is an American take on Flemish red that is drier and not as vinegary, but with the same deep berry and caramel flavors. It is similar to beers like Russian River Supplication and Jolly Pumpkin La Roja. The red wine barrel (or wine-soaked oak cubes) adds depth to the fruit flavors.

Ingredients
- 26% German Pilsner malt
- 27% German Munich malt
- 27% German Vienna malt
- 8% wheat malt
- 8% medium crystal malt (blend of 60°L crystal and CaraMunich®)
- 4% dark crystal malt (blend of 120°L crystal and Special "B")
- 15 IBUs of Hallertau (60 min.)
- Wyeast 1968 London ESB
- Wyeast 3763 Roeselare Blend
- Lost Abbey Red Poppy (or similar) bottle dregs

Boil time:	90 minutes
Original gravity:	1.060 (14.7°P)
Final gravity:	1.008 (2.1°P)
ABV:	6.8%
IBU:	15
SRM:	24

Directions
Mash at 157°F (70°C) for 60 min. Ferment around 65°F (18°C).

When primary fermentation is complete, rack to secondary with 0.15 oz./gal. (4 g/L) boiled and drained medium toast red–wine soaked French oak cubes (or ferment in a used French oak red wine barrel).

Carbonate to 2.2 volumes of CO_2.

Variations
A good candidate for red berries. It is also a terrific beer to dry hop with bold American varieties like Cascade, Amarillo, and Simcoe. Blended with an imperial stout to temper the sourness, the resulting combination is like cherries and chocolate.

Oud Bruin

This beer is an American interpretation of a Belgian oud bruin. The result is dark and malty, with complementary character from a bourbon barrel that has already had a couple of beers aged in it.

Ingredients
- 79.5% English pale malt (Maris Otter)
- 13% German dark Munich
- 3% 90°L crystal malt
- 3% melanoidin malt
- 1.5% chocolate malt
- 11 IBUs of Amarillo (45 min.)
- Safale US-05 Ale Yeast
- Additional *Brettanomyces* and bacteria of your choice

Boil time:	90 minutes
Original gravity:	1.069 (16.8°P)
Final gravity:	1.010 (2.6°P)
ABV:	7.7%
IBU:	11
SRM:	23

Directions
Mash at 155°F (68°C) for 60 min. Ferment around 65°F (18°C).

When primary fermentation is complete, rack to secondary with 0.15 oz./gal. (1 g/L) bourbon-soaked heavy toast American oak cubes (or age in a bourbon barrel that has already aged a couple of beers).

Carbonate to 2.2 volumes of CO_2.

Variations
Blending with a younger, sweeter beer would produce a beer closer to an Belgian oud bruin, as would aging it in a neutral fermentor (glass, stainless steel, or plastic).

Dave and Becky Pyle's Belgian-style Lambic[1]

Ingredients
· 50% Pilsner malt
· 50% wheat (malted or unmalted)
· 0.65 oz./gal. (4.8 g/L) aged (minimum 3 years), low AA% whole hops (60 min.)
· 0.3 oz./gal. (2.25 g/L) aged, low AA% whole hops (30 min.)
· No yeast pitched

Boil time:	60 minutes
Original gravity:	1.055 (13.6°P)
Final gravity:	1.015 (3.8°P)
ABV:	5.2%
IBU:	Low
SRM:	3

Directions
Mash grains at 150°F (66°C) for 75 minutes.

Transfer wort into rinsed barrel previously used to ferment a sour beer. Allow to ferment for a year at ambient temperature. Blend with batches brewed in other years to taste.

Bottle, aiming for 2.7 volumes of CO_2.

Remi Bonnart's Zed's Dead (Flemish) Red[2]

Ingredients
- 33.5% German Pilsner malt
- 33.5% Vienna malt
- 17% dark Munich malt
- 4% aromatic malt
- 4% CaraMunich malt
- 4% special "B" malt
- 4% wheat malt
- 14 IBUs of East Kent Goldings plug hops (60 min.)
- Wyeast 1764 Rogue Pacman Yeast
- Wyeast 3763 Roeselare Blend

Boil time:	90 minutes
Original gravity:	1.060 (14.7°P)
Final gravity:	1.008 (2.1°P)
ABV:	6.8%
IBU:	14
SRM:	16

Directions
Mash grains at 158°F (70°C) for one hour. Mash-out at 168°F (76°C) for five minutes. Add 0.2 tsp/gal. (1 mL/L) yeast nutrient to the boil. Pitch ale yeast for primary fermentation.

When the fermentation is complete, transfer to secondary and pitch Wyeast Roeselare Blend as well as 1.6 fl. oz./gal. (50 mL/L) of a previous batch. Age around 70°F (21° C) with a silicon airlock. Pitch additional bottle dregs occasionally during aging.

Soak medium toast French oak cubes in Daron Calvados for two weeks in preparation for next step. When the desired sourness is achieved, add 2 oz (57 g)* of the oak cubes along with a cup (237 mL) of the Daron Calvados they had been soaking in, and age the beer on them for three months.

When the desired oak character is reached, package aiming for 2.5 volumes of CO_2.

* Per 5 gallons brewed

Bretted Petite Saison

This low-gravity saison is a session ale for people who enjoy the bigger funky saisons out there, like Boulevard Saison Brett and the Bruery Saison de Lente. The Saison Dupont yeast strain is fickle and difficult to get good attenuation from, so the *B. claussenii* ensures that the beer finishes as dry as a light saison should. This is an easy beer to do from the second runnings of the mash of a higher alcohol beer.

Ingredients
· 95% Pilsner malt
· 4% flaked wheat
· 1% CaraPils
· 26 IBUs of Czech Saaz (45 min.)
· 4 IBUs of Czech Saaz (15 min.)
· 2 IBUs of Czech Saaz (5 min.)
· White Labs WLP565 Belgian Saison I
· White Labs WLP645 *Brettanomyces claussenii*

Boil time:	90 minutes
Original gravity:	1.046 (11.4°P)
Final gravity:	1.005 (1.3°P)
ABV:	5.3%
IBU:	32
SRM:	5

Directions
Mash at 154°F (68°C) for 45 min., and then raise temperature to 167°F (75°C) for 10 min. Ferment around 85°F (29°C).

Carbonate to 2.8 volumes of CO_2.

Variations
Pitch another strain of *Brettanomyces* to generate more aggressive funkiness. To provide fresh hop aromas, dry hop close to packaging with more Saaz, or another spicy hop like Hallertau or Sterling.

Session Brett Belgian Pale

Low gravity *Brettanomyces* beer inspired by Orval and Petite Orval.
Adding the *B. bruxellensis* in primary leads to an aggressively funky beer,
with more character than most session ales have. This is not a sour ale,
as the *Brettanomyces* only produces complex farmyard aromatics and
adds just a faint hint of tartness to the dry finish.

Ingredients
- 54% French Pilsner malt
- 23% German Vienna malt
- 23% wheat malt
- 28 IBUs of Czech Saaz (60 min.)
- 5 IBUs of Czech Saaz (10 min.)
- White Labs WLP550 Belgian Ale
- White Labs WLP650 *Brettanomyces bruxellensis*

Boil time:	90 minutes
Original gravity:	1.042 (10.5°P)
Final gravity:	1.005 (1.3°P)
ABV:	4.8%
IBU:	33
SRM:	3

Directions
Mash at 147°F (64°C) for 75 min. Ferment around 68°F (20°C).
Carbonate to 2.4 volumes of CO_2.

Variations
Add the *Brettanomyces* to the secondary fermentor to reduce the farmyard funk character, or choose a different strain for either a more or less
aggressive flavor contribution.

Courage Russian Imperial Stout Tribute

This recipe is based on the historic Courage Russian Imperial Stout; the current incarnation has no Brett character. If you want to have it retain much sweetness, you will need to kill the *Brettanomyces* by crash cooling when the beer reaches the target final gravity. Fine with gelatin, and add one Campden tablet per gallon (one tablet for every 4 L). The *Brettanomyces* provides a nice leather character and pairs well with the dark malt.

Ingredients
- 61% pale ale malt (Maris Otter or Golden Promise)
- 20% amber malt
- 4% black patent malt
- 12% dark candi syrup (kettle)
- 3% table sugar (kettle)
- 50 IBUs of Target (90 min.)
- Wyeast 1028 London Ale
- *B. anomalus* (a.k.a. *B. claussenii*)

Boil time:	95 minutes
Original gravity:	1.101 (24°P)
Final gravity:	1.020 (5.1°P)
ABV:	10.7%
IBU:	50
SRM:	55

Directions
Mash at 155°F (68°C) for 90 min., then raise the temperature to 166°F (74°C) for 10 min. Ferment around 65°F (18°C).

When fermentation is complete, rack to secondary and add 0.10 oz./gal. (0.8 g/L) medium toast French oak cubes (or age in a well-used oak barrel).

When the gravity reaches 1.020 (5°P) use heat, chemicals, or filtration to halt the fermentation.

Carbonate to 2.1 volumes of CO_2.

Variations
Aged at a cool temperature (below 50°F) for a decade or more, this beer only gets better with time.

English Stock Ale

A traditional English stock ale had big leathery *Brettanomyces* flavors. On its own the body of this beer may be lacking, but it is perfect for blending with a younger, sweeter beer. The malt character is right between toasty and roasty, with dark fruit flavors from the crystal malts.

Ingredients
- 84% English pale malt (Maris Otter)
- 3% 120°L crystal malt
- 3% 60°L crystal malt
- 3% pale chocolate malt
- 7% dark soft candi sugar (kettle)
- 35 IBUs of East Kent Goldings (115 min.)
- Danstar Windsor
- Safale US-05
- WLP645 White Labs *Brettanomyces claussenii*

Boil time:	130 minutes
Original gravity:	1.082 (19.8°P)
Final gravity:	1.011 (2.8°P)
ABV:	9.4%
IBU:	35
SRM:	23

Directions
Mash at 156°F (69°C) for 60 minutes. Ferment with the ale yeast around 65°F (18°C).

Pitch the *Brettanomyces* when transferring to secondary and add 0.10 oz./gal. (0.8 g/L) red wine–soaked medium toast French oak cubes, or age in a red wine barrel.

Carbonate to 2.1 volumes of CO_2.

Variations
Blend with a dark mild or a porter to get a taste of what drinking in England was like before Pasteur and Hansen's techniques cleaned the *Brettanomyces* out of breweries there.

100% *BRETTANOMYCES* BEERS

Sebastian God Damn

One hundred percent *Brettanomyces* session ale inspired by a recipe from fellow homebrewer Sebastian Padilla. Fermented hot, White Labs *Brettanomyces claussenii* makes a big peach character that meshes well with the hop aromatics. This is a quick beer to brew, and a good place to start playing with *Brettanomyces* if you do not like sour beers.

Innovation: Using *Brettanomyces* as the only microbe in the fermentation.

Ingredients
· 83% Belgian Pilsner malt
· 17% wheat malt
· 18 IBUs Sterling (50 min.)
· 2 IBUs Mt. Hood (10 min.)
· 1 IBUs Mt. Hood (5 min.)
· 2 IBUs Sterling (5 min.)
· 0.1 oz./gal. (0.8 g/L) Mt. Hood (0 min.)
· 0.1 oz./gal. (0.8 g/L) Sterling (0 min.)
· White Labs WLP645 *Brettanomyces claussenii*

Boil time:	90 minutes
Original gravity:	1.049 (12.1°P)
Final gravity:	1.009 (2.3°P)
ABV:	5.3%
IBU:	23
SRM:	3

Directions
Mash at 153°F (67°C) for 60 min., then raise the temperature to 168°F (76°C) for 15 min. Ferment around 80°F (27°C).

Carbonate to 2.6 volumes of CO_2.

Variations
Additional hops can be added at the end of the boil, or as a dry hop, for more hop aroma.

Inspired by Pizza Port Mo' Betta Bretta

Based on one of the first commercial 100% *Brettanomyces* beers brewed, Pizza Port's Mo' Betta Bretta. The flaked oats and CaraFoam® provide body, and the acid malt provides lactic acid for ethyl lactate production by the *Brettanomyces*. The result is fruity, with hints of funk, but without much sourness or bitterness.

Innovation: Adding lactic acid to spur ester production by *Brettanomyces.*

Ingredients
- 74% Belgian Pilsner malt
- 9% Belgian Munich malt
- 6.5% CaraFoam
- 6.5% flaked oats
- 4% acidulated malt
- 11 IBUs of Magnum (50 min.)
- *Brettanomyces anomalus* (a.k.a. *B. claussenii*)

Boil time:	125 minutes
Original gravity:	1.060 (14.7°P)
Final gravity:	1.011 (2.8°P)
ABV:	6.3%
IBU:	11
SRM:	5

Directions
Mash at 151°F (66°C) for 60 min. Ferment around 70°F (21°C). Carbonate to 2.3 volumes of CO_2.

Variations

To replicate the original, replace the acid malt with an equal amount of Pilsner, and sour a portion of the wort with *Lactobacillus* while the majority of the batch is boiling. For an autumnal character, add 4 fl. oz./gal. (32 mL/L) of Pinot noir wine and 0.25 lb./gal. (0.3 kg/L) of dried sour cherries. The flavor exhibits surprising spice notes along with the fruit.

Modern Times Beer Neverwhere

A 100% *Brettanomyces* version of American India pale ale, inspired by Super Friends. Tropical-citrusy aroma hops are an interesting match with the similar flavors produced by the *Brettanomyces* fermentation.

Innovation: Melding the ester profile of *Brettanomyces* with fruity American hops.

Ingredients
- 70% American pale 2-row malt
- 22% German wheat malt
- 4% CaraPils malt
- 4% acidulated malt
- 45 IBUs of Hop Extract (60 min.)
- 53 IBUs Centennial (60 min.)
- 0.4 oz./gal. (3 g/L) Centennial (0 min.)
- 0.2 oz./gal. (1.5 g/L) Citra (0 min.)
- 0.2 oz./gal. (1.5 g/L) Chinook (hop back)
- 0.2 oz./gal. (1.5 g/L) Citra (hop back)
- 0.5 oz./gal. (3.75 g/L) Citra (dry hop)
- 0.3 oz./gal. (2.25 g/L) Centennial (dry hop)
- 0.2 oz./gal. (1.5 g/L) Chinook (dry hop)
- White Labs WLP 644 *Brettanomyces bruxellensis* Trois, or BSI *Brettanomyces bruxellensis* var. Drie

Boil time:	75 minutes
Original gravity:	1.064 (15.7°P)
Final gravity:	1.010 (2.6°P)
ABV:	7.1%
IBU:	98
SRM:	4

Directions
Mash at 153°F (67°C) for 60 min. Ferment around 68°F (20°C). Carbonate to 2.4 volumes of CO_2.

Variations
The above hop bill produces a beer heavy with pineapple and mango. Try Amarillo, Simcoe, and Columbus in similar amounts for a more classic fruity, piney, dank West Coast IPA.

AMERICAN ORIGINAL SOURS

Quick Oud Bruin

A sour ale that mimics the flavor of an oud bruin without the wait.
The souring technique is based on the sour worting technique used by
several breweries (see Chapter 5), so the time from brewing to drinking
is much shorter than many other sour ales. The sourness comes off as a
clean tartness that gives depth to the dark malt character.

Innovation: Wort is soured before primary fermentation begins.

Ingredients
- 84.5% pale ale malt (Golden Promise or Maris Otter)
- 5% amber malt
- 5% Golden Naked Oats
- 3% American roasted barley (300°L)
- 2.5% Simpsons dark crystal malt
- 22 IBUs of Galena (60 min.)
- S-04 Safale English Ale

Boil time:	90 minutes
Original gravity:	1.056 (13.8°P)
Final gravity:	1.013 (3.3°P)
ABV:	5.7%
IBU:	22
SRM:	18

Directions
Mash at 154°F (68°C) for 60 min.

Take half of the wort pre-boil, chill and pitch a starter made from
the microbes living on a small amount of grain. Ferment around
80°F (27°C) to make a sour wort. Boil the remaining wort with the
hops and then ferment with the yeast around 65°F (18°C). When the
sour portion is sour enough (usually two or three days), bring it to a
boil for 30 minutes, cool, and combine it with the fermenting beer.

When primary is complete, rack to secondary with 0.25 oz./gal.
(2 g/L) medium toast French oak cubes.

Carbonate to 2.3 volumes of CO_2.

Variations
This one works with bold fruit, for example, a combo of blackberries
and black raspberries.

Bourbon Barrel Imperial Oud Bruin

Originally planned to be a wee heavy, but the microbes from the Flemish red in the barrel next to it had other ideas. The combination of vanilla and coconut in the nose makes for a surprising counterpoint to the bright acidity on the palate.

Innovation: Aging in a characterful spirit barrel.

Ingredients

- 82.3% pale ale malt (Maris Otter or Golden Promise)
- 11% Munich malt
- 3% 90°L crystal malt
- 3% melanoidin malt
- 0.7% chocolate malt
- 25 IBUs of Galena (60 min.)
- WY1728 Wyeast Scottish Ale
- Your choice of *Brettanomyces* and bacteria

Boil time:	90 minutes
Original gravity:	1.097 (23.1°P)
Final gravity:	1.014 (3.6°P)
ABV:	11%
IBU:	25
SRM:	20

Directions

Mash at 155°F (68°C) for 60 min. Ferment around 62°F (17°C).

When primary fermentation is complete, rack to secondary with 0.15 oz./gal. (1.1 g/L) bourbon-soaked heavy toast American oak cubes, or age in a bourbon barrel that has already aged a couple of beers.

Carbonate to 2.0 volumes of CO_2.

Variations

Vanilla beans will enhance the vanilla from the oak, and is an intriguing combination.

Wine Barrel Sour Single

Based on Russian River's original batch of Beatification (Redemption aged in barrels from New Belgium that previously held La Folie). The result is a crisp, mildly tart beer, with layers of complexity contributed by the barrel and its microbes.

Innovation: Reusing the barrel from one type of sour beer for another.

Ingredients
- 77% German Pilsner malt
- 15% wheat malt
- 4% acidulated malt
- 4% Vienna malt
- 24 IBUs of Fuggles (60 min.)
- White Labs WLP500 Trappist Ale Yeast

Boil time:	90 minutes
Original gravity:	1.052 (12.9°P)
Final gravity:	1.004 (1°P)
ABV:	6.4%
IBU:	24
SRM:	4

Directions
Mash at 154°F (68°C) for 60 min. Ferment around 68°F (20°C).

Allow to ferment to completion, rack to a second-use red wine barrel that previously held a Flemish red, and allow to age 18 months. Alternatively, pitch Wyeast Roeselare Blend and bottle dregs along with 0.2 oz./gal. (1.5 g/L) neutral French oak cubes.

Carbonate to 2.2 volumes of CO_2.

Variations
Zest from various citrus fruits (lemon, orange, grapefruit), or citrusy spices such as pink peppercorn, added in the last few weeks before bottling will add freshness to a well-aged beer.

Huge Funkin' Ale

Inspired by high alcohol sour beers like Brasserie des Franches-Montagnes' Abbaye De Saint Bon Chien. Sourness conceals the massive ABV, while enhancing port-like complexities, and huge dark fruit maltiness.

Innovation: Producing a beer that combines alcoholic strength and tartness.

Ingredients
- 52.5% Pilsner malt
- 15% Munich malt
- 8% English pale malt (e.g., Maris Otter)
- 6% CaraMunich malt
- 6% CaraVienna malt
- 6% flaked corn
- 0.5% chocolate malt
- 6% D2 dark candi syrup (kettle)
- 28 IBUs of Galena (90 min.)
- Ferment with yeast slurry from a Flemish red (e.g., Safale US-05 and Lost Abbey Red Poppy dregs)

Boil time:	135 minutes
Original gravity:	1.122 (28.4°P)
Final gravity:	1.020 (5.1°P)
ABV:	13.6%
IBU:	28
SRM:	24

Directions
Mash at 150°F (66°C) for 90 min. Ferment around 65°F (18°C). Carbonate to 1.8 volumes of CO_2.

Variations
Add to the character from the dark malts and candi syrup by adding dried fruits, such as dates, figs, or raisins, to boost the sourness. To cut residual sweetness, add tannins by using oak cubes or your choice of barrel aging.

Sour American

This recipe is for a lambic-like beer, but without as much work. The microbe blend pitched gave it a fruity flavor and a sharp acidity.

Innovation: Adapting the Belgian-style lambic tradition to a less versatile brewhouse.

Ingredients
- 68% German Pilsner malt
- 20% English pale ale malt (Maris Otter)
- 8% wheat malt
- 4% rolled oats
- 13 IBUs of Willamette (75 min.)
- East Coast Yeast ECY01 Bugfarm

Boil time:	120 minutes
Original gravity:	1.056 (13.8°P)
Final gravity:	1.005 (1.3°P)
ABV:	6.7%
IBU:	13
SRM:	5

Directions
Mash at 154°F (68°C) for 75 min, then raise the temperature to 169°F (76°C) for 15 min. Ferment around 68°F (20°C).

Allow to ferment to completion, then rack and add 0.2 oz./gal. (1.5 g/L) of red wine–soaked oak cubes, or age in a red wine barrel.

Carbonate to 2.5 volumes of CO_2.

Variations
A base that is just right for yellow peaches, or blended with a darker beer.

Inspired by Lost Abbey Cable Car
Blend of Red Barn Clone, Avant Gard Clone, and Amigo Lager Clone
This is one of my most complex batches, a blend consisting of 50% saison, 33% bière de garde, and 16.7% pale lager. It was based on the first batch of Lost Abbey's Cable Car, a special blend produced for the 20th anniversary of Toronado, the legendary San Francisco beer bar.

Innovation: Blending three different base beers to compose a unique sour beer.

Blended Beer
Original gravity:	1.060 (14.7°P)
Final gravity:	1.007 (1.8°P)
ABV:	7.0%
IBU:	23.6
SRM:	10

Red Barn Clone (50%)
Ingredients
- 83% Golden Promise
- 7% flaked wheat
- 3% quick oats
- 7% table sugar (kettle)
- 24 IBUs Target (60 min.)
- 4 IBUs Tettnang (15 min.)
- 2 g sweet dried orange peel (7 min.)
- 1 g ground black pepper (7 min.)
- 0.5 g ground dried ginger (7 min.)
- 0.5 g ground grains of paradise (7 min.)
- Wyeast 3724 Belgian Saison

Boil time:	90 minutes
Original gravity:	1.065 (15.9°P)
IBU:	28
SRM:	5.2

Directions
Mash at 150°F (66°C) for 60 min. Ferment at 82°F (28°C).

Avant Garde Clone (33%)
Ingredients
- 90% Golden Promise
- 7.5% home-toasted malt (pale malt toasted in a pie plate placed on a pizza stone at 400°F (204°C) for 25 minutes, stirring every few minutes, until it smelled like a Butterfinger candy bar)
- 2.5% honey malt
- 9 IBUs of Sterling (25 min.)
- 6 IBUs of Styrian Golding (25 min.)
- 4 IBUs of Saaz (15 min.)
- Wyeast 2206 Bavarian Lager

Boil time:	130 minutes
Original gravity:	1.060 (°P)
IBU:	19
SRM:	8.5

Directions
Mash at 147°F (64°C) for 60 min. Ferment around 60°F (16°C).

Amigo Lager Clone (16.7%)
Ingredients
- 70% German Pilsner malt
- 30% Golden Promise
- 16 IBUs of Magnum (60 min.)
- 4 IBUs of Saaz (15 min.)
- Wyeast 2206 Bavarian Lager

Boil time:	75 minutes
Original gravity:	1.048 (11.9°P)
IBU:	20
SRM:	4.3

Directions
Mash at 148°F (64°C) for 60 min. Ferment around 50°F (10°C).

Final Blended Beer
After all three beers are fermented out, combine them into a single fermentor and add the dregs from several bottles of sour Lost Abbey beers along with 0.2 oz./gal. (1.5 g/L) of red wine–soaked French oak, or age in a red wine barrel.

Carbonate to 2.4 volumes of CO_2.

Cherry Bourbon Belgian Dark Strong

This beer gets much of its character from the addition of four different caramelized or unrefined sugars. The combination of cherries, a strong dark base, and bourbon was inspired by Lost Abbey's Cuvée de Tomme. Replacing the other two sugars with more dark candi syrup and muscovado would get you most of the way there.

Innovation: Adding fruit to a strong, dark sour base beer.

Ingredients
- 35% Pilsner malt
- 21% Munich malt
- 14% English pale ale malt (Maris Otter)
- 4% aromatic malt
- 4% CaraMunich malt
- 1% chocolate malt
- 9% dark candi syrup (kettle)
- 8% muscovado (kettle)
- 3% dark soft candi sugar (kettle)
- 1% Brew Like a Monk caramel (kettle)
- 30 IBUs of East Kent Goldings (120 min.)
- 2 IBUs of Czech Saaz (15 min.)
- White Labs WLP530 Abbey Ale
- *Brettanomyces claussenii*
- Orval bottle dregs (or similar)

Boil time:	150 minutes
Original gravity:	1.095 (22.7°P)
Final gravity:	1.010 (2.6°P)
ABV:	11.3%
IBU:	32
SRM:	27

Directions
Mash at 154°F (68°C) for 45 min. Ferment around 70°F (21°C).

When primary fermentation is complete, rack to secondary with 0.15 oz./gal. (1 g/L) bourbon-soaked heavy toast American oak cubes (or age in a bourbon barrel), with 1 lb./gal. (0.12 kg/L) sweet dark cherries. Brew Like a Monk caramel is made from a recipe in the book of the same name that calls for heating corn syrup with an addition of diammonium phosphate (DAP) until it is a rich amber color.

Carbonate to 2.2 volumes of CO_2.

Variations
This recipe would work beautifully with dried cherries, and aged in a red wine barrel.

Floral Honey Wheat

A sour beer with a floral honey aroma. The honey malt contributes sweetness to complement the floral aromatics of the actual honey. Waiting to add the honey until after primary fermentation prevents the aromatics from being scrubbed out. This batch was inspired by Hanssens Mead the Gueuze, although that beer was actually a blend of two beverages rather than an addition of honey to lambic.

Innovation: Incorporating the aromatic qualities of honey into a sour beer.

Ingredients

- 45% German Pilsner malt
- 26% wheat malt
- 4% 10°L crystal malt
- 2% CaraPils
- 2% honey malt
- 21% orange blossom honey (secondary)
- 16 IBUs of Amarillo (50 min.)
- 0.04 oz./gal. (0.3 g/L) dried chamomile (0 min.)
- Wyeast 1056 American Ale
- *Brettanomyces* and bacteria of your choice (I used dregs from New Belgium's corked-and-caged La Folie, and Russian River)

Boil time:	80 minutes
Original gravity:	1.056 (13.8°P)
Final gravity:	1.008 (2.1°P)
ABV:	6.3%
IBU:	16
SRM:	5

Directions

Mash at 156°F (69°C) for 60 min. Ferment around 68°F (20°C).

After primary fermentation is finished, add the honey to the primary fermentor. Allow to ferment out before transferring to secondary. Add 0.4 fl. oz./gal. (15.5 mL/L) of 88% lactic acid to the fermentor if, like my batch, your beer is not adequately sour.

Carbonate to 2.3 volumes of CO_2.

Variations

Good blended with 2 lb./gal. white peaches (0.24 kg/L). This recipe would also work well with additional flowers, such as hibiscus, jasmine, lavender, rose, or heather.

Funky Rye Session Ale

A low gravity rye ale with a subtle *Brettanomyces* character. The toasty dark malt and *Brettanomyces* funk create a session beer than is satisfying during colder months when a lighter beer does not work.

Innovation: Creating a characterful sour beer at the low end of the alcohol spectrum.

Ingredients
· 79% Golden Promise
· 10% rye malt
· 6% 120°L crystal malt
· 2.5% pale chocolate malt
· 2.5% chocolate rye malt
· 19 IBUs of East Kent Goldings (50 min.)
· 5 IBUs of East Kent Goldings (15 min.)
· Wyeast 1275 Thames Valley Ale
· White Labs WLP645 *Brettanomyces claussenii*

Boil time:	105 minutes
Original gravity:	1.045 (11.2°P)
Final gravity:	1.009 (2.3°P)
ABV:	4.7%
IBU:	24
SRM:	4.5

Directions
Mash at 154°F (68°C) for 60 min, then raise the temperature to 168°F (76°C) for 15 min. Ferment around 68°F (20°C).
    Carbonate to 2.2 volumes of CO_2.

Variations
Good base for red fruits such as raspberries, currants, or red wine grapes.

Perpetuum Sour

A recipe designed to be fermented as a solera, so giving a regular payoff. Remove a quarter of the volume once a year and replace it with enough fresh wort to fill the barrel or fermentor. The result is similar to a lambic, but without as much mineral or lemon character.

Innovation: Applying the solera method to sour beer production.

Ingredients
- 42% German Pilsner malt
- 37% American pale malt
- 8% rolled oats
- 7% flaked wheat
- 6% wheat malt
- 11 IBU Willamette (60 min.)
- East Coast Yeast ECY01 Bugfarm

Boil time:	75 minutes
Original gravity:	1.058 (14.3°P)
Final gravity:	1.002 (0.5°P)
ABV:	7.4%
IBU:	11
SRM:	4

Directions
Mash at 156°F (69°C) for 90 min, then raise the temperature to 168°F (76°C) for 15 min. Primary ferment in a red wine barrel at around 68°F (20°C).

Carbonate to 2.5 volumes of CO_2.

Variations
Does not need to be aged as a solera. Add red wine grapes, citrusy dry hops, or elderflowers after the souring has progressed.

Sour Bourbon Barrel Porter

A dark porter (or is it a stout?) aged in a second-use bourbon barrel. It retained enough sweetness from the crystal malts and high mash temperature to balance the roasted malts. The vanilla and coconut notes from the barrel complement the dark malts, and the sourness adds drinkability that many bourbon-barrel stouts are missing.

Innovation: Souring a dark beer.

Ingredients
· 84% American pale malt
· 7% crystal malt (a combination of 55°L and 150°L)
· 5% chocolate malt
· 4% 500°L roasted barley
· 25 IBUs of Magnum (60 min.)
· Wyeast 1056 American Ale
· Your choice of *Brettanomyces* and bacteria

Boil time:	90 minutes
Original gravity:	1.080 (19.3°P)
Final gravity:	1.014 (3.6°P)
ABV:	8.8%
IBU:	25
SRM:	40

Directions
Mash at 155°F (68°C) for 60 min. Ferment around 65°F (18°C).

When primary fermentation is complete, rack to secondary with 0.15 oz./gal. (1 g/L) bourbon-soaked heavy toast American oak cubes, or age in a bourbon barrel that has already aged a couple of beers.

Carbonate to 2.1 volumes of CO_2.

Variations
A good beer for fruits like sour cherries, blackberries, or red wine grapes.

Sour Squash

A sour brown ale with subtle spicing in the boil and roasted butternut squash added to the mash. The squash adds a subtle character that dances right around the flavor threshold. With the blend of winey tartness, warming spices, and earthy squash, it tastes like autumn in a glass.

Innovation: Adding squash to a sour beer.

Ingredients

- 53% German Pilsner malt
- 15% German Munich malt
- 12% roasted butternut squash
- 8% wheat malt
- 4% 90°L crystal malt
- 4% 55°L crystal malt
- 2% flaked barley
- 2% melanoidin malt
- 1% Carafa Special II malt
- 17 IBUs of Amarillo (60 min.)
- 0.02 oz./gal. (0.13 g/L) cinnamon (0 min.)
- 0.01 oz./gal. (0.07 g/L) nutmeg (0 min.)
- Wyeast 1056 American Ale
- Your choice of *Brettanomyces* and bacteria

Boil time:	120 minutes
Original gravity:	1.067 (16.4°P)
Final gravity:	1.012 (3.1°P)
ABV:	7.3%
IBU:	17
SRM:	17

Directions

Mash at 156°F (69°C) for 90 min. Ferment around 65°F (18°C).

When primary fermentation is complete, rack to secondary with 0.2 oz./gal. (1.5 g/L) red wine–soaked medium toast French oak cubes, or into a red wine barrel.

Carbonate to 2.2 volumes of CO_2.

Variations

Consider adding additional spices, such as ginger, clove, and allspice, if you want a beer that tastes like Thanksgiving. It would also make a delicious oud bruin by omitting the spices and squash.

Funky Tripel

The addition of sourness and funk to a tripel makes for a more complex experience. There are a few sour and funky tripels I have been inspired by including, Allagash's Tripel Roselaire, and also La Buteuse Brassin Spécial, a complex funky elixir from Le Trou Diable.

Innovation: Using a refined sugar to lighten the body of a sour beer.

Ingredients
- 86% German Pilsner malt
- 4% flaked wheat
- 1% CaraPils
- 9% table sugar (post-primary fermentation)
- 16 IBUs of Simcoe (60 min.)
- Wyeast 3763 Roeselare Blend
- Wyeast 3787 Trappist High Gravity
- Russian River Temptation dregs (or similar)

Boil time: 90 minutes
Original gravity: 1.073 (17.7°P)
Final gravity: 1.010 (2.6°P)
ABV: 8.3%
IBU: 16
SRM: 6

Directions
Mash at 154°F (68°C) for 45 min., then raise the temperature to 167°F (75°C) for 10 min. Ferment around 68°F (20°C).

When fermentation is complete, rack to secondary with 0.25 oz./gal. (1.8 g/L) medium toast French oak cubes, or age in an oak barrel.

Carbonate to 2.8 volumes of CO_2.

Variations
Soak the oak in Calvados (or age in an apple brandy barrel) to give it an apple character that will result in a beer with a Quebecoise vibe (like La Buteuse Brassin Spécial).

Dark Winter Saison I

A saison inspired by Lost Abbey's Ten Commandments (Pizza Port SPF 8). It has a Christmas character from the piney rosemary and orange zest added to the boil. The funk gives it a loamy mushroom flavor. The first in a series of dark funky beers brewed with homebrewers Alex Howe and Noah Paci.

Innovation: Creating a saison for the holiday season.

Ingredients

- 87.5% Pilsner malt
- 3.5% Carafa Special II malt
- 3.5% CaraWheat malt
- 2% Special "B" malt
- 25 IBUs of Amarillo (first wort)
- 3.5% raisins: blackened, deglazed in wine, and pureed (0 min.)
- zest of two Valencia oranges per 5 gal. (20 L) (0 min.)
- one small sprig of fresh rosemary per 5 gal. (20 L) (0 min.)
- Wyeast 3725 Bier de Garde
- Bottle dregs from your favorite sour beers

Boil time:	100 minutes
Original gravity:	1.072 (17.5°P)
Final gravity:	1.003 (0.8°P)
ABV:	9.1%
IBU:	25
SRM:	23

Directions

Mash at 130°F (54°C) for 20 min., then raise to 152°F (67°C) for 90 min., and then to 168°F (76°C) for 15 min. Ferment around 78°F (26°C).

When primary fermentation is complete, rack to secondary with 0.2 oz./gal. (1.5 g/L) port-soaked medium toast French oak cubes, or age in a port barrel.

Carbonate to 2.5 volumes of CO_2.

Variations

Without the wild yeast and bacteria this makes a clean dark saison.

Dark Winter Saison II

The second iteration of our dark winter saison series. The more complex grist gives more dark roasted flavors. The black cardamom addition needs to be done sparingly, because it gives a smoky-medicinal aroma that reminds me of turpentine.

Innovation: Flavoring with a unique spice to compete with a strongly flavored beer.

Ingredients

- 83% American pale malt
- 4% CaraMunich malt
- 4% Special "B" malt
- 3.5% 40°L crystal malt
- 2% Belgian chocolate malt
- 1.5% coffee malt
- 1% Carafa Special II malt
- 1% flaked wheat
- 17 IBUs of Amarillo (60 min.)
- 0.02 oz./gal. (0.13 g/L) black cardamom seeds (2 min.)
- 4 oz./gal. (30 g/L) dates blackened and then deglazed with wort and red wine (2 min.)
- Wyeast 3711 French Saison
- Jolly Pumpkin bottle dregs (or similar)

Boil time:	90 minutes
Original gravity:	1.078 (18.9°P)
Final gravity:	1.004 (1°P)
ABV:	9.8%
IBU:	17
SRM:	32

Directions

Mash 90 min. at 154°F (68°C). Ferment around 78°F (26°C).

When primary fermentation is complete, rack to secondary with 0.2 oz./gal. (1.5 g/L) port-soaked medium toast French oak cubes (or a port barrel).

Carbonate to 2.4 volumes of CO_2.

Variations

As the beer already has big flavors, 2 lb./gal. (0.25 kg/L) red wine grapes makes a good addition.

Dark Winter Saison III

Buckwheat honey has an earthy flavor that is overpowering in large amounts, but at the right level it provides supporting flavors to the funk. Much like buckwheat itself, the honey also provides fatty acids, which are turned into fruity esters under the right conditions. The result is a unique fruity and earthy aroma.

Innovation: Creating a beer that can compete with the assertive flavor of buckwheat honey.

Ingredients

- 60% German Pilsner malt
- 15% German Munich malt
- 4% steel-cut oats (pre-boiled)
- 3% Carafa Special II malt
- 3% CaraMunich malt
- 2% Special "B" malt
- 8% fig puree (0 min.)
- 5% buckwheat honey (0 min.)
- 23 IBUs of Simcoe (70 min.)
- 0.02 oz./gal. (0.13 g/L) anise (5 min.)
- 0.01 oz./gal. (0.07 g/L) star anise (5 min.)
- 0.003 oz./gal. (0.025 g/L) cinnamon (5 min.)
- White Labs WLP565 Belgian Saison I
- White Labs WLP645 *Brettanomyces claussenii*
- Additional *Brettanomyces* and bacteria of your choice

Boil time:	85 minutes
Original gravity:	1.066 (16.1°P)
Final gravity:	1.006 (1.5°P)
ABV:	7.9%
IBU:	23
SRM:	23

Directions

Mash at 156°F (69°C) for 90 min. Ferment at around 78°F (26°C). Carbonate to 2.4 volumes of CO_2.

Variations

Adding oak cubes soaked in rum or another spirit could add depth to this brew.

Dark Winter Saison IV

A dark saison, with flavors inspired by Russian River's Consecration. The cold-steeped roasted barley adds a smooth chocolate flavor, avoiding a harsh roasted contribution in a dry beer. Aged on Zante currants and a wine-soaked oak stave, it becomes rich and vinous.

Innovation: Melding the flavors of wine and Zante currants to create a unique beer.

Ingredients
- 92% Vienna malt
- 2% Special "B" malt
- 2% American chocolate malt
- 2% Carafa Special II malt
- 2% roasted barley (cold extraction added at the start of the boil)
- 22 IBUs of Warrior added (75 min.)

- Wyeast 3726 Farmhouse Ale
- White Labs 670 American Farmhouse
- Wyeast 5112 *Brettanomyces bruxellensis*
- 5 oz./gal. (37 g/L) Zante currants (secondary)

Boil time:	60 minutes
Original gravity:	1.067 (16.4°P)
Final gravity:	1.005 (1.3°P)
ABV:	8.2%
IBU:	22
SRM:	29

Directions
Mash at 159°F (71°C) for 60 min. Ferment around 75°F (24°C).

After fermentation is complete, transfer off the yeast and onto 0.2 oz./gal. (1.5 g/L) of red wine–soaked oak.

Carbonate to 2.4 volumes of CO_2.

Variations
Age in a red wine barrel.

Inspired by McKenzie Brew House Saison Vautour (Du Bois)

Saison Vautour is named for the vultures that ominously circle the brewery on brew days. This is the recipe for McKenzie Brew House's multiple gold medal–winning rye saison directly from the brewer. It is a good example of how a simple recipe can result in a beer of extraordinary complexity. The clean version has an authentic rustic character from the rye and yeast, while the mixed fermentation by *Brettanomyces* and bacteria living in the wood adds tartness and funk to the barrel-aged version. It is fermented with saison yeast for two to three days in a conical tank. Once active fermentation peaks, the portion of the beer to be soured is pumped to the basement and into barrels, which are already colonized by a variety of strains of wild yeast and bacteria.

Innovation: A saison fermentation started in stainless steel, finished by a barrel's resident microbes.

Ingredients

- 74% Pilsner malt
- 18% rye malt
- 8% soft blond candi sugar (kettle)
- 23 IBUs Hallertau Tradition (60 min.)
- 2 IBUs Hallertau Tradition (15 min.)
- 3 IBUs East Kent Goldings (15 min.)
- 1 IBU Hallertau Tradition (5 min.)
- 1 IBU East Kent Goldings (5 min.)
- White Labs WLP566 Belgian Saison II

Boil time:	90 minutes
Original gravity:	1.057 (14°P)
Final gravity:	1.006 (1.5°P)
ABV:	6.7%
IBU:	30
SRM:	4

Directions

Mash at 145°F (63°C) for 60 minutes. Start fermentation at 60°F (16°C) and allow to rise to 82°F–84°F (28–29°C).

When the gravity stabilizes, bottle with enough priming sugar to reach 2.5 volumes of CO_2.

Variations

To mimic the barrel-aged version, rack to secondary and add 0.2 oz./gal. (1.5 g/L) medium toast French oak cubes (boiled to extract excess tannins and to sanitize), along with either Wyeast WY3278 Lambic Blend or the dregs from your favorite unpasteurized sour beer. Allow the gravity to stabilize before bottling, aiming for 2.5 volumes of CO_2.

McKenzie Brew House Irma

A saison, bière de garde and bière de miel mash-up my friend, Nathan Zeender, and I brewed with Ryan Michaels and Gerard Olson at McKenzie Brew House. The base beer was not sour, but a portion of the beer was aged with their house culture and various sugars in wine and apple brandy barrels.

Innovation: Aging the same beer in different types of barrels with different sugars before blending back together.

Ingredients
· 68% German Pilsner malt
· 9% English pale ale malt (Maris Otter)
· 4% German Munich malt
· 2% CaraMunich malt
· 11% soft blond candi sugar (kettle)
· 5% D2 dark candi syrup (kettle)
· 21 IBUs of East Kent Goldings (70 min.)
· White Labs WLP566 Belgian Saison II

Boil time:	90 minutes
Original gravity:	1.062 (15.2°P)
Final gravity:	1.006 (1.5°P)
ABV:	7.4%
IBU:	21
SRM:	15

Directions
Mash at 150°F (66°C) for 60 min. Ferment around 80°F (27°C).
Carbonate to 2.4 volumes of CO_2.

Variations

For Irma Extra, age in a used wine or apple brandy barrel (or with oak cubes), a house culture of microbes (or dregs), and add a sugar, such as wildflower honey or jaggery, to increase the alcohol and complexity. Irma Extra turned out to be a wonderfully complex saison, with big notes of apple and berry, and a pleasant lactic acid sourness. As it warms, a bit of oak comes out, but it maintains a highly drinkable balance.

Close-up of an apple brandy barrel at McKenzie Brew House.

Buckwheat Sour Amber

The only exposure most people have to buckwheat is in pancakes, but it is also toasted and sold as kasha (especially popular in Russia). The flavor is in the same general category as rye; buckwheat is slightly more rustic, grainy, and flavorful than more commonly used grains. Part of that character derives from buckwheat's caprylic acid content (*capr-* comes from the Latin for goat, so you can guess what sort of flavor it adds). The fortunate thing about many off-tasting fatty acids, like caprylic acid, is that *Brettanomyces* transforms them into appealing aromas by combining them with a molecule of ethanol (or another alcohol) to form an ester. In this case, the *Brettanomyces* will take caprylic acid and ethanol to create ethyl caprylate, an ester whose flavor is "waxy, wine, floral, fruity, pineapple, apricot, banana, pear, brandy."[3] Based on the base beer for Russian River's Supplication, this beer was brewed to explore what character could be obtained from *Brettanomyces*-produced esters derived from the fatty acids in buckwheat.

Innovation: Using buckwheat.

Ingredients
- 48% German Pilsner malt
- 22% German Vienna malt
- 17.5% raw buckwheat
- 11% 40°L crystal malt
- 1.5% Carafa Special III malt
- 17 IBUs of Styrian Goldings (60 min.)
- Safbrew T-58
- Jolly Pumpkin bottle dregs (or similar)

Boil time:	90 minutes
Original gravity:	1.056 (13.8°P)
Final gravity:	1.004 (1°P)
ABV:	6.8%
IBU:	17
SRM:	14.5

Directions
Boil the buckwheat in 3–4 qt. water per pound of buckwheat (6.3–8.3 L/kg).Mash the rest of the grains at 125°F (52°C) for 15 min., then combine with the buckwheat "porridge" and additional boiling water and hold at 149°F (65°C) for 45 min. Ferment around 73°F (23°C).

When primary fermentation is complete, rack and add 0.2 oz./gal. (1.5 g/L) of rum-soaked American oak cubes (or into a spirit barrel).

Carbonate to 2.6 volumes of CO_2.

Variations
Add sour cherries to the beer after it sours. Swap the buckwheat with spelt, emmer, or another heirloom grain to experience what these can add.

Red Wine Yeast Sour Red

I was inspired to try fermenting a beer with wine yeast by an interview with Shea Comfort on the Brewing Network's *Sunday Session*.[4] I selected Brunello BM45 (a red wine strain known for imparting berry jam-like aromatics) as the primary fermenter for a Flemish red. I had read that BM45 is excruciatingly slow to start fermenting, including stories of it taking three days before the onset of CO_2 production.[5] Despite knowing this, I pitched the rehydrated wine yeast simultaneously with East Coast Yeast Flanders Red (ECY02). By the next morning the fermentation was raging, most likely the ale yeast in the blend. Luckily, BM45 is a "killer" strain, so shortly after that became active the ale yeast would have been dead.

When I racked the beer to the secondary fermentor I pulled a sample that exhibited a coating viscosity in the mouthfeel. At first I was suspicious that it was a result of *Pediococcus*, but the manufacturer's description of BM45 reads, "BM45 produces high levels of polyphenol-reactive polysaccharides, resulting in wines with great mouthfeel and improved color stability."[6] The primary fermentation only reduced the gravity to 1.020 SG (5°P) from 1.068 OG (16.5°P), which left plenty of fermentables for the other microbes. After six months of souring, the beer developed an unpleasant sulfur character. After that phase passed, the finished beer contained many of the berry jam-like vinous aromatics I was hoping that the wine yeast would provide. The microbes disassembled most of the polysaccharides, leaving a mouthfeel that was similar to a batch fermented with brewer's yeast.

Innovation: Primary fermentation with red wine yeast.

Ingredients
- 40% German Munich malt
- 40% German Vienna malt
- 8% CaraMunich malt
- 4% flaked corn
- 4% flaked soft white wheat
- 4% Special "B" malt
- 16 IBUs of Sorachi Ace (60 min.)
- Lallemand BM45 Brunello
- East Coast Yeast ECY02 Flemish Ale

Boil time:	90 minutes
Original gravity:	1.068 (16.6°P)
Final gravity:	1.012 (3.1°P)
ABV:	7.3%
IBU:	16
SRM:	17.5

Directions

Mash at 158°F (70°C) for 60 min. Ferment with the wine yeast around 76°F (23°C).

When fermentation is complete, transfer and pitch the remainder of the microbes.

Carbonate to 2.4 volumes of CO_2.

Variations

Age on oak cubes soaked in red wine or port (or age in a wine barrel) to reinforce the wine flavors that come from the yeast. Wine grapes could be added, but this would overwhelm the subtle character generated by the wine yeast.

Wild Cider

A cider version of a sour beer, similar to the Basque ciders that have become a sensation in the last few years. Cider does not have the unfermentables of beer, so it gets funky, but only slightly tart.

Innovation: Applying the principles of sour beer to apple cider.

Ingredients
- 100% apple cider
- 0.25 tsp pectinase (pectic enzyme) per gallon of cider (0.3 mL/L)
- White Labs WLP300 Hefeweizen Ale
- Yeast slurry from a sour beer of your choice

Boil time:	0 minutes
Original gravity:	1.048 (11.9°P)
Final gravity:	1.000 (0°P)
ABV:	6.3%
IBU:	0
SRM:	2

Directions

Add pectic enzyme one hour before the yeast. Alcohol denatures the enzyme, so the earlier it is added the better. Ferment around 65°F (18°C).
    Carbonate to 2.6 volumes of CO_2.

Variations

Leave it uncarbonated for a more authentic Basque experience. If you are feeling lucky, buy unpasteurized cider and rely on the naturally occurring wild yeast to add the rustic character.

References

1. "2005 National Homebrew Competition Winner's List," American Homebrewers Association, Baltimore, MD, June 18, 2005, Accessed March 14, 2013, http://www.homebrewersassociation.org /attachments/0000/2535/2005_Winners_List.pdf.
2. "Zed's Dead Red NHC 2010," American Homebrewers Association wiki, *Homebrewopedia*, last accessed March 14, 2013, http:// wiki.homebrewersassociation.org/ZedsDeadRed.
3. Jeff Sparrow, *Wild Brews: Beer Beyond the Influence of Brewer's Yeast.*
4. Shea Comfort, interview on the *Sunday Session*, MP3 audio, Brewing Network, November 23, 2008, http://www.thebrewing network.com/shows/The-Sunday-Session/The-Sunday-Session -11-23-08-Shea-Comfort.
5. Brian S, "BM45," *Burgundian Babble Belt* homeBBBrew board, August 18, 2011 (12:33 p.m.), http://www.babblebelt.com /newboard/thread.html?tid=1108752780&th=1300465998.
6. "Yeast Selected from Nature," Lallemand Inc., last accessed April 24, 2013, http://www.lallemandwine.us/products/yeast_strains.php.

APPENDIX A: FRUIT AND BEER SUGGESTIONS

These charts give a quick reference for adding fresh or frozen fruit and vegetables to beer.[1] The Beer Flavor column provides a suggestion for the type of sour beer best suited for each fruit or vegetable. These are not firm rules, but serve as a guide based on extensive experience both tasting and brewing sour beers. The fourth column offers a range of fruit or vegetable concentrations, from subtle (but noticeable) to assertive. There are cases where you may venture outside this range to create either sub-threshold complexity (below the low end) or dominant fruit flavors (above the high end). Unless otherwise noted, the amounts reflect whole fruit (either fresh or frozen).

Table A.1—Fruit and Beer Suggestions Chart

Fruit	Commercial example	Beer flavor	Amount per gallon (per L)	Average sugar content of edible portion[2]
Apple (cider)	New Glarus Apple Ale	Light	0.5–4.0 lb. (60–480 g)	9.4%
Apricot	Cascade Apricot Ale	Light	0.5–2.5 lb. (60–300 g)	9.2%
Blackberry	The Bruery Wanderer	Light-Medium	0.5–2.0 lb. (60–240 g)	4.9%
Blueberry	Ithaca LeBleu	Light	1–3 lb. (120–360 g)	10.0%
Cherry (dark)	Double Mountain Devil's Kriek	Any	0.5–1.5 lb. (60–180 g)	12.8%

Fruit	Commercial example	Beer flavor	Amount per gallon (per L)	Average sugar content of edible portion[2]
Cherry (sour)	Cambridge Brewing Cerise Cassée	Any	0.5–2.0 lb. (60–240 g)	9.0%
Cherry (dried sour)	Russian River Supplication	Medium-Dark	0.25–1.0 lb. (30–120 g)	77.5%[3]
Citrus	Lost Abbey Veritas 008 (lemon)	Any	0.25–0.5 lb. (30–60 g)	Lemon: 2.5% Grapefruit: 7.0% Orange: 9.1%
Cranberries	New Belgium Kick	Light-Medium	0.25–0.5 lb. (30–60 g)	4.0%
Date	Cambridge Brewing Benevolence	Dark	0.25–0.5 lb. (30–60 g)	63.4%
Elderberry (dried)	Captain Lawrence Black and Brown Sour	Medium-Dark	0.1–0.25 lb. (12–30 g)	N/A
Fig	Cascade Figaro	Medium-Dark	0.25–0.5 lb. (30–60 g)	Raw: 16.3% Dried: 23.4%
Grape (red wine)	Captain Lawrence Rosso e Marrone	Any	0.5–1.5 lb. (60–180 g)	Varies (22%–25%)
Grape (white wine)	Cascade The Vine	Light-Medium	0.5–1.5 lb. (60–180 g)	Varies (22%–25%)
Lychee	Cambridge Brewing Double Happiness	Light	0.5–2.0 lb. (60–240 g)	15.2%
Peach	Lost Abbey Yellow Bus	Light	1.0–3.0 lb. (120–360 g)	8.4%
Persimmon	Upland Persimmon Lambic	Medium	0.25–5.0 lb. (30–600 g)	12.5%
Pluot	Russian River Compunction	Light	0.5–1.5 lb. (60–180 g)	n.d.
Prickly pear	Freetail Fortuna Roja	Light-Medium	0.5–1.0 lb. (60–120 g)	n.d.
Raisin	Lost Abbey Ten Commandments	Dark	0.25–0.5 lb. (30–60 g)	59.2%
Raspberry	Lost Abbey Framboise de Amorosa	Any	0.5–3.0 lb. (60–360 g)	4.4%
Strawberry	Upland Strawberry Lambic	Light	1.0–4.0 lb. (120–480 g)	4.9%
Tropical fruit	The Bruery–Cigar City ISO:FT (guava)	Any	0.5–2.0 lb. (60–240 g)	Papaya: 7.8% Guava: 8.9% Mango: 13.7%
Watermelon	Russian River Watermelon Funk	Light	0.5–2.0 lb. (60–240 g)	6.2%
Zante currant (dried)	Russian River Consecration	Dark	0.25–1.0 lb. (30–120 g)	67.3%

Table A.2—Vegetable and Beer Suggestions Chart

Vegetable	Commercial example	Beer flavor	Amount per gallon (per L)	Average sugar content of edible portion
Chile pepper	Upright Fatali Four	Any	0.05–0.1 lb. (6–12 g)	Green: 5.1% Red: 5.3% Dried: 41.1%
Rhubarb	Cantillon Zwanze 2008	Light-Medium	0.5–2.5 lb (60–300 g)	1.1%
Squash	Jolly Pumpkin La Parcela (pumpkin)	Medium	0.5–2.0 lb (60–240 g)	Butternut: 2.2% Pumpkin: 1.4%

References

1. United States Department of Agriculture, Agricultural Research Service, 2011, *USDA National Nutrient Database for Standard Reference*, Release 24, Nutrient Data Laboratory Home Page, http://www.ars.usda.gov/ba/bhnrc/ndl.

2. "Composition of Foods Raw, Processed, Prepared," *USDA National Nutrient Database for Standard Reference*, Release 25, U.S. Department of Agriculture, Agricultural Research Service, 2012, Nutrient Data Laboratory Home Page, http://www.ars.usda.gov/ba/bhnrc/ndl.

3. "Dried Montmorency Cherries," Eden Foods, product ID 103270, last accessed December 15, 2013, http://www.edenfoods.com/store/.

APPENDIX B: IMPACT OF FRUIT ON ALCOHOL CONTENT

To correctly determine the impact of adding fruit on the alcohol content, you will need to first establish the effective original degrees Plato of the beer. You can use this number along with the measured final gravity in a standard alcohol formula. The calculation to determine the effective starting gravity requires inputting five variables:

W_F : Weight of the fruit in lb. (not including pits, stems, and seeds)
P_F : °P of the fruit (from a refractometer or packing info)
P_B : Original °P reading of the beer
G_B : Original gravity reading of the beer
V_B : Current volume of the beer in gal.

To use the following formula with metric units, simply use the weight of fruit in kilograms for W_F and liters of beer for V_B, and remove the multiplication by 8.35 in the formula, because 1 L of water weighs 1 kg.

$$\text{Effective starting gravity in } °P = \frac{(V_B \times G_B \times 8.35) \times P_B + (W_F \times P_F)}{(V_B \times G_B \times 8.35) + W_F}$$

Sample calculation

If you have 4.5 gal. of (1.044 OG) 11°P beer onto 10 lb. of 1.057 SG (14°P) cherries:

Effective original gravity =

$$\frac{(4.5 \times 1.044 \times 8.35) \times 11 + (10 \times 14)}{(4.5 \times 1.044 \times 8.35) + 10} = 11.61°P$$

That is to say, the increase in the effective starting gravity was 0.61°P, enough to boost the alcohol by 0.3% ABV, assuming the same final gravity (about the same increase in alcohol from the priming sugar).

On the other hand, if you add the same 10 lb. of 1.057 SG (14°P) cherries into 4.5 gal. of 1.106 OG (25°P) imperial stout you would have:

Effective original gravity =

$$\frac{(4.5 \times 1.106 \times 8.35) \times 25 + (10 \times 14)}{(4.5 \times 1.106 \times 8.35) + 10} = 22.9°P$$

This represents a drop of 2.1°P, enough to reduce the alcohol by 1.1% ABV, assuming the same final gravity.

These two examples demonstrate a key insight: if the sugar concentration of the fruit is lower than the original gravity of the beer, the addition will lower the effective original gravity and reduce the percentage of alcohol, given the same final gravity. Conversely, if the sugar content of the fruit is higher than the beer, it will raise the effective original gravity and similarly the percentage of alcohol.

In general, fruits provide sugars that are more fermentable than mashed grains; even with the same starting gravity, fruit beers may result in a lower final gravity and thus marginally more alcohol. However, if you determine your effective starting gravity, this difference will be included in your alcohol content calculation when you take the final gravity reading.

While employing this complex formula will lead to a slightly more accurate measurement, the main lesson is that the change in alcohol resulting from the addition of fruit is small enough to be comfortably ignored in most cases. You may want to take it into account if you are adding fruit to a base beer that is exceptionally strong or weak, or when adding a large amount of a fruit that has a substantially different gravity than the base beer.

If adding a fruit juice that is low in sugar, such as watermelon, home-brewer Seth Hammond advocates freeze concentrating the juice before adding it to the beer.[1] This method (as opposed to concentration by evaporation) does not harm the fresh flavor contributed by the fruit.

References

1. Seth Hammond, personal communication with author, June 12, 2012.

BIBLIOGRAPHY

Aguilar Uscanga, M., M.L. Delia, and P. Strehaiano, 2003. "Brettanomyces bruxellensis: effect of oxygen on growth and acetic acid production." *Applied Microbiology and Biotechnology* 61(2):157. doi:10.1007/s00253-002-1197-z.

Allagash brew. "Allagash Brewing's First Traditional Spontaneous Brew." *Youtube* video. December 13, 2007. http://www.youtube.com/watch?v=wD_49kfVJeE.

Arthur, Tomme, Vinnie Cilurzo. "Cult Beers of California." Presentation at SAVOR. Washington, DC, 2009. http://www.craftbeerradio.com/savor/savor2009.html.

"At Logsdon, Ales For Every Seizoen." *Hood River News.* February 18, 2012. http://www.hoodrivernews.com/news/2012/feb/22/at-logsdon-ales-for-every-seizoen/.

Back, Werner. 1978 "Elevation of *Pediococcus cerevisiae* subsp. *dextrinicus* Coster and White to Species Status [*Pediococcus dextrinicus* (Coster and White) comb. nov.]." *International Journal of Systematic Bacteriology* 28(4):523. doi:10.1099/00207713-28-4-523.

Beer Judge Certification Program (BJCP). *BJCP Style Guidelines for Beer, Mead, & Cider*, 2008 edition (St. Louis Park, MN: Beer Judge Certification Program, Inc.). Accessed December 15, 2013. http://www.bjcp.org/stylecenter.php.

Belau, Ken. "Acidification in the Brewhouse." Presentation at the Master Brewers Association of the Americas Winter Conference. January 14, 2011. http://www.mbaa.com/districts/michigan/mash/Pages/PresentationsArchive.aspx.

Bokulich, Nicholas A., Charles W. Bamforth, David A. Mills. 2012. "Brewhouse-Resident Microbiota Are Responsible for Multi-Stage Fermentation of American Coolship Ale." *PLoS ONE* 7(4):e35507. doi:10.1371/journal.pone.0035507.

Bouckaert, Peter. "Brewery Rodenbach: Brewing Sour Ales." April 1996. Accessed February 24, 2013. http://hbd.org/brewery/library/Rodnbch.html.

Bouckaert, Peter and Eric Salazar. "New Belgium Brewing." Interview on *Basic Brewing Radio* podcast. October 19, 2006. Accessed April 22, 2013. http://media.libsyn.com/media/basicbrewing/bbr10-19-06.mp3.

Bouckaert, Peter, Ron Gansberg, Tomme Arthur, Tyler King and Vinnie Cilurzo. "A Comprehensive Look at Sour Ale Production," panel interview, Craft Brewers Conference, San Diego. MP3 audio, Item #1611-26, May 4, 2012. http://www.allstartapes.com/conferences/conference_1611.shtml.

"Brett Pack Beer Dinner." *Basic Brewing Radio* podcast. November 27, 2008. Accessed March 14, 2013. http://www.basicbrewing.com/index.php?page=basic-brewing-radio-2008.

Bruckner, David A, Paul Colonna and Bradley L. Bearson. 1999. "Nomenclature for Aerobic and Facultative Bacteria." *Clinical Infectious Diseases* 29(4):713. doi:10.1086/520421.

Buglass, Alan J., ed. 2011. "Malolactic Fermentation." In Vol. 1 of *Handbook of Alcoholic Beverages: Technical, Analytical and Nutritional Aspects.* Chichester: John Wiley & Sons, Ltd.

Calagione, Sam. 2012. *Extreme Brewing, A Deluxe Edition with 14 New Homebrew Recipes: An Introduction to Brewing Craft Beer at Home.* Beverly, MA: Quarry Books.

Chandrashekar, Jayaram, David Yarmolinsky, Lars von Buchholtz, Yuki Oka, William Sly, Nicholas J. P. Ryba, Charles S. Zuker. 2009. "The Taste of Carbonation." *Science* 326(5951):443. doi:10.1126/science.1174601.

Chatonnet, Pascal, Denis Dubourdie, Jean-noël Boidron, Monique Pons. 1992. "The origin of ethylphenols in wines." *Journal of the Science of Food and Agriculture* 60(2):165. doi:10.1002 /jsfa.2740600205.

Cilurzo, Vinnie. "Belgian Beers with Vinnie Cilurzo." Interview on *The Sunday Session*, audio podcast. Brewing Network. August 14, 2005. http://thebrewingnetwork.com/shows/The-Sunday-Session /The-Sunday-Session-08-14-05-Belgian-Beers-with-Vinnie -Cilurzo.

————. "Brewing Sour Beers at Home Using Traditional & Alternative Methods." Presentation at the National Homebrewers Conference. San Diego, 2011. (via "The Sunday Session" podcast. July 7, 2007. The Brewing Network. http:// thebrewingnetwork.com/shows/The-Sunday-Session /The-Sunday-Session-07-07-07-Meltdown-and-Sour-Beer.)

————. Interview with Brandon Jones. "Russian River Talks a New Beer, Their Coolship, 'Sonambic' and Future Beatification Blends." *Embrace the Funk* blog. January 9, 2012. http://embracethefunk .com/2012/01/09/russian-river-talks-a-new-beer-their-coolship -sonambic-and-future-beatification-blends/.

Cilurzo, Vinnie, Yvan de Baets, Jean Van Roy. "Barrel-Aged Sour Beers from Two Belgian's Perspectives." Panel discussion at the Craft Brewers Conference, San Francisco, 2011.

Claussen, N. Hjelte. 1904. "On a method for the application of Hansen's pure yeast system in the manufacturing of well-conditioned English stock beers." *Journal of the Institute of Brewing* 10(4):308. doi:10.1002/j.2050-0416.1904.tb04656.x.

Coghe, Stefan, Koen Benoot, Filip Delvaux, Bart Vanderhaegen, and Freddy R. Delvaux. 2004. "Ferulic Acid Release and 4-Vinylguaiacol Formation during Brewing and Fermentation: Indications for Feruloyl Esterase Activity in *Saccharomyces cerevisiae*." *Journal of Agricultural and Food Chemistry* 52(3):602. doi:10.1021/jf0346556.

Curtin, Chris D., Jennifer R. Bellon, Paul A. Henschke, Peter W. Godden, Miguel A. De Barros Lopes. 2007. "Genetic diversity of *Dekkera bruxellensis* yeasts isolated from Australian wineries." *FEMS Yeast Research* 7(3):471. doi:10.1111/j.1567-1364.2006.00183.x.

Daenen, Luk, Daan Saison, Femke Sterckx, Freddy R. Delvaux, Hubert Verachtert and Guy Derdelinckx. 2008. "Screening and evaluation of the glucoside hydrolase activity in *Saccharomyces* and *Brettanomyces* brewing yeasts." *Journal of Applied Microbiology* 104(2):478. doi:10.1111/j.1365-2672.2007.03566.x

Daenen, Luk, Femke Sterckx, Freddy R Delvaux, Hubert Verachtert, Guy Derdelinckx. 2008. "Evaluation of the glycoside hydrolase activity of a *Brettanomyces* strain on glycosides from sour cherry (Prunus cerasus L.) used in the production of special fruit beers." *FEMS Yeast Research* 8(7):1103. doi:10.1111/j.1567-1364.2008.00421.x.

De Cort, S., H.M. Kumara and H. Verachtert, 1994. "Localization and Characterization of alpha-Glucosidase Activity in *Lactobacillus brevis.*" *Applied and Environmental Microbiology* 60(9):3074.

De Keukeleire, Denis. "Fundamentals of beer and hop chemistry." *Química Nova* 23(1):108. doi:10.1590 /S0100-40422000000100019.

Guy Derdelinckx, 1978. "La refermentation de la biere en bouteilles [Bottled beer refermentation]." [French] *Cerevisia* 12(3):153–162.

De Vos, Paul, George Garrity, Dorothy Jones, Noel R. Krieg, Wolfgang Ludwig, Fred A. Rainey, Karl-Heinz Schleifer and William B. Whitman, eds. 2009. *The* Firmicutes. Vol. 3 of *Bergey's Manual of Systematic Bacteriology*, 2nd edition. New York: Springer.

Doss, Greg. "Brettanomyces: Flavors and performance of single and multiple strain fermentations with respect to time." Presentation at the American Homebrewers Association National Homebrew Competition. Cincinnati, OH, 2008.

Dueñas, Maite, Arantza Munduate, Aidé Perea, Ana Irastorza. 2003. "Exopolysaccharide production by *Pediococcus damnosus* 2.6 in a semidefined medium under different growth conditions." *International Journal of Food Microbiology* 87(1–2):113. doi:10.1016/S0168-1605(03)00060-6.

Ekre, Ryan. "Athos - A Biére de Garde fermented with Sherry Flor." *Ryan Brews* blog. December 19, 2010. http://ryanbrews.blogspot .com/2010/12/athos-biere-de-garde-fermented-with.html.

Fix, George. "Diacetyl: Formation, Reduction, and Control." *Brewing Techniques* 1, no. 2 (July/August 1993). Content republished online. http://morebeer.com/brewingtechniques/library /backissues/issue1.2/fix.html.

Germond, Jacques-Edouard, Luciane Lapierre, Michèle Delley, Beat Mollet, Giovanna E. Felis, and Franco Dellaglio. 2003. "Evolution of the Bacterial Species *Lactobacillus delbrueckii*: A Partial Genomic Study with Reflections on Prokaryotic Species Concept." *Molecular Biology and Evolution* 20(1):93. doi:10.1093/molbev/msg012.

Gibbs, Erich. *Measurement of Oxygen Transfer Rates for Carboy Closures and Air Locks.* November 10, 2011. http://www.mocon.com /pdf/optech/Closures%20-%20Oxygen%20Passage%20Study.pdf.

Great American Beer Festival (GABF). "Beer Styles." *2013 GABF Style Descriptions.* Accessed December 15, 2013. http://www .great-americanbeerfestival.com/the-competition/beer-styles/.

Great American Beer Festival (GABF). "GABF Winners." Accessed February 2, 2014. http://www.greatamericanbeerfestival.com /the-competition/winners/.

Goode, Jamie. 2005. *The Science of Wine: From Vine to Glass.* Berkeley: University of California Press.

Hall, Michelle. "'Autumn Fire' Catches On." *The Chestnut Grower* 11, no. 1 (Winter 2009). http://www.centerforagroforestry.org /pubs/chestnut/v11n1/v11n1.pdf.

Henick-Kling, Thomas, Christoph Egli, Jonathan Licker, Craig Mitrakul, and Terry E. Acree. 2000. "*Brettanomyces* in Wine." Proceedings of the 5th International Symposium on Cool Climate Viticulture and Oenology. Melbourne, Australia, 16–20 January 2000. Adelaide: Australian Society of Viticulture and Oenology. http://locale.mannlib.cornell.edu/gsdl/collect/wiwp/tmp/08a .THK.Brett%20in%20wine.html.

Henry, Jason. "Russian River Toronado 25th Anniversary Beer: Deconstructed." *Examiner.com.* August 15, 2012. Accessed March 14, 2013. http://www.examiner.com/article /russian-river-toronado-25th-anniversary-beer-deconstructed.

Hieronymus, Stan. 2010. *Brewing with Wheat: The 'Wit' and 'Weizen' of World Wheat Beers.* Boulder, CO: Brewers Publications.

————. 2012. *For the Love of Hops: The Practical Guide to Aroma, Bitterness and the Culture of Hops.* Boulder, CO: Brewers Publications.

————. "Ommegang Zuur and Goose Island Matilda." *Brew Like a Monk* blog. March 2, 2010. http://www.brewlikeamonk .com/?p=105.

Hornsey, Ian Spencer. 2007. *The Chemistry and Biology of Winemaking.* Cambridge: Royal Society of Chemistry.

Hui, Y. H. and George G. Khachatourians, eds. 1995. *Food Biotechnology: Microorganisms.* New York: John Wiley & Sons.

Jackson, Michael. 2008. *Michael Jackson's Great Beers of Belgium.* Boulder, CO: Brewers Publications.

Jackson, Ronald S. 2008. *Wine Science: Principles and Applications.* Burlington, MA: Academic Press.

Jeffries, Ron. Interview on "Can You Brew It: Jolly Pumpkin Bam Biere" podcast. *The Jamil Show.* Brewing Network. October 12, 2009. http://thebrewingnetwork.com/shows/561.

————. Interview on "Can You Brew It: Jolly Pumpkin Dark Dawn" podcast. *The Jamil Show.* Brewing Network. October 26, 2009. http://thebrewingnetwork.com/shows/567.

Kelley, William J. 1965. *Brewing in Maryland; From colonial times to the present.* Baltimore.

Kishimoto, Toru. "Hop-Derived Odorants Contributing to the Aroma Characteristics of Beer." Doctoral dissertation. Kyoto University, 2008. http://repository.kulib.kyoto-u.ac.jp/dspace /bitstream/2433/66109/4/D_Kishimoto_Toru.pdf

Kumara, H. M. C. Shantha, S. De Cort, and H. Verachtert. 1993. "Localization and Characterization of alpha-Glucosidase Activity in *Brettanomyces lambicus.*" *Applied and Environmental Microbiology* 59(8):2352. http://aem.asm.org/content/59/8/2352.

Lafon-Lafourcade, S., C. Geneix and P. Ribéreau-Gayon. 1984. "Inhibition of Alcoholic Fermentation of Grape Must by Fatty Acids Produced by Yeasts and Their Elimination by Yeast Ghosts." *Applied and Environmental Microbiology* 47(6):1246. http://aem.asm.org/content/47/6/1246.

Lallemand, Inc. "Yeast Selected from Nature." Accessed April 24, 2013. http://www.lallemandwine.us/products/yeast_strains.php.

Libkinda, Diego, Chris Todd Hittinger, Elisabete Valério, Carla Gonçalves, Jim Dover, Mark Johnston, Paula Gonçalves, and José Paulo Sampaio. 2011. "Microbe domestication and the identification of the wild genetic stock of lager-brewing yeast." *Proceedings of the National Academy of Sciences USA* 108(35):14539. doi:10.1073/pnas.1105430108.

LoverBeer Brewery (Birrificio Loverbeer). "BeerBera." Accessed March 15, 2013. http://www.loverbeer.com/

Mansfield, Anna K., Bruce W. Zoecklein and Robert S. Whiton. "Quantification of Glycosidase Activity in Selected Strains of *Brettanomyces bruxellensis* and *Oenococcus oeni.*" *American Journal of Enology and Viticulture* 53(4):303. http://ajevonline.org/content/53/4/303.

Markowski, Phil. 2004. *Farmhouse Ales: Culture and Craftsmanship in the Belgian Tradition.* Boulder, CO: Brewers Publications.

Martens, Hilde. "Microbiology and Biochemistry of The Acid Ales of Roeselare." Doctoral thesis. Catholic University of Leuven, Germany, 1996.

McGee, Harold. 2004. *On Food and Cooking: The Science and Lore of the Kitchen*. New York: Scribner.

McGovern, Patrick E., Juzhong Zhang, Jigen Tang, Zhiqing Zhang, Gretchen R. Hall, Robert A. Moreau, Alberto Nuñez, Eric D. Butrym, Michael P. Richards, Chen-shan Wang, Guangsheng Cheng, Zhijun Zhao, and Changsui Wang. "Fermented beverages of pre- and proto-historic China." *Proceedings of the National Academy of Sciences USA* 101(51):17593. doi:10.1073/pnas.0407921102.

McMahon, H., B. W. Zoecklein, K. Fugelsang, Y. Jasinski. 1999. "Quantification of glycosidase activities in selected yeasts and lactic acid bacteria." *Journal of Industrial Microbiology and Biotechnology* 23(3):198. doi:10.1038/sj.jim.2900720.

Methner, Frank-Jürgen and K. Wackerbauer, "The microorganisms of 'Berliner Weissbier' and their influence on the beer flavour." *Brauwelt—International* (1988). EBC Microbiology Group Meeting, Wuppertal, Germany June 13-15, 1988.

Mishra, Ankita. "The Effect of Wort Boil Time and Trub on Barley Malt Fermentability Through the Miniature Fermentation Method." Master's thesis. Dalhousie University, 2012. Accessed April 23, 2013. http://hdl.handle.net/10222/15434.

Mortimer, Robert, Mario Polsinelli. 1999. "On the origins of wine yeast." *Research in Microbiology*, 150(3):199–204. doi:10.1016/S0923-2508(99)80036-9.

Mosher, Randy. 2004. *Radical Brewing: Recipes, Tales and World-Altering Meditations in a Glass*. Boulder, CO: Brewers Publications.

Noonan, Gregory. 2003. *New Brewing Lager Beer*. Boulder, CO: Brewer's Publications.

Oliver, Garrett, ed., *Oxford Companion to Beer.* New York: Oxford University Press, Inc., 2012.

Palmer, John. 2006. *How to Brew: Everything You Need To Know To Brew Beer Right The First Time.* Boulder, CO: Brewers Publications.

Pasteur, Louis. 1876. *Etudes sur la Bière: ses maladies, causes qui les provoquent, procédé pour la rendre inaltérable; avec une théorie nouvelle de la fermentation.* Paris: Gauthier-Villars.

Perkins, Jason. "Spontaneous Fermentation." Interview by James Spencer. Basic Brewing Radio. April 30, 2009. http://media .libsyn.com/media/basicbrewing/bbr04-30-09spont.mp3.

Redner, Joey, Wayne Wambles, Patrick Rue, Tyler King. "Califlorida: A Tale of East Coast/West Coast Collaboration." Presentation at SAVOR. Washington, DC, 2011. http://www.craftbeerradio .com/savor/savor2011.html.

Richards, M., R. M. Macrae, 1964. "The significance of the use of hops in regard to the biological stability of beer II. The development of resistance to hop resins by strains of lactobacilli." *Journal of the Institute of Brewing* 70(6):484. doi:10.1002/j.2050-0416.1964 .tb06353.x.

Romano, P., C. Fiore, M. Paraggio, M. Caruso, and A. Capece. 2003. "Function of yeast species and strains in wine flavour." *International Journal of Food Microbiology* 86(1–2):169. doi:10.1016/S0168-1605(03)00290-3.

Rue, Patrick. "The Bruery." Interview on *The Sunday Session* podcast. November 2, 2008. Brewing Network. http:// thebrewingnetwork.com/shows/The-Sunday-Session/ The-Sunday-Session-11-02-08-The-Bruery.

Russian River Brewing Company. "Bottle Logs." Accessed February 5, 2014. http://russianriverbrewing.com/bottle-logs/.

Sakamoto, Kanta. "Beer Spoilage Bacteria and Hop Resistance in *Lactobacillus brevis*." Doctoral thesis, University of Groningen, 2002. Accessed March 11, 2013. http://dissertations.ub.rug.nl /FILES/faculties/science/2002/k.sakamoto/thesis.pdf.

Salazar, Lauren. Interview with Brandon Jones. "Lauren Salazar of New Belgium Q & A." *Embrace the Funk* blog. July 26, 2012. http://embracethefunk.com/2012/06/26 /lauren-salazar-of-new-belgium-qa/.

—————. "NHC: Tips and Tasting." *Basic Brewing Radio* podcast. July 19, 2007. http://www.basicbrewing.com/index .php?page=basic-brewing-radio-2007.

Schramm, Ken. 2003. *The Compleat Meadmaker: Home Production of Honey Wine From Your First Batch to Award-winning Fruit and Herb Variations.* Boulder, CO: Brewers Publications.

Shimwell, J.L. 1936. "Saccharobacillus infection." *Journal of the Institute of Brewing* 42(5):452. doi:10.1002/j.2050-0416.1936.tb05682.x.

Simpson, W. J. 1993. "Studies on the Sensitivity of Lactic Acid Bacteria to Hop Bitter Acids." *Journal of the Institute Of Brewing* 99(5):405. doi:10.1002/j.2050-0416.1993.tb01180.x.

Small, P., D. Blankenhorn, D. Welty, E. Zinser, J. L. Slonczewski. 1994. "Acid and base resistance in *Escherichia coli* and *Shigella flexneri*: role of rpoS and growth pH." *Journal of Bacteriology* 176(6):1729. http://jb.asm.org/content/176/6/1729.

Smith, Maudy Th., Wilma Batenburg-Van der Vegte, W. A. Scheffers. 1981. "*Eeniella*, a New Yeast Genus of the Torulopsidales." *International Journal of Systematic and Evolutionary Microbiology* 31(2):196. doi: 10.1099/00207713-31-2-196.

Smith, Maudy Th., M. Yamazaki, G.A. Poot. 1990. "*Dekkera, Brettanomyces* and *Eeniella*: electrophoretic comparison of enzymes and DNA-DNA homology," *Yeast* 6(4):299. doi:10.1002 /yea.320060403.

Snowdon, Eleanor, Michael C. Bowyer, Paul R. Grbin, and Paul Bowyer. 2006. "Mousy Off-Flavor: A Review," *Journal of Agricultural and Food Chemistry* 54(18):6465. doi:10.1021 /jf0528613.

Sparrow, Jeff. 2005. *Wild Brews: Beer Beyond the Influence of Brewer's Yeast.* Boulder, CO: Brewers Publications.

Stamer, J. R. and B.O. Stoyla. 1967. "Growth Response of *Lactobacillus brevis* to Aeration and Organic Catalysts." *Applied Microbiology* 15(5):1025. PMCID: PMC547135.

Stanga, Mario. 2010. *Sanitation: Cleaning and Disinfection in the Food Industry.* Weinheim, Germany: Wiley-VCH.

Staten, Christopher. "Native ales: A new state of beer." *Draft Magazine.* (March/April 2013). http://draftmag.com/features /native-ales-yeast/.

Staton, Caleb. "Exploring the American Sour Niche." *The New Brewer* (July/August 2010).

————. Interview with Brandon Jones. "Caleb Staton of Upland Brewing Company Q&A!" *Embrace the Funk* blog. October 19, 2012. http://embracethefunk.com/2012/10/19 /caleb-staton-of-upland-brewing-company-qa/.

Steele, Mitch. 2012. *IPA: Brewing Techniques, Recipes, and the Evolution of India Pale Ales.* Boulder, CO: Brewers Publications.

Stefanini, Irene, Leonardo Dapporto, Jean-Luc Legras, Antonio Calabretta, Monica Di Paola, Carlotta De Filippo, Roberto Viola, Paolo Capretti, Mario Polsinelli, Stefano Turillazzi, and Duccio Cavalieria. 2012. "Role of social wasps in *Saccharomyces cerevisiae* ecology and evolution." *Proceedings of the National Academy of Sciences USA* 109(33):13398. doi:10.1073/pnas.1208362109.

Strong, Gordon. 2011. *Brewing Better Beer: Master Lessons for Advanced Homebrewers.* Boulder, CO: Brewers Publications.

Teuber, M. and Arno F. Schmalreck. 1973. "Membrane leakage in *Bacillus subtilis* 168 induced by the hop constituents lupulone, humulone, isohumulone and humulinic acid." *Archiv für Mikrobiologie* 94(2):159. doi:10.1007/BF00416690.

Thomas, T.D., L.L. McKay, H.A. Morris. 1985. "Lactate Metabolism by Pediococci Isolated from Cheese." *Applied and Environmental Microbiology* 40(2):908. http://aem.asm.org/content/49/4/908.

United States Department of Agriculture, Agricultural Research Service. 2011. *USDA National Nutrient Database for Standard Reference*, Release 24. Nutrient Data Laboratory Home Page, http://www.ars.usda.gov/ba/bhnrc/ndl.

————. 2012. "Composition of Foods Raw, Processed, Prepared." *USDA National Nutrient Database for Standard Reference*, Release 25 Nutrient Data Laboratory Home Page, http://www.ars.usda.gov/ba/bhnrc/ndl.

United States Department of the Treasury, Alcohol and Tobacco Tax and Trade Bureau. "Classification of Brewed Products." July 23, 2008. http://www.ttb.gov/industry_circulars/archives/2008/08-03.html.

————. "Flavoring Substances and Adjuvants Subject to Limitation or Restriction." September 4, 2012. http://www.ttb.gov/ssd/limited_ingredients.shtml.

————. "Class and Type Designation." Chapter in *The Beverage Alcohol Manual: A Practical Guide.* Basic Mandatory Labeling Information for Distilled Spirits, Volume 2. 2007. http://www.ttb.gov/spirits/bam/chapter4.pdf.

United States Environmental Protection Agency. "*Acetobacter aceti* Final Risk Assessment." February 1997. Accessed March 12, 2013. http://epa.gov/biotech_rule/pubs/fra/fra001.htm.

Upright Brewing. "Fantasia & Blend Love." *Upright Brewing* blog. January 2, 2012. http://uprightbrewingblog.blogspot.com/2012/01/fantasia-blend-love.html.

Vaccaro, Scott. Interview on "The Sunday Session" podcast. *Brewing Network.* August 31, 2008. http://thebrewingnetwork.com/shows/The-Sunday-Session/The-Sunday-Session-08-31-08-OFF-WEEK.

Van den Steen, Jef. 2011. *Geuze & Kriek: The Secret of Lambic.* Tielt, Belgium: Lannoo Publishers.

Verachtert H. and D. Iserentant. 1995. "Properties of Belgian acid beers and their microflora. 1. The production of gueuze and related refreshing acid beers." *Cerevisia* 20(1):37.

Wahl R., M. Henius. 1908. *American Handy Book of the Brewing, Malting, and Auxiliary Trades.* 2nd edition. Chicago: Wahl-Henius Institute.

Webb, Tim, Chris Pollard, Siobhan McGinn. 2010. *LambicLand: A Journey Round the Most Unusual Beers in the World.* Cambridge, UK: Cogan & Mater.

White, Chris and Jamil Zainasheff. 2010. *Yeast: The Practical Guide to Beer Fermentation.* Boulder, CO: Brewers Publications.

Willaert, Ronnie, Hubert Verachtert, Karen Van Den Bremt, Freddy Delvaux and Guy Derdelinckx. 2005. "Bioflavouring of Food and Beverages." In Vol. 8B of *Applications of Cell Immobilisation Biotechnology*, edited by Viktor Nedovic and Ronnie Willaert. Dordrecht, The Netherlands: Springer.

WineMaker, Wine Wizard. February/March 2005. http://www .winemakermag.com/stories/wizard/article/224-could-you -provide-me-some-ideas-on-an-easy-and-cost-effective-way-to -properly-frame-a-stand-for-my-barrels.

Yakobson, Chad. "Pure Culture Fermentation Characteristics of *Brettanomyces* Yeast Species and Their Use in the Brewing Industry." Master's thesis. Heriot-Watt University, 2010. http://www .brettanomycesproject.com/dissertation/.

Yamada, Yuzo, Minako Matsuda, Kozaburo Mikata. 1995. The phylogenetic relationships of *Eeniella nana* Smith, Batenburg-van der Vegte et Scheffers based on the partial sequences of 18S and 26S ribosomal RNAs (Candidaceae). *Journal of Industrial Microbiology* 14(6):456. doi:10.1007/BF01573957.

Zoecklein, Bruce and Lisa Van de Water. "Practical Monitoring and Management of Brettanomyces." Presentation. Enology-Grape Chemistry Group, Virginia Tech. Accessed February 3, 2014. http://www.apps.fst.vt.edu/extension/enology/downloads /BZWU%20Brettanomyces.pdf.

INDEX